EUROPEAN
CINEMA

EUROPEAN CINEMA

Edited by **Elizabeth Ezra**

OXFORD

UNIVERSITY PRESS

12-14-2004
WW
$ 24.95

OXFORD
UNIVERSITY PRESS

Great Clarendon Street, Oxford OX2 6DP

Oxford University Press is a department of the University of Oxford.
It furthers the University's objective of excellence in research, scholarship,
and education by publishing worldwide in

Oxford New York

Auckland Bangkok Buenos Aires Cape Town Chennai
Dar es Salaam Delhi Hong Kong Istanbul Karachi Kolkata
Kuala Lumpur Madrid Melbourne Mexico City Mumbai Nairobi
São Paulo Shanghai Taipei Tokyo Toronto

Oxford is a registered trade mark of Oxford University Press
in the UK and in certain other countries

Published in the United States
by Oxford University Press Inc., New York

British Library Cataloguing in Publication Data

Data available

ISBN 0–19–925571–7

1 3 5 7 9 10 8 6 4 2

Typeset in 9/15pt Frutiger Light
by Graphicraft Limited, Hong Kong
Printed in Great Britain by
Ashford Colour Press Limited, Gosport, Hants

PREFACE

This book grew out of a series of film courses I developed with a colleague, Karl Leydecker, in the School of Modern Languages at the University of Stirling. It is intended to provide overviews of key movements in European film history, considering aesthetic developments and the contributions of individuals within a wider industrial (and more broadly historical) context.

Such a project is naturally bound to exclude at least as much as it includes, but the decision of which movements and traditions to cover was guided by what is generally being taught in European cinema courses today. As the political and economic entity known as 'Europe' expands and changes in the coming years, so will the cinematic traditions that come to international prominence, influencing in turn what is taught and written. In the meantime, it is hoped that this book will be of use to all those who wish to increase their understanding of an art form that extends far beyond Hollywood.

ACKNOWLEDGEMENTS

I am very fortunate to have had the privilege of working with such outstanding contributors, whose professionalism and expertise made the job much easier. I am also very grateful to my colleague Karl Leydecker, with whom I developed the courses that gave rise to this book, for his comments on the introduction. I wish to thank, too, the following people for their helpful suggestions and advice: Sue Harris, Alison McMahan, Martin Mellor, Martin O'Shaugnessy, Sandra Rutter, Jane Sillars, Sarah Street, and Sharon Wood. Once again, Alison Cooper's assistance was invaluable. Jennifer and Ken Porter and Peggy and Herschel Booth all provided welcome support during the preparation of the manuscript. Finally, my thanks go to Paul Jackson as ever for his patience throughout, and to Nathan, who began life halfway through this project, and whose cheerful presence enlivened things considerably.

CONTENTS

CONTRIBUTORS

Dudley Andrew, now at Yale University, taught for many years at the University of Iowa in a career that has engaged the history of film theory, French cinema, world cinemas, and issues in aesthetics. His forthcoming *The Politics and Poetics of Popular Front Paris* is a co-authored study that builds on *Mists of Regret: Culture and Sensibility in Classic French Film* (1995).

Martine Beugnet is a lecturer in Film Studies at the University of Edinburgh. She is the author of a series of articles and essays and a book on contemporary French cinema, *Sexualité, Marginalité, contrôle: le cinéma français contemporain* (2000). She is currently completing a book on the films of Claire Denis (forthcoming).

Peter Bondanella is Distinguished Professor of Italian and Comparative Literature at Indiana University. His publications on Italian culture and cinema include *The Eternal City: Roman Images in the Modern World* (1987); *Italian Cinema: from Neorealism to the Present* (3nd rev. edn., 2001); *The Cinema of Federico Fellini* (1992); *The Films of Roberto Rossellini* (1993); *Cassell's Dictionary of Italian Literature* (1996); *Umberto Eco and the Open Work* (1997); and *The Films of Federico Fellini* (2002). At present he is completing a study of Hollywood's treatment of Italians in the movies entitled *Hollywood Italians: Dagos, Palookas, Romeos, Wise Guys, and Sopranos.*

Paul Coates is Professor of Film Studies and Head of Department in the School of English and Film Studies at the University of Aberdeen, Scotland. His publications include *The Story of the Lost Reflection* (1985); *The Gorgon's Gaze* (1991); *Lucid dreams: the films of Krzysztof Kieślowski* (ed.) (1999); and *Cinema, Religion and the Romantic Legacy* (2002).

Thomas Elsaesser is Professor in the Department of Media Studies at the University of Amsterdam and Chair of Research in Film and Television Studies. He is General Editor of the series 'Film Culture in Transition' and Director of 'Cinema Europe-Media Europe', a research project at the Amsterdam School of Cultural Analysis. His books as author and editor include: *New German Cinema: A History* (1989); *Early Cinema: Space Frame Narrative* (1990); *Writing for the Medium: Television in Transition* (1994); *Fassbinder's Germany: History, Identity, Subject* (1996); *Cinema Futures: Cain, Abel or Cable* (1998); *The BFI Companion to German*

Cinema (with Michael Wedel, 1999); *Weimar Cinema and After* (2000); *Metropolis* (2000); *Studying Contemporary American Film* (with Warren Buckland, 2002); and *Früher Film und Kinogeschichte* (2002).

Peter William Evans is Professor of Spanish at Queen Mary, University of London. His recent publications include *The Films of Luis Buñuel: Subectivity and Desire* (Oxford); *Women on the Verge of a Nervous Breakdown* (British Film Institute), and (ed.), *Spanish Cinema: The Auteurist Tradition*. He has recently completed a book on *Jamón jamón* (Paidós), and is currently writing another, on Carol Reed (forthcoming).

Elizabeth Ezra is a Senior Lecturer in the School of Modern Languages at the University of Stirling in Scotland. She is the author of *Georges Méliès: The Birth of the Auteur* (2000) and *The Colonial Unconscious: Race and Culture in Interwar France* (2000); co-editor (with Sue Harris) of *France in Focus: Film and National Identity* (2000); and an editor of the journal *Studies in French Cinema*.

Sue Harris is Senior Lecturer in French Studies at Queen Mary, University of London. She is the author of *Bertrand Blier* (2001); co-editor (with Elizabeth Ezra) of *France in Focus: Film and National Identity* (2000); and associate editor of the journal *French Cultural Studies*. She has also published a wide range of articles and book chapters on French cinema and the performance arts.

Anton Kaes is Chancellor's Professor of German and Film Studies at the University of California, Berkeley. He is the author of *From 'Hitler' to 'Heimat': The Return of History as Film* (1989) and *M* (2000); he is also the co-editor of *Geschichte des deutschen Films* (1993) and *The Weimar Republic Sourcebook* (1995).

T. Jefferson Kline is Professor of French in the Department of Modern Foreign Languages and Literatures at Boston University. His publications include *André Malraux and the Metamorphosis of Death* (1973*); Bertolucci's Dream Loom: A Psychoanalytic Study of Cinema* (1987); *I film di Bertolucci* (1992); and *Screening the Text: Intertexuality in New Wave French Film* (1992). He has also co-edited *Bernardo Bertolucci: Interviews* (2000) and a posthumous edition of Charles Bernheimer's *Decadent Subjects* (2002). He is currently at work on a study tentatively entitled *The Cinema and Its Doubles*.

Rudolf Kuenzli teaches in the Department of Cinema and Comparative Literature at the University of Iowa. His publications include *Marcel Duchamp* (1989); *Dada and Surrealist Film* (1996); *André Breton Today* (1989); *Surrealism and Women* (1991); and *New York Dada* (1986). He edits the journal *Dada/Surrealism* and directs the International Dada Archive at the University of Iowa.

Gaetana Marrone is Professor of Italian at Princeton University, where she specializes in modern Italian literature and postwar Italian cinema. She is the author of *La drammatica di Ugo Betti* (1988), which won the American Association of Italian Studies Presidential Award; *New Landscapes in Contemporary Italian Cinema* (1999); *The Gaze and the Labyrinth: The Cinema of Liliana Cavani* (2000), awarded the Scaglione Prize by the Modern Language Association of America; and *Lo sguardo e il labirinto* (2003). She has also produced two award-winning films, *Woman in the Wind* (1990) and a documentary feature on Princeton's intellectual and social history, *Princeton: Images of a University* (1996).

Alison McMahan wrote *Alice Guy Blaché, Lost Visionary of the Cinema* (2002) based on her award-winning doctoral dissertation. From 1997 to 2001 she taught early cinema and new media at the University of Amsterdam in The Netherlands. She currently holds a Mellon Fellowship in Visual Culture at Vassar College and is writing a book on the work of Tim Burton.

John Orr is Professor Emeritus at the University of Edinburgh and the author of *Cinema and Modernity* (1993); *Contemporary Cinema* (1998); and *The Art and Politics of Film* (2000). He has recently co-edited a collection for Wallflower Press on the cinema of Andrzej Wajda, and is now working on the films of Roman Polanski.

Peter Schepelern, University of Copenhagen, has published a number of books on Danish cinema, mostly in Danish, including a monograph on Lars von Trier (2000), a Danish film history, and a Film Encyclopedia. He has also published a collection of Carl Dreyer's film journalism and articles on the Dogme 95 movement in collections including *Purity and Provocation* (2003).

Sarah Street is Reader in Screen Studies at the University of Bristol. She is the author of *British National Cinema* (1997), *British Cinema in Documents* (2000), *Transatlantic Crossings: British Feature Films in the USA* (2002), and *Costume and Cinema: Dress Codes in Popular Film* (2001). She is co-author (with Margaret Dickinson) of *Cinema and State: The Film Industry and the British Government* (1985); co-editor (with Linda Fitzsimmons) of *Moving Performance: British Stage and Screen* (2000), and (with Jill Forbes) *European Cinema: An Introduction* (2000). She is also an editor of the journal *Screen* and *the Journal of British Cinema and Television*.

Denise J. Youngblood is Professor of History and Vice Provost for Faculty and Academic Affairs at the University of Vermont. A specialist in Russian and Soviet silent cinema, Soviet cultural politics, and Soviet and post-Soviet historical film, she has published extensively on the subject. Her works include *Soviet Cinema in the Silent Era, 1918–1935* (1991); *Movies for the Masses: Popular Cinema and Soviet Society in the 1920s* (1992); *The Magic Mirror: Moviemaking in Russia, 1908–1918* (1999); and numerous articles. She is currently writing a book on Russian war films.

INTRODUCTION

A brief history of cinema in Europe

Elizabeth Ezra

What is European cinema? In some ways, it is difficult to speak of 'European' cinema at all, since so many supposedly European films are made with the strong financial backing of American companies, using international casts and personnel. European films are often associated with 'art' cinema, films considered challenging and open to multiple interpretations. These traits may well characterize the films that tend to be distributed internationally, but they do not necessarily reflect the majority of films made and shown in Europe; and conversely, films popular in their country of origin do not always travel well. European films are primarily seen by European audiences, whereas American films reach a much larger share of the world market. It is this economic disparity, more than anything else, that has had a defining impact on the film industries of Europe.

Before Hollywood: The European prequel

The first public film screenings in the world were held in Europe in 1895. Thomas Edison in the United States had been making films for two years, but he had never projected them before an audience: therein lies the distinction between film, the medium, and cinema, the public event. The history of cinema has largely been a reversal of this early division of achievement, which saw the Americans at the forefront of film form, with the Europeans attending to the audience. It would not be not long before European countries, despite producing some of the world's finest films, struggled to find the kinds of audiences that would flock to see Hollywood productions. European cinema has long been characterized by this dichotomy: films in Europe, so it is said, are created by artists, while in Hollywood they are manufactured by corporations. Of course, cinema every-where is a combination of art and industry, the product of both aesthetic and economic influences. But the distinction between Europe and Hollywood, while in many ways heuristic, has nonetheless played an important role in film history.

Until World War I, films circulated beyond the borders of individual countries and con-tinents with relative ease, and cinema was more the product of international collabora-tion than of national competition. The very invention of the medium, indeed, cannot be attributed to a single individual or even a single nation, but was instead the result of interaction and cross-fertilization among several entrepreneurs in France, the US, Britain, and Germany (see Chapter 1, 'Beginnings'). Although Max and Emil Skladanowsky of Germany beat the Lumière Brothers to the first public film showing by almost two months, it is the Frenchmen who are remembered (rightly or wrongly) for this achieve-ment, because they quickly capitalized on their invention by sending personnel and equipment all over the world to make and show their films. Their *cinématographe* was a camera/projector that used a claw-like mechanism to pause frames for a split second, thereby creating intermittent motion, which conveyed the impression of a moving image on screen. The Lumières' machine was exhibited in most European countries in 1896 or soon thereafter, and France became the biggest producer and distributor of films in the world, dominating even the US market for nearly twenty years.

In its first decade, cinema was a different animal from what we know today. For one thing, people did not go to the movies; the movies came to them. The first permanent cinemas were only built in the major European capitals around 1906. Before then, films were shown largely in traveling fairs that moved from town to town, and then in a vari-ety of venues including cafés, department stores, music halls, zoos, churches, and skating rinks. Initially less than a minute in length, films were interspersed among many other fairground and variety-show attractions. They were often presented by a live narrator who explained what was happening on the screen, perhaps adding the occasional sound effect; musical accompaniment, too, was part of the program whenever possible. Such active participation in the film screening gave those who showed the films (exhibitors) a considerable amount of creative input, to the extent that they were even able to cut up multi-scene films and reassemble them in whichever order they pleased. However, as the production process became increasingly mechanized, films began incorporating many of the features that had previously been added by exhibitors. For example, in 1899, the filmmaker Georges Méliès began using dissolves to link his scenes together, making it more difficult for exhibitors to rearrange them; then, around 1903, intertitles were intro-duced, diminishing the role of the film narrator; and in the late 1920s and early 1930s, the widespread implementation of synchronized sound (for which the technology had actually been developed, but unsuccessfully marketed, at the turn of the century) completed the drive to make films a complete entertainment package.

Not only was the experience of going to the movies different in the first decade of cinema, but films also looked different. While film historians used to speak of a 'primitive' mode of filmmaking prevalent prior to around 1907, they have more recently come to refer to the earliest non-actuality films as the 'cinema of attractions' (a term coined by Tom Gunning and André Gaudreault), which privileged dazzling tricks and effects over narrative involvement. There is no question that, from the very beginning, many films displayed a certain degree of formal sophistication and ingenuity. But it is no less true that, as films became more self-contained, they also became more narratively complex. The eventual development of cinematic techniques such as close-ups endowed characters with psychological interiority, providing more subtle forms of motivation for their actions, while editing came to be used as a means of guiding the viewer's attention to those aspects of the story that directors wanted to emphasize.

Films gradually increased in length, allowing time for story and character development, and audience identification with characters led to the cultivation of movie stars (actors only began to be credited in films routinely around the beginning of World War I). In the 1910s Italy became known around the world for its historical epics, culminating in the enormously successful, and influential, *Cabiria* (Enrico Guazzoni, 1914). Also in the early 1910s, Denmark acquired a reputation for producing both high-quality psychological dramas and sensationalistic melodramas set in liminal milieux such as the criminal underworld or the circus. Germany, which, despite its auspicious beginnings, had been relatively slow to develop its film industry, saw the emergence of the elite *Autorenfilm*, or 'authors' film', based on the work of prestigious literary writers, as well as more popular vehicles for rising stars such as Asta Nielsen. Sweden excelled in a variety of genres, many prominently featuring the country's rugged natural beauty. In France, Louis Feuillade began making his hugely popular crime serial films, and comedies starring the top-hatted Max Linder drew crowds worldwide. This golden age of European dominance in world cinema, however, was short-lived: the early 1910s was also the time that US distributors began an aggressive campaign to capture the European market.

War and revolution

Already in the years leading up to World War I, there were signs of decline in Europe's film industries. Méliès, the magician and entrepreneur who had established one of the world's first film studios in 1896, was forced out of business in 1912, ruined by a refusal to abandon his labour-intensive, artisanal mode of production, which left him unable to compete with firms that used more efficient, industrial methods. Nor could the British film industry sustain the initial success provided by the comedies of Cecil Hepworth in the first decade of the twentieth century; by the early 1910s, many British cinemas had exclusive contracts with American distributors, who were able to offer better rates than their European counterparts because their films had already broken even in the American market. But these difficulties paled in comparison with those encountered during the war itself.

World War I (1914–18) drained a large portion of Europe's financial—and human—resources, leaving most European film industries in ruins. Because the United States did not enter the war until 1917, its film industry was able to race ahead of those in Europe, bolstering capital investment and building up networks of production and distribution, both in Europe and in the US, while the Europeans were forced to abandon such activities in favor of the war effort. From the early 1910s, many American film companies had established headquarters in Southern California, and both the area and the industry were coming to be known metonymically as 'Hollywood'. While American firms became vertically integrated (branching out from production into distribution and exhibition, thereby controlling all sectors of the industry), the biggest French film company, Pathé, pulled out of production, leaving the field wide open. In Russia, the Bolshevik Revolution of 1917, subsequent civil war, and economic hardship all hampered film production in the short term.

The film industries of Spain and Sweden, countries that had avoided direct participation in the war, emerged relatively unscathed after the armistice in 1918. Germany, too, despite its devastating defeat, had been able to build up its film industry by banning foreign films, and was easily able to sell its films abroad in the years immediately following the war, when high inflation benefited the export market. But even countries with relatively stable film industries could not compete with the large number of films imported from the US. Everywhere in Europe, filmmakers found it increasingly difficult to match the big budgets lavished on Hollywood films afforded by profits made in the vast American market, and bolstered by the growing European market, both of which were now dominated by Hollywood.

In order to counteract this precipitous decline in the number of domestic films shown on their own screens, many European countries implemented the first in a long line of quotas and other measures designed to restrict the American hold on their markets. Attempts to pool resources and create mutually beneficial trade agreements resulted in the creation of a coalition known as Film Europe, which attempted to match Hollywood in size and strength. However, these measures ultimately did little to stem the tide of American films.

World War I may have marked the end of European cinema's domination of world markets (including Europe's own), but this decline also had the paradoxical effect of ushering in an age of stylistic innovation. Although European film industries could not compete with Hollywood in economic terms, they could distinguish themselves and garner international prestige through formal experimentation. Whereas before the war, a vogue for literary adaptations in countries such as France (begun in 1907 as the *film d'art*), Germany, Spain, and Russia had attempted to lend legitimacy to the new art form, after the war, many filmmakers began taking greater risks with material that did not derive from the realist novel or theater, but was instead influenced by the modernist trend in other arts such as painting, sculpture, and poetry. No sooner were filmic conventions established than filmmakers began experimenting with the range of aesthetic possibilities the medium offered. Filmmakers in France such as Abel Gance and Jean Epstein used optical devices and rhythmic editing to convey characters' subjective states, in what became known as the Impressionist style. In Germany, the Expressionist movement emphasized theatrical set design, the use of distorted and exaggerated visual motifs, and highly stylized acting techniques that complemented the extreme psychological states and supernatural themes depicted (see Chapter 3, 'Weimar Cinema'). In the Soviet Union, Lev Kuleshov's experiments in the 1920s highlighted the capacity of a given shot to influence viewers' interpretation of other shots, and Eisenstein's conception of montage emphasized the role of collision and contrast over continuity in editing. These theories resulted in a cinema of abstraction, which privileged the expression of (generally political) ideas over the flow of narrative (see Chapter 2, 'Soviet Cinema'). The juxtaposition of disparate images was also a device favored in Dada and Surrealist film, which, though anti-bourgeois, invested its passion in aesthetics rather than politics (see Chapter 4, 'Dada and Surrealist Film').

These artistic movements converged in the effervescent interlude between the devastation of World War I and the Great Depression of the early 1930s. Several European capitals in the 1920s were cross-cultural artistic hubs, as political refugees from the Soviet Union, fleeing the Bolshevik revolution and civil war, gravitated toward Paris, Vienna, and Prague. But although avant-garde experimentation did much to bolster the international reputations of the countries in which it was practiced, it did not draw large domestic audiences. The expansion of truly popular cinematic forms would have to wait for the widespread implementation of sound.

The transition to sound

When *The Jazz Singer* (Alan Crosland, 1927) premiered in the United States, Europe was still a few years away from being able to show films using the new technology in most of its cinemas, let alone to make fully synchronized films. The first 'talkies' were not made in

Europe until the end of 1929, just as the Depression hit, and it was 1930 or even later before most European countries were in a position to produce them. But when they did, the coming of sound ushered in a new era in film style.

The new technology, though embraced by the public, was greeted with scepticism by advocates of 'pure cinema', who felt that the silent format allowed for a lyricism specific to the medium, which might degenerate into little more than filmed theater if allowed to speak. Critics also warned that linguistic barriers would lead to a decline in cinema's status as a unified, international 'language'. To some extent, both predictions were borne out, but with rather more positive results than initially feared. Many countries did develop theatrical film styles, but these sometimes resulted in witty and engaging works, such as those by Sacha Guitry and Marcel Pagnol in France, or Basil Dean in Britain. And linguistic barriers did pose problems, but these were solved in a number of ways, the most notable of which was the system of 'multilinguals' in place briefly at the very beginning of the sound era. In 1929, some companies began shooting the same films in several different languages, reusing sets and costumes. Although many of these multilingual films were made in Hollywood, Paramount and the German company Tobis-Klangfilm made multilinguals in studios they built in Paris. By 1933, however, better dubbing technology made this practice obsolete.

Some emerging cinemas, such as those of Romania, Yugoslavia, and Bulgaria, initially suffered in the transition to sound, as production in the Balkan languages was effectively taken over by the large multinational firms. However, the Balkan industries—in particular that of Romania, whose linguistic market was the largest in the region—gradually regained ground in the mid-1930s after the demise of the multilinguals. Balkan audiences, like those in many other European countries, tended to prefer comedies, romantic melodrama, and costume dramas, often adapting Hollywood genres to their own cultural specifications (as in the Romanian *hajduk* film, which transposed plots from American Westerns to the conflicts between Romanian bandits and foreign warlords).

Although the coming of sound meant the waning of internationalism in a linguistic sense, the 1930s saw continued circulation of technical and artistic personnel fleeing persecution in Germany and the Soviet Union. Many of these artists had settled, at least temporarily, in Paris, where a cross-fertilization of talent resulted in many of the greatest classics of French cinema. France's piecemeal system of hundreds of small production companies, many of which only produced a single film, at least had the advantage of cutting down on centralized bureaucracy and rewarding ingenuity. In this atmosphere of creative independence, a genre such as Poetic Realism, the atmospheric precursor to American *film noir*, could flourish and gain international recognition (see Chapter 5, 'French Cinema in the 1930s').

The documentary form was also gaining legitimacy throughout Europe. The coming of sound provided new opportunities for the genre, which had its roots in the Lumières' early actuality films, and which, after undergoing an experimental and often abstract phase in Germany, France, Holland, and Belgium in the 1920s (typified in the 'city symphony' films) became increasingly politicized. In Britain, John Grierson's work for the General Post Office (GPO) Film Unit resulted in often lyrical educational films with a sociological bent.

More than anything else, though, the coming of sound encouraged the growth of popular genres such as the musical, which flourished in Spain (where *zarzuelas*—operettas—drew upon traditional folklore), France (where, especially in the first half of the decade, musicals were vehicles for music hall stars), Hungary, Poland, and Portugal. Musical comedies were also popular in the Soviet Union—Stalin was a big fan—despite the doctrine of Socialist Realism, imposed by the state in the mid-1930s, which required all films to impart unambiguously the virtues of Communism: these criteria resulted in a hybrid subgenre sometimes referred to as 'tractor musicals', in which workers happily labored on collective farms while singing snappy tunes.

In Britain, too, as in other European countries, musicals were among the most popular films, after comedies and thrillers. The new sound technology allowed the British public to hear familiar accents—which, if not usually identical to those heard on the streets of Bristol, Newcastle, or Glasgow, at least echoed the received pronunciation, or 'King's English' they heard on the radio (though many Scottish, working-class, and regional English audiences apparently preferred hearing American English to the upper-crust London accents used in many British films). In the 1930s, British film production reached an all-time high, largely due to the 1927 Cinematograph Films Act, which required that the percentage of British-made films shown in domestic cinemas rise to 20 per cent by 1936 (from less than 5 per cent in the mid-1920s). This act, also referred to as the Quota Act, compelled companies, often American-owned, to churn out the cheaply made films that came to be known as 'quota quickies', but also led to the development of the British studio system—a centralized, organized system in which the division of labour enabled the production of several films at once—which would continue to thrive through the following decade.

The early sound era also saw a flowering of cinemas aimed at specific linguistic communities. This was the heyday of Yiddish cinema, produced all over Central and Eastern Europe but based primarily in Warsaw. In Belgium, Gaston Schoukens directed popular comedies filmed in a Brussels dialect that combined elements of both French and Flemish, and Switzerland produced the first films in the Zurich dialect. Catalan-language cinema, too, flourished briefly before being banned when Franco came to power in Spain; in

Italy, Mussolini also banned the use of dialects and accents other than Florentine in film. Such cultural diversity was antithetical to the totalitarian policies of the leaders who came to prominence around this time.

However, though rendered more homogeneous through increasing restrictions and state control, the production of feature films (full-length films, usually fictional, intended for cinema exhibition) continued throughout the Fascist era, motivated both by profit and by the need to pacify the populace. In 1937, Mussolini himself inaugurated the Cinecittà film studios in Rome, which would remain the centre of film production in Italy for decades to come. Most German, Italian, and Spanish films produced under Fascist rule (as well as those produced in countries such as Hungary, under Communist control since 1919 but allied with the Fascists in the late 1930s) were light entertainment, escapist comedies, and melodramas, including the theatrical comedies known as 'white telephone' films because of their bourgeois domestic settings. Few films of the Fascist period were overtly political, despite the visibility of openly propagandistic films such as Leni Riefenstahl's *Triumph of the Will* (1935), which glorified Hitler's rise to power.

Feature filmmaking continued during World War II, though to varying degrees and in varying conditions. The bans imposed on American and other foreign imports in Nazi-occupied countries during the war had the effect of stimulating some film industries to produce more domestic works to meet the public's continued demand for movies. In France, those filmmakers who had not already fled to Britain or Hollywood initially went to the country's then-unoccupied southern zone to continue working, until the Nazis centralized film production in Paris in 1942. French filmmaking was allowed to continue under German occupation in part because Germany had financial interests in many sectors of the French film industry, and in part because the Nazis ultimately envisioned French cinema's prestigious international reputation as a jewel in the Reich's crown. Germany had similar plans for the Prague-based Czechoslovakian film industry, which it had expanded following its occupation of the country in 1938; Denmark's industry also grew under German occupation, boosted by the ban on film imports. Sweden, which remained neutral during the war, was also able to expand its film industry during this period, as was Britain, which exploited the studio system it had built in the 1930s. Documentary production, too, increased in all parts of Europe, a tool of propaganda considered a valuable part of the war effort. But this boom in domestic production, brought about to some extent by 'captive' audiences and by the absence of imported, particularly American, films, was short-lived. When the war ended, Europe's film industries, like Europe itself, entered a new era.

Postwar cinema

As World War I had done before it, World War II left much of Europe struggling to rebuild. The immediate postwar years were marked by economic deprivation and continuing shortages of staple commodities. There was no shortage, however, of American films, which flooded European markets after having been banned in German-occupied countries during the war. Yet once again, the crisis sparked by the overwhelming competition from Hollywood provided the catalyst for some desperate, but often inspired, solutions.

The privations suffered by the populations of Europe were both captured and transformed in the first great genre to emerge at the end of the war, Italian Neorealism. With the Cinecittà studios being used as a refugee camp, filmmakers such as Roberto Rossellini and Vittorio De Sica took to the war-torn streets, creating low-budget films by shooting on location with non-professional casts. These films, which recalled the gritty despair of French Poetic Realism of the 1930s, in turn influenced subsequent movements such as the *nouvelle vague* (French New Wave) and *cinéma-vérité*, the naturalistic documentary style. The enormous influence of Neorealist films, however, was disproportionate to their box-office appeal, and the movement only lasted through the end of the 1940s (see Chapter 6, 'From Italian Neorealism to the Golden Age of Cinecittà').

At the end of the war, a defeated Germany was occupied by Allied powers, and American companies effectively took over film distribution in the country, leaving less room for domestic production. The major German genre to emerge in the postwar years was the nostalgic *Heimatfilm*, which typically depicted idealized romances in an idyllic Black Forest setting. This extremely popular—and apolitical—genre stood in almost direct opposition to the *Trümmerfilm* ('rubble film'), which provided a hard-edged look at the difficulties of reconstructing postwar Germany. In 1949, the country's eastern, Russian-controlled zone became the German Democratic Republic (also known as East Germany), which, like other Eastern and Central European countries after the war, nationalized its film industry. In the late 1940s and early 1950s, filmmakers from Eastern bloc countries trained in the Soviet Union, learning the techniques of Socialist Realism, which dominated film production until Stalin's death in 1953.

During the de-Stalinization period of the mid-1950s, restrictions on filmmaking were relaxed somewhat, allowing greater artistic freedom. In Poland, the Lódz Film Academy produced filmmakers who rose to great international prominence, none more so than Andrzej Wajda, whose war trilogy depicted the tragic heroism of Poland's resistance fighters. Czechoslovakia also experienced a brief cinematic renaissance, with directors

Václav Krska and Vojtech Jasny producing formally innovative works, while filmmakers in Hungary such as Karoly Makk and Zoltán Fábri bolstered Hungarian cinema's international profile in the brief period before Soviet suppression of the attempted revolution in 1956. Throughout the 1950s, animated children's cinema and puppet films—which, it was thought, could more easily elude the censors—thrived, especially in Yugoslavia, Czechoslovakia, and Romania.

In the rest of Western Europe, the end of the 1940s ushered in an age of economic growth, which would last for nearly thirty years. In France, established directors made slick, glossy costume dramas and other big-budget, 'Tradition of Quality' productions, which would later be dismissed as the 'cinéma de papa' (dad's cinema) by New Wave filmmakers. In 1952, an agreement between France and Italy resulted in several co-productions between the two countries, which utilized post-synchronous sound (sound added to the soundtrack after filming) to avoid the language barrier. In Britain, Ealing studios became known for their comedies, which enjoyed international success, as did some of the films of Michael Powell and Emeric Pressburger (see Chapter 9, 'From Ealing Comedy to the British New Wave'). From Spain, there emerged a couple of directors, Juan Antonio Bardem and Luis Garcia Berlanga, whose work drew on Italan Neorealism to depict Franco's authoritarian rule in a critical light. And in Sweden, the films of Ingmar Bergman garnered great international prestige in the 1950s, building on the filmmaker's theatrical background in psychologically penetrating chamber pieces, which would later evolve into meditations on the nature of art, illusion, and faith (see Chapter 7, 'Postwar Scandinavian Cinema').

New Waves

In the years immediately following World War II, the French film critic André Bazin was energetically setting up ciné-clubs (film societies) and sharing his enthusiasm for cinema —in particular, Italian Neorealism—with all who would listen. For Bazin, cinema at its best was a medium that used artifice as unobtrusively as possible to enable viewers to grasp the intricate subtleties of the real world. Bazin's championing of a serious film culture had a profound effect on both film theory and practice in Europe. The journal that Bazin co-founded, Les Cahiers du cinéma, employed many of the young writer-directors who would become the founding figures of the nouvelle vague (French New Wave). Articles deriding postwar French cinema and championing certain American directors such as Orson Welles and Howard Hawks led to the development of the auteur theory of cinema, which celebrated the creative vision of filmmakers who wrote and directed their own films. The fact that auteurism, which has become one of the theories most strongly associated with European cinema, grew out of an appreciation of filmmakers working in the United States, exemplifies the reciprocal influence between Europe and Hollywood.

The New Wave, however, was not simply the product of individual talent. Material factors played a determining role in the development of the movement. First, new funding structures, such as the 'avance sur recettes' (advance on box office takings), were created in France to aid first-time directors working outside the studio system, and to encourage cinema that was not overtly commercial. Then, too, the development of faster film stock and lightweight cameras and audio equipment enabled filmmakers to shoot more easily on location, giving New Wave films their spontaneous feel. André Bazin did not live to see the work produced by his colleagues (including François Truffaut, Bazin's protégé; Jean-Luc Godard; Claude Chabrol; and Agnès Varda) in the late 1950s and early 1960s, but these directors' films, though much more playful (and experimental) in nature than Italian Neorealist cinema, were clearly influenced by the realist principles Bazin had advocated (see Chapter 8, 'The French New Wave').

The French *nouvelle vague* coincided with, and often inspired, other New Waves across Europe. In Great Britain, 'kitchen sink' realism grew out of the Free Cinema documentary movement of the mid-1950s, and depicted the grim lives of working-class characters, often using French New Wave techniques such as hand-held camerawork and location shooting (see Chapter 9). Portuguese cinema experienced its own New Wave, with veteran director Manoel de Oliveira joined by younger filmmakers such as Paolo Rocha and Fernando Lopes, who coalesced around the producer António da Cunha Telles. In East-Central European countries, whose film industries were gradually becoming more liberalized, imported films by Godard and Truffaut greatly inspired young filmmakers. Directors of the Czech New Wave such as Jiri Menzel and Milos Forman (who later went to work in the US) produced films that attracted attention all over the world. In Hungary, Miklós Jancsó made thought-provoking historical films, while the more youthful István Szabó depicted his own restless generation in films that owed much to the French New Wave. And in Poland, Roman Polanski launched an international career that would span several decades, winning an Oscar for his direction of *The Pianist* in 2003.

In the Soviet Union, Khrushchev's de-Stalinization campaign made it possible for a filmmaker like Andrei Tarkovsky to make the visually poetic *Ivan's Childhood* (1962), but by the time Tarkovsky had made his highly acclaimed second feature (*Andrei Rublev*, 1965), a new regime headed by Leonid Brezhnev refused to release it, sensing that it contained social criticism in allegorical form. Tarkovsky was something of an anomaly, though, in a country that remained largely isolated from filmmaking developments in the rest of the world. Censorship also continued to play a role in Franco's Spain, to where the Surrealist Luis Buñuel returned after having worked in Mexico after the war. His film

Viridiana (1961), despite winning a prestigious award at Cannes, was banned in Spain because it was deemed blasphemous by the Catholic Church.

The films with perhaps the most impact among international audiences of the 1960s were those made in Italy. Popular movie-making and 'art cinema' rubbed shoulders at the Cinecittà studios in Rome, nicknamed 'Hollywood on the Tiber' because they were used by American production companies to make toga-and-sandals epics, but which also became the working home of Federico Fellini, one of the era's great *auteurs*. Fellini had come to international prominence in the 1950s with *La Strada* (1954), before taking a definitive turn away from realism, delving into a spectacular and very personal dream-world derived from the milieux of the circus and the stage. Like many of his contemporaries, Fellini depicted the decadence of life in modern Italy, in the context of which he questioned the possibility of spiritual salvation. In 1960, the year in which Fellini's *La dolce vita* attracted huge international success, Michelangelo Antonioni, possibly the most modernist of the Italian directors of this era, released *L'Avventura*, which depicts the alienation of modern life through the use of meticulously-composed shots. The same year saw the release of *Rocco e i suoi fratelli* (*Rocco and his Brothers*) by Luchino Visconti, whose career had been launched during the war with *Ossessione* (1942). Later in the decade, the visionary work of poet and novelist Pier Paolo Pasolini would also win wide acclaim (see Chapter 6).

The 'death' of cinema

Just as these 'new waves' were breathing life into film traditions across Europe, cinema began to feel the effects of the biggest threat to its survival: television. Postwar prosperity and the growth of consumer society led to the dramatic proliferation of television ownership, which sparked an irreversible decline in cinema attendance. Since the 1960s, the 'death of cinema' has been proclaimed loudly and often, not because of a lack of creative initiative on the part of filmmakers, but because of cinema's precarious financial status brought about by the steep drop in audience numbers. Since then, the medium has seemed to lurch from one crisis to the next, somehow managing to retain and develop its distinctive features while, paradoxically, becoming increasingly reliant upon television for its very survival, with European television channels funding film production.

The postwar period also witnessed the birth of film studies as a recognizable academic discipline. Although film theory is nearly as old as film itself (with early filmmakers and critics such as Georges Méliès, Béla Balázs, Sergei Eisenstein, Sigfried Kracauer, and Jean Epstein analyzing the structure and functions of the medium), film studies as an institutional practice only dates from this era. What we know today as film theory grew out of literary theory, in particular structuralism, semiotics, and psychoanalysis, which gained ascendancy in France in the 1950s and 1960s through the work of Roland Barthes and Christian Metz, who built upon the earlier work of the linguist Ferdinand de Saussure. It was at precisely this time that cinema attendance began its precipitous decline in the wake of the proliferation of television. As cinema became less of a popular pursuit and more of a pastime for the educated elite, it came to be taken seriously as an object of study and site of intellectual and cultural debate, spawning university courses and departments, journals, film museums, and cinémathèques for the storage and preservation of films throughout Europe.

The wave of social unrest that spread across Europe in the spring of 1968, emblematized by the violent clashes in Paris and Prague, flagged up a general malaise that was evident in many films of the period. The most prominent movement of this time was the New German Cinema, which marked German film's return to international visibility after a long hiatus. An outgrowth of the Young Cinema movement which, in 1962, published a manifesto calling for a new cinema and criticizing postwar German cinema's links with the Nazi period, New German filmmakers Rainer Werner Fassbinder, Werner Herzog, and Wim Wenders revitalized Germany's reputation for producing serious art cinema (see Chapter 10, 'New German Cinema'). Although German filmmakers in this era consciously tried to break with the past, many of the films produced in the 1970s and 1980s revisited the war and the immediate postwar period.

Other European countries—especially France and Italy—were also beginning to grapple with the legacy of the war, in many cases confronting issues that had never been fully acknowledged. In France, Marcel Ophüls's epic, eight-hour documentary Le Chagrin et la pitié (The Sorrow and the Pity, 1971) exposed the 'banality of evil' (Arendt, 1994) that proliferated during the Vichy period, opening the floodgates to filmic and literary representations of France's ambiguous role in the war that would continue well into the turn of the century. Similarly, films of the early 1970s by Bernardo Bertolucci and Neorealist director Vittorio De Sica contributed to Italy's reappraisal of its Fascist past.

Slightly longer in coming was recognition of the painful legacy of colonialism, sparked by decolonization (notably the British empire's loss of India in 1945 and the independence of most French- and British-controlled African countries in the late 1950s and early 1960s), and brought to the fore by the problems experienced by immigrants from former colonies. In Great Britain, films of the 1980s focusing on second-generation immigrants presented a counterpoint to the policies of Thatcherism, while in France, filmmakers such as Claire Denis and Brigitte Rouan made films recounting their personal experiences of the colonial era and the Algerian War (1958–62). Significantly, it was also in the 1980s that the children of North Africans who had settled in France began making films known as 'beur' cinema, which typically showed the obstacles they faced in gaining acceptance.

These attempts to come to terms with the past coincided with the growth of film genres that deliberately glossed over uncomfortable truths. One such genre, which developed in France in the 1980s, became known as the *Cinéma du Look*, because it privileged a sleek visual aesthetic over any overt social or political content (see Chapter 11, 'The *Cinéma du Look*'). Another genre that arose in both France and the UK in the same period was the visually opulent literary adaptation known as the 'heritage film', which painted a rosy picture of the past that deflected attention from a troubling present. Extremely successful abroad, the heritage film in Britain was typified by the Merchant–Ivory producer–director team, which specialized in adaptations of E. M. Forster novels set in Edwardian England. In France, Claude Berri directed highly successful adaptations of Marcel Pagnol's novels, which presented an idealized picture of a provincial France untouched by industrialization. Italy's contribution to the genre was the tremendously popular and critically successful *Nuovo Cinema Paradiso* (*Cinema Paradiso*) (Tornatore, 1989), a nostalgic portrait of village life in Sicily, and of a lost age of cinema itself (see Chapter 12, 'New Italian Cinema').

Crisis and change

During the same period, a momentous transformation was occurring throughout Eastern and Central Europe. The era of *glasnost* (openness) and *perestroika* (restructuring) inaugurated by Soviet leader Mikhail Gorbachev in the mid-1980s culminated in the fall of the Berlin Wall in 1989, and ultimately led to the breakup of the Soviet Union in 1991 and the collapse of Communist regimes throughout East Central Europe. Film production in this region, however, though relieved of the burden of state censorship, now faced potentially even greater challenges. Where filmmakers in former Soviet bloc countries could once count on automatic funding from the state, they now faced the same difficulties raising funds as their capitalist counterparts; the role of the producer, virtually unheard of in the Soviet era, quickly became all-important. Moreover, as trade restrictions were lifted, cinema in these countries suddenly found itself competing with American films, a situation not previously encountered to this extent. As video copies of American and other foreign films (some legal, but many pirated) became cheaply and widely available, cinema attendance plunged dramatically. Finally, the general economic crises that plagued these countries in the 1990s resulted in severe under-funding of all sectors of the film industry. Today, filmmakers in former Communist countries rely heavily on international co-production, and must still often go abroad to make films, as Agnieszka Holland, director of *Hitlerjunge Salomon* (*Europa Europa*) (1990), and Krzysztof Kieślowski, director of the influential *Three Colors* trilog.y (1993–4), did in the early 1990s, and Emir Kusturika, the Bosnian director of the highly successful *Underground* (1995), did in the middle of the decade (see Chapter 14, 'East-Central European Cinema: Beyond the Iron Curtain').

The crisis in the former Soviet bloc, though attributable to historically specific circumstances, is in some ways a magnified version of the crisis gripping the rest of Europe's film industries. Since the official formation of the European Union in 1992, there have been a number of European-wide initiatives designed to boost both commercial filmmaking and art cinema. The most significant sources of funding for cinema in Europe currently come from television channels, both state-run and private, and subsidies from individual European states (including lottery funding and proceeds from taxes on box-office revenues), followed by inter-European funding bodies. Notable European initiatives to help both European co-productions and individual national cinemas have included Media Plus, a programme initiated in 2000 (following on the heels of its predecessors, Media I and II), and Eurimages. These funding bodies have responded to a recognized need by placing greater emphasis on distribution and promotion than did their predecessors.

Perhaps in reaction to more general problems such as high unemployment and a widening of the gaps between social classes, filmmakers in several European countries have responded by producing socially committed realist cinema, with the notable exception of Spain, whose most successful directors, Pedro Almodóvar and Julio Medem, are known for their melodramas and magical realist films (see Chapter 13, 'Contemporary Spanish Cinema'). In Britain, the landmark film *Trainspotting* (Danny Boyle, 1995) was followed by other films that highlighted social issues by well-established directors Mike Leigh and Ken Loach, and new directors such as Lynne Ramsey. Although still dominated by London, the British industry has recently been shifting its focus to regions such as the north of England and Scotland. France, too, has acknowledged the existence of life outside Paris in films by Erick Zonka, Bruno Dumont, and Robert Guédiguian (see Chapter 15, 'French Cinema of the Margins'). This tendency toward realism has been accompanied by a surge in violence, inaugurated by Mathieu Kassovitz in *La Haine* (*Hate*) (1995), which signalled the desperation of young people excluded by mainstream society, and culminating in the relentlessly raw films of Gaspard Noé and Claire Denis, as well as in films (again by Noé, and Catherine Breillat), that test the definition of pornography. The European realist revival found its fullest expression in the international Dogme 95 movement, launched in Denmark with Thomas Vinterberg's *Festen* (*The Celebration*) (1998), and which stipulated that filmmakers should abide by a rigid set of rules in a manifesto banning the use of artificial lights, sets, and props (see Chapter 16, 'New Directions in European Cinema').

The traditional association of European cinema with *auteur* films, films that bear the personal imprint of a particular director's artistic vision, takes for granted the conditions of production that enable the realization of such a vision in the first place. In Hollywood, where scripts are usually written by committee and where producers generally maintain control of the finished product (paradoxically transforming the 'director's cut' into an alternative version of a film), there is little scope for the expression of individual artistic identity. It is true that, in the late 1980s and 1990s, American independent cinema, or 'indie' film, emerged as a US brand of auteurism, in reaction to the big-studio blockbusters that had become Hollywood's own version of the much-maligned 'cinéma de papa'. But the majority of American films still differ from the majority of European films in the ways they are produced and financed.

This difference in approach was illustrated in 1993 at the Uruguay round of the GATT (General Agreement on Tariffs and Trade) talks when, at Europe's insistence, cinema and other audiovisual works were finally exempted from the agreement to lift European trade barriers. Spearheaded by the French, this 'exception culturelle' (cultural exception), as it came to be known, was the result of a hard-fought battle to classify films as expressions of national and cultural identity, rather than simply as industrial products like any other. As it turned out, the GATT talks did not resolve this thorny issue, but merely left the door open to further debate. The history of cinema in Europe remains, to a large extent, a history of these conflicting conceptions of the medium itself, of its function, and of its role in the construction of cultural identity.

Conclusion

Throughout its many manifestations, movements, and genres, European cinema has responded to almost continual crisis with a remarkable capacity for survival and innovation. From its nineteenth-century beginnings, through its development in the 1900s, cinema is now advancing through its third century, and new technologies such as digitization are changing the ways people make and watch films. In some ways, history is repeating itself, as individual viewing at Edison's early Kinetoscope machines has evolved into solitary viewing in front of the television or DVD player, and the cinema of attractions resurfaces in MTV and action films with large special-effects budgets. Although this brief account has necessarily highlighted the major developments that have occurred since the birth of cinema, film history is perhaps more accurately characterized, like the Lumières' first film projector, by a kind of intermittent motion, in which a series of tiny breaks creates the impression of movement.

Further reading

Finney, Angus, *The State of European Cinema* (London: Cassell, 1996). An account of individual conditions of production.

Forbes, Jill, and Sarah Street (eds.), *European Cinema: An Introduction* (Basingstoke: Palgrave, 2000). An excellent overview of the politics, economics, and aesthetics of European cinema from its beginnings through the end of the twentieth century, as well as a number of penetrating case studies of key films.

Holmes, Diana, and Alison Smith (eds.), *100 Years of European Cinema: Entertainment or Ideology?* (Manchester: Manchester University Press, 2000). A timely collection, with several essays devoted to popular cinema in former Communist-bloc countries.

Nowell-Smith, Geoffrey (ed.), *The Oxford History of World Cinema* (Oxford: Oxford University Press, 1996). An informative survey of cinematic movements all over the world.

—— and Steven Ricci (eds.), *Hollywood and Europe: Economics, Culture, National Identity 1945–95* (London: British Film Institute, 1998). The introduction offers an illuminating account of the institutional forces that have shaped European film history.

Sorlin, Pierre, *European Cinemas, European Societies 1939–1990* (London: Routledge, 1991). European cinema from a sociological perspective.

Stoil, Michael Jon, *Balkan Cinema: Evolution after the Revolution* (Ann Arbor, Mich.: UMI Research Press, 1982). A useful introduction to Balkan cinema up to the late 1970s.

Thompson, Kristin, and David Bordwell, *Film History: An Introduction* (New York: McGraw-Hill, 1994). An indispensable book, vast in scope and meticulously detailed, written in a clear, accessible style.

Vincendeau, Ginette, *Encyclopedia of European Cinema* (London: Cassell/British Film Institute, 1995). An extremely useful, comprehensive reference work.

—— (ed.), *Popular European Cinema* (London: Routledge, 1992). A groundbreaking collection of essays examining the hitherto neglected area of popular cinema in Europe.

EARLY CINEMA

Early Cinema Introduction

In 1895, Sigmund Freud published his first psychoanalytic work; Guglielmo Marconi pioneered wireless telegraphy; Minna Cauer founded the German feminist journal *The Women's Movement*; Captain Alfred Dreyfus, falsely accused of betraying French state secrets to the Germans, was imprisoned on Devil's Island; Great Britain, France, and Italy advanced into Africa in order to expand their respective colonial empires; and the capital flows between the United States and Europe reversed, with the US lending more than it owed for the first time in history. This was the year—and the world—in which cinema made its debut.

At its inception near the turn of the twentieth century, cinema performed several historical functions. In Britain and France, the two largest imperial powers, the exhibition of documentary footage shot in exotic locales furthered the colonial project by allowing metropolitan audiences to glimpse the populations that were being 'pacified' in their name. Cinema also provided a boon to the burgeoning leisure industry, as increasing automation in the workplace led to shorter working days. Then too, it fulfilled an important ideological function in the reinforcement of traditional gender roles at a time when these were being called into question by a growing demand for universal suffrage and other rights for women.

Not just the images projected onto screens but the development of the film industry itself reflected its historical context in a changing Europe. First, the transformation of cinema in its first decade from an itinerant fairground amusement to a primarily urban pastime reflected a more general demographic trend toward urban living and the rise of the city. Second, the nationalization of cinema, which for the first two decades of its existence (i.e., before the establishment of quotas and other protectionist measures) moved much more freely across borders, coincided with the rise of nation–states after World War I (1914–18). Finally, the eclipse of European cinema by the American industry in the second decade of the twentieth century can be seen as part of the larger shift in economic supremacy that occurred as the world's financial capital moved from London to New York.

The changing financial status of the world's largest film-producing countries was reinforced by the war itself, which brought far-reaching changes to cinema in Europe. The diversion of money and personnel to the war effort put European film industries at a serious disadvantage in relation to the US, which did not enter the war until 1917. In the 1920, filmmakers reacted to Hollywood's commercial dominance by fostering elite art cinemas. Modernist artistic influences from the worlds of painting and literature led to the development of avant-garde cinematic styles that privileged formal abstraction over storytelling. Filmmakers experimented with editing (Soviet Montage), sets and lighting (German Expressionism), and the disruption, or even abolition, of narrative continuity (Dada and Surrealism). The trend toward abstraction receded, however, with the widespread use of synchronized sound in Europe around 1930.

The coming of sound, combined with the increasingly ominous political climate of the 1930s, resulted in two opposing trends: frothy, escapist entertainment films, and the rise of forms of realism. In the former category, musicals and comedy (often combined) drew large audiences and made movie stars of music-hall performers. At the same time, economic hardship caused by the Great Depression deepened social and political divisions, leading to the adoption of film by both Left and Right as a tool of ideological persuasion, whether through documentary or, more frequently, through fiction. The establishment of Socialist Realism as the official artistic doctrine of the Soviet Union promoted a utopian vision of Communist life, while depictions of the marginalized strata of society by Leftist feature filmmakers, in France especially, emphasized the dangers of social exclusion.

By the time World War II loomed on the horizon, cinema was well established both as Europe's first mass medium and as a legitimate art form. The medium was no longer finding its feet technologically, nor was it yet seriously threated by what would soon become its great nemesis, television. In only four decades, European cinema had developed rapidly from the heady, pioneering days of its beginnings, to achieve its full blossoming as a privileged means of cultural expression.

1

BEGINNINGS

Alison McMahan

Film history is characterized by certain grand narratives. For example, it has long been held that it took the earliest filmmakers almost twenty years to establish the basic principles of filmic narration; that silent cinema came first, and synchronized sound cinema came belatedly after; and that live-action cinema is the umbrella paradigm from which all other media, such as animation, are derived. Yet there is an alternative way of looking at film history, which we can refer to as the grand narrative of mechanization. The development of moving picture machines, most of which projected images (whether photographed or drawn) that gave an illusion of life by being shown rapidly one after the other, were the product of the industrial drive to mechanization, the drive to measure, quantify, and ultimately automate every aspect of life. Moving pictures were born out of a science called motion studies, with the immediate goal of understanding human and animal locomotion in order to devise exercises to perfect the human soldier and solve the mysteries of flight. The by-products of this effort were live-action cinema and animation, both products of the same drive to capture, store, and replay motion at will.

Motion studies

One of the most influential of the motion studies pioneers was Eadweard Muybridge (who was born in the UK but worked in the US), a still photographer who was commissioned by Leland Stanford, the President of the Central Pacific Railroad, to photograph a horse at full trot to demonstrate, once and for all, whether all four hooves left the ground at any one point. Muybridge worked on this problem for years. Finally, in California in 1877, Muybridge managed to line up twelve cameras that could take exposures in 1/1000 of a second, triggered when the horse broke the strings set across the track. These pictures showed definitively that all four of the horse's hooves did leave the ground in mid-trot. Muybridge continued these experiments and photographed many sequences of animals and humans in motion. He lectured in the US and Europe and projected his images on a screen using his Zoöpraxiscope projector. Muybridge's work especially influenced Marey and Edison (Herbert and McKernan 1996: 99–100).

Muybridge's photographs of birds contributed significantly to the advancement of aerodynamics. The idea that was popular in most aerodynamic circles was that of the ornithopter, or a flying device modeled on birds (although some favored the idea of a rotating blade that would screw upwards, as in a helicopter). In order to build an ornithopter it was therefore necessary to study the flight of birds. Such studies had already been attempted, including graphic studies by Etienne-Jules Marey in 1869 and 1870 that produced line tracings from the flights of harnessed birds.

Marey continued his work on locomotion by adapting the photographic rifle that the astronomer Pierre-Jules Janssen had developed to photograph the passage of Venus across the sun, and he was galvanized by the publication of Muybridge's photographs of Leland Stanford's racehorse. In 1883 he was awarded money to erect a building on his *Station Physiologique*, his center for the study of locomotion. The money also enabled him to hire an associate, Georges Demenÿ, whose work would become well known in its own right.

Cameras

At first Marey used single large fixed plates where a series of images would all be imprinted, but the overlap in these images made it difficult to decipher the motions he wished to study. By 1888 he had developed the *chronophotographe sur bande mobile*, a motion picture camera that could register up to twenty images a second on paper. Because the roll of paper was not perforated it was not possible to make the images equidistant, thus making it unreliable in the capture and projection of true motion picture images. Marey was not concerned about this because his interest was the study of locomotion and not motion picture projection. By 1890, celluloid (the result of research by inventors all over the world but mostly commercialized by George Eastman) had become widely available. Marey patented his camera for use with celluloid in 1890.

Now Marey and Demenÿ began to produce motion pictures in earnest, always with the purpose of studying locomotion. Until 1892 Marey studied his images of locomotion by cutting them out and then attaching them equidistantly inside a zoetrope, a cylindrical viewing device. At this point, though, he began to feel the need for real projection. By November of 1892 many of his colleagues considered the projector he developed to have resolved the problems of projecting movement. However, Marey's projector, like his camera, did not use a perforated-film system, which made it difficult to ensure a steady movement.

Thomas Alva Edison, already well known as the inventor of the light bulb and the phonograph, among many other accomplishments, saw Muybridge present his zoöpraxiscope in Orange, New Jersey, in February 1888, and met with him privately two days later to discuss the possibility of connecting Muybridge's projection system with Edison's phonograph. This particular plan never came to fruition, but Edison continued to pursue the concept on his own. In 1888 and 1889 he first tried to have 42,000 images, each $\frac{1}{32}$ of an inch wide, imprinted on a cylinder that was the size of his phonograph records. These were to be taken on a continuous spiral with 180 images per turn. The spectator would watch the images through a microscope while listening to a phonograph. In June 1889, Edison hired Scottish inventor William Laurie Kennedy Dickson to pursue the second version of the project, now called a kinetoscope, which consisted of wrapping the cylinders with celluloid coated with a photographic emulsion. While Dickson pursued this approach, Edison went to Paris in the summer of 1889 for the *Exposition universelle* (World's Fair), and there he saw the *chronophotographe* and met with Marey. This showed him that his error was in a too-literal application of phonographic principles to the kinetoscope. Edison was able to demonstrate a horizontal feed system (rather than the vertical feed system used today) by 1891. Dickson had switched to vertical feed and a wider strip of film by 1892. In 1893 in New Jersey, Edison built his film studio, 'the Black Mariah', a small black room that could rotate to let in the light of the sun through the open roof. Dickson and William Heise, his partner on the kinetoscope project, then went on to film numerous scenes, usually vaudeville acts, that would be staged with a frontal presentation in the Black Mariah; spectators would watch these films through a peephole in a box (Musser 1990: 64–78).

Projecting images

Robert William Paul built the first commercial film projector in England. An electrical instrument-maker, he became the British film pioneer when two Greek entrepreneurs asked him to build replicas of Edison's kinetoscope (which Edison had not bothered to patent in Europe). In addition to making the copies for his employers, he made a few for himself. The kinetoscopes could only be used for viewing the films, but with the assistance of Birt Acres, Paul designed a cinematograph, the Paul–Acres camera, with which they shot their first film in March 1895. Most of the films were actualities, but they did make a fiction film in June entitled *Arrest of a Pickpocket*. These films, the first made in England, were shown at the Empire of India Exhibition in Earl's Court that same year. Paul worked on a projection device and completed his Theatregraph by February of 1896, the first of various projectors he would build; later he incorporated the use of the Maltese Cross, a shutter device still in use in film projectors today. Paul also built the first film studio in England, where he employed G. H. Cricks, Jack Smith, and Walter Booth to make trick films, comedies, and actualities; all of these men went on to successful film careers. Paul himself stayed in the film business until 1920 (Herbert and McKernan 1996: 107–8).

Also in the UK George Albert Smith, a hypnotist and lanternist who ran his own amusement garden in Brighton, followed on the heels of R. W. Paul by obtaining a camera and making over thirty-one films in 1897 alone. Frank Grey credits Smith with 'the remarkable interpolative use of close-ups, subjective and objective point-of-view shots, the creation of dreamtime and the use of reversing . . . and the development of continuity editing' (Herbert and McKernan 1996: 136). Smith's best-known films include *As Seen through a Telescope, Grandma's Reading Glass,* and *Let Me Dream Again*. Smith joined forces with Charles Urban in 1902 and focused his energies on the development of Kinemacolor, a two-tone color process, until he left the film business in 1915.

The first motion picture cameras appeared just in time to film the first successful flights of dirigibles and airplanes, as the same motion studies that had produced the cameras had demonstrated the futility of ornithopters and helped scientists conduct studies in drag, velocity, and wind tunnels that would lead to flight.

False starts

Meanwhile, Demenÿ continued to work on the improvement of Marey's inventions, and he was also eager to commercialize them. In July 1891 Demenÿ gave a demonstration of his *phonoscope* at the Musée Grévin, the Parisian wax museum.

The *phonoscope* was a projector designed to reproduce the living manner of a subject as s/he pronounced short phrases. (One film shows Demenÿ himself saying 'Vive la France'.) Demenÿ made a series of animated portraits of people, from women , children, and babies to workmen, each of which represents a character type. Sometimes he put these archetypal characters into scenes together, such as a man and a woman arguing, or a family group watching a child and grandfather play pat-a-cake. Though plotless, these *phonoscope* sequences can be seen as the first steps towards fiction film. The images were taken with Marey's *chronophotographe* and then laboriously transferred to a glass disc, from which they could be observed through the *phonoscope* peephole or projected. Demenÿ also gave some thought to synchronizing his *phonoscope* images with a phonograph, but apparently never actually did so. Gaumont purchased the rights to Demenÿ's patents for the *phonoscope* (patented in 1891) and the *biographe* (patented in 1893) after Demenÿ had tried to interest the Lumière brothers in them without success. Demenÿ's patent of 10 October 1893 became the basis for the Gaumont 60mm camera, also called a *chronophotographe*, which would be perfected in the first few months of 1896.

In Germany, the Skladanowsky brothers had the same vision as Demenÿ: that film should be projected for the amusement of a paying audience. Max Skladanowsky began experimenting with 'living photography' around 1887, inspired by Joseph Plateau's Phenakistiscope. After a number of failures he managed to construct a workable camera, and shot his first film footage in August 1892: forty-eight single frames of his brother Emil. The construction of a projector, the *Bioskop*, however, was delayed because of financial difficulties. By November 1895, Max Skladanowsky had developed and built all the necessary apparatus for a public screening: a film camera, projector, printer, and perforation machine. Since he had worked in vaudeville showing lantern slides, chromotropes or kaleidoscope images, and even x-rays, he was well equipped to become a film exhibitor, as films were first shown at circuses and vaudeville fairs; nickelodeons, as the first store-front cinemas were called, did not appear until around 1905.

The first film performance to a paying audience occurred when the *Bioskop* of the Brothers Skladanowsky was introduced to audiences at Berlin's leading vaudeville house, the Winter Garden, as the final number of the new programme of 1 November 1895. The Skladanowskys used a double projector. The negative was cut apart into single frames which were then remounted on two strips consisting of alternating images (even-numbered frames on one projector, odd-numbered frames on the other). Positive prints of both strips were then projected simultaneously, using a synchronized worm-gear transport system with sprockets. A comb-like moving shutter projected only one motionless frame at a time, while masking the moving image on the other projector. The projector ran at 16 frames per second. In 1895 Skladanowsky patented the worm-gear system, already in use in his film camera of 1892, and received the official German patent number 88,599. Through this invention he solved the problem of transporting images through a projector, while simultaneously bringing them to a momentary standstill for the split second of actual projection. The Skladanowsky brothers toured widely—though in Paris, their month-long engagement was cancelled after the historic Lumière screening, at which they were present. But they toured all over Germany and had extended runs in Norway and Copenhagen (Lichtenstein 1990: 313–25).

At the same time as Demenÿ and the Skladanowskys were working on their cameras and projectors, the Lumière Brothers were busy working on a *cinématographe* of their own invention. The Lumière camera used 35mm film and had innovatively solved the problem of stabilizing the film as it unwound by perforating the celluloid with sprocket holes along the edges, using these to hold the film in place with a registration claw while each individual frame was exposed. Because the Lumières solved the registration problem, and because they were credited as the first to project films to a paying public, on 28 December 1895 (though in fact the Skladanowky Brothers had done this somewhat earlier), and—last but not least—because they were better capitalized and better at promoting their film franchise, they are usually credited as the inventors of motion pictures. Although December 1895 is a convenient marker for the beginning of moving picture history as we know it, especially since their 35mm format is still the principal cinematographic format to this day, this date is not necessarily the most accurate marker of the birth of the medium.

Lumière vs. Méliès, and other fictions

For many years it was a given among film historians that the Lumières were 'the fathers of the non-fiction film' and that Georges Méliès was the 'father of the fiction film'. This idea was derived from the grand narrative mentioned earlier, namely, that it took early filmmakers almost two decades to develop the principles of classic cinematic narration, the standard today. It is true that the Lumières specialized in making actualities, as the earliest non-fiction films were called. These were usually one-minute, one-shot, one-location films with frontal presentation. The very first one, *Sortie d'usine* (*Workers Leaving the Factory*, 1895), was also the first commercial, as it showed workers leaving the Lumière photographic equipment factory. But, as Marshall Deutelbaum (1983) has shown, most of the Lumière actualities (all about 20 metres, or one minute long) display a narrational structure dominated by a linear, sequential process, a systematic series of events directed to some end, and closure that usually matches the film's opening. The Lumières actually directed few of the films themselves, but they turned their basic narrational structure into a set of principles that was imparted to the many cameramen they subcontracted to go all over the world making films and promoting the Lumière system. For many countries, a screening of Lumière films, including a handful taken in their own locales, formed their introduction to cinema.

Though more than two-thirds of the approximately 1,500 films produced by the Lumières were non-fiction films, a third of their output was fiction, including the very first fiction film, *L'arroseur arrosé* (*The Waterer Watered*, 1895), directed by Louis Lumière in early 1895. The structural principles developed for the actualities were applied to the fiction films as well. In *L'arroseur arrosé*, for example, there is a clear beginning (the gardener is watering the yard with a hose), a middle (the boy steps on the hose and cuts off the flow of water, then releases it when the gardener is peering into the hose so that he gets a face full of water), and an end (the gardener chases the boy, then drags him back to center screen to spank him). Most of the Lumière fiction films were directed by Georges Hatôt. The Lumière brothers eventually sold their film concern to Charles Pathé in 1902.

Léon Gaumont, Jules Carpentier (inventor and Gaumont's mentor), and Alice Guy were among those invited to witness an early demonstration of the Lumière *cinématographe* on March 22, 1895, for the *Société d'Encouragement pour l'industrie nationale à Paris*. Carpentier immediately offered to build more machines for the Lumière brothers. He also designed a *Défileur Carpentier-Lumière* that allowed longer bands of film to pass through the camera. The only film shown at the March 22 screening was the *Sortie d'usine*. (It is possible that as of March 22, 1895, *L'Arroseur* had not yet been made.) But this demonstration inspired Alice Guy to start her own filmmaking career; and she wrote, produced, and directed her first fiction film, *La Fée aux choux* (*The Cabbage Fairy*), sometime before May 1896, probably with the Demenÿ–Gaumont 60mm camera, thus becoming the first woman filmmaker. She taught herself the art by first remaking the fiction films released by the Lumière company, most of them one-minute, one-take, one-set 'cinema of attractions' films directed by Georges Hatôt. She also imitated Edison films and films by Méliès (McMahan 2002: 4–12).

The 'cinema of attractions' theory was developed by Tom Gunning and André Gaudreault (based on a term used by Eisenstein) (Elsaesser 1990: 56–61). According to this theory, the cinema of attractions dominated until 1902, and was characterized by frontal presentation, theatrical devices like entering and bowing, a lack of development of a diegesis (a story world), a lack of editing and montage, and no use of off-screen space. Other historians have developed counterarguments and alternatives to this theory (see, for example, Brewster and Jacobs 1997). In *Alice Guy Blaché, Lost Visionary of the Cinema*, I reached the conclusion (based on the work of Charles Musser, Edward Branigan, later essays by Gaudreault, and my own research) that the 'cinema of narrative integration', as early narrative cinema is referred to by scholars, existed from the very beginning of cinema; certainly it is present in single-shot films. I used three arguments to support this claim: that elements of the *mise-en-scène* of single-shot films can serve the same function as editing, such as the use of staging in depth or off-screen space; that certain single-shot films do suggest the passage of time; and that character development is clearly evident (McMahan 2002: 32–6 and 49–52). The cinema of attractions theory

■ Alice Guy (1873–1968)

Alice Guy was working as a secretary at the Gaumont Company when she began making films in 1896. She mastered most of the techniques of special effects quickly, but preferred to make dramas and comedies over trick films. Her great contribution to film was the development of cinematic storytelling technique. From the beginning her films focused on the emotional perspective of individual characters and she used every filmmaking tool available to her to tell stories of character growth, whether it was a mattress-maker coming to terms with her desires, a father dealing with his new wife's abuse of his son, or a pregnant woman coping with her irresistible cravings for phallic foods. This last film, *Madame a des envies* (*Madame has her Cravings*), probably made in 1904, contains one of the earliest extant dramatic uses of close-ups in film; in fact, the whole story is structured around them. Guy's skill at communicating a character's psychological state, and maintaining dramatic focus on that state throughout the duration of the film, was unmatched by her peers. Even when Ferdinand Zecca at Pathé plagiarized her films, he would improve the effects or arrange for more spectacular staging but he would lose the psychological focus.

In addition to a steady stream of silent films, Guy made over 100 synchronized sound films for the Gaumont Chronophone from 1902 to 1906 (the sound was recorded first, the

⏷ Alice Guy on set

picture filmed in sync with the sound playback, and the phonograph and cinematograph were synchronized together for exhibition). In 1907, Guy married Herbert Blaché, another Gaumont employee, and quit her job as head of film production at Gaumont in Paris to move with her husband to the United States, where her daughter was born in 1908. In 1910 she started her own company, Solax, and made silent films using the Gaumont studio in Flushing, New York. The Solax films were distributed by Gaumont through George Kleine. Guy built a $100,000 studio plant for Solax in Fort Lee, New Jersey, in 1912, the same year she had her second child, a son. Once Gaumont joined the ranks of the independents, Solax had to negotiate for distribution on a state-by-state basis.

For the two years in which it was successful, Solax made stars out of actors like Marion Swayne and Billy Quirk and provided a rich growth and learning environment for designers like Ben Carré and Henri Menessier. But by 1914 it was clear that the day of the short film was over. Due to his multiple business setbacks and the outbreak of the war in France, Gaumont pulled out of the US, as did other French companies except for Pathé. The Blachés remained, but Solax had to borrow money from bankers, the Seligmans, who then owned the majority share in the company. Partly to avoid being controlled by Seligmans, Blaché started up his own company, and by the late 1910s both Guy and her husband were direct-ing feature films for Blaché Features. After retooling themselves in various guises (US Amusement Corporation, etc.) Guy and Blaché began to join loose distributor coalitions with other filmmakers, such as Popular Plays and Players. Some of the films they directed for Popular Plays and Players were distributed by ALCO, the production entity that led to the formation of Metro-Goldwyn-Mayer in Hollywood. Guy also directed a series of 'painted woman' melodramas starring the great Olga Petrova, all of which appear to be lost. The couple divorced in 1920. In 1922 Guy chose to return to France, where for the next thirty years she lectured widely on film and wrote magazine fiction and novelizations of film scripts; but she never remarried, nor did she make another film. She died in New Jersey in 1968.

Alice Guy produced, or supervised the production of, thousands of films. She directed approximately 400 films herself; of these, 111 survive. Seventeen of her sound films survive, some of which are missing the soundtrack. Of her twenty-two features, only three survive, one of which is still unpreserved (*The Empress* at the Cinemathèque Française).

was developed to account for a more limited body of early films than we have available today, and primarily in relationship to the trick films of Méliès. However, Elizabeth Ezra has shown that the films of Méliès, used for years as the standard by which the cinema of attractions was defined, can in fact be categorized as narratives (Ezra 2000: 24–49).

Georges Méliès, a successful magician who had his own theatre, the Robert-Houdin, saw the first public Lumière screening at the Grand Café des Capucins on December 28, 1895, where *L'Arroseur arrosé* was screened. Immediately after the screening, Méliès offered Antoine Lumière (the brothers' father) FF10,000 for a *cinématographe*. M. Lumière refused. Not to be dissuaded, Méliès went to London in February of 1896, where he bought a Bioscope, a motion picture camera developed by William Paul. In April he used this camera/projector to screen films produced by Paul and Edison Kinetoscope films at his Theatre Robert-Houdin. In May he returned to London and bought some Eastman unperforated celluloid film stock, which he cut into strips and had perforated by a mechanic named Lapipe. In May or June he shot his first 20m film, which was an imitation of a Lumière film, entitled *Une partie de cartes* (*A Game of Cards*, 1896), shot in May 1896 in the garden of his house in Montreuil and featuring Méliès himself. Méliès went on to specialize in a genre of 'fairy films' known as *féeries* (though he also made dramas, non-fiction films, and slapstick comedies in his long career); he became the undisputed master of the trick film, relying primarily on the stop-action substitution technique. The technical virtuosity in Méliès' trick films still dazzles today, especially in films like *Voyage dans la Lune* (*Trip to the Moon*, 1902), *Voyage à travers l'impossible* (*The Impossible Voyage*, 1904), and *A la conquête du Pole* (*The Conquest of the Pole*, 1912). Méliès was successful enough—partly because he made filmed advertisements as early as 1898 and was the first to use product placements in his films in 1901—for his films to be copied everywhere, and he had his brother start an American branch of the company in the US. However, as audiences developed a taste for films with more complex narrative, and as the result of his inability to collect fees for the plagiarized films, he was forced to go out of business in 1915. His downfall can also be seen as a result of his inability to keep up with the drive toward mechanization: he stubbornly stuck to an artisanal, non-assembly approach to filmmaking that made it impossible for him to compete with more industrialized film manufacturers such as Charles Pathé.

Color and sound

In histories of the cinema, progress towards color film with synchronized sound is often interpreted as an unstoppable evolution toward increased realism. To the contrary, the drive to color and especially synchronized sound is another manifestation of the impetus to full mechanization. Synchronization and the optical soundtrack resulted not from audience demand for increased realism but from capitalist and industrial pressures to homogenize product and control distribution and exhibition. To put it another way, movies were never silent, they were only imperfectly mechanized.

Let's start by looking at the case of color. Many early films were actually made to be shown in 'color'. At first, color was applied by hand, then by stencil (the areas of the frame to be colored were cut onto matrix copies which were then placed on the positive prints; each color was applied to the film through the outlines thus obtained, with brushes or pads soaked in the appropriate dye), two processes previously used on lantern slides. It was not until 1906 that Pathé began to use the ad-line 'cinematography in natural colors', thereby accelerating the company's drive toward standardization of the product by promising an increase in realism. Hand-coloring was gradually replaced by tinting and toning, but was still being used on certain films as late as the early 1920s.

Tinting and toning—the uniform coloring of the film base—started as early as 1901 and was employed into the late 1920s, and was used on approximately 85 per cent of total film production. However, producers did not have final control over colors used on films exhibited abroad, as negatives were sent with coloring instructions that may or may not have been followed. Although a combination of hand-coloring, stenciling, and tinting and toning was sometimes used on quality productions and achieved a beautiful effect, the demands of standardization and mechanization were hardly met by this procedure, which was too expensive to be used widely. It was not until the advent of Technicolor (Gaumont began experiments with three-color processes as early as 1912) and its perfection around 1930 that the goal was achieved. In between—from 1911 to 1928—there was much experimenting with additive (the projection of a black-and-white image through color filters) and substractive (the subtraction of colors while filming so that only the desired colors appear during projection). Little is known about these processes now (Usai 2000: 22–34). What is clear is that film manufacturers aimed for standard, fast, and reliable methods of producing color film and continued to experiment until they were found. The search for color systems that will stand the test of time continues to this day.

A similar progression occurred with synchronized sound. The earliest known synchronized film to exist is the 'Dickson Experimental Sound Film'. The film was made in late 1894 or early 1895, or perhaps even earlier. The image has been known to film scholars and archivists for many years, but in spite of the film's name no one was sure it had ever really had a soundtrack. The successful preservation of the film in 1999 resulted in perfect sync between Dickson's violin as he plays an air from Pietro Mascagni's *Cavalleria rusticana* and the sound of the dancing men's feet on the wooden boards. And although Dickson succeeded in recording the sound and image of his film simultaneously, it is doubtful that the film was ever shown synchronized. The post-synchronized sound films such as the *phonoscènes* made for the Gaumont Chronophone, on the other hand, were recorded and filmed separately, but were exhibited regularly, properly synchronized, to paying audiences. (Pathé first did this in 1896, Gaumont in 1901; post-synchronized systems had commercial lives into the mid-1910s.) The Chronophone was not the only such device: in the US there was the Cameraphone, the Cort-Kitsee Device, and the Synchronophone. In England there was the Cinematophone, the Vivaphone, and, most successful of all, the Animatophone, developed in 1910 from Thomassin's Simplex Kinematograph Synchronizer (mismanagement forced the Animatophone Company out of business in 1911). In Germany, F. N. Messter had successfully created his Biophon, Alfred Dusker produced a Cinephon, Karl Geeyr built the Ton-biograph for the company Deutsche Mutoskop und Biograph GmbH, and Guido Seeber developed the Seeberophon and later used Messter's Synchronophon as a technical model for the German Bioscop. After the demise of Messter's Tonbilder, synchronized musical films continued to be produced in Germany from 1914 to 1929 on the Beck system, the Lloyd-Lachman device, and the Notofilm system. The proliferation of devices was matched by placid expectation in the print media: for example, from around 1906 to around 1915, *The Moving Picture World* discussed widespread synchronized sound film production and distribution as if it were just over the horizon, an inevitable and natural occurrence.

For about a decade many of the individual systems, including the Gaumont Chronophone, were commercially very successful. In Germany alone, by 1914, 1,500 negatives from 60 to 85 metres in length and 500 Biophons had been sold in Germany; Gaumont recorded 1,000 films for the Gaumont-Messter system, totaling 60,000 meters. According to Harald, as many sound films were produced in England as in France. His estimate of sound films produced worldwide is 3,500–4,500, totaling 250,000 or 300,000 meters. That all of these systems fell out of favor around the same time, in the mid-1910s, suggests that by then these systems represented imperfect mechanization; they were gradually replaced by optical sound systems (the outbreak of World War I was also a factor) (McMahan 2002: 47–69).

If we accept that at least certain types of silent film, such as films with diegetic sound events like explosions, or dance films, were meant to be shown with sound added at the exhibition venue, then we can see these as films with a low level of mechanization, which might be raised by the addition of printed speeches for the narrator or arrangements or orchestral scores for the musicians. Seen in this light, early silent films and early sound films are part of the same continuum in a period of cinema's history when mechanization was the driving force behind technological changes. In other words, films produced with various degrees of mechanization, at the level of both color and sound, existed side by side.

Stories and stars

Mechanization, in the form of standardization, also had an influence on the development of editing and narrative. At first, film manufacturers such as Charles Pathé sold their films outright to exhibitors, who selected and re-edited the films they purchased—assembling actualities, for example, into narrative sequences. Gradually, however, this process was taken over by film manufacturers. According to Richard Abel, Pathé-Frères took the lead in producing story films in order to wrest authorial and editorial control from exhibitors as it moved into mass production around 1904–5. The industrial switch from selling to renting films led to the standardization of length to one-reel and split-reels, setting the stage for the single-reel, pre-feature story film which dominated the film market from 1907 to 1911. With a running time of approximately fifteen minutes, one-reel films were long enough to tell complex stories, and many of the elements of what is now considered classic cinematic language were developed in the one-reel films before 1912 (Abel 1998 [1994]: xv).

The trend toward standardization and industrialization also led to the development of the star system. At first films carried no credits, apart from the title and the company logo (written or emblazoned directly onto sets at first to prevent the kind of pirating that ruined Méliès). Soon intertitles appeared to carry explanatory descriptions and, later, dialogue. As audiences learned to recognize certain actors and clamored to see their favorites again, credits with actors' names appeared, though credits for directors, producers, and screenwriters only came some time later. By 1912 the star system as we know it was in place.

From animation to digitization

When cinema and animation are looked at not in isolation, but in terms of the roles they play in the drive towards mechanization, it becomes clear that animation is not a sub-species of cinema; rather, cinema and animation were both born out of the same drive to capture, store, and replay motion at will. It also becomes clearer that cinema and animation were always much more intricately related than is commonly accepted. Even if their paths diverged after 1907 (though even this is debatable), there is no question that cinema and animation are merging again in the twenty-first century. By understanding how the drive to mechanization worked at the beginning of the last century, we can better understand the drive to digitization that already characterizes the current one; and in the case of certain nineteenth-century mechanized media, such as Reynaud's, we can see that digitization was already the goal.

Reynaud was making animated bands for his *praxinoscope* as early as 1877. From 1892 to 1900 he rear-projected more elaborate bands, which he now called *pantomimes lumineuses* (luminous pantomimes), onto a screen by means of a complicated mirror-and-lens system. The images were hand-painted on long strips of transparent celluloid and fitted into a leather band with perforations next to each frame; in other words, his apparatus in many ways prefigured that of cinematic projection, though all the images were hand-drawn and hand-colored by Reynaud himself. Reynaud also supplied narration and vocal sound effects during his performances, with music played by a phonograph or live musicians. This was animation with almost no mechanization.

In 1896 Reynaud adapted Marey's *chronophotographe* to make a motion picture camera-projector and made a handful of films. The first of these was a classic vaudeville act by two clowns, Footit and Chocolat (black or in blackface), loosely based on an episode of William Tell: Chocolat has an apple on his head (and takes bites out of it) and Footit shoots it off with a water rifle, soaking Chocolat in the process. Once Reynaud had shot the film (at 16 frames a second) he took a few frames from one part and a few frames from another. These short selected sequences were then reproduced on the transparent celluloid, improved by drawing and coloring applied by hand and then strung into a sequential loop by joining them within a perforated flexible metal band. Reynaud repeated this process with at least two other films, one entitled *Le Premier Cigare* (*The First Cigar*), in which a university student tried his first cigar and found it comically sickening, and another vaudeville act featuring a pair of clowns, called *Les Clowns Price* (*The Price Clowns*), made in 1898, which was never shown to the public. These experiments can be seen as mechanical versions of what today is referred to as digitization, in the sense that Renaud was taking analog material, reducing it to units of information (the cut-up sections), manipulating and transforming them by coloring and re-editing, and putting them back together to make a new product. Reynaud's artisanal drive to develop mechanical methods to digitize his films in the late nineteenth century would flower into ubiquitious digitization across the media industries by the end of the twentieth. Unfortunately, none of his early efforts survive.

By retouching cinematographic images so that the figures took on the appearance of cartoons or animation, Reynaud was applying a form of digitization similar to motion capture: the film provided him with the basic shape and motion, and he cut up the pieces to use as he wished, then drew and painted over them to give them a graphic appearance instead of a filmic appearance. A similar method was used in 1899–1900 by the Brothers Bing of Nuremberg, along with other German toy firms such as Planck, Bub, and Carette, and the French Lapierre company, all of whom made cartoons for use in toy viewers by tracing from live-action films in a technique that became known as 'rotoscoping' (Robinson 1991: 18).

The production of animation itself gradually became more mechanized. At first, artists like Emile Cohl, who began making animated films for Gaumont and Lux in 1908–9, and his US counterpart, Windsor McCay, produced every drawing for an animated film by hand. The laboriousness of this process was often highlighted in films, and live

⬆ *Drame chez les Fantouches*

action and animation were combined in order to reach the one-reel standard length while still staying within budget. As a result the animator himself, or at least his hand, appeared in the cartoon, which was often framed with opening and closing live-action scenes.

But in 1910 the philosophy of Taylorism, or scientific management, became popularized in the US, and inevitably affected the art of animation. It was at this time that animation studios were being established in the US, and John Bray, an animator with a regular production contract with Paramount studios, patented a series of inventions and, most important, a *system* of scientific management for animation studios. The idea was to automate the process so that a maximum amount of unskilled labor could be used for smaller tasks, and to organize the work of the skilled labor in the most efficient way possible. Bray established a strict hierarchical chain of command, spelled out the daily tasks for everyone on his staff, penalized those who did not finish the assigned work, and rewarded with bonuses those who finished ahead of time. This was in sharp contrast to the earlier workshop arrangements, but since animation studios were just getting established, the system of scientific management became the norm, and remains so to this day (even though scientific management fell out of fashion in other industries by the late

1910s). Scientific management of the animation studio spread to Paris with Lortac in 1921, who had observed the process at work in New York. Two-dimensional animation suffered in Europe during World War I, although some animators such as Lortac managed to survive by producing commercials and public service films (Crafton 1993).

Trick films and special effects

Slightly more successful in Europe were stop-motion animation films. Trick films made before 1908 by artists such as Méliès, working in his own studio, and Zecca and Segundo de Chomón, working for Pathé, included techniques such as stopping the camera and replacing one object with another (a process known as stop-substitution); filming in slow motion, so that when projected at normal speed the film would appear speeded up; combining such fast-motion through superimposition with a regular speed sequence, so that some characters moved at comically fast speeds and others at normal speed; cutting alternate frames out of a sequence to speed it up; shooting with the camera hanging upside down, so that the film when projected normally would play the action backwards; superimposing a fade in and fade out of a figure to simulate the apparition and dis-appearance of a ghostly image; and using objects such as removable limbs, miniature sets, and miniature props. The list of special effects actually used is much longer, but this gives an indication of the creativity of the film manufacturers working in live-action cinema before 1910.

Similar tricks were adopted in Europe and applied to stop-motion animation, often using animatronic figures and puppets that could be remotely controlled, with cables, for example. Ladislas Starevitch, who was born in Poland but did most of his work in France, made animated films using the carcasses of real insects such as grasshoppers and beetles, as well as the corpses of birds and other animals. He later began to work with puppets, and continued to make animated films into the sound era.

Emile Cohl worked briefly for Pathé in France in 1911, where he was only allowed to make animated films in between live-action film assignments. By 1913 he had migrated to the US where he worked with other French filmmakers at the Éclair Studio in Fort Lee, New Jersey. According to Donald Crafton, Cohl was the one responsible for disassociat-ing animation from the trick film genre (1993: 61). Unfortunately, the only films that survive from his years in the US are *He Poses for his Portrait* (1913), which used speech balloons, and *Bewitched Matches* (1913), a stop-motion film with matches as characters, an effect which was copied by René Clair in *Entr'acte* in 1924. Cohl's work also influenced another Surrealist filmmaker, Fernand Léger, who included an animated Charlie Chaplin cut-out in *Ballet mécanique* (1923–4). In spite of these efforts, Europe in general did not succeed in producing a viable animation industry, though many individual artists managed to produce works of great beauty and ingenuity, such as Lotte Reiniger working with her shadow puppets in Germany from 1918 to 1936.

As Crafton notes, when it came to content, early animators were inspired by early stop-motion films (1993: 74–6); but we must not forget that animation itself is a product of stop-motion substitution, as each drawing is replaced by the next, shot on another bit of film, until the whole gives the impression of movement. We can consider J. Stuart Blackton's *Haunted Hotel* (1907), for example, both as live action film and as a trick, or animated film.

However we choose to look at the relationship between cinema and animation in the last hundred years, there is no question that the paths of cinema and animation were joined at the beginning of their history and are joining up again now. The prioritizing of cinema over animation has made it all too easy to overlook the real historical process that we are still engaged in—the drive toward mechanization, which in the twenty-first century has become the drive to digitization.

Conclusion

A reconsideration of the earliest technologies that led to the invention of cinema as we know it also leads us to conclude that live-action cinema and animation are more intimately related than generally thought, and that both are primarily the products of the industrial drive to mechanization. The drive to mechanization gives us a better explanation of the transition to sound, the use of color, the development of editing, and even the development of narrative and the star system. Looking at cinema and animation as the outgrowth of the industrial drive to mechanization that occurred at the end of the nineteenth century and gathered its full strength in the twentieth, we are forced to reconsider the grand narrative that gives live-action cinema the pride of place. Especially now, when the drive to mechanization has mutated into the drive to digitization, it is worth reconsidering the nature of animation itself, the place of special effects within animation and cinema in general, and the relation of both to live-action cinema. By learning about the earliest technologies, and how their inventors were influenced by each other, we can gain a better understanding of the cinema of the past as well as the future.

Further reading

Abel, Richard, *The Ciné Goes to Town: French Cinema 1896–1914* (Berkeley: University of California Press, 1994). A very readable and engaging history of early French cinema; the book with which all researchers on the topic must begin.

—— *The Red Rooster Scare: Making Cinema American, 1900–1910* (Berkeley: University of California Press, 1999). They key text on how early French cinema, which dominated cinema worldwide until 1914, affected the American film industry.

Braun, Marta, *Picturing Time: the Work of Étienne-Jules Marey (1830–1904)* (Chicago: University of Chicago Press, 1992). The definitive text in English on the motion studies pioneer.

Crafton, Donald, *Before Mickey: The Animated Film 1898–1928* (Chicago: University of Chicago Press, 1993 [1982]). A unique and key study on early animation that covers both Europe and the US.

—— *Emile Cohl, Caricature and Film* (Princeton, NJ: Princeton University Press, 1990). The definitive text in English on this influential animation pioneer.

Elsaesser, Thomas, and Adam Barker (eds.), *Early Cinema: Space, Frame, Narrative* (London: BFI Publishing, 1990). An important collection of theoretical texts on early cinema.

Ezra, Elizabeth, *Georges Méliès* (Manchester: Manchester University Press, 2000). An overview of Méliès's work that argues for the importance of narrative in his films.

Herbert, Stephen, and Luke McKernan (eds.), *Who's Who of Victorian Cinema* (London: British Film Institute, 1996). An excellent reference on all of the players in the development of cinema in Europe and the US, including many little-known figures such as vaudeville performers, narrators, and exhibitors.

McMahan, Alison, *Alice Guy Blaché, Lost Visionary of the Cinema* (New York: Continuum, 2002). The only definitive study of the work of the first woman filmmaker and narrative filmmaking pioneer which re-evaluates many theories of early cinema.

Mannoni, Laurent, *The Great Arts of Light and Shadow: Archeology of the Cinema,* trans. and ed. Richard Crangle, introduction by Tom Gunning, preface by David Robinson (Exeter: University of Exeter Press, 2000). An encyclopedic text on just about every aspect of precinematic visual culture that had some bearing on the cinema.

Musser, Charles, *The Emergence of Cinema,* vol. 1: *The American Screen to 1907* (History of the American Cinema Series: New York: Scribner's, 1990). A readable, carefully researched overview of cinema in the United States by the foremost expert on the subject.

Williams, Alan, *The Republic of Images: A History of French Filmmaking* (Cambridge, Mass.: Harvard University Press, 1992). The key text in English on French cinematic history from the beginning to the late 1980s.

2

SOVIET CINEMA: THE OLD AND THE NEW

Denise J. Youngblood

'Cinema is for us the most important of all arts.' Attributed to Vladimir Lenin, this statement became the watchword of the Soviet film industry and was emblazoned in all Soviet movie theaters. The slogan signifies not only Lenin's interest in the potential of film as propaganda but also the centrality of cinema as a form of mass art and entertainment in the USSR. The motion picture industry had a considerable impact on culture, society, and politics throughout Soviet history, but at no point was it greater than during the 1920s. At this time, the influence of Soviet cinema spread far beyond its borders. Young Soviet directors like Alexander Dovzhenko, Sergei Eisenstein, Lev Kuleshov, Vsevolod Pudovkin, and Dziga Vertov literally revolutionized film art and earned themselves an enduring place in the history of European cinema.

Yet the achievements of this revolutionary avant-garde—and their eventual fall from grace—cannot be understood outside their historical context. Children of revolution, these filmmakers engaged in constant battles—with each other, the studio heads, the censors, and perhaps most of all with the 'old' directors of pre-revolutionary cinema—to win the hearts and minds of audiences. Their story transcends the politics of a bygone era and speaks to the transformative role of art on society. It also challenges the distinctions drawn between 'high' and 'low' culture, 'art' and 'entertainment,' and the 'old' and the 'new.'[1]

Early Russian cinema, 1896–1918

Before we can assess the degree to which early Soviet cinema was truly 'new,' we need to understand its prehistory. The movies came to Russia less than a year after the first screenings in France. They debuted on May 6, 1896 at the Aquarium amusement park in St Petersburg, then the country's capital. By summer, films became a popular attraction at the large trading fairs in the provinces.

Initially French films dominated, as they did elsewhere in Europe. Although French cinema, especially comedies, continued to be very popular with Russian audiences, the native industry grew rapidly after its inaugural production, Alexander Drankov's *Stenka Razin* (1908). Although the Drankov studio was located in St Petersburg, Moscow became the Russian Hollywood, home to two large Russian-owned studios, Khanzhonkov and Thiemann & Reinhardt.

With the outbreak of World War I in 1914, the native Russian film industry entered a 'boom' phase. There were two reasons. First, the war had a negative impact on trade, even with allies like the French; movies made by enemy nations, like Germany, were banned altogether. Second, Russian cultural nationalism was becoming increasingly important; no one could make the dark melodramas popular with Russian audiences better than Russian directors. As a result, by 1916 more than 100 studios in the empire produced about 500 pictures annually to fill the country's 4,000 theaters. Movie attendance was estimated at 2 million spectators daily (Youngblood 1999: ch. 1).

Early Russian directors made films in all genres, but they specialized in deeply erotic contemporary melodramas, often based on 'boulevard' novels. Although Russian cinema was 'star-driven'[2] (in sharp contrast to what we shall see in the early Soviet period), the industry did produce one great *auteur*, Yevgeny Bauer (1865–1917). Bauer successfully translated the 'psychologism' characteristic of Russian literature to the screen. His innovative camerawork and elaborately decorated sets raised artistic standards.[3]

The chaotic revolutionary year of 1917 proved disastrous for cinema. The overthrow of the Romanov dynasty in February ended media censorship, which naturally pleased filmmakers.[4] Their joy was short-lived. It soon became clear that the quasi-democratic Provisional Government could not provide political, economic, or social stability to a country on the brink of total anarchy. By the autumn of 1917, when the Bolsheviks staged their 'Great October' coup, electricity was in short supply and many theaters were forced to close. Bolshevik proclamations made clear that the new government intended to implement a Marxist program, starting with the abolition of private property. Russian studio heads ordered their companies to pack up and move south to the Crimea, where the counter-

revolutionary 'White' forces were marshalling strength. By 1920, when it was fairly obvious that the Bolsheviks would win the Civil War that followed the October Revolution,
Russia's filmmakers were on the move again, to Paris, Berlin, Prague, and even Hollywood.

Russian cinema was no more. The equipment and film stock were gone; the personnel
had emigrated; much of the repertory was lost. The movie theaters were in ruins. The
road was cleared for the creation of a totally new cinema . . . or was it?

The birth of Soviet cinema, 1918–1925

The Bolsheviks understood that force alone would not save their revolution. Their
recognition of the agitational potential of the movies was prescient, particularly in a
country with the lowest literacy rates in Europe. In 1918, revolutionary film committees
formed in a mainly futile attempt to resume production. On August 27, 1919, in a largely
symbolic gesture, the Bolshevik government 'nationalized' the film industry, turning
it over to 'Narkompros', the acronym for the People's Commissariat for Enlightenment
(i.e., Department of Education). Commissar Anatoly Lunacharsky became cinema's great
champion among the Bolshevik leadership.

The Civil War of 1918–21 devastated European Russia. Filmmaking took place under
extraordinarily difficult conditions of famine, cold, and brutality. Trained cameramen and
projectionists vanished, along with film stock and spare parts to fix broken-down equipment. Since most established directors, producers, and actors had already fled central
Russia for territories controlled by the White armies, young men and women with artistic
talent found themselves rapidly rising to positions of prominence in the revolutionary
cinema. These young people were drawn to film as the art of the future, the art of the
masses, the art that for them exemplified the possibilities of a socialist revolution.

Crisis sparked innovation. In addition to newsreels from the front, the Civil War repertory consisted of newsreels and 'agit-films' (agitki). Agit-films were schematic one- or
two-reel melodramas, with clear, simple, and direct political messages attacking the
bourgeoisie and supporting the worker–peasant revolution. Colorfully decorated 'agit-
trains' traveled the country, carrying portable electric generators, a necessity given that
rural areas had yet to be 'electrified.' The 'screen' for these impromptu shows was usually
no more than a linen sheet. The agit-trains also carried Bolshevik propagandists to read
the titles, explain the films, and check on the political allegiances of the audiences.
Important early innovators like Lev Kuleshov and Dziga Vertov honed their skills at the
front at this time.

A semblance of order was restored to most parts of the country by 1921, although
fighting and rebellion continued sporadically until 1922. At the end of 1921, Lenin

decided to end the draconian system of fixed prices, rationing, requisitioning, and forced labor known as War Communism, in favor of a mixed economy, the NEP (New Economic Policy). The NEP had the same salutary impact on the Soviet film industry that World War I had had on the pre-revolutionary cinema. In 1922, Goskino ('State Cinema'), the first state film trust, was formed, under the titular control of Narkompros; in 1924, after the formal establishment of the Union of Soviet Socialist Republics, Goskino was reorganized and renamed Sovkino (Soviet Cinema). Another important event was the opening of the non-government studio Mezhrabpom-Rus, which received its founding capital from a German Communist organization, the International Workers' Aid. Production of fiction films began to rise, from just twelve titles in 1921 to seventy-six in 1924 (Youngblood 1991: appendix 1).

By the end of the Civil War, most of Soviet Russia's future filmmakers had converged on Moscow, once again the country's capital city.[5] Because film stock was carefully rationed until the postwar economy recovered somewhat in 1924–5, young would-be directors had to content themselves with theory instead of practice. Organized into 'collectives,' many of them connected to the Proletkult (Proletarian Culture) theater, aspiring moviemakers rehearsed the experiments they hoped to film, which Lev Kuleshov dubbed 'films without film.' They also debated among themselves, writing combative theoretical essays for new film periodicals like *Cinema-photo*, *Cinema Gazette*, and *Prolet-cinema* (Youngblood 1991: ch. 1).

Given that the new socialist society privileged the masses over the individual, it is deeply ironic that early Soviet cinema was a director's cinema, with powerful personalities dominating the cinematic front. In Moscow, the leading director-theorists were Sergei Eisenstein (1898–1948), Lev Kuleshov (1899–1970), Vsevolod Pudovkin (1893–1953), and Dziga Vertov (1896–1954, born Denis Kaufman). In Petrograd[6] (renamed Leningrad after Lenin's death in 1924), the FEKS (Factory of the Eccentric Actor), led by Grigory Kozintsev (1905–73) and Leonid Trauberg (1902–90), were the leading aspirants.

Although he was only 18 years old at the time of the revolution, Lev Kuleshov quickly became the 'old man' of the young guard. Not only had he gained valuable filmmaking experience during the Civil War, Kuleshov had begun his film career before the revolution working as a set designer for director Yevgeny Bauer, discussed above. The Kuleshov collective became a magnet for young talent, with important directors like Boris Barnet and Vsevolod Pudovkin emerging from the collective as well as distinctive actors like Vladimir Fogel, Alexandra Khokhlova, and Sergei Komarov.

Kuleshov laid the foundations for the development of Russian 'revolutionary' film theory. He was the first to articulate the role of quick rhythmic cutting in creating a new kind of moving picture, distinctly different from the slow-paced psychological melodramas of pre-revolutionary Russian cinema. Kuleshov called this kind of editing 'American' montage in tribute to the American action picture. Kuleshov also stressed the role of body language in film acting and the importance of exercise and training ('Delsartism' and 'bio-mechanics') for his actor-model (*aktër-naturshchik*).

His most famous theoretical experiment, the 'Kuleshov effect', became the basis for relational montage. In this experiment, Kuleshov alternated the same shot of the pre-revolutionary star Ivan Mozzhukhin with shots of other objects, e.g., a plate of soup, a girl, and a coffin. Although some film historians doubt Kuleshov's recollections, viewers were said to believe that Mozzhukhin's facial expression changed depending on the ordering of the images; for example, that he looked hungry at the plate of soup, sad at the coffin, etc. (Kuleshov 1974).

Important as Kuleshov's contributions were to the development of Soviet film theory, the ideas of Sergei Eisenstein and Dziga Vertov had an impact that extended far beyond Soviet borders. The debates between Eisenstein and Vertov over 'acted' versus 'non-acted' cinema symbolized the most extreme positions in the theoretical conflicts among the revolutionary avant-garde. Eisenstein believed in 'acted' cinema, i.e., fiction films with actors playing parts. He disdained the glamorous theater actors who dominated pre-revolutionary cinema, favoring non-professional actors who would blend in with others in the ensemble to form a socialist 'collective hero'. Eisenstein's ideas about fictional narrative also differed markedly from those of 'bourgeois' cinema. Trite romances and melodramas were replaced with narratives driven by a 'montage of attractions' (editing in the service of abstract ideas rather than storyline), with the 'masses' as the protagonists (Eisenstein 1988; 1991).

Vertov, on the other hand, privileged documentary ('non-acted') films. He argued that the 'real' image, not the actor, should be the heart of a film. In one of his most famous proclamations, Vertov called the movie camera a 'cinema eye' (*kino-glaz*); his production collective became known as the Cinema Eyes (*Kinoki*). According to Vertov, the purpose of all cinema should be to capture 'life off-guard' (*zhizn vrasplokh*). Yet despite his protested allegiance to unvarnished 'reality', Vertov was an inveterate manipulator of time and space in his pictures (assisted by his wife, the gifted editor Yelizaveta Svilova). Vertov strenuously opposed narrative cinema. In his articles and his art, he proclaimed that a brilliantly constructed kaleidoscope of images revealed the contours of revolutionary life better than any fictional drama (Vertov 1984).

Other young directors, although less well known than Kuleshov, Eisenstein, and Vertov, also contributed significantly to the development of Soviet film theory. Grigorii Kozintsev was merely 17 years old and Leonid Trauberg only 20 when they published the FEKS manifesto, 'Eccentrism'. While these zany fragments of 'futurist' thought hardly constitute a coherent theory (and that was part of the point), Eccentrism attracted the attention of established futurist and formalist artists and critics. Boris Eikhenbaum,

■ The old: Yakov Aleksandrovich Protazanov (1881–1945)

Yakov Protazanov was the scion of a wealthy Moscow merchant family who was reluctant to take over his family's businesses. Well-educated and fluent in several languages, Protazanov 'discovered' the movies in 1905 on a trip to Paris, where he visited the Pathé studio. In 1907 he returned to Moscow to work in the new Russian film industry as an interpreter, actor, scenarist, and assistant director. By 1911 he had become a director for a major studio, Thiemann & Reinhardt, where in 1913 he co-directed *The Keys to Happiness* with Vladimir Gardin (who also became a Soviet moviemaker). This record-breaking 5,000-meter melodrama was the biggest box office hit in Russian cinema before the revolution, and Protazanov became one of Russia's best-known and highest-paid directors.

Protazanov early exhibited his versatility as a director. He excelled in the full-length adaptations from Russian classic and contemporary literature known as the 'Gold Series' of prestige pictures. When he joined the Ermolev studio in 1916, he began making sensational films that catered to the public's fascination with the supernatural and mysticism. Two of Protazanov's last films for Ermolev, both made in 1918 and starring the great Russian silent

◑ *Aelita*

actor Ivan Mozzhukhin, were among his finest work. *Little Ellie* and *Father Sergius* indicated an intriguing turn toward the psychological, the former exploring the psyche of a child murderer, the latter a priest tormented by his sexual desires.

Like most major Russian filmmakers, Protazanov emigrated when it became clear that the Bolsheviks would win the Civil War. He continued making films for Ermolev, in his new French studio, Albatross. Protazanov also worked briefly in Berlin before returning to Soviet Russia in 1923. In his Soviet persona, Protazanov embodied what came to be known as the 'Mezhrabpom director', that is, a maker of highly polished, well-acted, and entertaining blockbusters in the Hollywood style that the Mezhrabpom studio promoted. Protazanov's films always had a 'revolutionary' message, but it was clear to critics that the politics in his movies was window-dressing. The great popularity of Protazanov's pictures with Soviet audiences paid off for his studio. With the profits, Mezhrabpom could afford to finance the films of its young 'revolutionary' directors, notably Vsevolod Pudovkin.

Protazanov's most original Soviet film was his first, *Aelita* (1924), but he also made interesting melodramas situated in the revolutionary period. *His Call* (1925) concerned the moral rehabilitation of a young girl seduced by a conniving White guardist; *The Forty-first* (1927) adapted Alexei Tolstoy's story about a female sharpshooter in the Red Army during the Civil War who kills her lover, a White officer. Finally, there was *The White Eagle* (1928), which features the only surviving screen appearance of the important theater director Vsevolod Meyerhold.

As good as his melodramas were (and they kept getting better), Protazanov's greatest successes were his satirical comedies: *The Tailor from Torzhok* (1925), *The Case of the Three Million* (1926), *Don Diego and Pelageya* (1928), and *St Jorgen's Feast Day* (1930). In these films he skillfully skewered the absurdities of modern society, both Soviet and capitalist. *Don Diego and Pelageya* was a particularly sharp exposé of the arbitrariness of Soviet power in the countryside, showing a petty-minded station-master persecuting an elderly peasant woman.

Protazanov displayed a keen understanding of Soviet cultural politics: he stayed completely out of them. Unlike Sergei Eisenstein and Dziga Vertov, he wrote almost nothing and was amusingly laconic on the rare occasions when he was interviewed. He continued to maintain a low public profile from the 1930s until his death in 1945, but he worked steadily, his last film appearing in 1943. The best known of his late films was *Without a Dowry* (1937), an adaptation of Alexander Ostrovsky's play.

Vladimir Mayakovsky, Vsevolod Meyerhold, Viktor Shklovsky, and Yury Tynyanov praised FEKS for their impudent rejection of Russia's sacred high arts in favor of pop culture, technology, and 'Americanism' (Christie and Gillett 1987).

Vsevolod Pudovkin's theories on cinema as a revolutionary art were more sober-minded and, ultimately, longer-lived in terms of application and utility. Like Eisenstein, he borrowed the notion of the actor as 'type' from Kuleshov. Unlike Eisenstein, he placed individual human heroes at the center of the action. Like Eisenstein, Pudovkin believed that rapid montage was critical to successful 'revolutionary' filmmaking, but Pudovkin also argued that ideas and theme should determine the action, rather than the other way around. Pudovkin's editing style, which he described as a 'montage of associations', reinforced the socialist content of his films (Pudovkin 1970).

Bursting with ideas, these young artists had few opportunities to put them into practice. Leading directors from the old regime, like Peter Chardynin, Vladimir Gardin, and Yakov Protazanov (recently returned from abroad), were 'reinventing' themselves as Soviet filmmakers. Film censorship during the NEP was loose enough to allow all kinds of 'bourgeois' artists to work, so long as they were not openly counter-revolutionary. For example, Protazanov's first Soviet feature, *Aelita* (1924), was a lavish production loosely adapted from Alexei Tolstoy's popular science fiction novel about a workers' revolt on the planet Mars. Alexandra Exter, a leading constructivist artist, designed the film's fantastical Martian costumes. Although *Aelita* was criticized for the superficiality of its Communist message, it scored a major success at the box office and continued to do well in audience surveys for several years after its release (Taylor and Christie 1991: ch. 5).

Indeed, only one member of this young cohort succeeded in making a full-length feature film before 1925. Lev Kuleshov's debut feature, *The Extraordinary Adventures of Mr. West in the Land of the Bolsheviks* (1924), was a marvelous illustration of his theories and became one of the most popular films of the decade. This high-energy satire of the NEP and American stereotypes about Bolshevism starred future directors Vsevolod Pudovkin and Boris Barnet as well as Kuleshov's wife, Alexandra Khokhlova (Petrić 1993).

The golden age, 1925–1929

The conflict between the youth and their elders came to a head by the mid-1920s. One might well argue that competition sharpened the talents of both the old and the new. There were two main issues. The first was ideological, about the role of cinema in a socialist society. The avant-garde declared that socialist cinema needed to be revolutionary in form as well as in content. If the 'masses' had difficulty understanding highly stylized movies, they would learn. The 'old guard' directors, joined by younger filmmakers who also worked in a realist, narrative mode, argued that entertainment was as important as art.

The second issue was closely related to the ideological debate. During the NEP, the film industry, though still nationalized (with the sole exception of the Mezhrabpom studio), did not receive state subsidies. It was expected to pay for itself through ticket sales. The state film trust Sovkino therefore encouraged the studios to make entertainment films that would attract audiences. These profits would then be used in part to finance the 'politically correct' but less popular movies of the revolutionary avant-garde. Sovkino also imported large numbers of foreign films to boost its profits, with the result that for most of the 1920s, the majority of pictures on Soviet screens were foreign. Sovkino's policies worked in that they assured the industry's financial stability—but backfired in that 'bourgeois' entertainment films were clearly more popular than Soviet revolutionary films. Middlebrow films even had their own 'fan' magazine, *Soviet Screen*, which featured full-page 'pin-up' photos of stars, and gushing letters from star-struck young women. Audience surveys showed that Soviet filmgoers enjoyed Douglas Fairbanks and Charlie Chaplin more than 'tractor and factory films' (Youngblood 1992: ch. 3).

As rational and fiscally responsible as Sovkino's policies might have been, they put the artistically radical young directors at a disadvantage. A comparison of Sergei Eisenstein's and Dziga Vertov's early work and reception with Protazanov's shows this clearly. Protazanov followed the success of *Aelita* with two more hits in 1925: the melodrama *His Call* and a rollicking comedy, *The Tailor from Torzhok*, starring the popular comic actor Igor Ilinsky. These highly entertaining and well-crafted films were not breaking new artistic ground, but Protazanov faced no problems with financing and distribution because he knew how to make crowd-pleasers.

On the other hand, Eisenstein's first two feature films, *Strike* (1925) and *Battleship Potemkin* (1926), are powerfully original. *Strike*, a fact-based look at the workers' movement during the Revolution of 1905, was a brilliant debut that introduced Eisenstein's ideas about montage to amazed audiences. *Potemkin*, however, guaranteed him an enduring place in film history.

Potemkin was a single episode taken from an epic screenplay intended to chronicle the events of 1905. It is a largely accurate rendition of a true event, the June 1905 mutiny of sailors from the battleship *Prince Potemkin of Taurida* in the Black Sea. In Eisenstein's film, the sailors rebel because of the miserable living conditions on the ship, which leads to the summary execution of one of their number, Vakulinchuk. Several officers are killed as the sailors take over the ship. Sailing toward Odessa, the mutineers are politicized when they realize that the city has also revolted against tsarist authorities. After the sailors lay Vakulinchuk's body 'in state' at the Odessa wharf, the city's protestors congregate there, leading to the government's attack on unarmed men, women, and children.

Potemkin is a visual textbook of Eisenstein's theories. First, his concept of the collective hero is well illustrated. Most of the sailors do not have names; one who does, the martyr Vakulinchuk, is a symbol, not an individual. Eisenstein's skillful use of the 'type', the non-professional actor, is also apparent; the faces in this film are those of real people, not movie stars. The fetishization of technology, so important to the avant-garde, is prominent as well, in the 'person' of the massive battleship. Finally, the massacre on the Odessa Steps

■ ... and the new: Sergei Mikhailovich Eisenstein (1898–1948)

Sergei Eisenstein was born in Riga in 1898, a pampered only child. Eisenstein's parents separated in 1902, and the boy was raised by his father, an engineer. Although his wide-ranging intelligence, intellectual ambitions, and artistic gifts had been evident from an early age, Eisenstein dutifully prepared to follow in his father's footsteps, studying civil engineering at a Petrograd technical institute from 1915 to 1918.

The Revolution enabled the young Eisenstein's own personal revolution. Freed from the 'bourgeois' influence of his father (who emigrated to Germany), Eisenstein volunteered for the Red Army in 1918 as a technical expert. After demobilization in 1920, he entered the Proletkult Theater in Moscow and studied with the avant-garde director Vsevolod Meyerhold. By 1923 he was an instructor in the Proletkult theatre workshops and the head of a theater 'collective'. In 1924, under the influence of another Proletkult artist, Lev Kuleshov, Eisenstein's interests shifted from theater to cinema. He managed to convince Goskino to give him the chance to direct one of the films being commissioned to honor the twentieth anniversary of the 1905 Revolution.

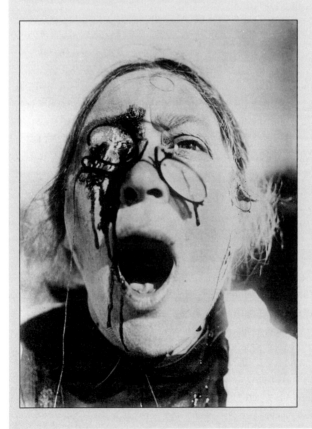

◉ *Battleship Potemkin*

Eisenstein was determined to make a film unlike any the world had ever seen. He succeeded. *Strike* (1925) generated extraordinary excitement at its premiere. The rapid pace, original shot compositions, and absence of an individual protagonist exemplified the collective energy of the revolution. Critics and competitors alike recognized that revolutionary cinema had found its genius. Eisenstein basked in the acclaim but did not allow it to quench his creative fires. *Strike* was quickly followed with another revolutionary masterpiece set in the 1905 revolution, *Battleship Potemkin* (1926).

Potemkin catapulted the young director to fame in the West, despite the suspicions against Soviet communist 'propaganda' in the capitalist world. Despite the success of *Potemkin* with Soviet critics, some disquieting notes began to emerge. The working-class audiences for whom the picture was intended disliked it, preferring films by 'bourgeois' or foreign directors.

Undaunted, Eisenstein forged ahead with *October*, a film based on American journalist John Reed's *Ten Days That Shook the World.* Commissioned for the tenth anniversary of the Revolution in November 1927, *October* was not released until 1928. The most persistent rumor was that the original version included the disgraced Bolshevik leader Leon Trotsky in key scenes. Trotsky had to be excised, and Eisenstein rearranged other scenes to conform better to the Party line.

Daunted but not cowed, Eisenstein was determined to restore his reputation as a politically reliable director. As a reflection of his self-confidence, he intended to call his movie about collectivization *The General Line*. Finally released in 1929 under the title *The Old and the New,* the film was a dreary failure, both artistically and politically.

Eisenstein received numerous invitations to travel to Europe and Hollywood, and this appeared to be the opportunity for a break. From 1929 to 1932 he was abroad, mainly in Hollywood. However, his genius proved incompatible with the aims of Hollywood's moguls. Gravely disappointed, he went to Mexico to make a movie titled *Qué viva Mexico!* Mexico proved a disaster, primarily because of conflicts with his financial backer, American novelist Upton Sinclair. The issues came to a head when Sinclair and his wife discovered a cache of Eisenstein's homoerotic drawings. They seized this 'pornography' and sent it to Stalin, who promptly ordered Eisenstein home. Disgraced, Eisenstein was not able to complete another movie until 1938. *Alexander Nevsky,* which depicted the victory of a Russian prince over the Teutonic knights in the fifteenth century, was hailed as a masterpiece but had to be withdrawn later that year when the USSR signed a non-aggression treaty with Nazi Germany. The film was immediately re-released in summer 1941 when the Germans invaded.

After the invasion, the Soviet government organized massive evacuations of the civilian population to the east, away from the front and the occupation zone. Along with other important members of the film community, Eisenstein ended up in Alma-Ata (now Almaty), Kazakhstan, in Central Asia, where a makeshift studio had been built. He was once again entrusted with an important commission, a biography of one of Stalin's favorite historical figures. *Ivan the Terrible*, part one, was filmed in Alma-Ata and premiered in January 1945. The second part was banned in 1946 and not released until 1958. Eisenstein's health collapsed under the stress of making *Ivan the Terrible.* Early in 1948, barely 50 years old, he died alone in his apartment of a massive heart attack.

is undoubtedly film history's most famous and most studied scene, a marvel of Russian montage. The rhythmic cross-cutting between extreme close-ups of the faces of the victims and the booted legs of the oppressors still evokes a powerful response from spectators (Bordwell 1993: ch. 2).

Both *Strike* and *Potemkin* brought Eisenstein the recognition he craved but also heightened his competition with Kuleshov and Vertov for cinematic supremacy. While most Leftist critics were unstinting in their praise of Eisenstein's first two movies, *Strike*, and especially *Potemkin*, failed to attract worker and soldier audiences. Attendance figures were inflated with compulsory showings at factories and clubs. Apart from the Odessa Steps sequence, which roused excitement, 'ordinary' people were puzzled by the absence of a classical narrative with a hero and a heroine. Abroad, however, *Potemkin* was hailed as a masterpiece.

Eisenstein's arch-opponent, Dziga Vertov, also had trouble making films that appealed to the mass audience. His feature-length documentaries *Forward, Soviet!* and *One-Sixth of the World* (both 1926) are remarkable examples of constructivism in film. They focus on the process of building socialism and on the impact of the revolution on daily life, providing a valuable archive of images of socialist construction and a positive political message. The 'proletarians' for whom Vertov intended his films were nonplussed. After a long day laboring in a factory, most workers did not choose to spend their limited leisure time and even more limited disposable income watching a movie about themselves— working.

Kuleshov's *The Extraordinary Adventures of Mr West* had shown his ability to make an entertaining film that was revolutionary in both form and content. Despite his early promise, his later efforts were much less successful, both at the box office and critically, although some display considerable artistry. Indeed, Kuleshov continued to grow as an artist, but his bold experiments failed to find an appreciative audience. *By the Law*, his stunning 1926 adaptation of Jack London's story 'The Unexpected', met the same derision as his failed attempt at science fiction, *Death Ray* (1925).

The FEKS team of Grigory Kozintsev and Leonid Trauberg, who made movies for the Leningradkino studio, never reached an audience outside the cultural elite, but their work is artistically important. Their experimental narratives like *The Devil's Wheel* and *The Overcoat,* the latter an adaptation of Nikolai Gogol's famous short story, perfectly realized FEKS's aspirations to adapt the principles of Expressionism and 'Eccentrism' to cinema. FEKS's movies deserve more careful attention than they have received to date (Youngblood 1991: ch. 4).

Among the early avant-garde, Vsevolod Pudovkin was the most consistently successful in translating revolutionary style and content for mass audiences. With well-developed plots and characters, as well as strongly realistic overtones, his films were the least radical in stylistic terms. His directorial debut, *Mother* (1926), was freely adapted from Maxim Gorky's famous novel. Pudovkin followed *Mother* with other well-received films on revolutionary themes: *The End of St Petersburg* (1927) and *Storm over Asia* (1928, also known as *The Heir of Genghis Khan*). Pudovkin's ability to elicit strong performances from actors was unusual among the avant-garde; he himself was a fine film actor, continuing to act even after he became a director.

None of these important avant-garde artists could compete commercially with the old guard, exemplified by Yakov Protazanov, who turned out hit after hit. No Soviet director could dethrone him, but several new realist filmmakers came close, among them Boris Barnet (1902–65), Fridrikh Ermler (1898–1967), and Abram Room (1894–1976). Barnet, the grandson of an Irish printer who emigrated to Russia in the nineteenth century, worked briefly as a professional boxer. He first came to public attention as an actor, playing 'Cowboy Jeddy' in *The Extraordinary Adventures of Mr West in the Land of the Bolsheviks*. Barnet left the Kuleshov collective immediately after making *Mr West*, but he skillfully applied Kuleshov's ideas about 'Americanism' in cinema in his own directorial work for the Mezhrabpom studio.

Barnet's directorial debut, *Miss Mend* (1926, co-directed with Fëdor Otsep), was an espionage adventure serial modeled after the Pearl White serials that Soviet audiences enjoyed. Loosely based on Marietta Shaginian's popular spy spoof, *Miss Mend* demonstrated how a 'Western' genre could easily be adapted to the Soviet worldview. This rollicking three-part film was an auspicious debut for the young director. He followed it in 1927 with a sparkling comedy, *The Girl with the Hatbox*, which exposed the shady dealings of the NEP era's private entrepreneurs. Both movies drew unusually large audiences for Soviet (as opposed to foreign) films. Barnet was commissioned to direct a tenth-anniversary film, *Moscow in October* (1927), but the revolutionary topic was not well suited to his talents. He returned to comedy in 1928 with a marvelous satire on the class contradictions of Soviet society, *The House on Trubnaya Square* (Youngblood 1992: ch. 7).

Fridrikh Ermler was a very different kind of narrative realist. A maker of penetrating social melodramas, he was among a minority of leading directors to be a 'card-carrying' Communist. He had joined the Party during the Civil War, where he served the Red Army as a spy behind German lines (and later as a member of the Cheka, the first incarnation of the Soviet secret police). Born Vladimir Breslav in a village in Latvia, he adopted 'Fridrikh Ermler' as his *nom de guerre* and continued to use it for the rest of his life.

Ermler's silent films were interesting, conventional tales about the problems of life during the NEP. Class consciousness and social criticism were foregrounded in every movie Ermler made, but his stories and characters were too complex for his work to be dismissed as mere propaganda. Indeed, he was often chided for being insufficiently 'Party-minded' in his work. He began to realize his promise as a director in his second feature, *Katka the Apple Seller* (1926), an exciting adventure and touching love story that explored Moscow's criminal underworld of black marketeers and speculators. *The Parisian Cobbler* (1927, released in 1928), showed a member of the Young Communist League (the Komsomol) recruiting a local gang of hooligans to attack and rape his pregnant girlfriend. This dark melodrama was a hit with moviegoers but drew murmurs of disapproval from critics for its sensational subject matter and unorthodox depiction of a Communist youth. The murmurs became a chorus after the previews of *The House in the Snowdrifts* (1927, limited release in 1928), based on a story by Yevgeny Zamyatin, a writer critical of the Bolsheviks. Even a Communist director could not be trusted to make 'politically correct' films.

In terms of artistic consistency and overall audience popularity, Abram Room was not in the same league as Barnet and Ermler. He must, however, be included even in a brief survey such as this because of the success and notoriety, at home and abroad, of his film *Bed and Sofa* (1927), released in the USSR as *Third Meshchanskaia Street*. Unlike Barnet and Ermler, Room was an active participant in the cinematic debates of the day and was a strong and articulate proponent of acted cinema. Room's first full-length films, *Death Bay* and *The Traitor* (both 1926), were 'revolutionary detective' adventures—lively but not particularly distinguished.

In *Bed and Sofa*, Room found his *métier* as a director of the urban social melodrama. The psychologically complex tale of a bored housewife who lives out her movie-fueled fantasies of romance in a one-room basement apartment, *Bed and Sofa* was the biggest box office hit of 1927. The Party's 'right-wing' moralizers were deeply disturbed that a film about a *ménage à trois,* with a petty-bourgeois heroine, should be so popular with Soviet audiences. Although Room ends with a positive message—the woman decides not to have an abortion, and leaves her husband and lover to live a productive life away from the big city —critics excoriated the director for failing to punish the miscreant males. This disapproba-tion was paralleled in the West, where *Bed and Sofa* was frequently banned (Graffy 2001).

Despite the predominance in early Soviet cinema of filmmakers who were either ethnically Russian or self-identified as such, moviemaking in this multi-ethnic state was not solely a Russian enterprise. Distribution politics often made it difficult, however, for films from Ukraine, Armenia, and Georgia to be considered more than 'exotica', at least as far as the Russian majority was concerned. The greatest artist to emerge from the non-Russian cinemas[7] was certainly the Ukrainian director Alexander Dovzhenko (1894–1956). Dovzhenko first gained widespread attention in 1928 with his fourth film, *Zvenigora*, a romantic and inventive celebration of folklore and folklife. None of Dovzhenko's previous films, which included the short comedy *Love's Berries* (1926) and the espionage thriller *Diplomatic Pouch* (1928), prepared viewers for the originality of *Zvenigora*. Sergei Eisenstein was thrilled by the kaleidoscope of images; studio and film trust executives were bemused; audiences were reportedly confused.

Nevertheless, a star had clearly been born. This was confirmed by Dovzhenko's next film, *Arsenal* (1928), a sweeping epic of war and revolution in the Ukraine that was criticized because it seemed to suggest that Dovzhenko's love for his native land was more important than his allegiance to the Soviet state and the Communist Party. Try as he might, his political messages were too mixed to satisfy cinema's increasingly alert watchdogs (Kepley 1986: chs. 4 and 5).

By the late 1920s, as the New Economic Policy era was coming to a close, Soviet cinema was flourishing. Cinema theaters had reopened in all provincial cities, and cinematic road shows served rural areas. A lively film press reflected a variety of aesthetic and political positions. Production was respectable, about 150 titles annually, despite the stiff competition from American and European studios. Yet clearly there were problems on the horizon. 'The people' did not like the films the critics liked—and vice versa. The young avant-garde directors were encouraged to be more 'accessible', while the old guard and the young realists were supposed to be 'less bourgeois'. From the Party's perspective, the artistic diversity of NEP cinema was unacceptable. More stringent control—before, during, and after production—ensued, and as a result, by 1933 production had plummeted to a mere thirty-five films (Youngblood 1991: appendix 1).

The cultural revolution in cinema, 1929–1932

Many factors contributed to the crisis in cinema that was part of the Cultural Revolution. First, in 1927 sound was introduced to cinema. This had significant artistic implications everywhere, but an impoverished developing country like the Soviet Union could not readily afford to develop the technology. Second, 'proletarianist' organizations like RAPP, the Russian Association of Proletarian Writers, and ARRK, the Association of Workers in Revolutionary Cinematography, were infiltrated by extremist elements who cared more about politics than either art or entertainment. These 'cadres' supported the government's aims to turn the Soviet film industry into a tool for propagandizing the collectivization and industrialization campaigns. The first All-Union Party Conference on Cinema Affairs in 1928 laid the groundwork for this. Third, in 1929 Anatoly Lunacharsky, the leading proponent of diversity and artistic freedom in cinema, was ousted as Commissar of Enlightenment. Massive purges of the film industry followed, lasting through the end of 1931.

Nevertheless, these troubled times saw the production of four great films, the last gasp of Soviet silent cinema. Fridrikh Ermler's *The Fragment of the Empire* (1929), which told the story of an amnesiac who suddenly recovers his memory to discover that Russia has been replaced by the USSR, was his most experimental film to date, skillfully employing unusual camera angles and cutting to show the man's overwhelming confusion (Youngblood 1992). Grigory Kozintsev and Leonid Trauberg cemented their reputation as the most daring experimenters of the Soviet avant-garde in their highly stylized and expressionistic *New Babylon* (1929), set during the events of the Paris Commune of 1870. In *The Man with the Movie Camera* (1929), a remarkable journey through Moscow, Dziga Vertov brilliantly realized his 'cinema eye' theory (Petrić 1987). Finally, Alexander Dovzhenko's *Earth* (1930), ostensibly intended to support Stalin's collectivization campaign to force peasants into state farms, was more remarkable as a celebration of the old way of life in rural Ukraine (Kepley 1986: ch. 6). The press of the time denounced all four pictures for their 'formalism', a code word meaning that they failed to conform to the state's preference for a simple style soon to be dubbed 'Socialist Realism'.

The end of an era

By the end of the Cultural Revolution, filmmakers understood that the era of artistic innovation was over. Movies and their makers were now 'in the service of the state' making art that must appeal to 'the millions'. 'Socialist Realism' was officially proclaimed the state aesthetic in 1934 and formally adopted by the film industry in 1935 at the All-Union Creative Conference on Cinematographic Affairs. Politically astute directors had, however, foreseen the inevitable. For several years, they had practiced 'self-censorship' by making movies set in factories or on collective farms that were only slightly more sophisticated than the *agitki* of the Civil War era (Youngblood 1991: ch. 9).

In the early 1930s, a few leading artists of the silent era attempted to adapt their experimental talents to the sound film. These efforts met with little success. Dziga Vertov's *Enthusiasm* (1931) and Lev Kuleshov's *The Great Consoler*, for example, were excoriated for their 'formalism'. The embittered Vertov began making hack documentaries, while Kuleshov spent the rest of his life sidelined into teaching at the state film institute.

By the mid-1930s, the situation was much worse. Sergei Eisenstein's *Bezhin Meadow* (1937), based on the case of Pavlik Morozov, a peasant boy who was supposedly murdered by relatives for denouncing his own father as a traitor, was banned outright. Film production plummeted, as directors tried to navigate the constantly changing 'Party line', and many projects were aborted mid-production. Stalin's intense personal interest and involvement in moviemaking greatly exacerbated the atmosphere of fear and tension in the film industry (Kenez 2001: ch. 7). Grigory Alexandrov, Eisenstein's longtime assistant director, provided a bright note to this dark scene, with his bouncy musical comedies like *The Circus* (1936) and *Volga-Volga* (1937).

Some of the early cinema avant-garde directors eventually rebuilt their careers. Grigory Kozintsev and Leonid Trauberg scored a major success with their popular and politically conformist adventure trilogy about the revolutionary era: *The Youth of Maxim* (1935), *The Return of Maxim* (1937), *and The Vyborg Side (1939)*.[8] Vsevolod Pudovkin avoided political confrontations by turning to historical films celebrating Russian heroes of old in *Minin and Pozharsky* (1939) and *Suvorov* (1941). Sergei Eisenstein likewise found a 'safe' historical subject in *Alexander Nevsky* (1938). Alexander Dovzhenko and Fridrikh Ermler compromised their artistic integrity by making movies that openly curried Stalin's favor. Ermler's *The Great Citizen* (two parts, 1937–9) is a notorious example of the impact of conformity on these great directors, as is Dovzhenko's *Shchors* (1938). This Civil War adventure was cut and recut to accommodate the twists and turns of the Party line on Ukrainian nationalist heroes (Kenez 2001: ch. 8).

Yet the legacy of Soviet cinema's golden age lived on, especially in Europe and North America. Soviet revolutionary cinema became a staple of film courses and film festivals, with Eisenstein's *Battleship Potemkin* regularly appearing on the lists of the greatest or most influential films ever made. The editing style of music videos owes a great deal to 'Russian montage', particularly to Dziga Vertov (whether or not the directors are aware of it). The style of the radical Soviet filmmakers of the 1920s has become part of the cinematic vernacular. And in the USSR, the revival of Soviet cinema after the death of Stalin owed a great deal to the filmmakers who learned the art of the cinema from the masters of the golden age.

Acknowledgments

I would like to thank Hilary Neroni, Kevork Spartalian, and Josephine Woll for their helpful remarks on an earlier version of this essay.

Further reading

Kenez, Peter, *Cinema and Soviet Society from the Revolution to the Death of Stalin* (London: Tauris, 2001). A specialist in Soviet propaganda discusses the politicization of cinema in the Stalin era; this is a reprint of the 1992 edition.

Leyda, Jay, *Kino: A History of Russian and Soviet Film* (London: Allen & Unwin, 1960). A colorful account written by a filmmaker who studied in the USSR in the 1930s, this classic history highlights the avant-garde directors with whom the author was acquainted.

Roberts, Graham, *Forward Soviet! History and Non-fiction Film in the USSR* (London: Tauris, 1999). The first full-length study of Soviet documentary filmmaking, dealing primarily with the silent era.

Taylor, Richard, and Ian Christie (eds.), *The Film Factory: Russian and Soviet Cinema in Documents, 1896–1939* (Cambridge, Mass: Harvard University Press, 1988). This volume is a thoughtfully selected and well-translated compendium of film criticism and theory.

—— (eds.), *Inside the Film Factory: New Approaches to Russian and Soviet Cinema* (London: Routledge, 1991). Leading specialists on Soviet cinema, including the editors, offer revisionist views.

Youngblood, Denise J., *Soviet Cinema in the Silent Era, 1918–1935* (Austin: University of Texas Press, 1991). A reprint of the 1985 edition, this is a study of the evolution of the early Soviet film industry, focusing on the cultural politics of the period.

—— *Movies for the Masses: Popular Cinema and Soviet Society in the 1920s* (Cambridge: Cambridge University Press, 1992). A study of the 'other' Soviet cinema—the commercially successful films of the golden age.

—— *The Magic Mirror: Moviemaking in Russia, 1908–1918* (Madison: University of Wisconsin Press, 1999). Explores the earliest years of Russian cinema.

Notes

1. The title of this chapter pays homage to Sergei Eisenstein's 1929 film *The Old and the New* (also known as *The General Line*).
2. The leading stars were Vera Kholodnaya (1893–1919) and Ivan Mozzhukhin (1890–1939). After the Revolution, Mozzhukhin emigrated to France and continued his film career as 'Mosjoukine'.
3. Some of Bauer's extant films are available on video cassette: *Twilight of a Woman's Soul* (1913), *Child of the Big City* (1914), *Silent Witnesses* (1914), *Children of the Age* (1915), *The Dying Swan* (1916), and *To Happiness* (1917).
4. At this time Russia went by the Julian calendar, thirteen days behind the Gregorian calendar used in the West. By the Gregorian calendar, the February Revolution took place in March; the October Revolution in November.
5. Moscow was Russia's capital until 1718, when Peter I moved it to St Petersburg.
6. St Petersburg was renamed Petrograd 1914–24, Leningrad 1924–92, and is now once again St Petersburg.
7. Although essentially unknown in the West, Armenia's Amo Bek-Nazarov (1892–1965) and Georgia's Nikolai Shengelaya (1903–43) made important contributions to early Soviet cinema.
8. Trauberg's career ended in the late 1940s, as part of the anti-Semitic 'anti-cosmopolitan' campaign, but Kozintsev made two extraordinary films late in his life: *Hamlet* (1964) and *King Lear* (1971).

WEIMAR CINEMA: THE PREDICAMENT OF MODERNITY

Anton Kaes

The beginnings of the Weimar Republic did not bode well for the future of Germany's first experiment with democracy. In November 1918 the Kaiser abdicated and disappeared along with his Reich; the German Revolution, meant to replicate the Russian Revolution of 1917, ended in bloodshed; and a harsh peace treaty, hyperinflation, and political violence further destabilized an already traumatized society. Born from Germany's devastating but unacknowledged defeat in World War I, Weimar democracy was fiercely contested until Hitler seized power in January 1933. The war had been fought, according to the ideologues, to defend traditional German *Kultur* against the onslaught of *Zivilisation*, i.e., the mechanization of life, democracy, and modern mass culture. While the fighting ceased in 1918, the cultural war for and against modernity continued. Cinema played a major role in this struggle, touching virtually every aspect of German society. Movies left their mark on art, lifestyle, sexuality, gender, and politics; they tantalized with images of luxury and freedom; they confronted provincial Germany with pictures from faraway worlds, broke taboos, created fashion fads, and encouraged mass consumption. Cinema contributed significantly to the modernization of German society during the Weimar Republic. At the same time, modernist Weimar cinema often critiqued and denigrated modernity, expressing a deep ambivalence vis-à-vis progress, technology, and the spectacle of cinema itself.

Germany's film industry, which began with the first film exhibition by the Skladanowsky brothers on 1 November 1895—predating the Lumière brothers' historic Grand Café show by some eight weeks—greatly profited from the war. Before 1914, German production of films hovered around 12 per cent; most came from France, Italy, and the United States. As these countries were declared enemies during the war, their films were banned in Germany, thus forcing the German film industry to increase production. Founded by the government in 1917 to make German propaganda films, UFA (Universum Film AG) soon became the largest production company of the 1920s, assembling a dazzling array of talent from the various arts. German companies pursued a double strategy, complementing their huge production of 300–500 popular films per year with a small number of prestige films that were meant to uphold the German self-image as *Kulturnation*, i.e., a nation defined by high culture. These artistically ambitious films drew heavily on modernist painting, architecture, design, and theater and experimented with new visual strategies and narrative forms that expanded film's expressive power. They were often exported and touted as 'German' films, thus creating the image of Weimar cinema as one of the richest and most innovative periods in film history. Exported films were also more likely to survive the onslaught of sound film which in Germany, as in other countries, led to the neglect and destruction of 'obsolete' silent cinema. It is a sad fact that more than 80 per cent of silent films are lost today. However, several hundred German films did survive, and a good number have been painstakingly restored in recent years. Some of these films have become classics of film history, prefiguring avant-garde cinema as well as Hollywood's genre films.

Horror picture shows: the Expressionist style

The opening of Robert Wiene's cult classic, *Das Cabinet des Dr. Caligari* (*The Cabinet of Dr. Caligari*), in February 1920 marks the beginning of Expressionist cinema as well as Germany's entry into the European and world cinema market. A daring experiment in its combination of crudely painted sets and stylized acting, of avant-garde art and murder mystery, *Caligari* stood out in the flood of films produced in Germany in 1919. Its blatant disregard for realism and its innovative visual language brought film as a medium into the purview of high modernism. Specifically, its use of abstraction, distortion, and fragmentation identified it as a product of Expressionism, a German art movement that had started in the first years of the twentieth century in painting and soon spread to poetry, prose, theater, and architecture. By 1920, Expressionism had become a catch-all

⊕ *Das Cabinet des Dr. Caligari*

term for a visual style that struck viewers as unsettling and bizarre; a style that stressed fractured narratives and split characters, and focused on extreme psychological states. *Caligarisme*, as the French called the film's distorted design, soon became synonymous with Expressionism in the visual arts.

The film's strikingly disjointed form reinforced a twisted tale of murder and mayhem. An inmate of an insane asylum narrates his hallucinated story about a murderous psychiatrist and his hypnotized patient in a flashback that blurs the lines between truth and deception, description and delusion. Functioning as a Freudian talking cure, full of ellipses, projections, and subjective distortions, the film silently references the mental wards of World War I where sadistic psychiatrists mistreated shell-shocked soldiers as malingerers. The traumatic experience of the first modern war, which cost the lives of two million young Germans, left its traces on all cultural production in the Weimar Republic; it inscribed itself with special force in Expressionist cinema with its focus on shock, insanity, and formal disorientation. The senseless mass death—in the battle of Verdun alone, one million German and French men were killed for no military gain on either side—returned after 1918 as stories of madness and mass murder. *Caligari*'s crazed visual form expressed the view, not uncommon in the aftermath of the war, of an entire world gone mad.

Friedrich Wilhelm Murnau's 1922 film *Nosferatu: A Symphony of Horror* similarly sets out to chronicle a strange world marked by 'mass death', as the first intertitle proclaims. Although the film is set in a small nineteenth-century North German town and draws on the ancient vampire myth, it alludes to the experience of mass death of World War I. Murnau's film was based upon Bram Stoker's novel *Dracula* (1897), but the names were changed to evade copyright laws. There is also a telling revision: the vampire is no longer killed by a stake through his heart, but by the sacrifice of a woman who eagerly embraces the monster to save the community. The film thus partakes of Germany's attempt to come to grips with war and defeat by reconfiguring the destruction as a tale of female sacrifice for a higher purpose. Nosferatu occupies the 'realm of phantoms', the very domain of filmic images. Silent cinema's dark contrasts, jerky movements, and strange flicker create a world that has a structural affinity with spiritualism and the occult. Once captured on celluloid, actors exist as ghosts, unable to die, 'undead' like Nosferatu. Whereas Stoker's literary text can only hint at the horror of Dracula, the film manages to make panic, fear, and anxiety palpable through special effects (such as time-lapse photography and negative film), lighting, camera angles, and abrupt editing. Hutter, the young man who visits Nosferatu in Transylvania, travels like millions of soldiers before him to the East, eager for adventure, but returns shell-shocked. If the repressed, according to Freud's 1919 essay on the uncanny, re-emerges in horrific form, then *Nosferatu* is about the repression of both death and sexuality. Expressionist film language is used here to destabilize viewing habits, to explore liminal mental conditions, and to focus on the hidden and repressed side of modernity.

Like other expressionist films of the period, Arthur Robison's *Schatten: eine nächtliche Halluzination* (*Warning Shadows*, 1923) resides in a no-man's-land between sanity and madness, waking and dreaming. A mysterious shadow puppeteer transforms the hidden sexual desires and murderous thoughts of high society members into living images—a metacinematic commentary on the hypnotic power of film as well as on film spectatorship. Similarly, Paul Leni's *Das Wachsfigurenkabinett* (*Waxworks*, 1924) plays with the idea of performance. A young poet is commissioned to create stories for three wax statues: the burlesque Caliph of Baghdad; the tragic figure of Ivan the Terrible; and the disturbed sexual murderer Jack the Ripper. The third episode in particular adopts Expressionist techniques, such as subjectively distorted point-of-view shots, superimpositions, and disorienting cuts that ignore the boundaries of time and space.

In the first years after the war, silent cinema became the preferred site for expeditions into the realm of irrational fears and violent visions. In silent film, where nobody speaks, everything speaks. Settings and objects acquire a life of their own, so that canted façades, twisted streets, and labyrinthine corridors come to signify the tormented interior landscape of the troubled protagonists. Expressionism expanded the emerging language of cinema to represent extreme psychological states. Visual motifs from such classics as *Caligari* and *Nosferatu* live on to this day in Hollywood's genre cinema of horror and vampire film.

Another German Expressionist film, Fritz Lang's *Metropolis* (1927), furnished the often-quoted genre prototype of the science fiction film. In production for more than two years, *Metropolis* opened in February 1927 with great fanfare as Europe's most expensive and ambitious film. Its visual style embeds Expressionist elements (including special lighting effects, stylized *mise-en-scène*, and startling point-of-view shots) within a modernist framework that glorifies technology and functionality. This framework is associated with a new art movement, Neue Sachlichkeit (New Objectivity) and Bauhaus, that began to supersede Expressionism by the mid-1920s. *Metropolis* tells the tale of a revolt of the 'heart', symbolized by the idealist, love-struck industrialist's son, against the idolatry of machines, represented by the cold father who controls the mechanistic universe of Metropolis. The film's unresolved tension between its high-tech aspirations (it was the most technologically sophisticated film of its time) and the maudlin love story, often ascribed to Lang's wife, the novelist Thea von Harbou, resulted in poor box office returns. However, this tension dramatizes precisely Germany's conflict with modernity. The Americanism of mass production and mass culture—the cult of machines, mechaniza-tion, and instrumental rationality that came with Germany's rapid modernization—were still fiercely contested in 1920s Germany. Fritz Lang claimed in 1926 that Hollywood, while technically superior, could not match the 'soul' and high cultural ambitions of German cinema. For him, movies were not to be mere entertainment, but instead cultural artifacts to uplift and educate the audience. For instance, *Metropolis* conjures up images of the Tower of Babel (in a film within a film) to show how disregard for the fate of the working class leads to discord and destruction. The film is deeply split between its fascination on the one hand with the beauty of gleaming machine parts that move elegantly by themselves, tall skyscrapers bathed in electric light, and on the other hand, with the repudiation of mechanized life. Only after the elimination of the Caligari-like mad scientist Rotwang, who has created a lifelike female robot as the ultimate worker of the future, does the film come to a conclusion—a provisional reconciliation between impetuous 'Expressionist' son and rational 'New Objectivist' father; between industrial management and working class; between American mass culture and German high art.

■ Fritz Lang (1890–1976)

The most accomplished and versatile modernist among German filmmakers, Fritz Lang shaped the emerging language of cinema as he explored the social and moral exigencies of modernity. From his earliest film in 1919 to his last in 1961, in more than forty films, he experimented with a wide array of cinematic forms, from German fairy tale to *film noir*; from science fiction to anti-Nazi film; from domestic melodrama to action and adventure film. Born into the multi-ethnic, highly cultured environment of turn-of-the-century Vienna, he served in the war and traveled widely before moving to Berlin in 1919, eager to participate in the booming German film industry. He began as a screenwriter but soon found commercial success with the adventure film serial *Die Spinnen* (*The Spiders*, 1919) and the meditative melodrama about love and death *Der müde Tod* (*Destiny*, 1921). The Expressionist film architecture of *Destiny*, which constructed a purely cinematic reality, soon gave way to a more realistic 'picture of the times' in *Dr. Mabuse, der Spieler* (*Dr. Mabuse, the Gambler*, 1922/3), which portrayed the moral cynicism of the postwar period. The role of the evil genius fascinated Lang throughout his life—in 1932 he directed *Das Testament des Dr. Mabuse* (*The Testament of Dr. Mabuse*), and in 1961 he concluded his career with another Mabuse sequel: *Die 1,000 Augen des Dr. Mabuse* (*The Thousand Eyes of Dr. Mabuse*). Each of the Mabuse films thematized new technologies of perception: the hypnotic gaze in silent cinema in 1922; the

⊕ *Metropolis*

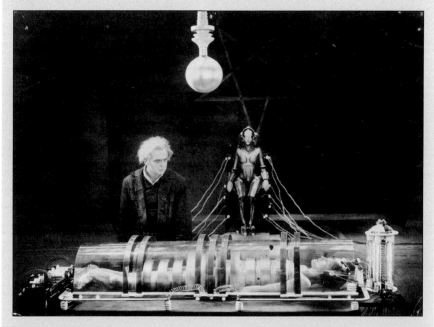

disembodied voice of radio and phonograph in early sound film in 1932; and the 'thousand eyes' of television and surveillance cameras in 1961. Lang, the modernist filmmaker, reflected on the act of seeing just as literary modernists were reflecting on the act of writing.

In Europe, Lang became known early on for making spectacular films that lifted a mass medium into the realm of high art. His two-part *Nibelungen* (1924) and three-hour *Metropolis* (1927) were lavish studio productions, one set in the Middle Ages, the other in the distant future; both took more than two years to make and boasted not only technical feats in film sets and trick photography but also unheard-of cost overruns. The *Nibelungen* recreated a mythical saga of betrayal and revenge, while *Metropolis* engaged the latest special effects for a dystopian vision of modernity. Airplanes negotiating their way between futuristic skyscrapers, rows of robotic workers, and the seductive female cyborg—these images have become part of an international image bank on which sci-fi films draw to this day.

When Lang, after some hesitation, finally made his first sound film, *M* (1931), he used the ear to challenge the primacy of the eye. The child-murderer in this urban crime film betrays himself by repeatedly whistling a tune that a *blind* man hears and recognizes. Once again, Lang reflects on the very material of his craft: vision and sound. The story also shows how the hunt for the murderer mobilizes millions of people, thereby creating a mob mentality that openly embraces Fascist practices. Two years later, when Hitler took power, Lang fled to Paris and, in 1934, to Hollywood. In exile, his ambitions of cinematic high art were curbed by the studio system, but flashes of his German film style still energize most of his twenty American films. Many of them, such as *Fury* (1936), *Scarlet Street* (1945), or *The Big Heat* (1953), revisit and work through narrative and visual tropes he had developed in complete artistic freedom in 1920s Berlin.

Next to *Caligari*, *Metropolis* has become the most influential film of Weimar cinema despite its fragmentary nature; for its American release it was cut by almost a third to better suit dominant tastes. Ultimately it may be less the convoluted story than the visual boldness of certain scenes—unfettered by any dictate of realism—that keeps inspiring us. A visionary, purely cinematic city, Metropolis has influenced innumerable horror scenarios of postmodern urban dystopias like Ridley Scott's *Blade Runner* or Luc Besson's *The Fifth Element*.

City streets: toward an urban cinema

From the beginning, German cinema has been preoccupied by the big city as a site of adventure and modernity. In *Leben und Treiben unter den Linden* (*Hustle and Bustle 'Unter den Linden'*, 1897), the camera was content to record the crowds on the streets and plazas of Berlin. The street became a staging ground for sex and crime, a setting where the individual encountered anonymous others, unsheltered and vulnerable. The prototype of the so-called 'street film', Karl Grune's film *Die Strasse* (*The Street*, 1923) narrates the adventures of a middle-aged man who flees the security of his apartment to enter the big city, where he encounters prostitutes and criminals, is framed for murder, and ends up in jail only to be rescued at the last minute. Exhausted, he returns home, where his wife warms up the dinner that he had abruptly abandoned when he broke out of his deadening routine. In the film's first scene, the magic of the street echoes the magic of cinema when he watches busy urban life as shadow-play on the wall of his living room. The street, not unlike the moviegoing experience, suggests a world of wonderment and alluring but dangerous excitement, allowing liberation and escape from the enclosure of the narrow bourgeois milieu. *The Street* also explores the value accorded to seductive mass culture by Germany's middle class, which found itself impoverished by the hyperinflation in 1923/24. The story ultimately punishes the man's uncontrollable desire for experience and adventure but captures the lure of the modern city—a motif that recurs time and again in American gangster and crime films of the 1930s and 1940s.

   No film represents the price of urban modernity more melodramatically than Murnau's *Der letzte Mann* (*The Last Laugh*), which premiered in December 1924. The film depicts the degradation of a hotel doorman (Emil Jannings) who can no longer keep up with the pace of modern life. Stripped of his uniform and demoted to the position of bathroom attendant, he hides his humiliation from his once-envious family and neighbors. The spatial organization of the film constructs stark contrasts between the darkly lit, narrow apartment buildings and the spacious luxury hotel with its revolving door. The camera is constantly in motion, descending from above—as in the first scene, which is set in a downward-shooting elevator. The 'unchained camera' of Karl Freund, the period's most innovative cinematographer, and its rapid series of subjective camera positions made it possible for Murnau to tell the story from multiple perspectives and almost without intertitles except for one that appears at the end: 'The film should actually end here. In real life, the unhappy old man would have nothing to anticipate but death. But the screenwriter took pity on him and imagined an almost impossible epilogue.' The second, ironic ending shows the doorman become a millionaire because an eccentric hotel guest from America made him his heir. Now his self-image and identity comes from money, not a uniform—clearly Murnau's comment on his times. The 'American' happy ending was also a sly commentary on the American Dawes Plan, which halted the German hyperinflation in 1924. Murnau's film depicts the painful dissolution of the old system, signified by the porter's Kaiser Wilhelm-style beard and the authority invested in his uniform, and the rise of a new order, symbolized by the significantly younger porter who replaces him. Progress and modernization, the film suggests, demand a high price.

Both *The Street* and *The Last Laugh* gestured toward a stylized realism propagated at the time by painters and designers associated with the New Objectivism. The Viennese director G. W. Pabst, who like Lang had moved to Berlin, built his reputation directing such New Objectivist style films as *Joyless Street* (1925) and *Die Liebe der Jeanne Ney* (*The Love of Jeanne Ney*, 1927). Although these films were still shot in a studio, Pabst made a conscious attempt to achieve a fuller 'realism effect' (Roland Barthes) than in earlier films. The resulting images of archetypal public arenas—nocturnal streets, hotel lobby, cabaret, office, bar, and bordello—are employed further in the social-critical films of the later 1920s, especially in the so-called *Dirnenfilme* (prostitute films); Bruno Rahn's *Dirnentragödie* (*Tragedy of the Street*, 1927) and Pabst's own *Tagebuch einer Verlorenen* (*Diary of a Lost Girl*, 1929).

One of the last silent films, Joe May's crime film *Asphalt* from 1929, exhibits all of the characteristics of the street film: forbidden sexuality, criminality, temptation, and punish-ment within the milieu of the dangerous but sensually thrilling metropolis. A young policeman falls in love with a pretty jewel thief and comes under suspicion for having murdered her former lover. Out of a sense of duty his father, a policeman himself, is forced to arrest him. But out of love for him, the woman testifies that he had acted in self-defense. The street in these films (as in later *film noir*) appears as the existential site of modernity, in which the individual is subjected to a series of incomprehensible and uncontrollable impulses and stimuli. Similar to Alfred Döblin's *Berlin Alexanderplatz* and other literary works about the big city, the street film bears witness to Germany's tormented relationship with the experience of modernity.

Although the vast majority of German films consisted of elaborate studio productions, short, unstaged documentaries about everyday life in Berlin began to appear in the mid-1920s. They corresponded to the new artistic trend that emphasized factual accounts over fiction, reports of the mundane over flights of fancy. Walter Ruttmann's 1927 film *Berlin, die Sinfonie der Grossstadt* (*Berlin: Symphony of a Big City*) records one day in the city of Berlin. A film without characters or story, *Berlin* presents the city itself as a machine—set in motion early in the morning, slowing down at noon, shutting down after midnight—a machine whose rhythm determines the lives of the people who live there. Partially filmed by a hidden camera, the daily ebb and flow of life in the big city was com-posed on the editing table according to the musical principle of a symphony with varying tempi. Inspired by abstract art, Ruttmann's early films, *Opus I* to *Opus IV* (1921–4), show hand-drawn squares, rectangles, and triangles constantly in motion: they dance with each other, collide, and change shapes. In order to represent the city as a complex and multi-dimensional mechanism, Ruttmann employs an editing technique in his Berlin film that juxtaposes similar patterns of motion by people and machines. In addition, he inter-laces abstract compositions into the flow of the images, as if to remind the spectator that the film is a construction.

Ruttmann's film established Berlin as the archetype of the modern metropolis in which cross-cutting connotes the intertwining of innumerable stories. In a similar manner, the camera in the collaborative film *Menschen am Sonntag* (*People on Sunday*, 1930) eschews a conventional story-line. A young man meets a young woman, invites her to the Wannsee, a local lake, on Sunday, and they each bring a friend. They flirt—and then Sunday is over. The energy of this film derives not from narrative conflict but from its attention to detail and its *cinéma vérité* style which, in conjunction with the fleeting irony of some scenes, results in the blurring of the border between documentary and fiction. *People on Sunday* has acquired cult status because of the collaboration of five budding directors, all in their 20s: Billie (later Billy) Wilder, Curt and Robert Siodmak, Edgar G. Ulmer, and Fred Zinnemann. Shortly afterwards, each was forced into exile by the Nazi regime. They started a new life in Hollywood and became successful American directors of *film noir*, the most urban of all film genres.

In 1930, when the silent *People on Sunday* appeared, sound films already outnumbered silent films. As a result, silent film emphasized the language of stolen glances and subtle gestures, the bodies of the amateur performers, and recognizable urban sites. The film coincided with a burgeoning debate about whether the introduction of sound would ruin the visual language of film—a language to which Weimar cinema had contributed so much.

As sound made its inroads in Germany around 1929, Fritz Lang, the acknowledged master of Expressionist cinema, fell silent. He believed sound could not match his architectural conception of cinema: the visual monumentalism of *Metropolis* would have dwarfed dialogue. When in May 1931, after a hiatus of one and a half years, Lang finally presented his first sound film, *M*, it was greeted with great expectations. He managed to employ sound in completely new, 'expressionist' ways. Instead of using dialogue and background noise to add realism to the images, he emphasizes the tension between silence and sound and between sound and image. More than half the film was shot as silent film. When he did use sound, it signified either danger (the honking of the horn of a car that one does not see), madness (the manic whistling from nowhere that sets in when the murderous impulse rises), or impending violence (the crescendo voices of the mob). Lang was fully aware of the effects of sound for the image and reflects on it with irony. For example, the clue to solving the identity of the murderer in *M* is an auditory sign (the suspect's whistling)—something a silent film would be hard pressed to deliver. It is, tellingly, a blind man who recognizes that whistle.

For his story, Lang used reports from the sensational mass murder trial of Peter Kürten. Moving the site of the crime from Düsseldorf to the bustling urban setting of Berlin, he changes the story of an individual criminal into that of a city crippled by communal hysteria and paranoia. In its search for the elusive psychopathic killer, the community monitors and represses itself. Everyone watches everyone else: the police, the authorities, the crime syndicates, and even the beggars. The police, whose newest methods of investigation and surveillance are introduced like a short documentary film inserted into the narrative, divide up and monitor the city, as does the well-organized crime network which demands: 'We must cast a net of spies over the city! Every square inch must be under constant surveillance. No child may take a step unnoticed.' Highly topical for a society ready to succumb to Nazism, *M* shows the emergence of Fascist mob mentality induced by fear. Anyone could be the murderer, as the original title, *A Murderer Among Us*, suggests. *M*'s Berlin is a city in which no intact families or friendships exist, only exhausted mothers, endangered children, criminals, beggars, corrupt police, and prostitutes. The city also appears as a place where mistrust, desire, sadism, and violence reign, where it is life-threatening to talk to a stranger. As the city seeks the murderer whose perversion throws off the delicate balance between police and criminals, an entire community finds itself confronted with sexuality and death. What to do with men who do not conform?

With its nexus of crime, sex, and urban anonymity, *M* follows the tradition of the street film, but here a terrifying dialectic emerges: in the same way that the big city overwhelms the individual, the individual is able to terrorize the big city. A chalk-marked palm slaps the letter 'M' on the suspect's back, thus brandishing him as a 'Murderer' (or 'Man'?). The crime syndicate finally succeeds in hunting down the murderer, putting him on trial before a self-appointed jury of criminals. Lang creates great tension in this scene through his use of camera and editing, cutting between long shots of the assembly and close-ups of various faces of the agitated and bloodthirsty courtroom. It is to this group that M, played by Peter Lorre, makes his confession: '. . . can I help it? Don't I have this horrible thing inside me? The fire? The voice? The torment? . . . How it screams and howls inside me! How I am forced to do it!' The psychoanalytic-clinical turn of his plea and the speech by his defense attorney resonate with arguments which had surfaced in this period in the debates about the death penalty and the reform of criminals. At the last second, the murderer is rescued from the lynch mob and turned over to the authority of the state, which Lang portrays throughout the film as weak and powerless. The exceedingly short final sequence further serves to undermine the state's last-minute intervention. Three mothers, like Sisters of Fate, speak directly into the camera and laconically pronounce the verdict 'of the people': 'This cannot bring our children back. We must take better care of our children.' The film constructs a deeply prophetic image of a destabilized German society a few years before Hitler's ascendance, a society without trust in the power of the state to maintain order, self-doubting, claustrophobic, and ready to become totalitarian to conquer insecurity—a society every bit as destructive as the murderer.

Fatal attractions: stars and mass entertainment

By the mid-1920s the so-called New Woman had emerged in Weimar Germany—gainfully employed, independent, self-confident, and contemptuous of the patriarchal order, which was already shaken by the shameful military defeat. Cinema related to the New Woman in two contradictory ways: while it created the incredible star power of Greta Garbo, Louise Brooks, and Marlene Dietrich, it also commodified their image as passive objects of visual pleasure. Whenever in Pabst's *The Joyless Street* the camera's gaze falls upon Garbo, the narrative comes to a momentary standstill and revels with close-ups and soft focus in Garbo's tableau-like posing. When she tries on the luxurious fur coat in front of a mirror, or appears in her skimpy dancer's costume in the nightclub, the spectator becomes a voyeur. It is no coincidence that female stars often played stage performers—Louise Brooks is a nightclub entertainer in Pabst's *Die Büchse der Pandora* (*Pandora's Box*, 1929), as is Marlene Dietrich in *Der Blaue Engel* (*The Blue Angel*, 1930), both proving to be fatal attractions to the men who fall for them.

When Pabst looked for an actress to play Lulu, the female protagonist in *Pandora's Box*, he first thought of Marlene Dietrich but found her too earthy and 'aware'. After a months-long search he chose Louise Brooks, a relatively unknown 22-year-old actress from Kansas, for the role of Lulu, the naïve and passive object of male (and female) desire. With her short hair, androgynous, athletic build, and no-nonsense approach to love and marriage, Brooks's Lulu embodied the ideal of the New Woman. Shot in 1929 as a silent movie, the film presents Lulu's life in a series of visually powerful scenarios: luxury apartment, revue stage, wedding reception, courtroom, gambling casino, foggy London street, and dark attic where she dies at the hands of Jack the Ripper. Despite its aesthetic brilliance, the film seems to say that the sexualized woman, unconscious of her own destructive potential, needs to be expunged for society to function.

The rise of Louise Brooks as a German film star also points to the vibrant give and take between Hollywood and Berlin. Concerned with Germany's competition with Hollywood—Germany had risen to the second-largest film industry in the 1920s—American studios managed to lure Germany's best talent away. Ernst Lubitsch, for instance, lived as a popular film director in Berlin before he was hired in 1922 by Mary Pickford, who wanted to play Gretchen in an American version of *Faust*. Although this project never came to pass due to major conflicts between the American superstar and the 'obstinate' German director, Lubitsch stayed in Hollywood for the rest of his career. In 1926, shortly after his own filmic adaptation of *Faust*, even Murnau, probably the most German of the German directors, received an offer by Fox he could not refuse. German film stars also started to act in American films—including Conrad Veidt, who had played Cesare in *Caligari*, and Emil Jannings, who even won the first Oscar for Best Actor in 1928. However, the vibrant transnational exchange of the late 1920s suffered with the introduction of sound film—Emil Jannings's heavy German accent was not tolerable in an American film.

The German accent is ironically alluded to in Josef von Sternberg's *The Blue Angel*, which features Jannings as a pompous English professor in a North German high school. He sadistically corrects a student who is unable to pronounce the English article 'the'. Jannings plays Professor Unrat, an autocratic character who loses his position, his dignity, and his life when he helplessly courts and defiantly marries the itinerant and vulgar singer Lola Lola, classically embodied by Marlene Dietrich in her defining role. *The Blue Angel* also created the cliché of Weimar's seductive decadence, and later imitations, such as Bob Fosse's *Cabaret*, still use the images that this film created. The commercial success of *The Blue Angel* also helped UFA regain the competitive edge it lost when Hollywood turned to sound.

Throughout the 1920s, the absence of sound had been perceived in Germany not as a lack but as an incentive to tell a story in strictly visual terms—an art that had reached remarkable heights by the end the decade. Not surprisingly, the German film industry dismissed the initial successes of Hollywood's experiments with sound. Only after early music films like *The Jazz Singer* became international box-office hits in late 1927 did Germany's film industry make frantic attempts to catch up. UFA, since 1917 Weimar Germany's unashamedly commercial production company, built Europe's most advanced sound studios in record time and modernized existing cinemas to accommodate the new technology. Within a year, film orchestras and, in smaller theaters, piano players, who had accompanied silent movies, had become superfluous. By 1930, more than 80 per cent of silent film production was destroyed because it seemed obsolete and useless. In 1929 only eight films used sound, but by 1930, sound films were already double the number of silent films. By1932 only sound films were in production.

Erich Pommer, who had produced *Caligari* and *Metropolis,* was also behind *The Blue Angel,* UFA's first high-budget sound film. He invited Josef von Sternberg, a Vienna-born filmmaker from Hollywood, to direct because he had experience with sound film and was known for his cosmopolitan touch. As in his earlier films, Pommer thought in terms of export. The script was based on Heinrich Mann's celebrated novel *Der Untertan*, but it commuted Mann's acerbic social critique of the German bourgeois class into the melodrama of an individual. It presented the professor's seduction by Lola, his rapid degeneration and pathetic death as the direct result of his deviation from the path of bourgeois order. The film associates this danger zone with sexuality, spectacle, and mass culture. The camera fetishizes Dietrich's legs and revealing costumes. But Lola Lola personified not only the vamp, but also a nurturing mother who strokes the beard of the starry-eyed professor and prepares breakfast for him after their first night together. By embodying both paradigms of femininity in the extreme—the mother and the whore —Lola represented a new kind of female figure. Lola is visually associated with the happily chirping canary, while the professor, a helpless victim of his desire, is reduced to a stammering child. The film revolves around the tension between voluntary subjugation on the one hand and the conscious exercise of power on the other. Professor Unrat's awakening of sexual desires weakens his main supports—Prussian discipline and author-itarianism—and plunges him into the depths of vacillation and self-doubt. The film overflows with images of this bewilderment: nets that entangle Jannings as he hesitantly enters the nightclub; mirrors that triple Lola's reflection as she puts on makeup; and the silent stare of the sad stage clown that foreshadows the professor's fate. *The Blue Angel* lives on in Germany as Marlene Dietrich's legendary film debut; it is further remembered to this day for Friedrich Hollaender's songs, which quickly became major hits. Like many early sound films, *The Blue Angel* was filmed in both German and American versions. On the evening of the film's Berlin premiere, Sternberg returned to Hollywood with his 'dis-covery', Marlene Dietrich, who was already under contract with Paramount for six more films under his direction, including such classics as *Morocco* (1930), *Shanghai Express* (1932), and *Blonde Venus* (1932).

The modernized German film industry became unabashedly commercial in the early 1930s. There were no more debates about film as high art; what counted now was enter-tainment value. Dialogue made the films more realistic and easier to follow; the camera remained stationary to record the actors speaking; lighting and sets no longer expressed the hidden psychological states of the protagonists; and words replaced visual language. Much of this light entertainment fare centered around singers and performers. Films with titles like *Ein blonder Traum* (*A Blonde Dream*) with stars like Lilian Harvey and Willy Fritsch, are certainly escapist fare, but they also suggest a utopian promise of better things to come. 'Somewhere in the world, there is a little bit of happiness,' sings Lillian Harvey in *A Blonde Dream*. Siegfried Kracauer, the foremost film critic of the Weimar Republic, wrote at the time about the new semi-proletarian audiences of shop girls and secretaries who sought in the movies what they could not get in their routinized and regimented lives. The star system that emerged late in Germany also fed into the desires of the masses, providing them with vicarious glimpses of intriguing lives, glamour, and style.

Moving the masses: political cinema

A politically charged and socially unstable period, the Weimar Republic produced many activist films that challenged the status quo and mobilized the masses. Germany's first democracy, precariously wedged between a smug monarchy and a militant Fascism, was consumed with constant struggles for legitimacy. Did the Weimar Republic ever have a chance? It came into being as a consequence of a devastating military defeat that went largely unacknowledged because the war was fought outside the nation's borders. Unlike the period after World War II, no cities lay in ruins to make war's devastation visible. The resentment over lost territory and the harsh punishments of the Versailles Treaty, as well as the bloody suppression and failure of a Soviet-style workers' revolution in 1918/19, weakened this developing democracy from the start. None of the professional classes that had propagated the war were replaced; courts, schools, and universities openly opposed the new democratic order. Although cinema often intervened in the daily political strug- gle, trying to address social ills and critique authority, it failed to promote democratic values or deal with the modernity of the new political system. The often changing but consistently impotent governments did not inspire moviemakers to make 'democratic' films. On the contrary: dramatic films need conflicts and clashes. The stark contrasts characteristic of black-and-white silent film corresponded to an emphatically binary, even Manichean worldview in which the old is set against the new, the rich against the poor, the strong against the weak. It consists, as in *Metropolis*, of catacombs or skyscrapers, domination or revolt, life or death, utopia or apocalypse. There was no democratically inspired appreciation of compromise, no nuance, and no negotiation within the system. Although many films enact the toppling of authorities and the old order, they do so (as in *Last Laugh* or *The Blue Angel*) in melodramatic terms.

Political activism found its most elaborate expression in the rejection of the war. Echoing the politics of the last years of the Weimar Republic, cinema of the Left found itself divided between a proletarian-revolutionary and a social-democratic, reformist wing. Pabst's anti-war films *Westfront 1918* (1930) and *Kameradschaft* (*Comradeship*, 1931) serve as examples of the latter, representing a humanistic rather than revolutionary position. Following the example of the American Lewis Milestone's filmic adaptation of Erich Maria Remarque's bestselling novel of 1927, *Im Westen nichts Neues* (*All Quiet on the Western Front*, 1929), several German films worked through the trauma of World

War I. It had taken more than ten years to find feature films addressing the human drama of war in direct form. Images of trench warfare, exploding shells, and fleeing soldiers, wounded and forlorn, were meant to immunize the viewer against the madness of war but may have had the opposite effect: the war became a dramatic historical backdrop for private stories about male bonding, female temptation, and the valorization of bravado and heroic courage. Pabst's *Kameradschaft* concentrates on understanding and cooperation between nations, and in particular between the wartime enemies Germany and France. The film interprets war between peoples as manipulation by the ruling classes, something against which the international proletariat must defend itself. The plot revolves around a successful rescue operation in a mineshaft in which German miners save French workers by removing the grill that marks the border between Germany and France. 'A comrade is a comrade,' says the German worker. 'We should not only unite in times of hardship. Or should we just stand by and watch until we have been so stirred up that we go after one another again? This coal belongs to everyone.' During this speech, German and French police forces restore the border grating—a sequence edited out by the censor as too inflammatory a commentary on the true political situation.

Sergei Eisenstein's celebrated *Battleship Potemkin*, and the notoriety it received because of the censorship battle that preceded its opening in Berlin, paved the way for a number of revolutionary film imports from Russia in the second half of the Weimar Republic. Eisenstein's visit to Berlin and his collaboration with the German composer Edmund Meisel, who wrote the score to *Potemkin*, helped to promote the film and also led to a lively transnational exchange of talent between Germany and Russia. The huge popular success of the film mobilized the German socialist-revolutionary community to make their own 'Russian' feature films, using traditionally Russian techniques of montage, close-ups of sharply lined faces, and revolutionary subject matter. During 1929 and 1930, no fewer than fifty Russian films were in distribution, including Eisenstein's *Ten Days That Shook The World* and Vsevolod Pudovkin's *Storm over Asia*. Class-conscious films like Piel Jutzi's *Mutter Krausens Fahrt ins Glück* (*Mother Krausen's Journey to Happiness*, 1929) provided painstaking details of Berlin's working class milieu and featured extras drawn from workers organizations. The narrative implies that solidarity and submission to the Party is the only alternative to self-destruction—the destitute and lonely mother Krausen kills herself and her grandchild. The film does not, however, end on this melodramatic note. The last shots show her daughter as she attempts to join the ranks of marching workers, first stumbling, but finally—in close-up—marching along in step.

This move from bourgeois individualism to collectivism as the solution to abject poverty and hopelessness also underpins the most original collaborative work of revolutionary filmmaking at the time, *Kuhle Wampe oder wem gehört die Welt?* (*Kuhle Wampe or Who*

Owns the World?, 1932). Bertolt Brecht wrote the screenplay, Slatan Dudow, a young Romanian student of Eisenstein, directed it, and Hanns Eisler, a protégé of Arnold Schönberg, composed the music. The name 'Kuhle Wampe' stands for a Berlin location where a tent city was erected for thousands of unemployed workers, evicted and penniless, who in their political apathy were still unwilling to join the Communist Party. The censorship board promptly banned the film in March 1932 because its images posed a threat 'to public order and safety and to basic interests of the state'. After some cuts were made, the film opened in one of the elite movie palaces of Berlin—praised as an avant-garde film, ignored by the working class. A mixture of feature film, documentary, and agit-prop, *Kuhle Wampe* replaced a linear narrative with episodes that illustrated a theory, thus distancing the viewer from emotional involvement. As in Brecht's Epic Theater, the spectator is not supposed to identify with the characters but to analyze them and learn from their behavior. Although without any impact in Germany only six months before Hitler's rise to power, the film inspired political filmmaking in 1960s France and Germany. Jean-Luc Godard emulated 'Uncle Bertolt,' as he calls him in *Two or Three Things I Know About Her* (1966) by incorporating documentary and non-narrative scenes and by breaking with Hollywood conventions of a cohesive narrative about psychologically rounded characters. Godard, like Brecht, argued that political opposition resided in the very form of the film.

The range and vibrancy of Leftist filmmaking had no match on the Right. There were monarchist films such as the four-part *Fridericus Rex* (1922/3), a biographical picture of Frederick the Great, the eighteenth-century founder of Prussia, which focused on discipline and order to counter the perceived lawlessness of the Weimar Republic. At the premiere the audience was allegedly so moved that it spontaneously stood up and sang the national anthem. Most of the Right's efforts went into attacking films that they considered to be anti-German; for instance, Nazi stormtroopers picketed and interrupted Milestone's *All Quiet on the Western Front* so frequently that its run was cut short.

Epilogue

In the transitional years of 1932/3, between the fall of Weimar and the rise of National Socialism, the movies opening in the theaters do not show a radical break. The escapist entertainment of revue and operetta films, musical comedies, and melodramas that formed the staple of popular cinema in the last years of the Weimar Republic continued and lived on throughout the Nazi regime. However, there were structural changes: within weeks of Hitler's rise to power, the entire film industry was put under complete control of Goebbel's Propaganda Ministry, which banned all films by Jewish or Leftist directors.

Although propaganda films represented only a small percentage of the Nazis' prodigious film production, and hardly any of their films showed the swastika, the political mission was never in doubt. A huge number of filmmakers, actors, and technicians chose to flee the country before the anti-democratic and anti-Semitic rhetoric turned into physical persecution. Two films of 1933 exemplify the tensions of the period. When Max Ophüls's *Liebelei*, the brilliant adaptation of Schnitzler's melancholic examination of love, friendship, honor, and death, opened in March 1933, the filmmaker had already left Germany. Gustav Ucicky's nationalist war movie *Morgenrot* (*Red Dawn*), on the other hand, premiered in February 1933 before an audience that included Hitler, Papen, and Hugenberg. It showed unconditional belief in the Führer, a willingness to sacrifice oneself, and a yearning for death. 'We Germans don't understand how to live,' remarks the submarine officer in this film, 'but we do know how to die.' Ucicky became one of the most prominent directors under the Nazis; Ophüls continued to make films in France and, after 1947, in Hollywood. Weimar cinema ended not only in Fascism but also in exile.

Did the modernist films of the 1920s foreshadow the rapid rise of National Socialism after 1933? Looking back in 1947, Siegfried Kracauer claimed in his polemical and influential book *From Caligari to Hitler* that the authoritarian figures of Weimar cinema paved the way to Fascism. He constructed a 'psychological history of German film' that pointed to a deeply troubled national unconscious expressed in the movies of the period. But Weimar's collapse cannot be explained on the basis of its films alone. Despite its troubled beginnings, it was not a foregone conclusion that Weimar would lead to a Fascist regime. Nor could it have been predicted that, after 1933, German filmmakers in exile would establish a 'Weimar on the Pacific' in Hollywood. The fact remains, however, that about 1,500 members of Weimar's vibrant film industry had to flee the country, and that German cinema never recovered from this massive loss of creativity.

Further reading

Bathrick, David *et al.* (eds.), Special Issue on Weimar Film Theory, *New German Critique* 40 (winter 1987). Essays and documents on the development of cinema as an institution in 1920s Germany; also pieces on Walter Benjamin, Siegfried Kracauer, and Béla Balázs.

Calhoon, Kenneth S. (ed.), *Peripheral Visions: The Hidden Stages of Weimar Cinema* (Detroit, Mich.: Wayne State University Press, 2001). A collection of articles that reinterpret canonical films of the period in light of current cultural theory.

Eisner, Lotte H., *The Haunted Screen: Expressionism in the German Cinema and the Influence of Max Reinhardt* (Berkeley: University of California Press, 1969). First published in 1952 in French, this classic study by a former Weimar film critic living in exile in Paris focuses on the influences of painting and theater on Expressionist cinema.

—— *Fritz Lang* (New York: Oxford University Press, 1977). The first exhaustive monograph on Lang, with numerous quotations from Lang's correspondence with Eisner in which he comments on his films.

—— *Murnau* (Berkeley: University of California Press, 1993). Authoritative study of the life and works of Friedrich Wilhelm Murnau.

Elsaesser, Thomas, *Weimar Cinema and After: Germany's Historical Imaginary* (London: Routledge, 2000). New perspectives on the German film industry, on Weimar films and filmmakers as well as popular genres in the context of avant-garde modernity and social modernization.

Gunning, Tom, *The Films of Fritz Lang: Allegories of Vision and Modernity* (London: British Film Institute, 2000). The first sustained analytical examination of Lang as *auteur*, it interprets his films as self-aware contributions to cinema's role within modernism.

Kaes, Anton *et al.* (eds.), *The Weimar Republic Sourcebook* (Berkeley: University of California Press, 1994). A documentation in English translation of Weimar's most important cultural and political debates; it also contains chapters on popular culture and cinema.

—— *M* (London: British Film Institute, 2000). A new-historicist study that opens up Lang's favorite film in new ways by relating its visuals and narrative to the social pressures of the last years of the Weimar Republic.

—— *Shell Shock: Cinema and Trauma in Weimar Germany* (Princeton, NJ: Princeton University Press, forthcoming). The book argues for the unspoken presence of the traumatic experience of World War I in Expressionist Cinema from *The Cabinet of Dr Caligari* to *Metropolis*.

Kracauer, Siegfried, *From Caligari to Hitler: A Psychological History of the German Film* (Princeton, NJ: Princeton University Press, 1947). Written in exile, the controversial book claims that Weimar cinema and its authoritarian protagonists foreshadow the Nazi regime. Despite criticism of its teleological trajectory and its reductive method, the book has shaped the master narrative of Weimar cinema during the last half-century.

—— *The Mass Ornament: Weimar Essays*, ed. and trans. Thomas Y. Levin (Cambridge, Mass.: Harvard University Press, 1995). Collection of Kracauer's critical reflections on Weimar society and mass culture, including cinema.

DADA AND SURREALIST FILM

Rudolf Kuenzli

The experience of World War I made many artists and writers rethink the values in the name of which that slaughter was glorified as the highest achievement of European culture. This rethinking coalesced into two related, but ultimately different, artistic movements that were to a large extent defined by their rejection of these values. The first movement, designated by the purposely childlike name 'Dada', was nihilistic in nature, bent on demonstrating the absurdity and moral bankruptcy of a culture that could sanction such a war. The second movement, Surrealism, grew out of Dada but departed from its predecessor in its insistence on the creation of new meaning out of the ruins of senseless destruction.

In opposing the conflict, the Dada movement attempted to short-circuit the war mentality. Writers and artists founded the movement in 1916 in Zurich, Switzerland, which due to its neutrality became a refuge for European pacifists, revolutionaries, and anti-war protesters. In stark contrast to the raging nationalism in most European countries, the Dada movement was decidedly international, and in Zurich included Jean Arp from Alsace; Tristan Tzara and Marcel Janco from Rumania; Emmy Hennings, Hugo Ball, Richard Huelsenbeck, and Hans Richter from Germany; Viking Eggeling from Sweden; and Sophie Taeuber from Switzerland. According to these writers and artists, the grenades of war not only killed millions of people, they also shattered European culture, social myths, art, language, and morality—in short, the very values society used to justify the massacre. In this sense, the Dada activities, which included cabaret performances, art, and writing, can be seen as a demystification of all the cultural idols and taboos in a radical Nietzschean sense; they can be interpreted as a questioning of all values.

In 1918, when the war had ended and the borders were open again, the Dadaists left their refuge in Switzerland. Huelsenbeck went to Berlin and formed the group of Berlin Dadaists; Jean Arp travelled to Cologne and formed Cologne Dada with Max Ernst and Johannes Baargeld; and Tristan Tzara left for Paris, where he became the center of the Paris Dada group, which included André Breton, who had worked as a medic with shell-shocked soldiers during the war, Paul Eluard, Louis Aragon, Philippe Soupault, and Francis Picabia. Disillusioned and disgusted by the senseless war, these young French writers returned from their military service to Paris and welcomed Tzara's anarchic spirit, his 'great negative work of destruction,' and the large provocation-demonstrations that he initiated, at which these Dadaists denounced literature and art and rejected the ideas of progress, logic, nationalism, and capitalism. Paris became the international center of Dada activities in the early twenties. The American photographer and artist Man Ray, who had tried to found a New York Dada movement with Marcel Duchamp, joined the group in Paris, and Max Ernst arrived there from Cologne.

The year 1920, when Dada performances and provocations were discussed in most of the newspapers, was the high point of the Paris Dada movement. Yet after two years of Dada activities, Breton grew tired of these meaningless performances and decided to launch a constructive movement. In 1922, he organized an International Congress in order to give direction to the 'New Spirit.' Having rejected Tzara's radically nihilistic, anarchic vision of Dada, Breton and his group set off on a new road toward Surrealism.

While both Dada and Surrealism rejected rationalism and logic, Surrealism attempted to overcome Dadaist nihilism by valorizing dreams and the unconscious as a higher reality. In the *First Manifesto of Surrealism* (1924), Breton defined the movement as 'based on the belief in the superior reality of certain forms of previously neglected associations, in the omnipotence of dreams, in the disinterested play of thought'. At the beginning of his *Second Manifesto of Surrealism* (1929), Breton explained Surrealism as the meeting point of the real and the imagined, past and future, high and low, life and death. Breton also invoked Salvador Dalí's definition of paranoia as 'ultra-confusional' activity, in which reality is constantly transformed through obsessional ideas and desires. According to Breton, the Surrealists achieve the 'marvelous' through the spark that originates by juxtaposing two or three objects that ordinarily are not grouped together, and he refers to the passage in Lautréamont's poem *Maldoror* about the chance encounter between an

umbrella and a sewing machine on a dissecting table. This notion of unusual juxtapositions served Surrealist writers, painters, and filmmakers as a guide, and they achieved
them by recollecting bizarre and haunting nightmares and dreams, by hallucination,
paranoia, and 'mad love'.

Dada films

The connections between films labelled 'Dada' or 'Surrealist' and the respective movements are complex. Hans Richter's and Viking Eggeling's abstract films can be seen as
an extension of painting. Cubist, Futurist, Dadaist, and Constructivist painters, obsessed
with capturing the sensation of physical movement in their work, saw in film a means of
overcoming the static nature of painting through 'moving pictures'. The rhythmic movement of squares, rectangles, curved shapes, and lines in Richter's *Rhythmus 21*, *Rhythmus
23*, and *Rhythmus 25* (1921–5), and Eggeling's *Diagonal Symphony* (1924) represent
part of Dada's tension between destructive and constructive tendencies. The connection
between Dada and Constructivism is very noticeable in the works of Janco, Richter,
and Eggeling in Zurich, Schwitters in Hanover, and Theo van Doesburg in Holland.
While participating in the 'great negative work of destruction', Richter's and Eggeling's
kinetic experiments attempted to produce nothing less than an elemental, universal
pictorial language, a grammar and syntax of contrasting relationships between geometric forms.

   Marcel Duchamp's experiments with optics and movements, which he began in his
painting *Nude Descending a Staircase* (1912), can also be considered as an attempt to
overcome the static nature of painting. From 1920 to 1926 he collaborated with Man
Ray on experiments that gave two-dimensional geometric designs on plates or disks the
illusion of three-dimensionality through rotary movement: *Rotary Glass Plates* (*Precision
Optics*) (1920), *Rotary Demisphere* (*Precision Optics*) (1925), and experiments in stereo-
scopic cinema. His film *Anémic cinéma*, which he produced with the help of Man Ray
and Marc Allégret in 1926, can thus be seen as an exploration of visual and verbal multi-
dimensionality. Rotating disks with geometric spirals regularly alternate in a slow rhythm
with disks containing spirally printed verbal puns. The motor that rotates the disks thus
transforms the different lines and words into indifference, stability into instability, decid-
ability into indecidability. Duchamp's radical questioning of the certainty and stability of
optical vision and language, which serve as the social, 'scientific' guarantors of truth, was
very central to Dada's critique of cultural myths of 'fact' and 'reality'.

   Man Ray's first film, with the highly ironic title of *Retour à la raison* (1923), is a kinetic
extension of his photographs. Only five minutes in length, it was put together by Man

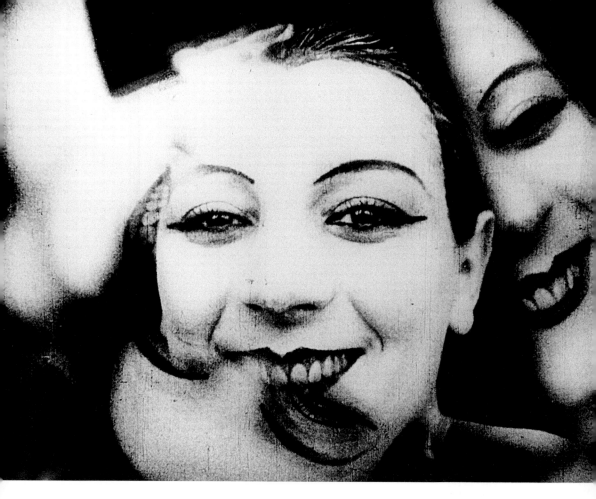

⬆ *Ballet mécanique*

Ray in one night for Tristan Tzara's *Soirée du cœur à barbe* (Evening of the Bearded Heart), the last Dada manifestation in Paris, where it was shown together with Richter's *Rhythmus 21*. Man Ray made this film partly without a camera by sprinkling salt and pepper and throwing pins and thumb-tacks directly on the film celluloid, a technique that he used for his Rayographs. Other short sequences resemble films of sculptures. But instead of the camera turning around the object, sculptural objects such as an egg crate and his *Lampshade* (1919) rotate in front of the static camera. *Retour à la raison*, commissioned by Tzara, expresses through its anarchic arrangement the Dada spirit of spontaneity and chance, which were the Dadaists' strategies for disrupting logic and rational order.

Three years after Breton and his followers had forcefully broken up Tzara's Paris Dada, Man Ray, with generous financial backing from Arthur Wheeler, attempted to make a Surrealist film with his 'ciné-poème' *Emak Bakia* (1926). This film is Man Ray's exploration of the camera's potential to transform the familiar world, and thus to create Surreality. The film opens by introducing the camera, the apparatus of transformation, and the film ends with a woman (played by Kiki, Man Ray's mistress) facing the camera. Viewers think that she has her eyes open, but they soon realize, when she opens her eyes, that the other eyes were only painted on her eyelids. The two pairs of eyes—seeing the familiar world vs. 'seeing' with eyes closed in dreams—suggest the two different kinds of vision: reality and Surreality. Yet the Surrealists regarded this film still as a Dada film, because Man Ray completely disregarded the conventions of storytelling, broke the cinematic illusion by pointing to the film as a product of the camera, and reused the abstract Rayographs he had made for *Retour à la raison*.

Fernand Léger's and Dudley Murphy's *Ballet mécanique* (1924) recalls sequences of Man Ray's first film, but Léger's carefully calculated choreography of ordinary objects and actions often lacks the spontaneity and chance of *Retour à la raison*. Everything in *Ballet mécanique* is caught in machine-like, contrasting rhythms, from the slow movement of the woman on the swing to numbers, geometric figures, machine parts, Christmas ornaments, and the woman climbing the stairs. Everything dances in this ballet according to calculated, changing tempos. Although Kiki also opens and closes her eyes in this film, these repeated sequences do not suggest two different visions, as they do in Man Ray's *Emak Bakia*, but are used here as yet another instance of rhythmic movement, similar to her mouth breaking rhythmically into a smile.

Entr'acte

One month after the first showing of *Ballet mécanique*, Francis Picabia presented his 'instantanist' ballet *Relâche,* and during intermission René Clair's film *Entr'acte*, for which Picabia wrote the outline of the sequences. Picabia's 'instantanist' movement was directed against Breton's group, especially against the *First Manifesto of Surrealism*, which had been published two months earlier. Unlike Léger's fascination with non-narrative mechanical movements of objects, *Entr'acte* consists of spontaneously invented and loosely connected narrative sequences. The actors are Picabia's friends, who in 1924 were neither in Tzara's nor in Breton's camp: Marcel Duchamp, Man Ray, Eric Satie, and members of the Ballet Suédois. The ballet and film were conceived as a total performance that was meant to attack the viewers' conventions and values. In the program for the performance Picabia wrote: '*Entr'acte* does not believe in very much, in the pleasure of life perhaps; it believes in the pleasure of inventing, it respects nothing except the desire to *burst out laughing*.' The ballet opened with a 'curtain raiser' in the form of a short film sequence: Picabia and Satie's cannon-shot aimed at the audience. After the first act of the ballet, the actual film *Entr'acte* was shown at intermission, between the two acts.

The film consists of a series of humorous gags: Picabia 'hosing down' Duchamp's and Man Ray's game of chess on top of a roof in Paris; a dancing ballerina filmed from underneath, only to be revealed as a bearded man; a huntsman shooting an ostrich egg, only to be shot himself; a funeral hearse drawn by a camel, and the chase of the funeral procession after the hearse; and finally the huntsman dressed as magician climbing out of the coffin. Although these gags are in the script, René Clair playfully explores the full cinematic potential of Picabia's proposed scenes by using the whole inventory of cinematic tricks and techniques, changes in tempo, superimpositions, sudden disappearances and transformations. Through Clair's montage, Picabia's illogical sequence of scenes receives an imagistic continuation. The discontinuous episodes of the chess game, the ballerina, and the shooting of the ostrich egg are connected through superimposed and interjected lyric images of rooftops and buildings of Paris.

The main section of the film begins with a series of eleven different long shots of houses and roofs seen diagonally or completely upside down. The sequence of the chess game is interspersed with different shots of the columns of the august Parisian landmark La Madeleine which, through dissolves and superimpositions, are defamiliarized to the extent that they become a play of geometric forms. The shower of water that finishes the chess game leads to the lyrical sequence of a superimposed paper boat floating over the rooftops of the city. The chase scene, which makes up almost half of the entire film, again indicates the differences between Picabia's 'instantanist' plans and Clair's film. Picabia's intent to lampoon the social conventions of funerals becomes for Clair a pretext to explore cinematographically movements of all kinds, from slow motion to mere blurs. At the end of the film, he even reveals cinema directly as an illusion-producing apparatus. The word 'End' appears on the screen. Suddenly a man in slow motion jumps through the 'film screen', and thus breaks the cinematic illusion. In this sense, *Entr'acte* constantly undermines and explodes not only social conventions but also the logic and norms of conventional filmmaking.

With the exception of the early abstract films of Richter and Eggeling, all other Dada-related films were made in Paris, where a network of ciné-clubs provided possibilities for showing these works. Dada-related films have several characteristics in common: they disrupt the viewers' expectations of a conventional narrative, their belief in film as presenting reality, and their desire to identify with characters in the film. Dada films are radically non-narrative, non-psychological; they are highly self-referential by constantly pointing to the film apparatus as an illusion-producing machine. Through their cinematic defamiliarization of social reality they attempted to undermine the norms and codes of social conventions, and thus of conventional filmmaking.

Surrealist films

While the relationship between Dada and film has remained largely unexplored, several studies have examined the connection between Surrealism and film. Already in 1925, one year after the publication of Breton's *First Manifesto of Surrealism,* Jean Goudal published his essay 'Surrealism and Cinema', in which he expressed hope and enthusiasm for film to become *the* ideal means for realizing Breton's notion of Surreality and of the marvelous. According to Goudal, cinema is the perfect art to simulate the metamorphoses and illogical sequences of dreams, hallucinations, and obsessions via the techniques of superimposition, dissolves, montage, and slow motion. The Surrealists were indeed great fans of cinema. Their favorite films were the very popular serials *Fantômas* (Feuillade, 1913–14), *Les Vampires* (Feuillade, 1915–16), as well as American films by Charlie Chaplin, Mack Sennett, and Buster Keaton. They rejected the avant-garde films of the Impressionists—Louis Delluc, Marcel L'Herbier, and Jean Epstein—who attempted to create a 'pure' cinematic art. The Surrealists liked popular films precisely because they were not examples of bourgeois art, and could in fact be regarded as an anti-art medium that could spark its own oneiric activities. Charged and inspired by the image sequences of popular films, the Surrealists began to write cinematically. As early as 1917 Philippe Soupault wrote 'cinematographic poems', in which he used filmic devices such as metamorphoses of objects, sudden disappearances, and abrupt changes. The fluidity of Breton's and Soupault's *Les Champs magnétiques* (*Magnetic Fields*, 1921) is certainly related to the flowing images in cinema. Goudal even suggests in his essay 'Surrealism and Cinema' that Breton's illogical sequences in *Poisson soluble*, which he published with his *First Manifesto*, should be read as film scenarios.

Although the Surrealists loved popular films, their own cinematographic writing, their numerous film scenarios and critical writings on film called for a new genre of films that would reproduce the illogical world of dreams or Breton's desire to create a new reality via the superimposition and montage of everyday reality and the dream world. Yet of the numerous Surrealist film scenarios, only very few were made into movies: Robert Desnos's *L'Étoile de mer* (*The Starfish*), Antonin Artaud's *La Coquille et le clergyman* (*The Seashell and the Clergyman*), and Salvador Dalí and Luis Buñuel's two collaborative scripts, *Un Chien andalou* (*An Andalusian Dog*) and *L'Age d'or* (*The Golden Age*). This small number of Surrealist films is probably due to Surrealism being primarily a movement of writers and artists, and not of filmmakers. While the viewing of popular films incited the Surrealist spectator to actively transform these 'readerly' films (i.e., those viewed passively) into 'writerly' ones (i.e., those that inspire creative acts), the truly Surrealist films put the viewer in a passive role, since their montage of incongruous sequences aimed at breaking open the spectator's unconscious drives and obsessions. Cinematographic techniques were thus a means of disrupting the symbolic order and of letting the unconscious erupt.

The Seashell and the Clergyman

The first Surrealist film was *The Seashell and the Clergyman*, which Germaine Dulac made on the basis of Artaud's scenario. According to Artaud in the 1920s, cinema was much more powerful than theater, since it had the capability of expressing the inner life of the mind in all its chaotic non-linearity. He wrote several scenarios, among them 'Eighteen Seconds', which registers a man's disparate thoughts while he stands at a street corner; but the only film produced from his many scripts was *The Seashell and the Clergyman*. Dulac, known for her earlier feminist film, *The Smiling Madame Beudet* (1923), followed Artaud's script very closely and used an impressive array of technical virtuosity, from superimpositions and slow motion to split screens, in order to visualize the clergyman's phantasmic world of hallucinations and obsessions. The film begins and ends with the clergyman as alchemist with his seashell alone in his laboratory. In the opening sequence the clergyman (Alex Allin) pours a black liquid from the seashell into glasses, which he then drops on the floor. A much-decorated officer (Lucien Bataille) enters the laboratory in slow motion, takes the seashell, breaks it with his enormous sword, and leaves. The clergyman follows him by crawling on all fours. A coach with a beautiful lady (Génica Athanasiou) and the officer pass by, whom the clergyman follows to a church, where he finds the officer and the lady in a confessional. Although much smaller and weaker, the clergyman pounces on the officer, his rival, who does not resist. While he strangles him, the officer's uniform changes into the white frock of a priest, and his head splits in two. In subsequent scenes, the clergyman is shown alternately pouncing on the woman, ripping off her clothes, chasing her, strangling her, and beheading her. Close-ups of the woman's face show her sticking out her tongue. After several scenes containing more images of severed heads, the film ends when the clergyman drinks from a shell containing the image of his own head floating on the black liquid that he poured in the opening scene of the film.

This brief account of *The Seashell and the Clergyman* may explain why the British Board of Censors banned this film on the grounds that it was not understandable. Clearly the film erases any demarcations between reality, dreams, and obsessions, and thus creates a Surreality that visualizes the chaotic processes of the clergyman's mind. Yet the repetition of images of fear, obsession, aggression, and violence suggest that once the solitary life of the clergyman is disrupted, he becomes obsessed with the beautiful lady as the supreme object of love. He desires her, and at the same time acts violently against her body. It seems as though he only wants to capture the spiritual part of the woman, symbolized by her severed head in the bowl, and is afraid of the woman's body. The film's beginning and ending suggest that the clergyman is only at peace alone, away from the physical presence of women, absorbed in his alchemical, narcissistic endeavors.

By the time of the film's first showing at the Studio des Ursulines on 9 February 1928, Artaud was seething with anger. Having played the role of Marat in Abel Gance's *Napoléon*, he had wanted to act the part of the clergyman, especially since his close friend Génica Athanasiou played the lady. He also wanted to be part of the editing of the film, but Dulac kept him at a distance. Artaud was sufficiently worried about the faithfulness of the film to have published his scenario, together with his view of how the film should have been made, three months earlier in the November issue of the *Nouvelle Revue française*. At the first showing of the film, Artaud and his friends protested violently and called Dulac a cow. However, a comparison of Artaud's script and the film indicates that Dulac followed the scenario very faithfully. Yet it seems that Dulac critiqued Artaud's phantasmic rendition of male desire by choosing the slight Alex Allin, and not the powerful screen persona of Artaud, for the role of the clergyman. Alin appears short even next to the woman; he is balding, and his running after her on his toes and with his arms stretched out which strikes viewers as rather ridiculous. Dulac's choice and directing of Allin as a rather annoying, adolescent-like clergyman might very well have been her critique of Artaud's hallucinations and expressions of male desire, violence, and fear.

L'Étoile de mer

The second Surrealist film, Man Ray's *L'Étoile de mer*, had its first showing three months after the noisy opening of *The Seashell and the Clergyman*. This film is very different from Man Ray's earlier Dada films *Retour à la raison* and *Emak Bakia*, in which he had explored objects in movement. The reason for this change might be that in filming *L'Étoile de mer*, Man Ray closely followed the thirty-three numbered sequences of the scenario written by his friend Robert Desnos, who was one of the great film enthusiasts among the Surrealists. Desnos wrote that he owned a starfish which for him became the embodiment of a lost love, and he tellingly added, 'a love well lost'. As in *The Seashell and the Clergyman*, the theme of this film is again the male protagonist's intent to alchemically transform the elusive, resisting woman into a spiritual abstraction, in order to possess and control her.

The film opens with a fairly coherent section. A man and a woman (André de la Rivière, a friend of Desnos, and Kiki) walk along a path. The woman lifts her coat and seductively adjusts the garter of one of her stockings. This action is punctuated by the intertitle 'The teeth of women are such charming objects that one should only see them in one's dream or at the moment of love', thus warning the viewer of the danger that woman poses. The two enter a house and go upstairs into a room, where she completely undresses, while he sits fully dressed on a chair looking away. When she has made herself comfortable on the bed, the man gets up, and the intertitle 'Adieu' appears. He kisses her hand, leaves, and the intertitle 'Si Belle! Cybèle!' ('So beautiful! Cybele!') follows. Again, the homonym 'Si Belle—Cibèle' reveals, as did the intertitle earlier about the teeth, a danger for the male protagonist. Cybele was a goddess of Phrygia, the mother of all gods, and as such connotes matriarchy. This section is followed by the same woman selling newspapers in the street. The male protagonist takes her arm, and they both look at a glass jar with a starfish in it. He takes the jar to his room and closely examines the living starfish. Then a sequence of movements (newspapers blown away, trains and ships moving) is juxtaposed to a flower in a flowerpot, image of feminine beauty, accompanied by the intertitle 'If the flowers were made of glass'. When the woman walks along the path by herself, the intertitle 'Beautiful, beautiful as a flower made of glass' appears, followed by the image of a dead starfish. This transformation of organic, living beings into immobile, fixed objects recurs throughout the second part of the film, and these two different worlds appear simultaneously. When the woman climbs the stairs with a long, threatening knife in her hand, the image of a dead starfish is superimposed. When the woman leaves the protagonist for another man (Robert Desnos), the intertitle 'How beautiful she was' appears. The protagonist looks at the starfish, and this sequence is accompanied by the intertitle 'How beautiful she is', thereby signalling the transformation of the mutable, fickle woman into the immutable image of the starfish, which he holds in his hands and can thus control. This alchemical change recalls the clergyman's severing of the lady's head and preserving it in a bowl in *The Seashell and the Clergyman*.

Desnos and Man Ray present the woman's independence as a threat to the protagonist, which they express most memorably via the shot of the woman dressed in a tunic and a Phrygian cap holding a spear. Intertitles such as 'And if you find on this earth a woman who loves sincerely' are accompanied by the image of the woman wearing a mask. Even the musical selections, which are clearly marked in the manuscript of the scenario, further underline the overall theme of love lost and turned into permanent memory. The film begins with the lyrics 'The pleasure of love lasts only a moment' of the popular song 'Plaisir d'amour', and concludes with the lyric 'Love's sorrow lasts an entire life' from the same song. The protagonist can only give permanence to his love relationship by turning the fickle woman into the permanent object of the starfish. The film presents this alchemical process in which everyday reality and the world of imagination interpenetrate, where flowers turn into glass as in Baudelaire's artificial paradise, and where threatening and independent women turn into beautiful starfish. It is this trans-formative process of the protagonist's mind that the film expresses above all. Man Ray's use of a gelatine filter for approximately half of the shots creates a very painterly, dreamy, poetic effect, which might also suggest that the protagonist does not recall very clearly some scenes from the past, and recalls others, such as the woman with the spear or the violent ending with the shattering of the glass, only too clearly.

Unlike the collaboration between Artaud and Dulac, the working relationship of Man Ray and Desnos on this film was very harmonious. Having unsuccessfully tried to make a Surrealist film with *Emak Bakia* in 1926, Man Ray used his own money and the help of Desnos' scenario to finally succeed. Desnos was very pleased with the realization of his script, and stated that Man Ray granted him the most flattering image of himself and his dreams. He did not even object to the seemingly playful long takes of newspapers scattered and blown by the wind, houses and trees filmed from the moving train, or the division of the screen into twelve sections, all of which recall sequences from Man Ray's earlier Dada films.

Un Chien andalou

The collaboration of the Spaniards Luis Buñuel and Salvador Dalí produced *Un Chien andalou* (1929) and *L'Age d'or* (1930), the two greatest Surrealist films. The two met at the Residencia de Estudiantes at the University of Madrid in a group of writers that included Federico García Lorca and Juan Ramón Jimenez. After his studies in entomology and his degree in history in 1925, Buñuel went to Paris, where he began his apprentice-ship in cinema as an assistant to Jean Epstein. Buñuel's mother provided him with the money to make his own first film, *Un Chien andalou*. For the scenario Buñuel sought the collaboration of his friend, the painter Salvador Dalí. They were two outsiders who had read Freud, Breton, and especially the works of Benjamin Péret, and who wanted to join the Surrealist group in Paris. In writing their film script they used fragments of their own dreams, but the composition, according to Buñuel, involved much more than automatic writing. Dalí would mention a series of disparate images and fragments, and Buñuel would interject his ideas and his dreams. Whenever images were too understandable, they were discarded. It is for this reason, too, that they chose the title of one of Buñuel's earlier collections of poems as the purposely nonsensical title of the film, which deals neither with dogs nor with Andalusia.

Un Chien andalou begins with the intertitle 'Once upon a time', followed by one of the most horrific sequences in all of cinema. A man (Buñuel) sharpens a razor, looks up and sees a narrow band of clouds passing in front of the full moon, and then is shown slicing the eye of a woman in a graphic close-up (it was actually a cow's eye that was used). A new intertitle, 'Eight years later', signals the next sequence. A man (Pierre Batcheff) decked out in feminine frills carries a striped box and rides a bicycle through the empty streets of Paris. A woman (Simone Mareuil) in a room reads a book that is opened at a reproduction of Vermeer's *Lacemaker*. After a premonition that something dreadful will happen, she goes to the window and sees the bicyclist fall off his bike. She runs down and kisses him. Back in her room she opens the striped box and arranges its content, a striped tie, with the frills and a collar, on her bed. The bicyclist is suddenly in the room and watches ants crawl from a wound in his hand. The woman and the bicyclist then observe from her apartment window an androgynous-looking person poking a severed hand with a stick in the street. Men surround the androgyne, until a policeman puts the hand into the striped box, which the woman then embraces.

After a series of encounters between the woman and the cyclist that are both violent and sexual, a new intertitle, 'Sixteen years earlier', is followed by the man/bicyclist facing his younger self whom he shoots, and whose body slides down the naked back of a woman in a park. Men carry away the dead body, and a series of long shots as well as the accompanying music suggest that this is the end of the film. But suddenly the woman opens the door to her room. She sees a moth, which the camera enlarges to the point that the image of a human skull is visible on the back of the moth. The man/cyclist, whose mouth is suddenly covered by the hair of the woman's underarm, appears, and the woman scornfully sticks out her tongue at him, opens the door, and directly steps onto a beach, where she kisses a different man, with whom she walks along the shore. The two find the now broken striped box and the feminine frills among the stones. The new man throws the box and frills away, and they happily continue their walk to tango music. A last intertitle appears, 'In the Spring', followed by a still tableau of the new man and the woman buried up to their chests in sand and devoured by insects.

This film obviously does not follow conventional narrative patterns, since it dislocates traditional notions of time and space not unlike illogical dream sequences. It is this illogical flow of scenes and images that Dalí and Buñuel wanted to evoke in order to convey figurations of masculine obsessions, phantasms, and fears. One of the provisional titles of this film was 'It is dangerous to lean inside', a play on the window signs in railway cars ('It is dangerous to lean outside'), through which Buñuel and Dalí probably wanted to suggest that this was a film in which viewers had to take the risk of 'leaning inside' to experience the workings of the unconscious.

Although Buñuel and Dalí believed that they created an incoherent, and therefore inexplicable film, certain sequences and images seem to cry out for interpretation. The slashing of the woman's eye in the prologue is undoubtedly the most viscerally experienced

■ Luis Buñuel (1900–1983)

In 1961 Buñuel wrote: 'There is no other way than that of *rebellion* in a world that is in such a mess.' His thirty-six films form his revolt against all forms of oppression and repression, be they religious, sexual, political, or economic. This sense of rebellion forms a continuity from his collaboration with Salvador Dalí in *Un Chien andalou* (1929) to his last film, *That Obscure Object of Desire* (1978). He wanted to provoke, shock, and attack a society that he found corrupt. Although he was a member of the Surrealist movement for only three years, he insisted that his films were marked by his 'Jesuit education and Surrealism' in the form of his biting anticlericalism and the Surrealist notions of obsession, mad love, and the irrationality of dreams.

Despite the fact that Buñuel embraced anarchy, obsession, and chance, he was one of the most disciplined directors, who often needed only one take and more often than not completed filming in two to four weeks. As one of the great film *auteurs*, he collaborated on each of his thirty-six scenarios, and when he did not write the story himself, he integrated his own worldview into the story that he adapted. After a very promising beginning with *Un Chien andalou* (1929), *L'Age d'or* (1930), and *Las Hurdes* (*Land without Bread*, 1932), the Spanish Civil War, the rise of Franco, and the Second World War interrupted his filmmaking for more than ten years, during which he worked on Spanish versions of anti-Fascist film projects in Hollywood and New York, which were distributed in Latin America.

⊙ *Un Chien andalou*

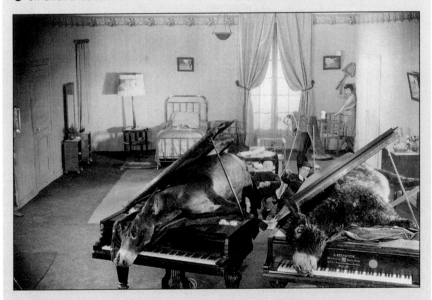

In 1946 Buñuel went with his family to Mexico, where after a hiatus of ten years he began to make films again. Though celebrated as the greatest Spanish film director of the twentieth century, Buñuel made most of his films in Mexico, where he lived in self-imposed exile until his death in 1983. His first Mexican film of note was *Los olvidados* (1950), an unflattering depiction of life in the slums of Mexico City. Inspired by Vittorio De Sica's *Sciuscià* (*Shoeshine*, 1946), Buñuel combined Neorealism with Surrealist devices and dream-like sequences. The film received the award for best directing as well as the International Critics' Prize at Cannes in 1951. At the age of 60 and after several years in Mexico, he returned to Spain in order to make *Viridiana* (1961). This film received the first prize at Cannes, but was promptly banned by the Spanish government because of its attack on religion, especially the beggars' travesty of the Last Supper. Buñuel then returned to Mexico to make his next film, *Exterminating Angel* (1962), for which he received the International Critics' Prize at Cannes.

With the film *Diary of a Chambermaid* (1964, starring Jeanne Moreau), he began a series of six French productions, for which he collaborated on the scenarios with Jean-Claude Carrière. *Belle de Jour* (1966, with Catherine Deneuve), which was awarded the Grand Prize at Venice, tells of the fantasies, dreams, and nightmares of a rich married woman who deals with her boredom and masochism by working in a brothel in the afternoons. *The Milky Way* (1969) is a Surrealistic trip through the fanaticisms of Christian heretics. Buñuel composed the whole dialogue using only quotes from religious literature. His next film, *Tristana* (1971, with Catherine Deneuve), combines many of Buñuel's recurring themes and obsessions: foot fetishism, necrophilia, hatred for blind persons, decadent priests, older men (Fernando Rey, Buñuel's alter ego) obsessed with younger women, dreams, and chance encounters. For his next film, *The Discreet Charm of the Bourgeoisie* (1972), Buñuel again wrote the story himself. The theme is frustration, as the characters are repeatedly prevented from having a dinner together. Buñuel made his last film, *That Obscure Object of Desire* (1978), at the age of 77. For the female role he depicted two different types of woman, the virgin and the temptress, played by two different actresses, in order to intensify the portrayal of the irrationality of male desire.

sequence of the film. Generally explained as Buñuel's and Dalí's demand for a new vision, a new cinema that portrays the inner workings of the mind, male viewers may experience it as an extreme gesture of sadism or as an act of castration, while female viewers may regard it as an instance of ultimate male aggression and violence toward women. Several sequences focus on male sexual desire. The cyclist, after sadistically enjoying the death of the androgyne, corners the woman in her room and attempts to rape her to the accompaniment of an Argentine tango. He is, however, stopped by the woman, who barricades herself in a corner of the room and threateningly holds up a tennis racket. It is at this moment that the man grasps two ropes on the floor and pulls the immense load of two priests and two rotting donkeys on two grand pianos. This burden might suggest social influences—the church (priests), work ethic (donkeys), bourgeois values (grand piano)—that inhibit his pursuit of what Breton called 'amour fou', mad love.

Some of the images seem to stem from Dalí's repertoire of obsessions, such as the ants and the severed hand, since they also occur in several of his paintings. The cut-off hand as well as the hand caught in the door might well suggest his preoccupation with masturbation. Other sequences are simply humorous gags, such as the dissolve, following the crawling ants, between the underarm of a female sunbather and a spiny sea urchin, or the woman's underarm hair around the man's mouth. This latter image, however, also seems related to the recurring instability of gender identity: the cyclist is dressed in feminine frills, and the androgyne poking the cut-off hand is a woman who looks like a man.

It is most curious that the film seems to end with the death of the cyclist's younger self in the park. The long shot of the men carrying the body is accompanied by the last measures of 'Tristan's Death' from Richard Wagner's *Tristan and Isolde*. Yet instead of 'The End', a different film seems to begin, which presents a changed woman who is now strong and assertive, and who is no longer the bicyclist's victim. She sticks her tongue out at him in disdain, leaves him, and joins another man at the seashore, with whom she tangoes along the beach. This sequence, including the new man's rejection of the rediscovered striped box and feminine frills, is the happiest moment for the woman. The last shot, however, shows the two dying.

When the Surrealists first saw *Un Chien andalou* in a private showing at the Studio des Ursulines on June 6, 1929, they were enthusiastic, declaring that this film was indeed a great Surrealist work. They immediately received Buñuel and Dalí with open arms as members of the Surrealist group. Jean Mauclaire of Studio 28 bought the film, which had a successful eight-month run. Buñuel, who published the scenario in the final issue of *La Révolution surréaliste*, stated in his introduction: 'It expresses, without any reservation, my complete adherence to Surrealist thought and activity. *Un Chien andalou* would not exist if Surrealism did not exist.' Yet Buñuel was distraught and disgusted by the enjoyment the film seemed to afford viewers. In the same introduction he wrote: 'But what can I do . . . about this imbecilic crowd that has found beautiful or poetic that which, at heart, is nothing other than a desperate, impassioned call for murder.'

L'Age d'or

Buñuel tried to make sure that his next film, *L'Age d'or*, was sufficiently scandalous, blasphemous, and revolutionary that viewers were not easily tempted to find it beautiful. He set out to explode bourgeois notions of religion, family, morality, and society through images of violence: the male protagonist kicks a blind man to the ground, hits a marquise in the face, and throws a bishop out of a window; a father kills his son, and Jesus Christ is the Marquis de Sade's Comte de Blangis, the most outrageous libertine, who kills a young woman at the end of the movie.

The film begins with footage from an educational documentary depicting scorpions fighting with each other. These animals are presented as antisocial, cruel, purely instinct- ive and violent. Buñuel and Dalí's title, *The Golden Age*, might well denote the instinctive, animalistic life of these scorpions, and thus the raw passion, 'l'amour fou', of the two prot- agonists, whose behavior transgresses social codes at every turn. This is most obvious in the highly official ceremony of the founding of Rome, which is interrupted by the pas- sionate shrieks of a couple rolling ecstatically in the mud. According to Buñuel and Dalí, this film is about the irresistible force of passion, mad love, that clashes with patriotism, social responsibility, religion, and the sacred ideals of civilized society. Although both *Un Chien andalou* and *L'Age d'or* are powerful expressions of Surrealist revolt, these two films are quite different from each other. *L'Age d'or* is one hour long, almost four times the length of *Un Chien andalou*, and it is one of the early French sound films. Its structure and message seem more coherent, probably because Dalí's collaboration was less exten- sive in their second film.

The Prologue, taken from the pedagogical film *Le Scorpion languedocien* (1912), including the intertitles, recalls Buñuel's interest in entomology, and may suggest attempt to equate the behavior of scorpions with that of human beings at the outset of this film. The film's five segments traverse chronological and narrative boundaries with bewilder- ing frequency, depicting desire as pure excess, thwarted by bourgeois convention, as the two lovers are constantly prevented from being together. The epilogue is a tribute to de Sade's *The 120 Days of Sodom*, which Buñuel discovered in 1929 when the Vicomte de Noailles, who provided the money for the making of *L'Age d'or*, purchased the original manuscript. Buñuel and several Surrealists hailed this work by Sade as a recipe for a new morality and cultural revolution, that would lead men (and only men) back to their basic instincts of passion and violence. In his *Second Manifesto of Surrealism*, Breton, like de Sade, called for abolishing institutions of civilization: family, country, religion. When the Surrealists saw *L'Age d'or* in a private screening in October 1930, they hailed it as the most perfect Surrealist film, since it focused on mad love in all its excesses, perversions, and revolt.

Unlike *Un Chien andalou*, this film was a collaborative project of the Surrealist group with the participation not only of Dalí but of Max Ernst and his second wife, Marie-Berthe Aurenche, Pierre Prévert, Paul Eluard, and Roland Penrose and his first wife, Valentine Boué, all of whom acted in the film and contributed to the many gags. For the opening of the film at Studio 28 on November 28, the Surrealists prepared a forty-eight-page gold-covered program which included Dalí's summary of the film, in which he clearly identifies the Comte de Blangis as Jesus Christ, and rather general texts by Breton, Crevel, Éluard, and Thirion on mad love and revolt. Dalí, Ernst, Arp, Man Ray, Tanguy, and Miro contributed drawings for it. In addition, the Surrealists combined the showing of L'Age d'or with an exhibition of paintings and books. The film showings went smoothly from November 28 to December 2. On December 3, members of the Anti-Jewish League and the League of Patriots disrupted the projection with shouts of 'Down with the Jews!' and 'There are still some Christians left in France!' They damaged the screen with ink, threw stink bombs, and smashed the Surrealist paintings in the entrance hall. Instead of taking reprisals against these Fascist thugs, Jean Chiappe, the chief of police, confiscated the film and withdrew its permit. Enraged by the actions of the police, the Surrealists published their tract 'The L'Age d'or Affair', in which they included excerpts from the Fascist press about the film, photographs of the damaged paintings, and a questionnaire that included the following question: 'Since when are the police in the service of anti-Semitism?'. The Surrealists' protest did little to increase the availability of the film, which for the next fifty years could only be seen in rare special screenings.

The attacks on L'Age d'or indicate that Surrealist films shock and scandalize through quite understandable sequences of images: Jesus Christ depicted as de Sade's murdering libertine, a woman's eye cut with a razor, a woman's face violently shattered. Surrealist films rely on characters, narratives, and optically realistic effects, which hook the viewer into the world portrayed by the film. Only through the viewers' identification with the familiar world invoked by the film can the film's sequential disruptions open up suppressed unconscious drives and obsessions. In the four Surrealist films, these obsessions and anxieties are predominantly those of the male protagonist, who seems afraid of losing control over the female lover, whom he does ultimately lose. Female independence is depicted as a threatening Phrygian woman warrior, as a woman full of disdain sticking out her tongue, as a lover who has dangerous teeth. The frequent use of male violence and aggression in these films might in part be related to this male anxiety and crisis. It is at the very moment when Lys leaves Modot that the drum roll of the Sadean epilogue begins in L'Age d'or, and Kiki's face is shattered shortly after she leaves the male protagonist in L'Étoile de mer. While ostensibly celebrating free love, these Surrealist films tend to depict male desire thwarted by independent, taunting women who are often shown being punished for their disloyalty. These films represent masculinity in crisis, fueled by the anxieties of a generation that lived through the most brutal slaughter the world had yet known.

Conclusion

Surrealist films obviously disoriented viewers through their subversions of the logic of space and time, and the mixing of dream and reality, the conscious and the unconscious. Yet, unlike Dada films, Surrealist films rarely used technical virtuosity or formal experimentation; they did not present the filmic images as yet another illusion. The Surrealist filmmakers used the cinematic apparatus as a realistic means to portray the symbolic order, which they then disrupted with incongruous, shocking images. The difference between Dada and Surrealist films thus lies in their different strategies of defamiliarizing social reality. Surrealist filmmakers largely relied on conventional cinematography (narratives, optical realism, characters) as a means to draw the viewer into the reality produced by the film. By contrast, the incoherent, non-narrative, illogical nature of Dada films, which constantly defamiliarize the familiar world through cinematic manipulations, never lets the viewer enter the world of the film.

Despite their differences, both Dada and Surrealism shared a contempt for the values they considered emblematic of bourgeois hypocrisy, whose veneer of civility ultimately concealed a deep-seated brutality. The emphasis on defamiliarization in the films of these movements gave viewers a means of seeing the world anew, and made them realize that this was a world that had stopped making sense.

Further reading

Breton, André (1969) *Manifestoes of Surrealism,* trans. Richard Seaver and Helen R. Lane (Ann Arbor: University of Michigan Press, 1969). Breton's important explanations and definitions of Surrealism in his Manifestoes of 1924 and 1929.

Buñuel, Luis, *My Last Sigh* (New York: Random House, 1984). Buñuel's memoirs.

Evans, Peter William, *The Films of Luis Buñuel: Subjectivity and Desire* (Oxford: Oxford University Press, 1995). An extended analysis of Buñuel's films using psychoanalysis and gender theory.

Hammond, Paul, *L'Age d'or* (London: British Film Institute, 1997). Commentary and analysis of the film with discussion of the 'L'Age d'or Affair'.

—— (ed.), *The Shadow and Its Shadow: Surrealist Writings on Cinema*, 3rd edn. (San Francisco: City Lights, 2000). Translations of major texts by Surrealist writers, artists, and filmmakers on the medium of film.

Kovács, Steven, *From Enchantment to Rage: The Story of Surrealist Cinema* (Rutherford, NJ: Farleigh Dickinson University Press, 1980). A study of the major Dada and Surrealist films, with an emphasis on the films by Man Ray.

Kuenzli, Rudolf (ed.), *Dada and Surrealist Film* (Cambridge, Mass.: MIT Press, 1996). A collection of critical essays on the major Dada and Surrealist films. Includes bibliography.

Matthews, J. M., *Surrealism and Film* (Ann Arbor: University of Michigan Press, 1971). A general study of Surrealist films that includes chapters on Surrealist aspects of commercial cinema and more recent Surrealist films.

Pérez Turrent, Tomás, and de la Colina, José, *Objects of Desire: Conversations with Luis Buñuel* (New York: Marsilio, 1992). A collection of interviews.

Richter, Hans, *Dada: Art and Anti-Art*, trans. David Britt (London: Thames & Hudson, 1997). An illustrated survey of the Dada movement.

Screen 39(2) (summer 1998). Includes relatively recent critical essays on Surrealist film.

Williams, Linda, *Figures of Desire: A Theory and Analysis of Surrealist Film* (Berkeley: University of California Press, 1992). Provides a psychoanalytic theory for the analysis of Surrealist films and includes close readings of early and late films by Luis Buñuel.

5

FRENCH CINEMA IN
THE 1930s

Dudley Andrew

 The affection felt in retrospect for the 1930s is akin to what is often felt for any period of adolescence: the time, inevitably troubled, of coming into one's identity, just before being shoved into the realities of a much larger world. For despite its august history and its victory in 1918, France in the 1930s appears as an uncertain youth standing before modernity. A fragile contrivance surrounded by totalitarian nations, its ethos came from a vulnerable humanism already outsized by the realities of the century. France, and particularly Paris, was the beloved refuge of Europe's political refugees. It had already become the cultural refuge of American writers and artists. The City of Light simply had to withstand the inhumane political and economic oppression whose dark specter was everywhere evident. If the human still mattered, it mattered most in Paris.

This feeling for—or memory of—an adolescent sincerity and vulnerability stands behind the affection expressed by critics from the 1930s to our own day for the exceptional aesthetic that incubated in the era, the so-called school of Poetic Realism, and for its icon, Jean Gabin. In films like *La Belle Équipe* (1936, Julien Duvivier) Gabin would disingenuously claim to be an everyman, that is, to be no icon at all; but in an entertainment system that marketed stars, he was a magnet for aspirations of social justice, if not for simple sociality. While Gabin was not quite the most popular star of the day, just as Poetic Realist films were not always the biggest hits, both have come down to us as the image of the era, as its best and most characteristic face.

However, a history of Poetic Realism can hardly stand in for that of a national cinema. To the student of popular culture these eighty films of 'dark pessimism' constitute merely one type among others within the larger system of the French film industry. Moreover, when treated as part of the chief 'popular entertainment medium' of the day, Poetic Realism hardly fulfills the vaunted social claims its apologists have made for it. Short-sighted and morally anemic, Poetic Realism tended to evade pressing political problems and wallow in regret. Indeed, few French films of the time, none of them commercially viable, lifted their heads out of the sand to confront the Depression and the Fascist threat head on. The fact is that none of the writers or directors in the industry came from the working class. This is evident when one tallies up the problems fussed over in film after film (virginity, for example, or paternity); problems that apply to a petit-bourgeois moral code that was officially promulgated in the nation but that did not keep the proletariat awake at night. Too lax in its 'social' ambition, perhaps too pretentious in its 'cultural' ambition, Poetic Realism has been lionized chiefly for a purely aesthetic appeal that may obscure whatever work cinema as a whole performed in its social context.

That social context comes clearer when we attend to faces other than Gabin's. Older men like Raimu, Alerme, Harry Baur, comics like Fernandel, Milton, Bach, and *ingénues* like Simone Simon, Anabella, and Michele Morgan played with and against one another in standard entertainment genres such as the historical drama, the military comedy, the theatrical farce, and the boulevard *mélo* (melodrama). Seldom before 1960 did cinema anywhere in the world seem so capable of satisfying or equilibrating art and entertainment, and of doing so with minimal state or studio supervision. French cinema would have to await the invasion of the Nazis before serious regulations and government rationalization would be set in place. As for business conditions, the same disorganization made this cinema truly a cottage industry, at least in comparison to the studio system in Hollywood or Japan. Ninety-five per cent of the theaters were owned by individual families, and dozens of distributors cropped up to bid for the scores of films made by one-shot producers. Scattered and without a long-term strategy, French cinema could only adopt a comparatively modest look. Seldom spectacular, these films aimed to speak to a wide social spectrum on a human scale, and they did so neither under the crass guise of rationalized commercial product nor under that of high art, but as the result of the everyday exercise of talent and tradition.

The coming of sound

It was in an ambience of sound that the films of the period huddled together (not always harmoniously) under the umbrella term 'French cinema of the 1930s'. New audio technology, including phonographs and radio, helped democratize a notion of culture that an elite had always believed it alone defined. Hybrid musical genres resulted from the mix of classical compositions and ribald singers available on airwaves. Popular modes of theater attracted playwrights like Jean Cocteau and anarchist poets like Robert Desnos. The latter, for instance, prepared a radio version of *Fantômas* in 1932, bringing his idiosyncratic sensibility to thousands of listeners who would never pick up a copy of his Surrrealist poems.

In luring to cinema a formidable array of writers, actors, and composers, and with proud traditions in theater and music, sound markedly changed the look and feel of French cinema. Journals and newspapers carried the protests of traditionalists against this amalgamation of media and audiences, while modernists saluted the collapse of artificial distinctions between popular and elite expression, between visual and literary modes, and between the officially mandated categories of 'spectacle' and 'art'. Meanwhile, sound technology advanced irrevocably across the country, driven by Hollywood's financial power and accelerated by German and American technological competition.

France could put up little resistance to the new powers of international cinema. Despite a run of famous masterpieces (*Napoléon*, 1928, Abel Gance; *La Passion de Jeanne d'Arc*, 1929, Carl Theodore Dreyer; *L'Argent*, 1929, Marcel L'Herbier; *Thérèse Raquin*, 1928, Jacques Feyder), the 1920s closed in a bleak fashion for French cinema overall. In 1929 only sixty of the 400 films projected in France were French, and 80 per cent of all receipts found their way back to Hollywood. Bringing with it both immense capital and up-to-date technology, Paramount of Paris immediately became France's leading production company. As a consequence the French populace must have assumed that the movies were a rightful Hollywood phenomenon, for they routinely watched more American than French films.

How had such a situation developed? First of all, the structure of Hollywood gave it an unbeatable advantage. A virtual monopoly held by eight vertically integrated studios kept foreign films from all but a few designated import theaters in New York. Production, distribution, and exhibition in France, on the other hand, competed with one another, giving foreign interests a foothold. With nearly all French movie theaters being independent and unchained, power lay in distribution. Subsidiaries of Hollywood studios quickly began to control distribution, pressuring theaters into exclusive deals. After all, they could provide Hollywood stars and spectacle. And so, while their facilities and personnel were capable of turning out 250 films a year, in the 1930s France produced half that number.

Not only was this a financial loss and a failed opportunity for idle artists, the massive importation of American films had invisible consequences for cultural identity. From 1925 onwards an alarm decrying this situation was sounded in French trade papers, an alarm that continues to this day. A panoply of emergency economic strategies has been deployed: taxes on imported films and on the dubbing of films; the required employment of French personnel in dubbing; quotas limiting imports, then limiting the number of weeks theaters might play foreign films; the blocking of funds made by American companies from leaving France.

Far more interesting are those textual strategies aimed at product improvement and differentiation. This is defense by counterattack, with consequences for the history of film style. Since, with its vast technical and financial resources, Hollywood was unassailable in the realm of spectacle, certain French producers introduced guerrilla tactics, launching distinctively French offerings that emphasized regional characters, dialects, tales, and lore that Hollywood could never copy or assimilate. Because the international language of the silent film exploded in 1930 into a Babel of dialects, the possibility was raised of innumerable independent fiefdoms ruling over local terrain. French stage plays, cheap to reproduce on film, could bring to a large French audience the witty and often socially attuned dialogue that playgoers in Paris enjoyed. And this dialogue could be spoken by actors the whole country had heard about but few had ever had the opportunity to see in person. From 1930 to 1934 the national theatrical genius flowed onto film in the form of farces, satires, boulevard comedies, and melodramas. Many, particularly Marcel Pagnol's, were spiced with regionalisms. His *Angèle*, shot cheaply on location near Aubagne, was the most lucrative hit in 1933, out-drawing the best the Hollywood studios had to offer.

A second strategy flowed from the magic words 'cinema of quality', first pronounced with missionary zeal in this context of trade around 1930. With 'quality', the French would dare to strike back not at regional outposts but at the center of American power. Quality was to match up with, and defeat, the ungainly American cinema of 'quantity', and not just in France alone, for this would be designated an export line of movies. Hollywood was pictured as an assembly-line factory, whereas all films made in France were thought to develop in an individual, hence more natural and human, manner. The standardized genres and studio styles of the factory were countered by the healthy diversity of French subjects, each treated in a style tailored specifically to it. As for working conditions, the alienated writers and contract performers in Hollywood were said to lack the morale maintained on French projects by talent who considered themselves artisans, heirs of a medieval guild system. Furthermore, these artisans could take pride in their devotion to a grand project as well as in their relations to co-workers with whom they formed a team or *équipe*.

Such an argument had a material basis. The absence of an integrated studio system in France meant that most films developed as unique ventures, with only a handful of producers involved in more than a single film, particularly after the collapse of Gaumont, Pathé, and Paramount around 1934. By 1937 you can't find a producer involved in more than six films. Hollywood studios, by contrast, turned out as many as fifty films each. Export films of high quality were built around the writer–director team who offered a project to a producer (frequently a friend). Jacques Prévert and Marcel Carné formed the most famous of such teams, but there were many others. Generally a star actor was included in the package which, once under way, grew with the addition of a trusted cameraman, designer, and composer. Such teams frequently traveled together from project to project, getting to know and respect one another. This contributed to that wholeness of atmosphere that bathes each of the famous Poetic Realist films—this and the fact that in a system of such liberty, where projects develop along lines of friendship, often the very best artisans were eager to join up.

Since no single producer planned for more than a couple of films each year, French cinema developed haphazardly. Without the convenient genre categories of Hollywood, without a governmental body to speak for it (the only major European cinema left to fend for itself in this way), and without a vertically integrated industry (indeed, without a substantial production company after 1934), French cinema appeared on screens in piecemeal fashion, the names of stars serving as the primary guide for viewers. Domestic trade journals like *La Cinématographie française* and foreign ones like *Variety* continually report an ongoing 'crisis' of French cinema throughout the first decade of sound. The cost of introducing sound cinema to France's more than 5,000 theaters was immense and could scarcely be born by most owners, predominately individual 'shopkeepers'. Hence for a few years in France, as in many countries, sound cinema was an exclusively urban entertainment, dominated by Hollywood pictures and filling the coffers of the Americans and Germans who owned the patents, if not the theaters and the films themselves.

Hollywood's strategy to control the European market can be broken into three phases. At first, foreign versions of certain designated scripts were filmed in southern California. Personnel from every country were imported for the hasty rewriting, acting, and direction required to turn a $300,000 English-language film into four $100,000 European versions. Jesse Lasky and Walter Wanger, chiefs of Paramount, were responsible for Hollywood's second European strategy. They equipped the Joinville studios in Paris with the same Western Electric sound that the company used at home. Already by 1930 the plant had been refurbished until it rivaled the best in Hollywood production facilities: that year, the studio turned out an incredible 100 features and fifty shorts in as

■ Jean Renoir (1894–1979)

There are good reasons for treating Jean Renoir as an independent force, orbiting French cinema from the lofty space to which he was launched by his prestigious family connections (the son of Impressionist painter Pierre-Auguste Renoir) and by his incalculable talent. But Renoir can just as easily serve to illuminate the national cinema to which he contributed. Never an average filmmaker, he nevertheless faced the same kinds of aesthetic, social, and business problems and options as did his colleagues during the 1930s. He made enough films, and under a sufficiently diverse set of circumstances, to support the claim to have belonged to this period as much as any industry hack.

Until 1937 Renoir's genius went unnoticed outside his homeland, while in France he was thought something of an amateur, whose wealth and family fame permitted him to experiment. He tried farces (*On purge bébé*, 1931), detective stories (*La Nuit du carrefour [Night at the Crossroads]*, 1932), light comedy (*Chotard et cie. [Chotard and Company]*, 1932), adaptations (*Madame Bovary*, 1933), social satire (*Boudu sauvé des eaux [Boudu Saved from Drowning]*, 1932), lurid *faits divers* (*Toni*, 1935), and social comedy (*Le Crime de M. Lange [The Crime of Monsieur Lange]*, 1936). Because of this very independence, and because of the Leftist sympathies exemplified in the latter two films, the Communist Party enticed him

⊕ *La Grande Illusion*

to coordinate their propaganda effort for the Popular Front elections of 1936, *La Vie est à nous*. The success of the elections coincided with Renoir's popular success as well. Awarded the first prize given by the French for direction (for *Les Bas Fonds*), he then made his most beloved film, *La Grande Illusion* (*Grand Illusion*, 1937), starring Jean Gabin. Up until the war, no one made films that were more ambitious, more costly, or more prestigious. He became a giant in these years with *La Marseillaise* (1938), *La Bête humaine* (*The Human Beast*, 1938), and *La Règle du jeu* (*Rules of the Game*, 1939). He also found time to direct a people's film cooperative, *Ciné-Liberté*, to write a column in the Communist weekly *Ce soir*, and to plan a host of other films for a company he helped found in 1939.

'The most French of directors', as André Bazin dubbed him, Renoir always set his dramas within densely realistic milieux, shooting on location whenever possible. He chose actors, sometimes against type, so that their interplay on these complex sets might allow miraculous discoveries of social psychology. Long takes, location sound, deep-focus photography, and a frequently mobile camera increased the chances that his recipe mixing just the right script, setting, and people would spark a reaction powerful enough to shock and illuminate the spectator. A thoroughgoing democrat in his politics and on the set, he also knew how to coax people (and somehow reality itself) to adopt shapes that he knew would be beautiful and morally revealing. While his films often speak to the grave social situation that brought down the Third Republic, their concerns and their form are clearly in dialogue with Montaigne, Beaumarchais, Rousseau, and other moral thinkers in the French tradition, giving his work a resonance that still seems up to date.

many as fourteen languages, prompting locals to call it 'the Tower of Babel'. Paramount spent staggering sums in Paris, allocating $8,000,000 in the single month of April 1931 for French productions, a sum equal to around 20 per cent of their total production budget.

Ultimately, though, the American obsession with efficiency reached a peak in the single-take, multiple-version method that stationed up to four teams of actors in glass booths surrounding the sound stage to deliver, in their particular tongues, simultaneous versions of the action taking place. Paramount turned out multiple versions of international high-life comedies at the rate of more than one a month, until actual dubbing technology was sufficiently perfected late in 1932. This would prove the longest-lasting strategy of colonization. By that date, however, Paramount was starting to reel from the first effects of the Depression, and nearly ceased production of original French films at Joinville. Joinville became a dubbing center that supported many technicians but no longer dominated European filmmaking.

An industry of entertainment

Today Marcel Pagnol and Sacha Guitry appear exceptional talents, but in 1930 they were part of a general migration of theater personnel to sound cinema at a time when upstart producers were backing any sort of drama that could be shot quickly on the newly equipped sound stages. The French public demanded familiar songs, singers, and stage routines. These could be cheaply transposed to celluloid, since they required little rehearsal time and even less scriptwriting and set design. Their previous stage life gave such films an immediate advertising advantage. By and large lost and forgotten, as a genre such films launched local production and provided invaluable experience to French producers, actors, and technicians. At Pathé as at Paramount, directors (including giants of the silent era like Marcel L'Herbier and Raymond Bernard) were demoted in favor of the soundman who belonged in fact to Western Electric and the scriptwriter who was invariably a playwright. Powerful artists fought this trend to homogenize French cinema and make it little more than an auditorium or broadcast medium for stage productions. The genius of directors like Jean Renoir and Jean Grémillon could already be felt as they argued for a new conception of script and sound in *La Chienne* (produced in 1930 by Braunberger-Richebé) and *La Petite Lise* (produced in 1930 by Pathé), but both were lost in the immediate avalanche of theatrical adaptations.

The dominance of the theatrical model in French cinema has been attributed to the particularly powerful pact between actor and audience that claims precedence over all other considerations, outweighing obligations to the film as a well-made object or work of art. A Jules Berry, a Raimu, or a Pierre Larquey might be pleased to act in films so long as they were given the chance on occasion to show off and act directly to the spectator. Plot, dialogue, and decor were designed to prepare for those moments when the actor could play himself and remind the audience of the special relationship they enjoyed. Picture Palaces such as the 4,000-seat Rex, built in 1932, exploited this connection to live enter-tainment by including stage acts in the price of admission, and by copying many of the luxurious accoutrements of music halls. But even in tiny cinemas in the suburbs, the pact between actor and audience was the chief component of an unbroken popular theatrical tradition whose function changed little as it fluctuated between stage and screen.

This standard *cinéma du samedi soir* ('Saturday night' fare) was a popular but not a populist cinema, and the working class learned from it very little that would help them bring into existence a culture of their own. Its actors exhibited the high life of the bour-geoisie in their real-life personas, and the values of that same class in the roles they played. Historian Ginette Vincendeau believes that the joy French viewers took in applauding their stars is the most visible symptom of the regressive function played by the movies in a decade she aptly sums up with the phrase 'a cinema of nostalgia' (Vincendeau 1985). She refers here naturally to the way the past is evoked as a lost haven in serious films like *Pépé le Moko*. Less obvious is the pervasive presence of nostalgia as a form of entertainment experience. Through the direct address of stars, the cinema evoked the memory of simpler forms of pleasure, of a lost community surrounding street singers, of revelers at spontaneous outdoor stage shows, of good times in the army, and so forth. Throughout the Depression, the cinema conveyed the persistence of an endless and secure *belle époque*. Evidently nostalgia was far easier to market, even during the Popular Front, than was social struggle. In any case, the taste for the theatrical finds its way into virtually all French films of the decade; it does so not just in the acting styles of most stars, but in the overuse of reaction shots to cue the audience's reactions, and in the inevitable song or dance number that finds its way even into trenchantly poetic works by Carné, Duvivier, and Renoir.

More than in other countries, theater was a crutch that enabled sound cinema to hobble and then walk upright in France. Under pressure from sound technology, French producers made use of every aspect of the nation's varied theatrical past; production doubled between 1929 and 1937, so that native offerings finally surpassed imports in box-office receipts at home. Ironically, sound cinema pulled spectators out of the music halls and the boulevard theaters at a tremendous rate from 1930 to 1936. Establishments that once were café-concerts, music halls, and theaters were refurbished for talkies; in five years cinema receipts more than doubled, while those for live entertainment were halved. The modern medium had conquered tradition, but only by usurping its look, its personnel, its appeal—in short its function.

Sources and style of Poetic Realism

The *longue durée* of 1930s popular culture, in which a fairly constant number of films—generally half native, half imported—satisfied a paying public can serve as the background to a more pointed history of artistic highs and lows. For the regulated mechanism of the system was not airtight; it was subject to the ambitions of powerful artists, whose mission is ever to shape the medium to suit their vision. It was also affected by invasions from the outside. French producers hoped to capitalize on ideas they picked up from the more than 1,500 films imported onto French screens from abroad during the decade. Statistics show that in 1938 *Snow White* (Walt Disney) outscored at the box office France's top offering, *Le Quai des brumes* (Marcel Carné). Weekly stories in the trade magazine *Pour vous* indicate that *Our Daily Bread* (1933, King Vidor) caught the attention of the filmmaking community, no matter what its success with the general public may have been. Another source of foreign ideas was the experience of French filmmakers abroad, who brought back routines and methods used by the far more elaborate industries of Hollywood and Germany. In these ways, the status quo of cinematic practice in France was continually subject to scrutiny and comparison.

An even more direct source of change came via the unusually high flow into Paris of immigrant artists, most from east of the Rhine. Russian emigrés even had their own studio, Albatros Films, led by Alexandre Kamenka. Dozens of White Russian actors and artists were employed both at Albatros and then throughout the industry. Most of these, like Eugène Lourié (eventually Renoir's chosen designer), were trained as painters in their native country and arrived in Paris needing work. The best of them, Lazare Meerson above all, contributed a distinctive atmosphere to the projects they were involved with, indispensable to the great Poetic Realist works.

The move away from theatrical cinema toward an atmospheric one was boosted by the arrival of a number of German-speaking directors who had grown up within the milieu of expressionism and its alternatives. Robert Siodmak, Max Ophüls, Victor Trivas, and G. W. Pabst increased the efficiency and ambition of French productions. As foreigners they naturally shifted attention from acting to the image, aided by experienced German cameramen like Eugen Shüfftan and Curt Courand. Marcel Carné, who was to hire both of these men, was poised to respond to the German influence. As a critic, he had championed Murnau and Expressionism. When in 1934 he published his essay 'Quand le cinéma descendra-t-il dans la rue?' ('When will cinema take to the streets?') he must have been responding to Trivas' *Dans les rues* (1933), which effectively shifted the ground of German street films to Paris. Carné's essay argued that a stodgy theatrical cinema ought to give way to productions that followed the most interesting trends in fiction. He specifically identified novelists like Pierre Mac Orlan who take advantage of the picturesque quality of urban drama. Why not 'study certain Parisian *quartiers* and seize the hidden spirit under the familiar facade of those streets'? Carné also mentions Eugène Dabit and his great novel *Hôtel du Nord*, which he was to adapt in 1938 following his phenomenally successful version earlier that year of Mac Orlan's novel *Le Quai des brumes*. Suddenly atmosphere and populism were abundantly popular, as the success of Brassaï's haunting photographs of 'Paris by Night' made clear. Brassaï was close to Mac Orlan and Prévert, both of whom worked with Carné. All were susceptible to an aesthetic of mystery and crime. The same was true for Francis Carco, an author fascinated with exotic locations and low-life characters. He aimed to update an urban mythology traced back to Eugène Sue and Victor Hugo. Producers recognized that money could be made in this somber style, a style baptized 'Poetic Realism' by an admirer of Chenal's *La Rue sans nom* (1933), from the Marcel Aymé novel.

By the end of the decade, cinema's rapport with prose fiction, and particularly with the *récit* (story), gained ascendancy, infecting even original scripts with an aesthetic that demanded the subtle participation of visual artists and composers. Directors strove to incorporate dialogue into a balanced orchestration of all cinematic registers. Significantly, not a single film in the Poetic Realist canon was drawn from the stage. The rapport between fiction and French film was aided by SYNOPS, a tiny office established within the publishing empire of Gaston Gallimard, which funneled the work of Gallimard's stable of famous authors to actors, directors, and producers. SYNOPS fielded scripts by Jean Giono, Antoine de St Exupéry, Pierre Mac Orlan, André Beucler, and Paul Morand. In the five years of its existence, SYNOPS was responsible for the adaptation of thirty novels into films, a large number of which figure among the classics of the decade.

By the time the war interrupted the increasing momentum of their international success, the Poetic Realist films of Carné, Duvivier, Grémillon, and Chenal seemed no longer to be played by characters on a set or actors on a stage. The theatrical model had been superseded and a novelistic, romantic aesthetic had taken its place. The visual world inhabited by the figures on the screen had become a breathing milieu, bearing down on them, often indistinguishable from them. Designed to be ingested in a single hypnotic experience, this 'figural space' is the visual correlate of the evocative novels and *récits* inspiring Poetic Realism.

Exceptional cinema

Given the 'crisis' of the century's worst economic moment, the 'crisis' of an impending international conflict, and the concurrent 'crisis' of French cinema, most films of the decade are remarkably unruffled and reassuring. This can be attributed to the hegemony of a relatively restricted number of established actors whose very reappearance in film after film was comforting. Their particular manners of projecting themselves, in one drama after another, amounted to an inventory of 'Frenchness', a *habitus* on the screen with which all citizens could identify. Also restricted was the number of screenwriters who adapted literary works (plays primarily, as we have seen) or concocted scripts on a template featuring acting and actors of this sort. One important study, *Générique des années trente* (Lagny *et al.* 1986), goes so far as to imply that the true subject of the entire decade's output was nothing other than the credits—the actors' names that appeared in every film—permuted each time as they played different characters and played against each other in different arrays. A virtually self-generating system without an overseer, it generated nothing other than an image of entertainment. French cinema of the 1930s has been called a theatrical display of nothing other than itself.

This, at least, is the impression conveyed by the routine fare. Exceptional films (those that aimed to capture a crucial topic and bring it forcefully into the light) were very few and, by definition, required extraordinary production resources. Among them one would want to count the films of the PCF (Parti Communiste Français). In addition to numerous shorts, they were involved in two features: *La Vie est à nous* (1936, Jean Renoir) and *Le Temps des cerises* (1938, Jean-Paul le Chanois), both of which carried explicit propagandistic messages inside the homilies of their stories. Probably the decade's largest and most anticipated political project, Renoir's *La Marseillaise* (1938), was financed in part through contributions of members of a Communist labor union, but gathered support wherever it could find it across the spectrum of the Popular Front coalition. The disappointing reception of this film illustrates the very problem of bucking the star system. For Renoir rebuffed the offers of a host of famous actors begging for roles in this national epic. Striving to be true to the philosophy behind the Popular Front, *La Marseillaise* modestly claimed to be a mere 'Chronicle of some happenings that contributed to the fall of the monarchy', everyday happenings for the most part, played out by citizens, not by politicians or heroes. Falling somewhere between the strident PCF films and the uplifting historical dramas of the standard cinema, *La Marseillaise* pleased few, especially when compared to Renoir's successful Popular Front features *Le Crime de M. Lange* (1936), *Les Bas-Fonds* (1936), and *La Grande Illusion* (1937).

On the other side of the political spectrum, one exceptional feature that scored a stunning box-office success was *L'Appel du silence* (1936, Léon Poirier). A biography of Charles de Foucauld, the dashing military rake of North Africa turned religious mystic and hermit and martyred during a native uprising at the outset of World War I, this film was financed by collections taken up in parishes across the country (and nearly 70 per cent of French in this period were practicing Catholics). While it mixed stunning location shots in North Africa with dull studio scenes, *L'Appel du silence* seems to prove both that French filmgoers were more responsive to Rightist rather than Leftist national anthems, and that they responded best to sagas of heroes, played by lionized actors (in this case Jean Yonnel, famous in the Comédie Française).

The decade contains its share of standard realist works, led by literary adaptations from the canon of French realism and naturalism such as the heavily promoted *Les Misérables* (1934, Raymond Bernard) and *La Bête humaine* (1938, Jean Renoir). Primarily vehicles for star actors, this genre could be said to address current social concerns only very indirectly. Cinematic realism requires the use of unfamiliar faces, and few French producers dared to buck the actor system so entrenched in the 1930s. A small number of melodramas that treated the plight of children displayed new faces without makeup. The most notable of these, *La Maternelle* (1934, Marie Epstein and Jean Benoît-Lévy), locates its subject in urban poverty, shot largely on location in Paris. But its realism is blunted somewhat by its literary source and by the featured performance of a star, Madeleine Renaud. The same contradictions mitigate the power of a couple of ambitious anti-war efforts that promised to rub the nation's nose in the reeking trenches of World War I. *Les Croix de bois* (1932, Raymond Bernard) was shot on location and simulated its battle scenes with scrupulous attention to authenticity. But the audience is not abandoned to the terrifying chaos of the unknown, for *Les Croix de bois* comes from a prizewinning novel and features a number of well-known actors. For the most part, and more than is usual in other countries and other eras, the French cinema of the 1930s comforted a national audience with its familiarity, even when advertising its depiction of 'real life'.

Of course neither all filmmakers nor all spectators were satisfied with the familiar. Some were intent on destroying it. Among the first sound films produced in France was the scandalous *L'Age d'or* (1930, Luis Buñuel and Salvador Dalí), sponsored by the Comte and Comtesse de Noailles, who also underwrote *Le Sang d'un poète* (1930, Jean Cocteau). *L'Age d'Or* had no immediate distribution, being banned after violence at its first public screenings. But the legacy of Surrealism, and particularly its desire to shock through bizarre images and juxtapositions, filtered into a number of more mainstream productions. Jacques Prévert and his brother Pierre, both Surrealist fellow travelers for a time, worked up short satiric films for the Leftist acting troupe known as the Groupe Octobre, leading to their participation in Renoir's *Le Crime de M. Lange*. Jean Vigo, whose single critical proclamation about cinema was an homage to Buñuel, injected a wild Surrealist spirit into an otherwise anodyne script about domestic life on a barge, *L'Atalante* (1934). Père Jules, the crusty old shipman who sets the tone of the film, keeps relics from around the world in his cabin (mechanical instruments, old photos, a knife from the South Seas, a pair of pickled hands). This veritable gallery of Surrealist 'found objects' enlivens the constricted life of the married couple on a barge that plies its dull trade up and down the Seine. Through the unpredictable ingenuity of Père Jules, a surrogate for the director, music magically sounds from a broken gramophone and the couple, full of watery visions, fall in love again. Vigo died as he finished this masterpiece and before he could reanimate standard French cinema with his spontaneity, animality, and irreverence, with his love of that which was different. *L'Atalante* was one of four French films sent to the 1934 Venice film festival, but its distributor was already cutting it and changing its soundtrack so that it might not startle the pathetically small audience that saw it before it was withdrawn.

The larger French audience to which Vigo aspired had its own ideas about difference, easiest to recognize in the ample genre of the 'colonial film'. Robust adventure tales of Africa that were common to the silent screen transformed themselves, after the Colonial

⬆ *L'Atalante*

Exposition of 1931, into quieter yet more desperate expressions. Addressing anxieties about identity, sexuality, and difference, these films suggest that the foreign—figured most often as Africa—had become a necessary idea in France's self-conception. *Le cinéma colonial* traded on the contradictions involved in that self-conception, and did so by summoning up such earlier expressions as Orientalist painting, romantic poetry, and the fiction of Carco and Mac Orlan, not to mention the famous novels of André Malraux and Louis-Ferdinand Céline. These plot a mythographic trajectory that French cinema traveled, in its fear of and attraction to 'the other', from the outlandish exoticism of the Sahara to the polyglot docks of foreign ports, right into the more sinister parts of Paris.

Julien Duvivier used the unsettling quality that African settings implied for French audiences in three of the most popular films of the decade: *Les Cinq Gentlemen maudits* (1932), *La Bandera* (1935), and *Pépé le Moko* (1937), each of which flirts with a dreadful irrationalism that overtakes the hero (Jean Gabin in the latter two films) on the other side of the Mediterranean. While providing a thrillingly exotic picture of the Casbah, *Pépé le Moko* explicitly intones a debilitating nostalgia for Paris, that is, for French identity. In the final scene Pépé stabs himself, expiring behind bars as he watches the beautiful Parisienne Gaby (Mireille Balin) sail from the harbor of Algiers. A more complex play between nationality and identity infuses *La Maison du Maltais* (1938, Pierre Chenal), for this time the main character, Matteo (played by Marcel Dalio), is not Parisian but North African. His love affair with a French prostitute (Viviane Romance) will bring him to Paris when she is taken there to be the wife of a wealthy benefactor. Matteo, a free spirit and a storyteller, will be blocked from caring for the bi-racial baby she gives birth to in France. Penniless and out of place, he lives in a North African ghetto of Montmartre. Nearly a preview of current films about the desperation of the *beur* in the *banlieue*, *La Maison du Maltais* ends with Matteo's ritual suicide. He is comforted knowing that his child, being raised in the sixteenth arrondissement, will grow up protected and privileged, but in a Paris to which he as an outsider would never have had access.

As is evident from even a brief consideration of these melodramas, French cinema may not have directly addressed the pressing issues of French society at the end of the Third Republic, but those issues (of nation, purity, gender, class) undergird the dramatic and figural appeal of the more interesting films. By the end of the decade, as in *Le Jour se lève* (1939, Marcel Carné), those issues became distilled to such a point that they required a new narrative form. The famous fatalism associated with this film stems both from the social predicament of its hero (Jean Gabin, once again), an orphan living in an anonymous tenement and working in inhuman industrial conditions, and, more certainly, from the flashback structure of the film which recounts a life that is effectively over in the very first scene.

Le Jour se lève was not the only work that at the end of the decade turned away from social hopes and inward to the solitary self. Aside from the full catalog of Poetic Realist films, we can locate in French culture of the late 1930s innumerable expressions up and down the ladder that share its attitude. At the lowest rung, the *chansons réalistes* of Fréhel and Edith Piaf as well as the joyful Charles Trenet tunes are an index of the nation's focus on personal sentiment and sentimentality. Like *Le Jour se lève*, these songs scarcely hint at the social or domestic framework surrounding private experience, and when they do, it is in the key of nostalgia. The same myopia, this time strategically employed, shapes the insights of the developing philosophy and literature of existentialism, the most famous example of which is Jean-Paul Sartre's *La Nausée* (1938). Few works of art of this time, fewer than in most times, directly address the social conditions out of which they arose; moreover, the songs and cinema of the 1930s most often sought a hypnotic rapport with an audience too absorbed in the experience to ask about its relevance. Nevertheless, one can listen to these songs, novels, and films as if they poignantly respond to questions posed by the spiritual and social issues of the day.

This chapter, like most accounts of the period, concludes with *La Règle du jeu* (1939, Jean Renoir). Not only a magnificent achievement of directorial prowess, the film makes the entire decade stand out because of its sheer difference. Refusing to indulge in the hypnotic aesthetic of Poetic Realism, it uses multiple perspectives to bring into sharp focus the spiritual state of France just before World War II was declared. Relentlessly honest and eschewing simple and satisfying solutions, it takes up such themes as social class and pacifism, fidelity and sincerity, art and tradition, organizing them in its three-dimensional space until they take on a distinctiveness previously unknown to cinema. Renoir's intelligence, full of both tenderness and irony, shines harshly on this difficult moment, so harshly that the film was a box-office failure before being banned by a government that found it demoralizing. Often named the inaugural film of the 'modern cinema', *La Règle du jeu* incubated in Renoir throughout the decade: its very existence is a tribute to that decade. It depends first of all on Renoir's genius, but also on his experience directing, in the course of eight years, fifteen very different films in different circumstances. It depends on the technological improvements in sound, lenses, set design, and lighting; it required formidable financial backing yet freedom for the director; it aimed at a new kind of sophisticated spectator. It was, in short, an ambitious project impossible to have imagined ten years before. As a marvelous aberration, *La Règle du jeu* shows us the limitations of the cinematic and cultural world it so tellingly accuses, but—with Renoir himself playing a key role—accuses from the inside and with affection.

Further reading

Andrew, Dudley, *Mists of Regret: Culture and Sensibility in Classic French Film* (Princeton, NJ: Princeton University Press, 1995). Examines 1930s French cinema in its cultural context.

—— and Steven Ungar, *Popular Front Paris: The Politics and Poetics of Culture* (Cambridge, Mass.: Harvard University Press, forthcoming). Analyzes many different aspects of French culture of the 1930s, including cinema.

Crisp, Colin, *The Classic French Cinema, 1930–60* (Bloomington: Indiana University Press, 1993). Discusses many aspects of film production and distribution from the 1930s through the following two decades.

—— *Genre, Myth and Convention in the French Cinema 1929–1939* (Bloomington: Indiana University Press, 2002). Examines mythic patterns in films as well as film magazines of the 1930s.

O'Shaugnessy, Martin, *Jean Renoir* (Manchester: Manchester University Press, 2000). A detailed study of Renoir's work.

Sherzer, Dina (ed.), *Cinema, Colonialism, Postcolonialism: Perspectives from the French and Francophone World* (Austin: University of Texas Press, 1996). Contains a number of chapters on cinema of the 1930s.

Slavin, David, *Colonial Cinema and Imperial France, 1919–1939: White Blind Spots, Male Fantasies, Settler Myths* (Baltimore: Johns Hopkins University Press, 2001). A detailed study of the *cinéma colonial* of the 1930s and its silent-era precursors.

Vincendeau, Ginette, *French Cinema in the 1930s: Social Text and Context of a Popular Entertainment Medium* (Ph.D. Thesis, University of East Anglia, 1985).

——, *Stars and Stardom in French Cinema* (London: Continuum, 2000). Includes a chapter on Jean Gabin, one of the biggest French stars of the 1930s.

—— and Keith Reader (eds.), *La Vie est à nous: French cinema of the Popular Front 1935–38.* (London: British Film Institute, 1986). A collection of essays on cinema made during the Popular Front era.

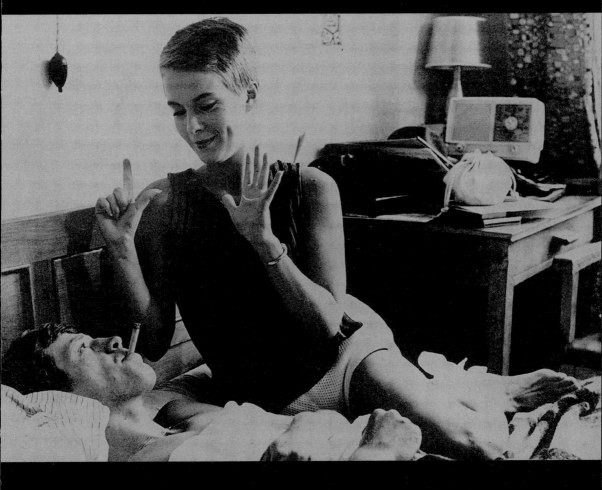

POSTWAR CINEMA

Postwar Cinema Introduction

The decades following World War II brought economic prosperity, technological innovation, and new artistic currents, which combined to produce what is often regarded as Europe's cinematic golden age. Film industries benefited from certain aspects of the political and economic climate, but they also faced new challenges, which they met with great ingenuity.

At the end of the war, a defeated Germany was occupied by the four Allied powers (the US, the USSR, Great Britain, and France). By the end of the 1940s, tensions between the US and the USSR had led to the division of Germany, and of Europe more generally, into 'Eastern' (Communist-controlled) and 'Western' (US-allied) zones. When, in the mid- and late 1940s, European cinemas were overrun with the tremendous backlog of Hollywood films that had not been distributed during the war, Western Europe was effectively forced to accept what many saw as US cultural imperialism along with the substantial economic aid it received in return for its political alliance against the Soviet Union. Yet this aid further enabled the development of European film industries, not only boosting popular cinema but giving rise to the 'art' cinema movements that would capture a niche market and gain an international following.

The economic prosperity that Europe enjoyed after the initial deprivations of the immediate postwar years was a double-edged sword for cinema. Although there was more money for the production of films and more disposable income for consumers to spend on movies, increased wealth also resulted in the proliferation of television owner-ship, which had a devastating and virtually irreversible impact on cinema attendance. The threats posed both by television and by Hollywood's economic domination prompted two different responses. While some filmmakers chose to imitate the Hollywood style, producing slick, spectacular, entertainment-driven films, others took a different path, making artistically challenging, ambiguous works that were self-consciously opposed to Hollywood's formulaic plots and happy endings. This art cinema revived, in attenuated form, the modernist aesthetic that had characterized the avant-garde films of the 1920s; but although they tended to be more challenging than popular European and Hollywood genres, the cinematic 'new waves' sweeping across Europe did not altogether abandon narrative coherence or dramatic tension. Postwar art cinema was characterized by two main tendencies, the realist and the theatrical. The first of these was the most predominant, beginning with Italian Neorealism in the years immediately following the war. Upon learning that the Cinecittà studios in Rome were being used as a refugee camp, Neorealist filmmakers made a virtue of necessity, shooting on location in the war-torn streets of Rome and Berlin. The use of non-professional actors and the grainy look of footage shot on low-grade film stock, both effects of wartime shortages, gave Neorealist films an urgent immediacy that heightened their dramatic impact for many viewers. This realist aesthetic would later influence other postwar film movements such as Britain's Direct Cinema and the subsequent 'kitchen sink' realism, as well as the French New Wave.

The theatrical tradition was most notably represented in the work of Swedish director Ingmar Bergman, who became the doyen of European art cinema in the 1950s, reviving Scandinavia's international (and, since the 1910s, long-dormant) reputation as a centre for art cinema. Artifice was also highlighted in the films of Federico Fellini, who returned to the Cinecittà studios to film his spectacular flights of fantasy. Later, Rainer Werner Fassbinder's films, with their theatrical aesthetic, would bring international reknown to the New German Cinema in the 1970s.

Whether theatrical or realist, though, the postwar tradition was one of tremendous innovation and creativity, in which individual *auteurs* rewrote the rules and made a lasting impact on film culture.

6

FROM ITALIAN NEOREALISM TO THE GOLDEN AGE OF CINECITTÀ

Peter Bondanella

Postwar Italian Neorealism: origins and innovations

During the two decades (1922–43) that the Italian Fascist regime of Benito Mussolini ruled Italy, the Italian commercial cinema had few foreign markets open to its products and was virtually unknown in the English-speaking world or outside Germany and Spain. Consequently, in 1945, when international audiences were first introduced to films made in a style that was dubbed 'new realism' (*neorealismo*), non-Italians falsely assumed that the Fascist cinema had been devoted primarily to propaganda. Yet the search for realism in the postwar Italian cinema owes major debts to a similar desire for a portrait of the 'real' Italy expressed by the best directors working in what the Italians were to dub 'the black twenty years' (*il ventennio nero*). The regime actually confined its propaganda to the newsreels produced by the Istituto Nazionale Luce (acronym for L'Unione Cinematografica Educativa), formed in 1924–5, an agency that had a monopoly over all newsreels shown in Italy after 1927. And the regime built Cinecittà, inaugurated by Mussolini himself in 1937, and still today one of the world's great production complexes. Earlier in 1935 the regime had founded an important film school, the Centro Sperimentale di Cinematografia, which did much to acquaint Italian filmmakers with film theories imported from abroad (including those of Eisenstein and other non-Fascist thinkers). Several film journals—the Centro's *Bianco e nero*, the official organ of the Centro, and *Cinema* (edited by Mussolini's son Vittorio)—helped to place the cinema at the forefront of intellectual life shortly before the outbreak of World War II. A number of important documentary films produced for the Italian armed forces by Francesco De Robertis (1902–59) and his young protégé Roberto Rossellini (1906–77) began experimenting with the use of on-location shooting, grainy action photography, non-professional actors, and what Luigi Freddi (1895–1977), the enthusiastically Fascist director of Cinecittà from 1940 to 1943, defined as a 'fictional documentary' (*documentario romanzato*), or the combination of actual historical events in a film plot with a fictionalized (usually romantic) story.

Many of the postwar Neorealist classics would follow precisely these aspects of cinematic style, with quite a different sort of political ideology in their content. No more than a few dozen of the more than 700 feature films produced between the advent of sound in 1930 and the fall of the regime in 1943 actually praised the truly unique aspects of Italian Fascist rule, such as the theory of the corporate state, the anti-democratic violence by gangs of its followers (*squadrismo*) that characterized its rise to power, or the regime's fulsome praise of the need for warfare to 'test' the strength of a nation. Even the documentaries produced by De Robertis and Rossellini for the armed forces, such as *La nave bianca* (*The White Ship*, 1941) and *Un pilota ritorna* (*A Pilot Returns*, 1942), combine an understandable nationalism typical of every national cinema during wartime with moments of real doubts about the nature of the conflict the films were intended to chronicle.

Few foreign audiences in 1945 were aware of the prewar origins of Italian Neorealism or the contributions of the Fascist regime to the creation of a cinema of realism. Even fewer Italians wanted to say anything positive about a regime that had fallen, destroying the reputations of not a few actors and directors too closely identified with the old regime's ideology and politics. Thus, the myth of a sudden and miraculous emergence of Italian Neorealism in 1945 without any links to an embarrassing past was born, and survived critical scrutiny for several decades. When international audiences were introduced to Italian films through a few great masterpieces by Roberto Rossellini, Vittorio De Sica (1901–74), and Luchino Visconti (1906–76) in the decade following the end of the war, they saw an abrupt break between the Fascist period and the postwar period that, in reality, never existed.

Nevertheless, there was something essentially new in the air. Italian Neorealist films stressed social themes (the war, poverty, the Resistance, unemployment); they seemed to reject traditional dramatic and cinematic conventions associated with Hollywood happy endings; they stressed on-location shooting rather than studio work, as well as the documentary photographic style favored by many directors under the former regime; and they often employed non-professional actors in original ways. However, Neorealist directors rarely denied traditional cinematic conventions or rejected Hollywood codes out of hand. Film historians have unfortunately tended to speak of Neorealism as if it were an authentic movement with universally agreed stylistic or thematic principles. The basis for the fundamental change in cinematic history marked by Italian Neorealism was less an agreement on a single, unified cinematic style than a common aspiration to view Italy without preconceptions and to employ a more honest, ethical, but no less poetic cinematic language in the process.

The masterpieces of Neorealism are Rossellini's *Roma città aperta* (*Rome Open City*, 1945) and *Paisà* (*Paisan*, 1946), two parts of what is known as his 'anti-Fascist trilogy'; De Sica's *Ladri di biciclette* (*The Bicycle Thief*, 1948); and Visconti's *La terra trema* (*The Earth Trembles*, 1948). These four seminal works, all original contributions to film language, were, with the exception of *Roma città aperta*, unpopular within Italy, and achieved critical success primarily among audiences, critics, filmmakers, and intellectuals abroad. One of the paradoxes of Italian Neorealism is that the ordinary people such films set out to portray were relatively uninterested in their image on screen. Italians flocked to see Hollywood films after the fall of the Fascist regime opened the market to American major studios. Of the approximately 800 films produced between 1945 and 1953 in Italy, only a relatively small number (about 10 per cent) can be classified as Neorealist, and most of these films were box-office failures.

Roma città aperta so completely reflected the moral and psychological atmosphere of the immediate postwar period that its international critical success alerted the world to the rebirth of Italian cinema. With a daring combination of styles and moods (due in great measure to brilliant scriptwriting by Sergio Amidei (1904–91) and a young Federico Fellini (1920–93)), Rossellini captured the tension and the tragedy of Italian life under German occupation and the partisan struggle out of which the new democratic republic was subsequently born. Although contemporary audiences interpreted the film's plot as a form of realism, in retrospect the film seems all too obviously based upon melodrama, and its brilliant script belies the commonplace that Neorealist films rejected a Hollywood plot. *Paisà* reflects to a far greater extent the conventions of the newsreel documentary, tracing in six separate episodes the Allied invasion of Italy and its slow process up through the 'boot' of the peninsula. Yet the grainy film, the awkward acting of the non-professional actors, the authoritative voice-over narration, and the immediacy of subject matter we associate with newsreels do not completely explain the aesthetic qualities of the work. Rossellini depicts the historic encounter of two alien cultures, resulting in initial incomprehension but eventual kinship and brotherhood.

De Sica's *Ladri di biciclette* represents the finest example of non-professional acting in Neorealist cinema. While De Sica employs non-professionals, on-location shooting, and social themes (unemployment, the effects of the war on the postwar economy) typical of many Neorealist films, the appeal of *Ladri di biciclette* cannot be explained completely by its superficially realistic style. The mythic structure of the plot—a quest for a bicycle, ironically a Fides ('Faith') brand, that has been stolen—suggests to the viewer that De Sica is not merely offering a political film denouncing a particular socio-economic system. De Sica's pessimistic perspective denies the possibility of changing the world by social reform in a society in which the loss of a mere bicycle spells economic disaster. No attempts at social engineering or even revolution will alter the basic facts of life in De Sica's universe—solitude, loneliness, and alienation.

Visconti's *La terra trema* is a far more ambitious ideological and aesthetic undertaking. To make the film, the Milanese aristocrat combined a plot adapted from the naturalistic novel by Giovanni Verga, *I Malavoglia* (*The House by the Medlar Tree*, 1881), with some of the Marxist theories of Antonio Gramsci (1891–1937). In many ways the film fits the traditional stereotypical definition of Italian Neorealism better than other equally famous films from the same period. No studio sets or sound stages were used, and the cast was selected from the Sicilian fishing village of Aci Trezza, the novel's setting. Visconti even refused to dub the film into standard Italian, preferring the more realistic effects of Sicilian dialect and synchronized sound. The film's visuals underline the cyclical, timeless quality of life in Aci Trezza. Visconti's typically slow panning shots with a stationary camera, or his long, static shots of motionless objects and actors, produce a formalism that bestows dignity and beauty on humble, ordinary people.

The birth of a new Italian film culture

While Italian Leftist intellectuals and social critics preferred a cinema devoted to social change, the public was more interested in imports from Hollywood or Italian films with less explicit ideological goals. Even the greatest Neorealist directors and scriptwriters associated with the early rise of Neorealist style became uncomfortable with the restrictive boundaries imposed upon their subject matter or style by such well-meaning but ideologically motivated critics. In Italian film history, the transition beyond Neorealism is often called the 'crisis' of Neorealism. In retrospect, the only individuals 'in crisis' were the Marxist film critics, whose Stalinist criteria for aesthetic judgements proved incapable of understanding or explaining aesthetic changes within Italian film culture. Italian scriptwriters, directors, and technicians were not 'in crisis' but were going through a natural process of evolution in Italian film language during the 1950s, toward a cinema concerned

◉ *Ladri di biciclette*

with more complex psychological themes and a new camera style no longer dominated by programmatic calls for non-professional actors, on-location shooting, documentary style, and a focus upon social problems. Crucial to this historic transition are a number of early works by Michelangelo Antonioni (1902–); several works starring Ingrid Bergman by Rossellini; and the first films directed by Federico Fellini. In *Cronaca di un amore* (*Story of a Love Affair*, 1950), Antonioni's first feature film, the director borrows a plot from James Cain's novel *The Postman Always Rings Twice* (as did Visconti in his earlier precursor to Neorealist cinema, *Ossessione* [*Obsession*, 1942]). Antonioni produces an Italian version of an American *film noir*, but his distinctive photographic signature is already evident: characteristically long shots, tracks and pans following the actors; modernist editing techniques reflecting the slow rhythms of daily life; and philosophical concerns with obvious links to European existentialism. In *Viaggio in Italia* (*Voyage to Italy*, 1953), Rossellini abandons the melodramatic plot of *Roma città aperta* or the pseudo-documentary style of *Paisà* to embrace an abstract psychological realism that also reflects the emphasis upon alienation typical of contemporary postwar European philosophy. Like Antonioni, Rossellini relied upon lengthy shots and non-intrusive editing. Both Antonioni and Rossellini focused upon anti-dramatic and introspective sequences that depended, in large measure, upon modernist photography. Alienation—and not large-scale macro-economic social problems such as unemployment among the working class—becomes the dominant theme of the Italian cinema.

Fellini's early films

It is with Fellini's early films that the Italian cinema moved resolutely beyond a preoccupation with social problems, although his works certainly reflect a deep understanding of Italian culture that no other Italian director has ever matched. His first three feature films—*Luci del varietà* (*Variety Lights*, 1950), *Lo sceicco bianco* (*The White Sheik*, 1952), and *I vitelloni* (1953)—constitute what may be defined as a 'trilogy of character'. In them, Fellini departs from a conception of character shaped by environment or social class (the Neorealist formula) and embraces a modernist analysis of the very notion of character itself, ultimately indebted to Pirandello's similar operation in the theatre. His comic portraits of likeable but flawed Italian males who have never grown up focus upon the clash between their social personas and the more authentic feelings and emotions concealed underneath—in Pirandello's theatrical terms, the clash between 'mask' and 'face.' *I vitelloni*, for example, follows six daydreamers around a thinly disguised seaside resort resembling his native Rimini on the Adriatic coast. A Neorealist director would have analyzed their wastrel existence as an example of middle-class decadence, but Fellini was fascinated by their fantasy lives and their daydreams. In spite of the difference in tone between the two works, American director Martin Scorsese points to this early work as the inspiration for his breakthrough film *Mean Streets* (1973) in a recent documentary on Italian cinema entitled *Il mio viaggio in Italia* (*My Voyage to Italy*, 2002). *I vitelloni* was also Fellini's first commercially successful film within Italy.

Fellini's next three feature films—*La strada* (1954), *Il bidone* (1955), and *Le notti di Cabiria* (*The Nights of Cabiria*, 1956)—continued a natural evolution toward a cinema expressing a personal or poetic view of the world. They may be defined as the 'trilogy of grace and salvation', since they all employ metaphors of transcendence borrowed by Fellini from traditional Catholic faith to fit his secular themes. The first and the third works in this trilogy made Fellini an international celebrity and introduced the world to Giulietta Masina, Fellini's wife, who starred in them both. Both films earned Fellini Oscars for Best Foreign Film.

La strada employs a picaresque and open-ended plot to follow the adventures of carnival people, producing a moving fable about the need for love in a cruel and spiritually vapid world. An inarticulate circus strongman named Zampanò (Anthony Quinn) learns only too late the meaning of love from a slightly addled young girl named Gelsomina (Giulietta Masina). Through Gelsomina's meeting with a strange circus acrobat named 'The Fool' (Richard Basehart), she comes to believe that her existence has some higher purpose. The three characters represent *commedia dell'arte* types, and the film is basically a parable, but one difficult to interpret. The film's ambiguity is intentional, but it is most certainly not a simple-minded apology for Catholic dogma, as so many of the Marxist critics in Italy asserted when they attacked it relentlessly. Its picaresque structure underlines the notion of the quest for self-knowledge. Its imagery has affinities with the Metaphysical school of painting represented by Giorgio De Chirico. It is a timeless fairy tale, a version of the 'Beauty and the Beast' narrative where Gelsomina (Beauty), mediated by the traditional angelic messenger (The Fool), transforms the Beast (Zampanò), but too late to save herself. *La strada* has been explained as both a metaphor for the difficulty of human communication and as an image of the cruelty men inflict upon women.

In *Le notti di Cabiria* (the inspiration for director Bob Fosse's *Sweet Charity* [1969]), Masina plays a prostitute who never fails to respond to the disappointments of her life with hope for the future. The subject matter of this film, the world's oldest profession in Rome, would have made an ideal Neorealist topic and a study in social class. However, as in *La strada*, Fellini refuses a strictly realistic portrayal of such a theme to reveal a new poetic dimension, one motivated by a personal vision and a particular Fellinian mythology concerned with spiritual poverty and the necessity for grace or salvation. Like Antonioni and Rossellini, Fellini thus based his works on a sense that postwar Italian society had produced a situation characterized by anxiety and alienation and chose, in this case, the classic example of a marginalized figure, the streetwalker. But unlike other more polit-ically motivated Italian directors who felt more at home with a Marxist explanation for the psychological alienation they portrayed on the silver screen, Fellini defined such alienation in terms that owed a great deal to traditional Italian Catholic ideas about redemption and salvation.

New Directions: the golden age of Cinecittà from the late 1950s to the late 1970s

In the decade between 1958 (a time when the so-called 'crisis' of Neorealism had clearly passed) and 1968 (a year when all over Europe turbulent social and political upheavals would begin that shook Italian society to its foundations), Italian cinema reached a level of artistic quality, international popularity, and economic strength it had never before achieved. Its excellence continued to shine while it began to falter in the subsequent decade, but from the late 1950s to the late 1970s no other national cinema in Europe had such an impact upon film history. Film production continued at well above 200 films per year in Italy, while a prolonged crisis in Hollywood reduced American competition within the Italian market and abroad. Not only did Italy boast a number of distinguished auteurs (Antonioni, Fellini, De Sica, Rossellini, Visconti) whose names had become household words everywhere and whose greatest films were being produced at this time, but the Italian cinema witnessed the arrival of a second generation of brilliant young directors who had apprenticed with these masters and whose first films would represent an intellectual response to and, in some cases, a revisiting of Italian Neorealist cinema: Pier Paolo Pasolini (1922–75), Bernardo Bertolucci (1940–), Marco Bellocchio (1939–), Gillo Pontecorvo (1919–), Ermanno Olmi (1931–), Francesco Rosi (1922–), Elio Petri (1929–82), brothers Paolo Taviani (1931–) and Vittorio Taviani (1929–), and Sergio Leone (1921–89).

Perhaps most important, the industry made huge profits in the international market by exporting a number of identifiable Italian products abroad. Besides the 'art film' classics that did relatively well at the box office during this period, the industry found a market for the *commedia all'italiana*, the Italian comic film that was generally far more polemical in its social satire and critique of Italian daily life than was typical of its Hollywood counter-part. In addition, three genres produced at relatively low cost in Italy were tremendously successful all over the world: (1) the 'peplum' film, historical costume films set in the classical period that recalled Italy's initial success with this genre during the silent period; (2) the 'spaghetti Western', a novel interpretation of a film genre usually associated with Hollywood but which Italians revolutionized, making a star out of Clint Eastwood in the process; and (3) over-the-top, camp versions of horror films, dubbed the 'spaghetti nightmare' in homage to the international success of the 'spaghetti Western'. Finally, during this creative period Italian cinema became identified with a genre called the 'political film' that managed to combine commercial appeal with provocative ideological positions. For perhaps the first and only time in the history of the postwar European cinema, the Italian film industry offered an alternative to the colossus of Hollywood, which was then undergoing a severe economic and intellectual crisis that opened up the vast American market to Italian productions.

Italian film comedy and social criticism in the 1960s

Many critics of the Left denigrated *commedia all'italiana* as merely 'commercial' cinema without artistic value, just as they ignored the Italian contribution to the Western genre. Their ideological bias ignored the fact that Italian comic films often contained more biting social criticism than the more acceptable ideologically oriented 'political films' of the period. The great comic films of the decade from 1958 to 1968 provide an amusing but often accurate mirror of changing Italian customs and values. They helped to force the average Italian into a greater awareness of conflicting moral standards; they attacked age-old prejudices; and they questioned the rule of inept governing elites and institutions. Taken as a group, comedies during this era embody a black, even grotesque vision of contemporary Italian society, and the laughter in these works rings bittersweet.

The international hit best reflecting the combination of social criticism and humor characteristic of the *commedia all'italiana* is Pietro Germi's *Divorzio all'italiana* (*Divorce, Italian Style*, 1961). Made before Italian law permitted legal divorce, Germi's satire of Sicilian sexual mores chronicles the comic attempts of a Sicilian nobleman (one of Marcello Mastroianni's most brilliant performances) to force his hated wife into adultery so that he can murder her, receive a light sentence for a crime of honor (hence the film's title), and marry his mistress. Utilizing a complex narrative juxtaposing the director's critical view of this affair with the Sicilian's biased justifications of his misdeeds, Germi recreates the oppressive atmosphere of Sicilian provincial life that forces men and women to commit violent crimes in order to obtain sexual fulfillment. An equally successful comedy providing a grotesque vision of Italian migrant workers abroad is *Pane e cioccolata* (*Bread and Chocolate*, 1973) by Franco Brusati (1922–93), a devastating indictment of the conditions experienced by Italian 'guest workers' in what is depicted as a racist Switzerland.

The most original director of Italian film comedies in the postwar period was Ettore Scola, who served an important apprenticeship working on scripts during the 1950s and the early 1960s. At the height of the Italian cinema's commercial success in the mid-1970s, Scola produced three comic masterpieces—*C'eravamo tanto amati* (*We All Loved Each Other Very Much*, 1974), which employed a meta-cinematic narrative to treat the history of Italian cinema itself; *Brutti, sporchi e cattivi* (*Dirty, Mean and Nasty*, 1976), essentially a comic remake of De Sica's Neorealist comedy about class struggle in *Miracolo a Milano* (*Miracle in Milan*, 1951); and *Una giornata particolare* (*A Special Day*, 1977), which pairs two of Italy's top stars, Marcello Mastroianni and Sophia Loren, in a classic reversal of their usual romantic roles as Latin lover and sweater girl, with Mastroianni playing a homosexual and Loren an aging housewife.

The most controversial comic director of this period was Lina Wertmüller (1928–), who burst upon the international scene with a series of excellent films that made a great deal of money in America—*Mimì metallurgico ferito nell'onore* (*The Seduction of Mimi*, 1971); *Film d'amore e d'anarchia* (*Love and Anarchy*, 1972); *Travolti da un insolito destino nell'azzurro mare d'agosto* (*Swept Away*, 1974). Wertmüller's film style combined an exuberant imagery, indebted to Fellini, with a particular concern for polemical approaches to political issues, all set within the conventions of traditional Italian film comedy, with its vulgarity, stock characters, and frontal attack upon society's values. By far the most successful of Italian women directors, Wertmüller nevertheless aroused the ire of many non-Italian feminists, as her works did not conform to what many Anglo-American academics considered to be a politically correct treatment of women's issues.

The peplum film, the spaghetti Western, and the spaghetti nightmare

Even before the success of the Italian Western, a number of commercially successful film directors in Italy had begun to mine a thematic resource with a long tradition in Italian film history that went back to the early success of Italian silent cinema. This was what has been variously dubbed the 'neomythical' or peplum film (peplum referring to the characteristic skirt-like garment worn by the protagonists of such works). Between 1957 and 1965, peplum films accounted for 10 per cent of Italian film production. The peplum, like the Italian spaghetti Western, embodied a very non-American brand of violence, strange humor, and camp parody. Set vaguely in classical times and populated by mindless musclemen—often played by American bodybuilders such as Steve Reeves and Gordon Mitchell—and buxom Italian starlets, the peplum film appealed to a predominantly male audience that thrived on violent action and strong, anti-intellectual heroes. The incredibly stilted dialogue of these works was often unintentionally amusing, especially in dubbed versions abroad, thus increasing its camp appeal to film buffs. Its protagonists—Hercules, Maciste, Samson, Spartacus—came from classical times but managed to fight Aztecs in Mexico, appear in scripts anachronistically set in centuries outside the classical era, and often pop up together in the same film. Peplum films were eventually superseded in popularity by the Italian Western after a blazingly brief lifespan of about a decade.

Italian directors produced almost 500 Westerns in a very brief period of time, and a single man dominated this hybrid genre: Sergio Leone. The peplum film's characteristic emphasis upon action was continued by the Italian Western. Between 1963 and 1973 over 400 such westerns were produced in Italy, but none of them had the impact of Leone's trilogy about a merciless bounty killer known simply as the Man With No Name (Clint Eastwood): *Un pugno di dollari* (*A Fistful of Dollars*, 1964); *Per qualche dollaro in più* (*For a Few Dollars More*, 1965); and *Il buono, il brutto, il cattivo* (*The Good, the Bad, and the Ugly*, 1966). This group of films revolutionized what was at the time an almost exhausted Hollywood genre by a conscious departure from what had come to be known as the 'classic' Western formula. Leone plunges us into a violent and cynical world far removed from the traditional West of John Ford or Howard Hawks. Leone's bounty hunter is motivated by the same greed as the evil bandits and hunts wanted men for money, not out of a sense of justice. Leone's graphic violence, combined with grotesque comic gags and mannered close-ups indebted to Eisenstein, created a new Western screen style.

After the successful trilogy, Leone's style moved toward an epic presentation of the conquest of the American West actually shot, not in rural Spain, in southern Italy, or at the Cinecittà studios in Rome (typical locations of cheaply produced Italian Westerns), but in John Ford country itself—Monument Valley in the United States. The resulting high-budget film—*C'era una volta il West* (*Once Upon a Time in the West*, 1968)—scripted in part by two young aspiring film buffs soon to become directors themselves, Bernardo Bertolucci and Dario Argento (1940–)—presents an impressive collection and reinterpretation of all of the myths associated with the traditional American Western. In a stroke of genius, Leone cast Henry Fonda as a murderous outlaw who kills innocent women and children, an obvious reversal of his heroic role as the crusading marshal Wyatt Earp in Ford's *My Darling Clementine* (1946). At one time the entire Italian film industry seemed to be working on producing Westerns, and each of the various sharpshooting protagonists invented by Italian scriptwriters and directors (Django, Sartana, Ringo, to mention only the most successful) were, like their peplum counterparts, reproduced endlessly in film sequels with only slight changes in plot or locale.

The final popular and low-budget genre that produced generous box office returns for the Italian film industry in this period was the horror film, the so-called 'spaghetti nightmare'. Pioneers in the Italian horror genre were Mario Bava (1914–80), Lucio Fulci (1927–96), and Riccardo Freda (1909–90), whose directorial debut, *La maschera del demonio* (*Black Sunday*, 1960), made a cult figure out of British actress Barbara Steele, whose unique face photographed in close-up shortly thereafter inspired Fellini to cast her in a memorable role in *Otto e mezzo* ($8\frac{1}{2}$, 1963). The most successful horror director is Dario Argento, recognized by many critics as an *auteur* in his own right. Argento's early works, very successful commercially but definitely low-budget in quality, include *L'uccello delle piume di cristallo* (*The Gallery Murders*, 1970) and *Il gatto a nove code* (*The Cat o' Nine Tails*, 1971). Argento's films combined the excessive gore and violence of the traditional B-film within more elaborate and complex visual settings. Italian horror films have earned a cult following due in part to the praise such works have received from American directors Quentin Tarentino and John Landis and writer Stephen King.

■ Marcello Mastroianni (1924–96)

Born in Fontana Liri, a small town near Rome, on 26 September 1924, Mastroianni would eventually make over 170 films and perform in a wide variety of dramatic and cinematic roles during a career that included collaboration with the greatest of Italian and foreign directors (Visconti, Fellini, De Sica, Scola, Germi, Altman, Monicelli, Polanski, Angelopoulos, Ferreri, Malle, Blasetti). At the age of 11 Mastroianni was introduced to both the cinema and

⊕ *La dolce vita*

the theater. Entering the gates of Cinecittà for the first time then, he was cast as an extra during the filming of a grape harvest and was delighted to be able to eat grapes all day and receive money for doing so. The experience may have been the first of many occasions when his work seemed more like a pastime than a vocation, as he was frequently to declare throughout his career.

While his work in the theater included works by Arthur Miller, Tennessee Williams, Goldoni, Chekhov, and Shakespeare, Mastroianni's best work in the cinema was in essentially comic roles. He became identified with Fellini's alter ego in *La dolce vita* and *Otto e mezzo*, but in Pietro Germi's *Divorzio all'italiana* he gave a no less brilliant performance. The range of Mastroianni's acting talents was indeed wide, and reflected his extensive training as a dramatic actor. He played a labor organizer in Monicelli's *I compagni* (*The Organizer*, 1963), an assassin in a futuristic film by Elio Petri entitled *La decima vittima* (*The Tenth Victim*, 1965), and a nineteenth-century revolutionary in *Allonsanfan* (1974) by the Taviani brothers. Two of his best comic performances in films by De Sica—*Ieri, oggi, domani* (*Yesterday, Today and Tomorrow*, 1964) and *Matrimonio all'italiana* (*Marriage Italian Style*, 1965)—were both nominated for Best Foreign Language Film (the first film won). In 1992 Mastroianni and Sophia Loren presented Fellini with his fifth Oscar, for lifetime achievement. He died in Paris on 19 December 1996.

The golden age of the 'art film'

One of the remarkable features of this period in Italian film history was its ability to produce great art that also turned a handsome profit, especially those works made by Fellini, Antonioni, and Visconti. Although these three directors began working during the Neorealist era, by this period their works had undergone highly complex stylistic shifts away from any interest in film realism. Works such as Fellini's *La dolce vita* (*La Dolce Vita*, 1959), Visconti's *Il gattopardo* (*The Leopard*, 1962), or Antonioni's *Blow-Up* (*Blow-Up*, 1966) not only made money at the box office but also opened new directions for the Italian cinema in plot, photography, and editing.

Fellini

Fellini's *La dolce vita* held the European box-office records for decades. Its impact upon Italian and European society was not unlike that of *Gone with the Wind* or *The Godfather* in America: it marks the end of one generation and the beginning of another. It created several new English words or expressions such as *paparazzi*, the gossip column photographers so ubiquitous in Rome's Via Veneto café society; the term *dolce vita* itself, literally meaning a 'sweet life' but actually pointing to a life that is bittersweet and decadent. It announced the triumph of the Italian economic miracle and the birth of a culture based upon public relations, press conferences, and false images. It marks the beginning of Fellini's collaboration with Marcello Mastroianni (1924–96), who functions in this film and three others made with Fellini as the director's alter ego. *La dolce vita* also begins an entirely new direction in Fellini's work: now he gives his introspective fantasy world and brilliant, baroque vision free rein, producing a kaleidoscope of images that are forever detached from the Neorealist desire to chronicle reality simply and directly. As he put it, the cinema needs to imitate the visual arts and to create films like Picasso painted Cubist canvases, cutting up the narrative and examining it from a variety of perspectives. In *La dolce vita*, Mastroianni's performance as a jaded journalist underscores the emptiness of much modern life. His famous bath in the Trevi Fountain with actress Anita Ekberg is justly remembered as one of the most famous sequences in film history: it is an indelible image that emphasizes life lived as a publicity stunt in a society that has come unglued and dis-connected from the important values it has inherited from the past.

Fellini's genius is nowhere better expressed than in his masterpiece, *Otto e mezzo* ($8\frac{1}{2}$, 1963), a work that embodies its creator's belief that the cinema exists primarily for the purpose of individual self-expression, not historical investigation or abstract photo-graphy. Fantasy, rather than reality, is its proper domain, because only fantasy falls under the director's complete artistic control. The harried protagonist of the film, the film dir-ector Guido Anselmi (Marcello Mastroianni), possesses many of Fellini's personal traits and preoccupations as a film director. Fellini's narrative moves rapidly and seamlessly between Guido's 'reality', his fantasies, and flashbacks to the past of his dreams—a discontinuous story line with little logical or chronological unity. The influence of psychoanalysis is obvious in the view Fellini presents of sexuality in the film, as personal problems prevent Guido from achieving artistic fulfillment. In no other film by Fellini was there to be such a perfect synthesis of his personality, his introspective style, and cinematic bravura. *Otto e mezzo* is generally regarded as one of the greatest European films of the postwar period. Its influence has been pervasive and the work has been widely imitated by such directors as Bob Fosse, Lina Wertmüller, and Woody Allen, as well as virtually any director who wishes to treat the nature of cinematic creativity.

After *Otto e mezzo*, Fellini produced a long series of more and more elaborate works, relying upon the resources of Cinecittà to produce brilliant set and costume designs: *Giulietta degli spiriti* (*Juliet of the Spirits*, 1965), *Satyricon* (*Fellini's Satyricon*, 1969), *Roma* (*Fellini's Roma*, 1972), *Amarcord* (1973), and *Il Casanova di Fellini* (*Fellini's Casanova*, 1976). *Satyricon* became a cult film in the psychedelic era and was assimilated into the counterculture of the times. *Amarcord*'s comic satire of the roots of Italian Fascism in a provincial seaside resort that resembled Rimini, Fellini's birthplace, became an interna-tional hit and was Fellini's last commercial success. It also won another Oscar for Best

Foreign Film. *Il Casanova di Fellini*, although a brilliant work that still rewards study, began a series of near misses and commercial failures that continued until the director's death. Now, however, the films made after *Amarcord* are being critically re-evaluated, and seem even more original and groundbreaking than those made during the first two decades of his career.

Visconti

Visconti's films during this period paint large historical canvases, and owe an obvious debt both to grand opera and to the European novel. *Rocco e i suoi fratelli* (*Rocco and His Brothers*, 1960) treats internal migration of Southern workers to a sometimes hostile Milan. Rocco (Alain Delon) and his brother Simone (Renato Salvatori) attempt to work their way out of poverty by becoming prizefighters, but their Southern Italian nuclear family is torn apart by their love for the same woman, a prostitute named Nadia (Annie Girardot). In a melodramatic denouement indebted to the grand opera Visconti often staged at La Scala rather than to any form of cinematic realism, Simone murders Nadia just as Rocco achieves a great victory in the ring. A third brother denounces Simone to the police (breaking the cardinal rule of the South, *omertà* or silence) to complete the destruction of the family, cast adrift in a world with values alien to their ancient culture.

Il gattopardo (*The Leopard*, 1963) adapts Tomasi di Lampedusa's bestselling novel about the Risorgimento in Sicily to Visconti's aristocratic pessimism about the possibility of social revolution. It contains Burt Lancaster's greatest performance as the Sicilian Prince Fabrizio Salina, whose skepticism about the possibility of social change taken verbatim from the novel ('Things have to change in order to remain the same') also reflects a similar belief in Visconti, himself a member of the most ancient Italian nobility. The film set a standard that very few films since have been able to match for the sumptuousness of its decor and the elegiac style of its camerawork. Visconti obviously loves this aristocratic world even as he realizes, as a Marxist, that its time has passed. And he employs the novel's adaptation to make a caustic commentary on Italy's present. In *La caduta degli dei* (*The Damned*, 1969) and *Morte a Venezia* (*Death in Venice*, 1971), Visconti turns to a consideration of Germany during the Nazi period and European decadence, with the novels of Thomas Mann as inspiration. *La caduta degli dei* provides a powerful visual metaphor for the infernal nature of moral degradation, a pathological case history of Nazi Germany underlined by the violent and hellish colors that dominate the film's visuals. From a visual point of view, *Morte a Venezia* constitutes one of the most successful literary adaptations in the postwar Italian cinema. Its chilling images of death and plague in a quarantined Venice of the imagination offer a fascinating treatment of the role of art in the intellectual life of its protagonist and combines the literary text of Thomas Mann with the music of Gustav Mahler. Dirk Bogarde's performance as Gustav von Aschenbach matches in brilliance that of Lancaster in *Il gattopardo*. Visconti was extremely good at obtaining excellent results from foreign actors, just as his skill as a stage and opera director at *La Scala* and other major theaters and opera houses in Paris, Rome, and Venice set the standards for the era. No other Italian director was so attentive to the cultural and historical potential of the Italian cinema. Perhaps no other figure could combine such a refined aesthetic taste with a Marxist ideology.

Antonioni

Antonioni's brilliant modernist photography finds its best expression in the black-and-white trilogy of *L'avventura* (*The Adventure*, 1960), *La notte* (*The Night*, 1961), and *L'eclisse* (*The Eclipse*, 1962), and in his innovative treatment of color in *Il deserto rosso* (*The Red Desert*, 1964). *L'avventura*'s originality resides in its de-emphasis of the dramatic potential of plot with its traditional trajectory of exposition, complication, and resolution through conflict of the major characters. Instead, Antonioni practically jettisons the idea of a well-made plot entirely. The film begins as a wealthy woman named Anna disappears on a Mediterranean cruise, and continues as her lover, Sandro (Gabriele Ferzetti), and Anna's best friend, Claudia (Monica Vitti), search for her, fall in love, and wander around in what seems at first vision to be an aimless quest. Antonioni's style emphasizes absolute control of the composition of each individual frame of the film: characters are frequently photographed as objects, framed as if in a work of art by windows, doorways, long halls, and corridors as if to stress their separation from each other and their failure to communicate. The themes of failed communication and human alienation that mark this trilogy of films also underline Antonioni's interest in the ideas of European existentialism, the philosophy that permeated the culture of the period.

La notte replaces the Mediterranean of Sicily with the gritty northern industrial city of Milan as its location. Again, Antonioni's characters reflect an emotional poverty and a sense of personal alienation he believes is typical of their upper-middle-class background. Giovanni (Marcello Mastroianni) and his wife, Lidia (Jeanne Moreau), discover they are no longer in love as Antonioni follows them during a single day that ends when Lidia reads an old love letter from Giovanni to her and he does not recognize it. Desperate to reach out to each other, they make love on the grass in a gesture of mutual pity that will probably not resolve their personal sufferings. In *La notte* Antonioni employs long tracking or panning shots to match the characters' time with his film time. As a result of such techniques, many insensitive critics proclaimed that 'nothing' ever happens in his films. *L'eclisse* pushes this increasingly abstract style to its limits, and once again plot takes second place to technique. The film turns around the love affair between Vittoria (Monica Vitti) and a young but shallow stockbroker named Piero (Alain Delon). It concludes with a justly famous sequence that captures the failure of the two lovers to meet at an appointed rendezvous: characters disappear altogether as Antonioni focuses on the objects, people, and places associated with the two people who are destined never to meet there again.

In *Il deserto rosso*, color photography pre-empts the central function of traditional plot and character by concentrating upon the relationship between characters and their environment, represented by the machinery and contemporary technology of a modern oil refinery in Ravenna. In spite of Antonioni's lack of interest in traditional plot, Monica Vitti delivers a brilliant performance as Giuliana, a woman who has experienced a mental breakdown. Antonioni's color photography is thoroughly modernist (only a single scene, Giuliana's dream of a desert island, is shot in what we have come to consider as 'natural' film color). Its hues come from the world of industrial plastics, chemicals, and artificial fabrics. In some cases, the director even changes the colors of natural objects (grass, fruit) to reflect the psychological states of his disturbed characters. And he frames each shot as if he were a contemporary abstract painter, asking us to consider objects from the world of technology primarily as art forms and only later as objects with a utilitarian function. Antonioni's greatest commercial success was the international hit *Blow-Up* (1966), a color film shot in English and one that seemed to capture the essence of swinging London of the 1960s. Its central scene, that of an enlargement of a photograph that seems to prove a murder has taken place under the nose of the film's protagonist, a fashion photographer, provides a metaphor for the search for truth and meaning in a world dominated by images from advertising and fashion magazines. Unlike the langorous speed of the earlier trilogy in black and white, which emphasized long shots to capture the characters' empty lives, *Blow-Up* is edited with the dynamic speed of a modern commercial and represents Antonioni's attempt to capture the energy of the period. Since the film offers a mystery plot, *Blow-Up* also represents a change of direction in Antonioni's normal rejection of traditional narrative structure.

Post-1968 cinema

Italian society underwent a number of major changes between the end of the war and the decade beginning in 1968. Student protests over an essentially authoritarian and patriarchal society spilled over from neighboring France into Italy, as universities suffered from paralyzing demonstrations and eventually riots. Labor unrest proclaimed that the postwar economic miracle had hit some snags. Conflicts between political parties on the Right and the Left reflected the tensions of the Cold War and anti-American sentiment increased during the Vietnam War. The scourge of terrorism raised the level of political struggle to a new high that had not been witnessed in Italy since the Fascists and Communists battled in the streets before 1922 or during the open civil war between the Fascists and the partisans after the fall of Mussolini's regime in 1943. The assassination of a former prime minister, Aldo Moro, by Red Brigade terrorists in 1978 represented the nadir of such troubles. As the art form most closely linked to social problems in Italy, the cinema quite naturally reflected this time of troubles in a number of ways. Politics and ideology played a major role in the cinema, moving even normally apolitical directors (such as Fellini) to treat political themes.

With *Medea*, Pier Paolo Pasolini employs the classic tragedy by Euripides as a metaphor to explore the confrontation of Western, industrialized society with the pre-industrial cultures of the Third World. In *Il Decameron*, Pasolini transforms Boccaccio's panoramic portrait of the rise of middle-class, mercantile culture in an age dominated by the city of Florence into an amusing portrayal of the sub-proletariat of Naples and its sexual adventures. The film not only underlines the class-oriented nature of the original literary source, but also proposes liberated sexuality as a characteristic of non-industrialized cultures and uses this innocent sense of sexuality to critique modern Western values.

Bertolucci's *Il conformista* and Fellini's *Amarcord* provide two very different interpretations of Italy's Fascist heritage. Bertolucci employs a complicated plot with frequent flashbacks, portraying the creation of a Fascist assassin. Bertolucci's mature grasp of his craft is evident in the famous tango scene between two women, with its quickly shifting camera angles, positions, graceful motions, and skillful editing, a virtuoso performance due in large measure to the brilliant cinematography of a young Vittorio Storaro (1940–). While Bertolucci's technique is masterful, the content of the film is somewhat heavy-handed, as it accepts Wilhelm Reich's discredited theories linking Fascism and homosexuality (a theory also espoused by Alberto Moravia, the author of the novel *Il conformista* from which Bertolucci's film was adapted)—a criticism that can also be leveled at Visconti's *La caduta degli dei*. As avowed Marxists, both Bertolucci and Visconti seem more intent on proving that Fascism arises from a decadent middle-class background than with providing their works with serious historical foundations. Fellini's *Amarcord* is much less stridently ideological but is no less a condemnation of Fascist restrictions of individual freedom. In an unforgettable evocation of life in a sleepy provincial town, Fellini combines a nostalgic view of his childhood with a searing indictment of Italian conformity during the Fascist period.

The period's interest in political cinema produced several memorable treatments of the Holocaust. Two were the controversial creations of Italy's best-known women directors, Lina Wertmüller and Liliana Cavani. Wertmüller's comic vision in her masterpiece, *Pasqualino Settebellezze* (*Seven Beauties*, 1975), was attacked by some critics as irreverent, even though there was a clear cinematic precedent for such a perspective in Chaplin's *The Great Dictator* (1940). However, its tragi-comic treatment of such sensitive subject matter and her memorable portrait of the hellish life inside a concentration camp found important critical defenders, while the virtuoso performance of the actor playing its protagonist, Giancarlo Giannini (1942–), made him an international star. Equally controversial, Cavani's *Il portiere di notte* (*The Night Porter*, 1974) presented a morbid portrait of a love affair between a woman in a death camp and a sadistic German officer, a relationship renewed in the postwar period after a chance encounter between the two in Vienna. The Italian treatment of the Holocaust that elicited almost unanimous praise (except from Giorgio Bassani, the novelist whose book was its source) was Vittorio De Sica's *Il giardino dei Finzi-Contini* (*The Garden of the Finzi-Continis*, 1971), a lyrical, elegiac portrait of the Jewish population of prewar Ferrara awarded the Oscar for Best Foreign Film in 1972.

The high-water mark of Italian cinema's success was probably achieved by the international acclaim bestowed upon Bertolucci's *Ultimo tango a Parigi* (*Last Tango in Paris*) and Fellini's *Amarcord*, two masterpieces devoted respectively to sexuality and Italian Fascism by representatives of the two very different generations that had combined forces to produce Cinecittà's golden age. Fellini's last box-office success underlined the strength of the tradition of Italian cinema. Bertolucci's phenomenal rise to fame as a result of a scandalous treatment of sexual relations between an American expatriate, played brilliantly by Marlon Brando, and a young French girl seemed to promise that a new generation of *auteurs* had emerged to take center stage in European cinema. As a result of the success of these two works, Fellini and Bertolucci earned the ability to move into the big-budget range of their Hollywood competitors with Bertolucci's *1900* and Fellini's *Il Casanova di Fellini*. Neither film, however, lived up to expectations. Perhaps the decline of the Italian film industry as a protean force in European and world cinema may be dated from the time these two films were released: 1972–3. After that period the Italian film industry began a slow but steady decline in economic importance and artistic innovation, a decline that was to be followed by other European national cinemas. Now the various national cinemas had to compete with a newly revived American cinema launched by a generation of young directors (Scorsese, Coppola, Lucas, Spielberg, De Palma) who had learned a good deal of their trade from their Italian and European masters.

Further reading

Armes, Roy, *Patterns of Realism: A Study of Italian Neo-Realism* (Cranbury, NJ: A. S. Barnes, 1971). A classic treatment of Italian Neorealism, covering not only the masterpieces but also the many lesser-known films.

Bacon, Henry, *Visconti: Explorations of Beauty and Decay* (New York: Cambridge University Press, 1998). This is the most recent and most useful treatment of Visconti in English.

Bondanella, Peter, *The Cinema of Federico Fellini* (Princeton, NJ: Princeton University Press, 1992). A comprehensive study of Fellini, emphasizing his origins in popular culture and his artistic development from Italian Neorealism to a personal cinema of fantasy and imagination.

—— *Italian Cinema: From Neorealism to the Present*, 3rd rev. edn. (New York: Continuum, 2001). An analytical survey of Italian cinema with emphasis on its artistic achievements from 1942 to the present.

Brunetta, Gian Piero, *Storia del cinema italiano* (4 vols.: Rome: Editori Riuniti, 1993). The most comprehensive history of Italian cinema in print today.

Brunette, Peter, *Roberto Rossellini* (New York: Oxford University Press, 1987). An exhaustive treatment of all of Rossellini's films.

Chatman, Seymour, *Antonioni: or, The Surface of the World*. (Berkeley: University of California Press, 1985). A fine examination of Antonioni's entire career, with particular emphasis upon his imagery.

Fanara, Giulia, *Pensare il neorealismo: percorsi attraverso il neorealismo cinematografico italiano* (Rome: Lithos, 2000). The most recent study of Italian Neorealism, the best in Italian.

Freyling, Christopher, *Spaghetti Westerns: Cowboys and Europeans from Karl May to Sergio Leone* (London: Routledge & Kegan Paul, 1981). A persuasive analysis of the Italian Western.

Marcus, Millicent, *Filmmaking by the Book: Italian Cinema and Literary Adaptation* (Baltimore: Johns Hopkins University Press, 1993). A fine study of various directors (Fellini, Pasolini, De Sica, the Taviani brothers, Visconti) and their adaptations of classic literary texts.

Palmerini, Luca, and Gaetano Mistretta, *Spaghetti Nightmares: Italian Fantasy-Horrors as Seen through the Eyes of their Protagonists* (Key West, Fla.: Fantasma Books, 1996). An indispensable treatment of this genre in English.

POSTWAR SCANDINAVIAN CINEMA

Peter Schepelern

Most Scandinavian cinema is relatively unknown to the international film world. But from time to time at least Denmark and Sweden have fostered remarkable filmmakers who have made groundbreaking film art. Scandinavian cinema has alternated between shining moments and unique, internationally visible personalities, and long periods where Scandinavian films have primarily been a local affair.

Danish and Swedish film have had some interaction during their hundred-year histories, but they have for the most part run parallel courses. Both countries enjoyed a brief international success in the silent years. After this followed decades of domestic success until the threat of television created a crisis in the early 1960s. Both countries took initiatives to protect national film production through legislation and state support. As a consequence, private film companies were weakened and the state influence on film production strengthened. From being a lucrative private market in the first half of the century, film has increasingly become an official cultural institution, financed and controlled by the state. In recent times the Scandinavian film industries, like other European film industries, have tried to hold on to their national audience but also to challenge the dominant American blockbusters by producing international films in English or by participating in international co-productions, as a kind of collective European effort against Hollywood.

For many non-Scandinavians, Scandinavian culture is characterized by a number of traits: a certain gloom, an austere despair—often with religious overtones—and, in contrast, a frank approach to eroticism and sex. Yet if we take a general look at Scandinavian films, particularly those of the postwar era, we will typically find harmless entertainment, characterized by jovial musical comedies, popular farce, and rustic melodrama. The most popular films are, in fact, far from philosophical, and no more explicit in sexual themes than are films from other Western countries. The two most important figures of Scandinavian cinema, Carl Theodor Dreyer and Ingmar Bergman, are atypical of Scandinavian cinema. They are uncompromising individualists, unbending personalities who tower above most of their contemporaries. They are giant artists from small countries, yet it is through their work that we can perhaps learn the most about the traditions from which their films emerged.

Danish cinema

In Denmark, the first film shows took place in Copenhagen in the summer of 1896, and in the following years royal photographer Peter Elfelt made the first Danish productions—short films in the style of the Lumière brothers. The Danish film industry on a larger scale began with producer Ole Olsen's establishment of Nordisk Film in 1906, that is still one of the leading companies in Danish and Scandinavian film (and television) production. Around 1910, films from Denmark had a huge international success in Europe, but World War I ended the Danish film industry's international prominence. Nordisk Film went bankrupt in 1928, but was soon reconstructed as a sound film company. Nordisk had acquired the rights to a sound system developed by two Danish engineers, Petersen and Poulsen, which was presented as an experiment in 1923. But with the first Danish talkie in 1931, Danish cinema, like many small national cinemas, lost its international potential, though it continued to attract home audiences. The major companies in the sound era were Nordisk and the new Palladium, which had enjoyed huge international success in the late 1920s with the comic duo Fyrtårnet and Bivognen (The Lighthouse and the Sidecar), known as Long and Short or Pat and Patachon.

Danish films were very popular with the Danish public through the 1930s and 1940s, and this box-office success continued in the 50s. During World War II, with Denmark occupied by German forces, films from the Allied nations could not be shown, but after the war American films regained their dominant position. In the 1950s, approximately 60 per cent of all titles were American and they took around 50 per cent of the grosses, compared to the 25–30 per cent taken by Danish films. The decline in cinema attendance started in the early 1960s, when the effect of television, which had been introduced in the mid-1950s, began to make its mark. In the mid-1960s, a new film law was established to support the production of artistic films, a policy that continued with the establishment in 1972 of the Danish Film Institute. The average output of Danish feature films was four-teen films a year in the 1950s and nineteen films a year in the 1960s.

Carl Theodor Dreyer: the early films

Carl Theodor Dreyer (1889–1968) is the classic figure in Danish cinema. He began his career as an audacious reporter and balloonist, before landing a job as a script supervisor and writer in 1910, and later as an editor as well, at Nordisk Film, the dominant film production company. At the time, Danish cinema had a leading role in European film—a brief golden age especially known for erotic melodramas such as Urban Gad's *Afgrunden* (*The Abyss*, 1910) featuring Asta Nielsen, who with her intense yet subdued acting became one of the first stars of European cinema, and August Blom's *Ved Fængslets Port* (*The Temptations of a Great City*, 1911), featuring the leading male star Valdemar Psilander in the prototypical story of an upper-class man attracted to a young woman of humble means.

By the end of the decade, when Dreyer himself began directing films like the melodrama *Præsidenten* (*The President*, 1919) and *Blade af Satans Bog* (*Leaves from Satan's Book*, 1920), influenced by D. W. Griffith's *Intolerance*, the golden age of Danish cinema had already passed, and it would soon lose its international status. Despite this, in the 1920s Dreyer was able to build an international career, working in Denmark, Sweden, Norway, Germany, and France. His charming Danish comedy *Du skal ære din Hustru* (*Thou Shalt Honour Thy Wife*, 1925), about the downfall of a tyrannical master of the house, led to an invitation, from the French company Société Générale de Films, to make a film about a great historical figure of his own choice.

La Passion de Jeanne d'Arc (*The Passion of Joan of Arc*, 1928), which already at its pre-miere was hailed as a masterpiece of silent cinema, is one of the most original works in film history. Dreyer's film tells the well-known story of Joan's trial, sentence, and death at the stake in a very personal and very minimalist, ascetic manner. He had the film company build an enormous set, yet in the film the buildings are hardly seen at all. For most of the film, the camera focuses with enormous intensity on faces—the judges, the soldiers, and Joan herself, played by Maria Falconetti, an Italian actress from the Boulevard Theatre, on whose naked face Dreyer expresses Joan's suffering and transfiguration. It is not Joan the warrior we meet, but Joan the maiden, for whom victory is martyrdom and for whom death is liberation (as stated in the famous line of the friendly young monk, played by the French writer Antonin Artaud).

Dreyer made an early sound film, *Vampyr* (1932). Shot in France in 1930, it was privately financed by the Baron Nicholas de Gunzberg (also known as Julian West), who also plays the main character who arrives at a small village haunted by vampires. In contrast to horror films such as the German expressionist *Nosferatu* or the American *Dracula*, Dreyer's film is a strangely poetic rendering of material, loosely based on a tale by Sheridan Le Fanu. Instead of night-time scenes and frightening gothic horror, he employs hazy, eerie visions of a summer night, giving the film a bizarre, dreamy atmosphere.

After *Vampyr*, Dreyer's career came to a standstill. He experienced a mental crisis and was involved in an aborted project, a French-Italian film that was to be shot on location in Africa. Shooting in Somalia did actually start, but Dreyer left the film abruptly, returning to Denmark, where he subsequently worked for a number of years in a humble position at a Copenhagen newspaper. By this time he had made ten films, yet the Danish film industry showed no interest in him. His austere, uncompromising film style was in complete contrast to the jovial Danish cinema of the 1930s, where popular musical comedies dominated the scene.

It was not until World War II, when Danish cinema took a turn in a new direction, that film producers again approached Dreyer. After making the documentary *Mødrehjælpen* (*The Good Mothers*, 1942), about adoption—a theme that interested Dreyer, who himself was adopted—he was given the opportunity to shoot a feature film, *Vredens Dag* (*Day of Wrath*, 1943), which premiered during the darkest hours of the Nazi occupation of Denmark.

Based on a play (1908) by a minor Norwegian writer, Hans Wiers-Jenssen, *Day of Wrath* tells a story set in Denmark in the 1620s. Young Anne lives in a loveless marriage with the elderly vicar Absalon, whose aged mother has never accepted the young woman as mistress of the house. We are given to understand that Absalon actually married Anne in return for not accusing her deceased mother of witchcraft. When Absalon's son from his first marriage returns from abroad, he and Anne fall in love. When she confesses this relationship to Absalon, he dies of a heart attack. At his funeral, Absalon's mother accuses Anne of witchcraft, and betrayed, by her lover and convinced that Absalon actually died because she willed it, Anne accepts her fate. The film contains powerful scenes, like those of a harmless old woman being interrogated, tortured, and burnt at the stake, and the pictorial style—influenced by seventeenth-century Dutch painters such as Rembrandt and Frans Hals—lend the film a monumental effect. The slow, restrained rhythm and long, searching camera movements were criticized by contemporary critics, but were deemed essential by Dreyer: 'Isn't it true that great dramas are played quietly, that people try to cover their feelings and avoid revealing on their faces the storms that are really raging within them?' (Dreyer 1973).

German forces occupied Denmark in April 1940, and both the government and the public tried to find a way to accept the situation. The result was a policy of cooperation, albeit involuntary, with Nazi Germany. But gradually resistance grew, and in October 1943 the Resistance movement successfully organized an action, which brought most Danish Jews to safety in neutral Sweden. Most Danish films from the occupation years were escapist entertainment, although there were also a number of dark melodramas and suspense films, but due to censorship none of these films ever made a direct reference to the war or to the occupation. With its story of torture and persecution, *Day of Wrath* was generally interpreted as an implicit commentary on the German occupation, though Dreyer explicitly denied that he had this interpretation in mind (Manvell 1947: 67).

After the premiere Dreyer, too, moved to Sweden. He had several plans for film projects in Sweden—among them a film about the Arctic explorer Andrée who in 1897 attempted to reach the North Pole by balloon, a film project realized many years later by Jan Troell in *Ingenjör Andrées luftfärd* (*The Flight of the Eagle*, 1982). The one film that Dreyer did produce in Sweden was the *Kammerspiel* (chamber piece) *Två människor* (*Two People*, 1944), a psychological crime drama. The minimalist story, presenting only two characters in a room, was an unsuccessful experiment and Dreyer wanted it withdrawn from circulation. It was never released in Denmark.

Dreyer's later films

After World War II, Danish film—as was the case for European film in general—discovered a new realism, a more direct and fearless approach on screen to social problems. Although there was no Danish Neorealism as such, a sudden break with the escapist comedic style of the 1930s was evident in such new Danish films as Bjarne Henning-Jensen's *Ditte Menneskebarn* (*Ditte Child of Man*, 1946), based on Martin Andersen Nexø's classic novel of a poor girl's tragedy, and Johan Jacobsen's *Soldaten og Jenny* (*Jenny and the Soldier*, 1947), which, in the French style of Poetic Realism, confronts the arbitrariness of justice through the story of an illegal abortion and its consequences. Dreyer earned his living as a director of short documentaries and the poignant fable *De naaede Færgen* (*They Caught the Ferry*, 1948), based on a story by Nobel Prize winner Johannes V. Jensen, about a couple hurrying on a motorcycle across the island of Funen in order to catch a ferry and, instead of catching the ferry they expected, finding themselves on a vessel taking dead souls to the underworld. The film was produced for the Council for Better Road Safety. For a time, Dreyer had plans for a British film about Mary Stuart, but this plan was aborted. He also started work on his most ambitious project, a

⬆ *Ordet*

film about Jesus Christ, which would consume much of his time and energy during the remainder of his life. Dreyer's manuscript was published in 1968 and has been staged theatrically, but it has never been made into a film. In the 1950s Dreyer was able to secure his income as a cinema owner in Copenhagen, but he made only two more films during the next two decades. The first of these, *Ordet* (*The Word*, 1955), was the greatest success of his career and received the Golden Lion in Venice in 1955.

The film is based on a well-known Danish play, written by the vicar Kaj Munk, who had for a time in the 1930s admired the European Fascist leaders but who later changed his political opinions and was subsequently murdered by the Germans in 1944. Munk wrote the play in 1926. It was originally performed as a stage play with great success in 1932, and the Swedish director Gustaf Molander had already made a film of it in 1944. The story is set in Jutland, where the peasant population was divided into two religious factions: one upholding a positive, life-affirming form of Christianity based on the ideas of Grundtvig, a great poet and religious leader of enormous influence in the nineteenth century; the other upholding the fundamentalist views of the evangelical branch of the

Church of Denmark (Indre Mission), in which life on earth is sad and sinful. This conflict serves as the backdrop for the story, culminating in a powerful scene in which Inger, a young mother who has died in childbirth, lies in her coffin, and her other child, a little girl, persuades her uncle, the mentally disturbed Johannes, to 'say the word', to call Inger back to life—and miraculously she comes back to life.

For the most part, Danish cinema of the 1950s had again sunk to trivial entertainment, exemplified as its best by the two most popular film series of the time, both directed by the prolific Alice O'Fredericks: *De røde heste* (*The Red Horses*, 1950) and *Far til Fire* (*Father of Four*, 1953). *De røde heste* was the first in a number of idyllic agricultural melodramas; a kind of Danish *Heimat* film, based on the novels of the popular kitsch writer Morten Korch, it was seen by more than 60 per cent of the population in the first six months after its release. The *Far til Fire* films were cosy comedies reflecting the new suburban family life (similar to *Leave it to Beaver* and other American sitcoms). These were the quintessential representatives of Danish film in the 1950s. Set against this backdrop, *Ordet* stands out as an unparalleled work of art, embodying an artistic intensity unseen in contemporary Danish cinema.

The 1960s arrived on the scene with young initiatives and styles in European film; a new wave had also hit Scandinavian cinema. Influence of the innovative trends from the French *nouvelle vague* and the new cinemas in Italy, Great Britain, and Eastern Europe were evident in such new films as Palle Kjærulff-Schmidt's *Weekend* (1962) and *Der var engang en krig* (*Once There Was a War*, 1966), written by the most innovative literary figure of the period, Klaus Rifbjerg. Other notable films were Henning Carlsen's *Sult* (*Hunger*, 1966), a Scandinavian co-production based on the novel by Knut Hamsun, and Sven and Lene Grønlykke's *Balladen om Carl-Henning* (*The Ballad of Carl-Henning*, 1969). In the 1960s, however, it also became increasingly evident that artistic films were being threatened by the decline in cinema attendance brought on by the arrival of television. Television made its breakthrough in Denmark in the mid-1950s, and cinema attendance dropped from 52 million tickets sold in 1950 to 23 million in 1970. In 1965 a new film law went into effect, giving financial support to the production of artistic films. This would lead to the establishment of the Danish Film Institute in 1972; but a few years later it was clear not only that artistic films required state support in order to survive but that all Danish film production had become dependent on state funding of some kind.

In the 1960s the Danish government allocated extra funding to Dreyer's Jesus project, but it was too late. Dreyer also worked on an uncompleted film project of *Medea*, a color film with Maria Callas in the title role (a casting that would later be realized by Pasolini in his *Medea* of 1970). He did succeed, though, in making one last film. *Gertrud* (1964) once again tells the story of a tormented woman in a man's world. Based on a play (1906) by the important Swedish writer Hjalmar Søderberg, it tells the story of a woman from upper-class Copenhagen society and her painful relationships with the men in her life: first a celebrated poet, then an official who is appointed Minister of Justice, and finally a young pianist. Ultimately she leaves them all, because for them work is more important than love. She ends her days in solitude, with the realization that we are all subject to 'carnal lust and the irredeemable loneliness of the soul'. Dreyer's film, a highly stylized melodrama told in long searching camera takes and employing an acting style full of pathos, was considered anachronistic in an era of modernity, and in Denmark it was little understood. It did, however, receive praise from French directors such as Jean-Luc Godard and Eric Rohmer (who were not able to recognize the archaic use of the Danish language). In the revolutionary year of 1968, Dreyer died.

Years later, his uncompromising art and deliberate distance from the conventions and norms of Danish style and approach would serve as inspiration to Lars von Trier (born 1956), the most original talent of a new generation of Danish filmmakers. Von Trier paid tribute to Dreyer with his innovative television production of *Medea* (1988), based on Dreyer's unrealized script, as he did with his international film breakthrough *Breaking the Waves* (1996), and again with his Cannes winner *Dancer in the Dark* (2000), both of which rework the Dreyeresque themes of the suffering woman and the miracle of faith. In an unforgettable TV happening in 1989, celebrating the 100th anniversary of Dreyer's birth, von Trier praised Dreyer's work and knelt at his grave.

Swedish cinema

Like Denmark, Sweden had its first film shows in 1896. The first Swedish films were made by royal photographer Ernest Florman in 1897. With Svenska Bio (later Svensk Filmindustri under the control of producer Charles Magnusson from 1909), Sweden got its most important production company, which still dominates the Swedish film industry. Swedish cinema had its golden age during the silent era when Victor Sjöström made *Terje Vigen* (1917) and *Körkarlen* (*The Phantom Carriage*, 1920) and Mauritz Stiller made *Erotikon* (1920) and the epic *Gösta Berlings* saga (*The Atonement of Gösta Berling*, 1924); the latter giving Greta Garbo her breakthrough and the beginning of her international career.

As was the case in Danish cinema, the arrival of sound around 1930 meant a change of direction from international scope to provincial nationalism (dominated by comedies and agricultural melodramas), and restricted the Swedish film market to Sweden—a rare exception being the melodrama *Intermezzo* (1936), which was remade in Hollywood in 1939 introducing the new Swedish star, Ingrid Bergman. During World War II, when

Sweden kept its neutrality (harboring exiles from occupied Denmark as well as allowing German traffic through the country), Swedish film had a big home market. But after the war the interest in Swedish films dropped and the industry suffered from labor disputes. The leading company was still SF (Svenska Filmindustri), but companies such as Sandrews and Terra were also important. TV arrived in Sweden in the mid-1950s, and ten years later the country enacted film reform legislation. Svenska Filminstitutet (SFI), the Swedish Film Institute, was established, along with a support system that protected and secured the artistic blossoming of Swedish films. In Sweden the competition from television was clearly seen in the period 1955–63, when the number of households with a television grew from zero to two million and cinema attendance dropped from 80 million tickets a year to 40 million. The average output of Swedish feature films was thirty-one a year in the 1950s and twenty-three a year in the 1960s.

Ingmar Bergman

In the early 1940s, the most important film director in Sweden was Alf Sjöberg (1903–80), also an outstanding director of theater, and it was Sjöberg who in 1944 made a film based on a manuscript by a young new talent named Ingmar Bergman (b. 1918). *Hets* (*Frenzy*, 1944) is an intense story of a high-school boy, tormented by a cruel Latin teacher, who falls in love with the girl at the tobacco store around the corner and finds that this sadistic man, too, has tormented her. The film—featuring Alf Kjellin and Mai Zetterling in the roles of the young couple (they would later have international careers)—was made in an Expressionistic style and was widely admired. Bergman was then given the opportunity to direct his own film, the rather clumsy debut *Kris* (*Crisis*, 1945), a melodramatic story of a young woman torn between her adoptive and biological mothers.

In the following years, Bergman made approximately one film a year, and was soon accepted as the promising young name in the New Swedish cinema. He would eventually become the leading figure in Swedish cinema, and subsequently one of the most important directors in the world. He has been of immense importance for Swedish film, but it has often been hard for other filmmakers to develop in his shadow.

In the nearly fifty films and TV productions he has made, he constantly returns to the same themes and the same dominating issues. His father was a stern Protestant minister, and from his earliest films Bergman deals with religious and existential questions. Often his protagonists desperately seek an answer from God, only to meet with disillusion and emptiness. Another of his themes is the artist in conflict with society, the artist as a humiliated victim of the common world. Bergman, who has been married a number of times and is the father of ten children, has always used the relationship between men and women as one of his great subjects; and his work analyzes these relationships with sarcasm and sharpness. He has been celebrated as a male director with a special ability to depict women and their world.

Bergman's early work

Bergman's early work often focused on the desperation and anxiety of young people in the postwar years, and already at this stage of his career he was describing personal, psychological, and spiritual conflicts rather than social and economic conditions. He was concurrently developing into one of the major theater directors of the century—working in Hälsingborg, Malmö, and later Stockholm at the Dramaten, in a career that would span more than sixty years and some hundred productions. Through his work in the theater, he assembled a group of actors he used in his films (made mostly during the summer when the theaters were closed): Max von Sydow, Gunnar Björnstrand, Harriet Andersson, Bibi Andersson, Ingrid Thulin, Erland Josephson and, in the early films, Birger Malmsten and Stig Olin (father of Lena Olin, who was discovered by Bergman).

His films were influenced by the trends of contemporary theater such as French existentialism (Jean-Paul Sartre, Albert Camus) and the psychological realism of Tennessee Williams. He was also influenced by the major works of the great Swedish dramatist August Strindberg—seen both in the numerous dream sequences present in his films and in the often cruel depictions of marital life—and his visual style borrowed elements from the German Expressionism of the 1920s and the sombre Poetic Realism of French cinema in the 1930s. A typical theme in early films like *Frenzy* is the struggle of young people against a hostile, old-fashioned world, trying to find room for their love but most often ending in defeat—as is the case in *Det regnar på vår kärlek* (*It Rains on Our Love*, 1946), *Musik i mörker* (*Night is my Future*, 1947), and *Hamnstad* (*Port of Call*, 1948). *Fängelse* (*Prison* or *The Devil's Wanton*, 1949) is an important film, with its strange experimental tale of a journalist attracted to a young prostitute. Together they flee her pimp and her cynical sister who has murdered their newborn baby; they have a short time together before destiny catches up with them and she commits suicide. The framework of the story revolves around an old man who wants his former pupil, now a filmmaker, to make a film about Hell, which he finds in the here-and-now. The film is the first mature work in which Bergman demonstrates his sense for desperate atmospheres, disillusioned characters, and haunting dream sequences.

Bergman soon became a true *auteur*—some of his early films were based on literary material, but he wrote the great majority himself. Two marital dramas followed, *Törst* (*Thirst* or *Three Strange Loves*, 1949) and *Till glädje* (*To Joy*, 1950), and the beautiful

Sommarlek (*Summer Interlude*, 1951), a poetic, tragic love story set in the Swedish summer, a special season that would also figure in the popular *Sommaren med Monika* (*Summer with Monika*, 1953), a story of two young people who board a ship looking to escape from their social and personal misery and hoping to find love and freedom, only to end disillusioned when the summer is over. *Gycklarnas afton* (*Sawdust and Tinsel*, 1953) was an unusual masterpiece about a troupe of touring circus artists. Here we find the memorable sequence in which the clown finds his wife bathing naked in the sea with a regiment of soldiers who are ridiculing him, told in disturbing overexposed shots, accompanied by the experimental music of Karl Birger Blomdahl.

In 1955 Bergman made his sixteenth film, an erotic comedy called *Sommarnattens leende* (*Smiles of a Summer Night*, 1955). With a delightful plot of erotic intrigues set on a Swedish country estate in the mid-nineteenth century, this rare excursion into comedy was the vehicle for Bergman's international breakthrough. The film won the Golden Palm at Cannes and was later turned into a Broadway musical by Stephen Sondheim (*A Little Night Music*, 1973, filmed in 1978).

The year 1957 witnessed two major Bergman films: the first, *Det sjunde inseglet* (*The Seventh Seal*); the second, *Smultronstället* (*Wild Strawberries*)—both central works of their era, both hailed as masterpieces. *The Seventh Seal*, based on a play that Bergman wrote and directed at an actors' school in 1954, is set in medieval times. A knight (Max von Sydow) has returned from the Crusades to a plague-devastated country, and one morning is confronted by Death. The knight manages to engage Death in a game of chess, thereby receiving an extension of his life. He then performs a good deed by helping a travelling player, his young wife, and their newborn baby—a holy family (their names are Jof and Mia)—escape the dark destiny, while other sinful characters are seen, in the end, in silhouette dancing the dance of Death. The film, which created a convincing medieval Sweden in just thirty-five days of shooting and on a very small budget, can be seen as an allegory of the contemporary political situation in the Western world during the Cold War, dominated by fear of atomic destruction. Bergman has stated that it is a film about the fear of death. It is also a reflection on faith and doubt—the knight calls out in vain to God, but he cannot give up the idea of God: 'Faith is a tough disease,' he says.

Wild Strawberries was another Bergman triumph, perhaps the most praised of all his films. An aging professor of medicine, Isak Borg, is about to be awarded an honorary doctorate at the University of Lund. Instead of flying from Stockholm to southern Sweden, he decides to drive, accompanied by his estranged son's wife, Marianne. The long trip becomes a journey through his past, in which he not only relives his own cold and self-righteous treatment of his wife, but also the summer of his youth when he lost

Sara, the girl he loved; he has ugly nightmares where he fails at the big exam of life, but he also meets Sara again both in the past and in the present—she is sitting at the secret spot where the wild strawberries grow, *smultronstället*. Gradually, when confronted with his life and his shortcomings, he comes to terms with himself and ultimately reconciles himself to his life. The film resonates with a belief in humanity that is such an important theme in postwar films like Kurosawa's *Rashomon* (1950) and Fellini's *La strada* (1954). Bergman operates effectively with multiple temporal layers, an idea he borrowed from Alf Sjöberg's adaptation of Strindberg's *Fröken Julie* (*Miss Julie*, 1951), where Julie the child and Julie the woman are seen together in the same scene.

Bergman continued with films such as *Ansiktet* (*The Face/The Magician*, 1958), a story set in the 1840s about a hypnotist/magician, Vogler, and the Oscar-winning *Jungfrukällan* (*The Virgin Spring*, 1960), a cruel and powerful tale of medieval Sweden in which a rich peasant executes the three men who raped and killed his young daughter. The dark nature of this work announced the emergence of a new, somber style for Bergman, which would reach its fullest expression in his next three films.

The dark films

Bergman was at the height of his career, but his films now took a turn toward the more somber and difficult, and were characterized by torment and crisis. This dark period began with three films that would later be presented as a trilogy—the Oscar-winning *Såsom i en spegel* (*Through a Glass Darkly*, 1961), *Nattvardsgästerna* (*Winter Light*, 1962) and *Tystnaden* (*The Silence*, 1963). The three films, though unrelated in terms of plot, share common reflections on existentialist and religious questions.

Through a Glass Darkly is an intense chamber play about a middle-aged novelist (Gunnar Björnstrand) whose daughter (Harriet Andersson) is gradually succumbing to mental illness. She hears voices talking to her from within the walls, and it is certainly no help to her condition when she reads in her father's diary of his fascination with studying her mental decline. At the end of the film she envisions divine salvation coming to her rescue, but it is only a helicopter that has come to take her away from the island where she lives. The film delivers an intense portrait of the psychotic woman, but it is also a film about the morality of an artist who uses others for the sake of art, and who is himself isolated in his suffering.

Winter Light is an austere story about a vicar (Björnstrand) in a northern Swedish county, where the winters are dark and life is harsh. One of his parishioners, a carpenter and family man, commits suicide because he is frightened by the world, making the vicar feel powerless and tormented. He is unable to accept the love offered to him by the organist (Ingrid Thulin), and yet he continues. It is perhaps Bergman's darkest film, a study in human loneliness and desperation.

In *The Silence*, two sisters, the refined Ester (Thulin again), who is seriously ill, and the sensual Anna, who is with her young son, interrupt their journey in a foreign country and stop at an old hotel. Ester's condition becomes worse, and while the young boy lingers in hotel rooms and corridors, the other sister takes to the city and has sex with a total stranger. The film takes place in a symbolic universe, in a city without language (actually mostly Estonian—Bergman's wife of that time was the Estonian pianist Käbi Laretei), which is mobilizing for an approaching war. The film was seen and interpreted as a reflection on the absence—or silence—of God in the modern world, and on the absence of love and genuine human contact among people in a hostile world. Only music— Johann Sebastian Bach—is a spiritual contact, between the sick sister and the old hotel servant, seemingly a divine presence. There are echoes of Sartre's famous play *Huis clos* (*No Exit*), where hell is presented as a hotel room with three strangers. Yet the fact that *The Silence*, an austere allegory of the pain and misery of modern existence, became an enormous box-office hit both in Sweden (where it was seen by 1.5 million viewers) and abroad, is hardly due to the existential questions it raised, but to a number of rather explicit sex scenes—the sick woman masturbating, a couple having sex in a theater during a matinée, the sister with a strange man. The film contributed to the general impression that Scandinavian cinema dealt with sexual themes in a daring manner—an impression reinforced by Denmark's 1969 abolition of laws against pornography—which remains in force today (despite the fact that global pornographic film production has long been dominated by the United States). Danish pornography quickly disappeared again, but the myth of Scandinavia as a haven for pornography exists to this day.

In the 1960s, a new generation of young Swedish filmmakers inspired by the New Wave arrived on the scene. Just as François Truffaut had attacked the so-called tradition of quality in established French cinema in his early articles in *Les Cahiers du cinéma*, so the young Bo Widerberg (1930–97), who together with Jan Troell (b. 1931) was the most important new filmmaker, published a pamphlet in 1962 in which he assailed the state of Swedish cinema in general, and in particular its father figure, Bergman. Widerberg criticized Bergman for being out of touch with the social realities of everyday life, instead using his artistic talent to contemplate religious themes: 'A lost God, a lost wild strawberry patch, a lost summer, are, of course, motives for filmmaking. But I think that this private nostalgia, if allowed to become a trend, is dangerous for the development of Swedish cinema' (Widerberg 1962: 31). Throughout the decade the new generation made their mark. Widerberg made *Kvarteret Korpen* (*Raven's End*, 1963), an intense and lyrical description of growing up in the poor neighborhoods of Malmö during the 1930s, and—alongside the romantic love story *Elvira Madigan* (1967)—politically engaged films such as *Ådalen 31* (*The Adalen Riots*, 1970), dealing with an incident that led to a change in Swedish politics, and the American *Joe Hill* (1971) about the life of the legendary labor leader. Jan Troell made *Här har du ditt liv* (*Here Is Your Life*, 1966), based on Nobel prize winner Eyvind Johnson's novel quartet about childhood and youth in northern Sweden at the beginning of the twentieth century, followed by the epic saga of Swedish emigration to the United States during the late 1800s, based on Vilhelm Moberg's popular novels *Utvandrarna* (*The Emigrants*, 1971) and *Nybyggarna* (*The Immigrants*, 1972), and featuring two of Bergman's favorite actors, Max von Sydow and Liv Ullmann.

While the young directors eventually approached historical subjects and themes not far from Bergman's, Bergman himself experimented with new forms of cinematic expression. His next films depart from religious themes, focusing more on the plight of the artist.

In *Persona* (1966), told in a style that disrupts and deconstructs the narration, an actress (Liv Ullmann, the Norwegian actress who would be Bergman's companion over the next years) suddenly ceases to speak. As part of her treatment, a psychiatrist moves her—together with a young nurse—to a summer cottage on an isolated island (shot on Fårö, close to Gotland, where Bergman has lived since the 1960s). Gradually, the two women merge with one another, and finally, in a disturbing shot, the two faces melt together. The film uses Brechtian *Verfremdung* (estrangement, or critical detachment) with interruptions where we see the film projector, and the film losing focus, melting, and spilling out of the machine. In this way it is also a film about Cinematography (the working title). Here it is the middle-aged Bergman, rather than the young directors, joining the international modernist search for a new form of cinematic expression, alongside Antonioni, Resnais, and Godard.

In *Vargtimmen* (*Hour of the Wolf*, 1968), a painter (Max von Sydow) moves to a small island with his pregnant wife (Liv Ullmann, who at the time was pregnant with Bergman's daughter Linn, later to become a successful novelist). Here the painter finds himself not only tormented by the hypocritical upper classes of the local estate (who admire his art but also take pleasure in humiliating him) but also tempted by an ex-mistress and haunted by demons.

Skammen (*The Shame*, 1968) can be viewed as a response to the criticism of Bergman's lack of involvement with political issues. It is a story of a small society plagued by war but, typically for Bergman, presented as an abstract and mysterious phenomenon, without political analysis, only as the cruel events that befall the population. Two musicians, played by Max von Sydow and Liv Ullmann, are drawn into the turmoil of events, and we watch as he becomes increasingly cynical and egoistic while she remains good and altruistic.

After *Riten* (*The Rite*, 1969), *En Passion* (*The Passion of Anna*, 1969), and *Beröringen* (*The Touch*, 1970), all bitter and cruel stories from the marital trenches, Bergman created

■ Liv Ullmann (1938–)

Liv Ullmann started in Norwegian film in the 1950s and became Bergman's female star in the years 1966–78, where they made masterpieces such as *Persona*, *Cries and Whispers*, and *Autumn Sonata* as well as the TV series *Scenes from a Marriage*. The Bergman roles that showed her great emotional range and humane expressivity lead to international fame and a rather mixed group of British and American films such as *Pope Joan* (Michael Anderson, 1972), *Lost Horizon* (Charles Jarrott, 1973), *Forty Carats* (Milton Katselas, 1973), and *A Bridge Too Far* (Richard Attenborough, 1977). In later years, she has turned director, starting with two historical dramas of women's fates. *Sofie* (1992), made in Denmark, is a melancholic story of a Jewish woman in the late 1800s; the epic *Kristin Lavransdatter* (1995), made in Norway and based on the novel by Nobel Prize winner Sigrid Undset, is a love story, set in medieval Norway, about the pure and religious Kristin's controversial love for the reckless knight Erlend. Ullmann had an international success with *Trolösa* (*Faithless*, 2000), a bitter infidelity drama, based on a script by Bergman. She returned to acting in a last film with Bergman, *Saraband* (2003), where Johan and Marianne from *Scenes from a Marriage* meet again after 30 years. Liv Ullmann has published two autobiographical books, *Changing* (1977) and *Choices* (1984).

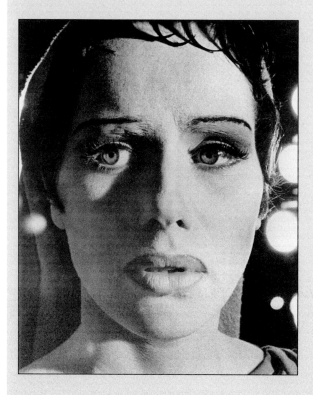

↩ *Persona*

a new masterpiece with *Viskningar och rop* (*Cries and Whispers*, 1972), his first major film in color. The story of three sisters who meet at a country estate sometime in the early 1900s, is told with the color red as the dominant stylistic element (the sequences also fade out in red). The unmarried Agnes (Harriet Andersson) is dying of cancer, and we learn of the marriages of the two other sisters, one of whom (Ingrid Thulin) lives in a cold relationship with her husband—at one time she cuts her vagina with a piece of glass in order to prevent him from having intercourse with her—while the other sister (Liv Ullmann) has an affair with the house doctor, driving her husband to try to kill himself with a knife when he discovers her infidelity. Agnes finally dies a horrible death, but awakes again in the night. The dead sister goes from door to door, seeking comfort, but her sisters refuse to let her in. Eventually she finds succor in the nursemaid, who takes her to her bosom in a Pietà scene.

Bergman's later career

Bergman's ensuing work was a six-part TV series, *Scener från ett äktenskap* (*Scenes from a Marriage*, 1973), released in several countries in a shorter cinema version. The story of a married couple, played by Erland Josephson and Liv Ullmann, who split up, find new partners, and sporadically get together again, met with enormous success in Scandinavia, where it was a popular breakthrough for Bergman, who had generally been seen as a rather elitist filmmaker. He also made the charming and colorful *Trollflöjtan* (*The Magic Flute*, 1975), based on Mozart's opera.

The following years were marked by crisis. One day in the autumn of 1976, in the midst of a rehearsal at the Dramaten in Stockholm, the Swedish police arrested Bergman on suspicion of tax evasion and fraud. He was later cleared of all charges (and some high-ranking tax officials were fired), but the incident had a traumatic impact on him. He left Sweden in anger, and after a time settled in Munich, Germany. During the succeeding years he made *The Serpent's Egg* (1977), shot in Germany in English, a story set at the time of the emergence of Nazism (Bergman had spent a summer as a teenager in Nazi Germany in 1934). In Norway, he shot *Höstsonaten* (*Autumn Sonata*, 1978), an intense psychological mother/daughter drama with Ingrid Bergman (no relation of his), as a world-renowned pianist and Liv Ullmann as her neglected daughter. He also made the cruel marital and crime drama *Aus dem Leben der Marionetten* (*From the Life of the Marionettes,* 1980), shot in German.

Ultimately, Bergman was exonerated, and returned to Sweden and Swedish film with the Oscar-winning *Fanny och Alexander* (*Fanny and Alexander*, 1982). This monumental three-hour film (also made in a five-hour version for television) was the epitome of his work, the embodiment of all his art, his themes, and his work with actors. It is a magical story, which takes place early in the 1900s, of two children growing up in the world of theater, who suddenly, after their father's death and their mother's remarriage to a stern bishop, find themselves prisoners in a tyrannical household, eventually rescued by the occult powers of a Jewish antique dealer and the mysterious Ismaël.

Since then, he has made a number of TV films such as *Efter repetitionen* (*After the rehearsal*, 1984) and *Larmar och gör sig till* (*In the Presence of a Clown*, 1997), about a mental patient who dreams of inventing sound film in 1925. He also wrote his autobiography, *Laterna Magica* (*The Magic Lantern*, 1987), in which he offers us a merciless view of his artistic and personal life, giving credence to Henrik Ibsen's famous dictum that 'to write is to make judgment over one's self'. He has also written scripts for other filmmakers, such as *Den goda viljan* (*The Good Will*, 1990–91), the story of Bergman's parents, directed by the Danish director Bille August; *Söndagsbarn* (*Sunday's Children*, 1992), about Bergman's relationship with his father, which was directed by his son, Daniel Bergman; and more recently, *Trolösa* (*Faithless*, 2000), a story of marital infidelity, directed by Liv Ullmann.

For more than half a century Bergman has been a leading figure in Scandinavian culture. He is one of the world's most profound filmmakers and he has given Swedish cinema respectability and elevated its cultural standards. Looking back on his career, he has said: 'Today I feel that in *Persona*—and later in *Cries and Whispers*—I had gone as far as I could go. In these two instances, when working in total freedom, I touched wordless secrets that only the cinema can discover' (Bergman 1994: 65).

Conclusion

During its hundred-year history, Scandinavian cinema has alternated between domestic film culture marked by provincial scope and moments of greatness that stand out in the history of film art. Bergman, now in his 80s, is still a presence in Swedish culture. He has directed a new film, announced as his last, the TV production *Saraband* (2003), that continues *Scenes from a Marriage* with Erland Josephson and Liv Ullmann thirty years later. Dreyer's spirit has also continued to wield its influence. His uncompromising art and deliberate distance from the conventions and norms of Danish style and approach would serve as inspiration to (among others) Lars von Trier, the most original talent of a new generation of Danish filmmakers. In the midst of the considerable attention that Scandinavian cinema has recently attracted, most notably with von Trier's Dogme 95 movement, it is clear that Bergman and Dreyer still remain as the classical masters, whose influence lives on in the work of new generations.

Further reading

Bergman, Ingmar, *The Magic Lantern* (New York: Viking, 1988). Bergman's memoirs.

—— *Bergman on Bergman* (New York: DaCapo, 1993 [1973]). Bergman discusses his films with leading Swedish critics.

—— *Images: My Life in Film* (New York: Arcade, 1994). Bergman's own commentary on his films.

Bordwell, David, *The Films of Carl-Theodor Dreyer* (Berkeley: University of California Press, 1981). A stylistic analysis of Dreyer's films.

Dreyer, Carl, *Four Screenplays* (London: Thames & Hudson, 1970). The manuscripts for *Joan of Arc*, *Vampire*, *Day of Wrath*, and *The Word*.

—— *Dreyer in Double Reflection* (New York: Dutton, 1973). An annotated collection of Dreyer's essays on film.

Drum, Jean, and Dale D. Drum, *My Only Great Passion: The Life and Films of Carl Th. Dreyer* (Lanham, Md.: Scarecrow, 2000). Dreyer's life and work.

Gado, Frank, *The Passion of Ingmar Bergman* (Durham, NC: Duke University Press, 1986). An interpretation of Bergman's films.

Steene, Birgitta, *Ingmar Bergman: A Guide to References and Resources* (Boston: G. K. Hall, 1987). A useful bibliography of Bergman literature.

THE FRENCH NEW WAVE

T. Jefferson Kline

An artistic wave, like the works of art which compose it, is not a 'substance' around a definable 'essence', but a response to pressures and influences converging from many different 'layers' of reality—social, political, economic, ideological, artistic and personal.

Raymond Durgnat

The scene is Paris. It is late summer in 1959. Flâneurs along the Champs-Élysées cast nervous sidelong glances at a handsome young couple ambling down the boulevard, preceded by a laundry cart, shrouded on three sides by curtains. Hiding in this improvised tracking truck, the young Raoul Coutard aims a hand-held Cameflex camera at the couple. No battery of floodlights illuminates this scene, shot in what Jacques Rozier was to dub 'tournage à la sauvette' (shooting on the run), because Coutard has discovered that 18-m lengths of highly sensitive Hilford HPS film can be spliced together into reels of 120 meters—enough to capture a sequence of this film. When night falls on the City of Light, shooting will continue, still without floods, because Coutard has worked out a special emulsion at the nearby GTC labs, creating a degree of sensitivity equivalent to an 800 ASA reading, thus enabling him to record images without a lot of light. Jean-Luc Godard has begun, in this single dramatic endeavor, his surreptitious pursuit of Jean-Paul Belmondo (alias Laslo Kovacs, car thief) and his full frontal assault on the bastion of the

French film industry. The result will be *A bout de souffle* (*Breathless*), a film that was to change forever the way we think about cinema.

What had driven Godard, Coutard, Belmondo, and Jean Seberg into the streets, freely inventing both story and film technology as they went? What allowed Godard to spend his nights writing notes for the next day's shooting in utter defiance of the traditions of careful *découpage* (division of scenes into a shooting script) and minutely planned takes and decors? Who would finance such a zany enterprise and why?

The decline of the French film industry after the war

The answers to all of these questions lay in the catastrophic decline of the French film industry after World War II. Following the Occupation, a variety of pressures and influences converged to devastate a war-weakened institution. Perhaps the greatest of these threats came from within the industry itself. For years, films had been shot at the great studios surrounding Paris, and at the Liberation there were still fifteen studios in operation, principally at Billancourt and Boulogne. Indeed, it was perhaps prophetic that the studios at Montreuil, built in the 1920s, were called 'Albatros', for the studio system of the late 1940s hung around the necks of its practitioners like Coleridge's omen of disaster. Shooting in studios required enormous and elaborate sets, crowds of extras (who had their own labor union), complicated technologies of lighting, and sufficient expertise in management to coordinate this vast division of labor. Not surprisingly it was the producers, not the film directors, who were the ultimate arbiters on the set. Nor was it a secret that the training for such work required certification by the prestigious IDHEC (Institut des Hautes Études Cinématographiques, the national film school), followed by long years as an apprentice spent learning the 'craft' at the feet of established directors and cameramen. Given the expense of every detail, and the authority of the producer, film directors were considered principally technicians, slaves to commercial efficiency rather than masters of style. Their job was to provide beautiful images, with high production values to illustrate the screenplays approved by the producers. Directorial debuts were usually made after the age of forty and usually well after any spark of creativity had been carefully replaced by adherence to convention and academic tradition. Innovation and risk were the last things on the producers' minds, who sought instead tried and true formulas and imitation of what already 'worked'.

It didn't help matters that the industry was reeling financially after the war. Nor did the government's attempt to intervene really help. By signing the Blum–Byrnes accords of 1946, supposedly designed to put the French cinema back on its feet, the government guaranteed French films exclusivity a mere sixteen weeks a year. That left thirty-six weeks open to a steady influx of Hollywood films. Nor did increasing the French share to twenty weeks in 1948 make matters much better. By that time, the industry had settled on the solution of trying to compete with Hollywood with a series of movies that had an 'international' appeal, strong production values, well-known stars, and, generally, a highly mannered style removed from everyday reality. This taste for convention and artificiality was also likely spurred by the belief that audiences preferred to turn away from the harsh reality of postwar France and unwelcome memories of the Occupation. Thus, far from portraying the culture and concerns of their audiences, screenwriters turned increasingly to adaptations of classic novels to help their audiences escape from the realities of the day. Films like René Clair's *Les grandes manœuvres* (*The Grand Maneuver*, 1955), Clouzot's *Le Salaire de la peur* (*The Wages of Fear*, 1953) and Autant-Lara's *Le Rouge et le noir* (*The Red and the Black*, 1954) emanated from a belief that cinema was nothing more than an elaborate way of illustrating a story, whose clever dialogue displayed a kind of cynical one-upmanship of the kind later foregrounded in Patrice Leconte's *Ridicule* (1996). Indeed, the studio system increasingly resembled a morose vision of Louis XVI's court, where producer and favored screenwriters were kings and chosen counselors and there prevailed what Jean Douchet (1999: 31) calls a form of 'congenital despair', and what Cédric Anger (in de Baecque and Tesson 1998: 20) terms 'une plastique du malheur' (the malleable art of unhappiness). French cinema had become the obsequious handmaiden of screenwriters like Jean Aurenche and Pierre Bost, whose 'genius' as Eric Rohmer was to say, lay in a 'duty-bound use of the legacy of their precursors and a familiarity with all the ways that, by some kind of conditioned reflex, particular emotional reactions could be provoked in the audience' (Hillier 1985: 205).

Two fathers of the New Wave: Langlois and Bazin

Thoroughly disenchanted with what they were to term 'le cinéma de papa' (Dad's cinema) or 'la tradition de qualité' (the tradition of quality), a small but very vocal group of critics began in the early 1950s the work of sapping the foundations of this tottering edifice. Jean-Luc Godard, François Truffaut, Jacques Rivette, Jacques Doniol Valcroze, and Claude Chabrol had been trained not at the IDHEC but at the Cinématheque, and their professsors were not skilled technicians but two deeply thoughtful amateurs of the seventh art, Henri Langlois and André Bazin. Since 1936 Langlois had been collecting, archiving, and showing rare and classic films from the world over at the Cinémathèque. Truffaut, Godard, Rivette, and their companions became regular visitors to Langlois's screenings beginning in 1949. Langlois's unusual approach to programming was to have

POSTWAR CINEMA

a formative effect on these young cinephiles, for he frequently grouped together silent films, and films from different countries, genres and periods, many of which had no French subtitles. The desired effect, he was to argue, was that his viewers learned to make connections between many different national styles and had to rely for their viewing pleasure on the purely visual aspects of the films (the 'how') rather than on conventional storytelling (the 'what'). Thus Langlois could legitimately claim to have taught an entire generation of French directors how to see a film. Langlois's pedagogy was complemented by Bazin's. The latter had begun writing serious film criticism in the 1940s, and, from 1946 to 1949 had published several major theoretical statements on film in Jean-Georges Auriol's *La Revue du cinema*. In March of 1948 Auriol also published Alexandre Astruc's hugely influential 'Naissance d'une nouvelle avant-garde: la caméra stylo' (Birth of a new avant-garde: the camera-pen), in which Astruc claimed that, far from being a mere slave of the concretely visual, 'the camera could become a means of writing as supple and as subtle as written language and the cinema could truly make itself the expression of thought'. Bazin took up this idea in his 'L'Evolution du langage cinématographique' (The evolution of film language), in which he focused on the notion of cinematic language as the chief object of the critic's concern.

When Auriol died in a car accident in 1950, *La Revue du cinema* failed and Bazin was forced to find other outlets for his energies. He first founded Objectif49, a ciné-club that showed new films and invited directors to speak about their work, among them Orson Welles, Roberto Rossellini, and Jean Renoir. Frustrated with the tradition-bound selections at Cannes, Objectif49 also sponsored a 'Festival du film maudit' (Festival of condemned films) at Biarritz (no doubt hoping to restage the crucial lift given to Impressionism in painting by the Salon des Refusés (Rejects' Exhibition) of 1874). At Biarritz, Jean Vigo's *L'Atalante* (1934) and Jean Renoir's *The Southerner* (1945) were viewed for the first time. After the second attempt at a 'Festival du maudit' failed, Bazin, Lo Duca, and Jacques Doniol Valcroze turned to Leonid Keigel to secure funding for a new journal baptized *Les Cahiers du cinéma*, whose first issue appeared in April 1951.

The founding of *Les Cahiers du cinéma*

Bazin's influence on the future of French cinema cannot be overstated: not only did he help found *Cahiers* and set the tone for serious film criticism, but he marshalled the troops who were to make the assault on the bastion of cinematic tradition. Bazin met the 16-year-old François Truffaut at his film club, and not only twice bailed him out of serious trouble (including a heroic effort to have him released from a military prison in 1951 after he was arrested for desertion) but virtually adopted him at his home at Bry sur Marne.

Truffaut then introduced Bazin to Godard, Chabrol, and Rivette, and the troops were assembled for battle. Indeed, one could almost date the birth of the New Wave from the November 1953 issue of *Cahiers*, which included articles by Rivette, Truffaut, and Chabrol. Under Bazin's leadership, *Cahiers* adopted a strategy of refusing to review the standard French fare, articulating a new aesthetic and standard for film criticism, highlighting experimental cinema and introducing the best international filmmakers to the French public. Bazin had also propounded a belief in the relationship between film technique and metaphysics, and convinced the younger contributors to *Cahiers* that a film's meaning should be sought in its formal structure.

This belief that cinema was an art (i.e., the product of individual genius and a particular sensibility, and not merely an industry), capable of rendering a metaphysical meaning in its own specifically cinematic language, was to become the rallying cry around which *Cahiers* would organize its *politique des auteurs* (*auteur* policy) and, consequently, its attacks on *la tradition de qualité*. And, although Bazin had discovered these qualities in Robert Bresson, a highly individualistic and independent director, his younger colleagues immediately applied his ideas to directors whom we might today consider the antithesis of Bresson. Jacques Rivette proclaims 'the genius of Howard Hawks, a director of intelligence and precision, the only American director who knows how to draw a moral' (*Cahiers* 23, May 1953). François Truffaut lauds David Miller and compares his films to those of Bresson (*Cahiers* 21, March 1953), but is not content merely to praise the American.

From the moment of his arrival at *Cahiers*, Truffaut displays an almost obsessive hostility to the French film industry, so much so that the editors hesitate to invite him into their midst. It is not enough to applaud American directors like Miller; Truffaut castigates French film as nothing more than 'three hundred continuity shots stuck together a hundred and ten times a year' (Andrew 1978: 184–5). Despite a flurry of requests to the *Cahiers* editors to rein him in, Truffaut's venom was to reach its apogee in his now famous 'Une certaine tendance du cinéma français' ('A Certain tendency within French cinema', *Cahiers* 34, January 1954). If the cinema was reborn after the war in the Poetic Realism of films like *Quai des brumes*, Truffaut argues, it died again when Claude Autant-Lara, Jean Delannoy, René Clément, and Yves Allégret, and their screenwriters Jean Aurench and Pierre Bost, replaced Poetic Realism with 'psychological realism'. These perpetrators of *la tradition de qualité*, Truffaut rants,

aim at realism [but] always destroy it at the very moment of capturing it, so concerned are they to lock up their actors in a closed world, barricaded by formulas, by puns and maxims, rather then letting them show themselves as they are . . . This so-called superiority of the authors over their characters turns them into infinitely grotesque [beings].

Opposed to these 'villains', Truffaut proclaims, there are a few cineastes with vision: Jean Renoir, Robert Bresson, Jean Cocteau, Jacques Becker, Abel Gance, Max Ophüls, Jacques Tati, and Jacques Leenhardt—who by a 'curious coincidence . . . are *auteurs* who often write their own dialogue and . . . even invent the stories they film' (Truffaut 1987: 233).* And if it isn't already clear that this is a war, Truffaut trumpets, 'I do not believe in the peaceful coexistence of *la tradition de qualité* and a cinema of *auteurs*' (1987: 225–6).

Auteur politics

That Truffaut is supported in this onslaught by his fellow 'young Turks' is obvious, for, in his first short film, *Tous les garçons s'apellent Patrick* (*All the Boys Are Called Patrick*, 1959), Godard will insert a shot of himself filmed next to his young heroine in a café reading an issue of *Arts* that sports in huge type the headline to Truffaut's other famous barrage: 'LE CINEMA FRANÇAIS CREVE SOUS LES FAUSSES LEGENDES' (French cinema is collapsing beneath the weight of false legends). In this essay Truffaut refines his idea of the *auteur*:

We could declare quite simply that, contrary to what has been written in histories of film, contrary to statements made by film directors themselves, a film is no more a question of teamwork than a novel, a poem, a symphony, or a painting. The great directors, Jean Renoir, Roberto Rossellini, Alfred Hitchcock, Max Ophüls, Robert Bresson, and many others, themselves write the films they shoot. Even if they are inspired by a novel, a play, a true story, the point of departure is merely a pretext. A filmmaker is not a writer, he thinks in images, in terms of *mise-en-scène*, and writing things down bores him. (Truffaut 1987: 234–5)

Truffaut goes on to codify what was to become the founding justification for the *politique des auteurs*:

I don't believe in good or bad films, I believe in good and bad directors . . . A director [*metteur en scène*] possesses a style that you find in all of his films and this is true of the worst filmmakers and their worst films. The differences from one film to the next, a more ingenious screenplay, better photography, whatever they may be, have but little importance, for these differences are most often due to external factors, more or less financing, more or less time for shooting. The essential thing is that an intelligent and gifted director remains intelligent and gifted no matter what film he makes. I am a partisan of judging (when it comes time to judge) not films but filmmakers. I will never like a film by Delannoy. I will always like a film by Renoir. (Truffaut 1987: 247)

There has never been a more forthright and succinct statement of auteur politics. With this highly romanticized notion of creative genius, Truffaut accomplishes two major

* All translations from works in French quoted here are mine.—*TJK*

objectives: he establishes personal style (*mise-en-scène*) as the sole criterion of aesthetic judgment, and he elevates himself (and his cohorts at *Cahiers*) as the sole arbiters of admission to the cinematic pantheon. His emphasis on arbitrary (and, indeed, a priori) choices and on personality makes his articulation of the *auteur* less a theory than a politics—nay, a polemics. For the *Cahiers* critics, Autant-Lara was bad; Hitchcock was good. Delannoy was awful, but Nicholas Ray was a genius. Eventually, the exaggeratedly polemical side of auteurism was to cause its originator, André Bazin (among others), to condemn its most glaring abuses and contradictions as a 'hazardous adventure' (*Cahiers* 70, April 1957); but Bazin's reaction glossed over what may have been the most important aspect of *auteur* politics—its articulation of a prolegomena for a new French cinema under the guise of praising Hollywood directors.

And if this new cinema was too pluralistic to have a single *ars poetica*, it nevertheless needed a rallying cry, and François Truffaut provided one:

A film costing 300 million francs must please every possible audience in every country. A film costing 60 million can make a profit in France alone or by touching certain groups in different countries. Tomorrow's film will not be made by camera technicians but by artists for whom shooting a film constitutes a formidable and exalting adventure. Tomorrow's film will resemble its author . . . Tomorrow's film will be an act of love. (*Arts*, 15 May 1957; in Truffaut 1987: 248–9)

This pronouncement derives from two complementary imperatives: *auteur* politics and financial austerity. To gain a foothold in the bastion of French cinema, each of these 'commandos . . . in the front line of battle' (Godard's phrase) had to find a way to make movies for one-fifth to one-tenth of the cost of studio productions. Austerity would in turn dictate the means of production, which in turn would have profound aesthetic implications. Ironically, every budgetary restriction implied an increase in creative liberty. In abandoning the studio, the young directors would be giving up elaborate decors, crowds of extras, established cameramen, scriptwriters, gaffers, continuity people, big stars, and, of course, the well-heeled producers who paid for and organized all of these crowds. By taking to the street to escape the heavy-handed rule of these producers, each became, in his/her own way, a keen observer of everyday life, telling simple tales interpreted by unknown actors whose innocently maladroit gestures were captured by hand-held cameras. Everything about the *tradition de qualité* that had been condemned by the *Cahiers* critics would be abandoned in their first cinematic endeavors as much for financial concerns as for aesthetic ones. Yet by proclaiming an intensely personal cinema, Truffaut guaranteed a community of individual styles and methods rather than a school with a common program.

Program or not, critical dust storm notwithstanding, no school or collection of individuals would likely have emerged for their directorial debuts had the film industry not entered upon increasingly hard times. Between 1958 and 1963, attendance at cinemas throughout France dropped by roughly 100 million, to 290 million. Some producers had begun to question the financial wisdom of backing hugely expensive studio productions that were increasingly running on empty at the box office.

Chabrol seizes the moment

It was in this climate of concern that the young Turks seized the moment. It fell to Claude Chabrol to get things rolling. Chabrol was doubtless inspired by the examples of Jean-Pierre Melville and Agnès Varda, whose films *Le Silence de la mer* (1947) and *La Pointe courte* (1954), respectively, had been produced entirely outside any controls by government or labor unions. Both films had been hailed by the *Cahiers* critics as inspirational breakthroughs against the tight restrictions of the industry. With funds his wife had inherited, Chabrol created his own production company, AJYM (based on his wife's and childrens' initials), borrowed a Gévaert 36 camera, convinced Henri Decae to be his cameraman, and headed off to Sardent to film *Le Beau Serge* (1958). Shot entirely on location over a seven-week period, using relatively unknown actors, a small band of technicians, and a Citroen 2CV for tracking shots, *Le Beau Serge* emerged as a model of low-budget but high-quality film production. Its evocation of life in a small provincial town radiated a sense of authenticity and raw emotional power.

Meanwhile, the French government, concerned by the ever-growing dominance of foreign films, had passed in 1948 *la loi d'aide au cinéma* (the law in aid of cinema), which redistributed to the French film industry monies raised from taxes on all movie houses in France. These monies were directed to filmmakers on condition that they be reinvested in new films. This law was modified in 1953 to include a jury who would award these monies to 'quality' projects'. *Le Beau Serge* was considered to be just the sort of film the Centre National de la Cinématographie (CNC, the body in charge of distributing funds) was looking for. Awarded 35 million francs, Chabrol's film was shown at the Festival de Cannes in 1958, where Edmond Tenoudji saw it and decided to distribute it. Given the austerity of Chabrol's production methods—he economized on sets, makeup, sound, and actors—35 million francs all but paid for his first film, and allowed him to turn immediately to a second project, *Les Cousins* (*The Cousins*, 1959).

Like *Le Beau Serge*, Eric Rohmer's first film, *Le Signe du lion* (1959), contributed to the sense of a group aesthetic, for it was based on a screenplay by Rohmer himself and was filmed primarily in the streets of Paris, as Rohmer and his cameraman, Nicolas Hayer, spent the month of August following Jess Hahn around the French capital. The film has all the raw street feeling of some of the Italian Neorealist works idolized by the *Cahiers* group, and in the main eschews plot lines for a kind of slow documentary recording of the gradual degradation of the main character. Hahn's peregrinations through the different neighborhoods of the capital, including a painful trek on foot from Neuilly to the Ile de la Cité, introduce a theme that was to become, at least momentarily, dear to many of the debuting *Cahiers* filmmakers: an intimate portrait of Paris. This was a direct challenge to the *tradition de qualité* filmmakers, who had created what C. Anger (de Baecque and Tesson 1998: 20) calls 'a décor for seduction and gallantry' out of their studio versions of the city.

Truffaut: from pariah to prince of Cannes

Like Chabrol, Truffaut did not sit idly by waiting for his chance, and, like his colleague, he used family money to found his own production company, Les Films du Carrosse (a title that pays homage to Renoir's *Carrosse d'or* (*The Golden Coach*, 1952)). François Truffaut had met Madeleine Morgenstern in the summer of 1956 and, the following year, convinced his future father-in-law, Ignace, to help find backing for his first film. When Ignace Morgenstern informed his daughter's impetuous friend that he'd lined up 'a mere' two million francs, Truffaut was forced to abandon his dreams of a full-length feature and turn to a short subject, *Les Mistons* (*The Mischief Makers*, 1957), based on a story by Maurice Pons (whose expenses-paid visit to the set ate up one-eighth of the film's entire budget). After another 'anonymous' financial intervention by Ignace Morgenstern, the film was completed and shown at the Festival de Tours in November 1957, and went on to garner prizes at the Brussels and Mannheim film festivals and a Blue Ribbon award in the US. Ironically, however, the success of this first effort did not carry over to Cannes, for Truffaut's harsh criticisms of the Cannes choices and jury resulted in his expulsion from the festival in 1958. Furious, Truffaut wrote, 'I'm going to toss off a thing so sincere that it will scream with truth and be formidably powerful; I'm going to show them that truth pays and that my truth is the only truth!' (*Arts* 652). And so he would!

Unable to attract the support of Pierre Braunberger, one of the more adventurous film producers around, Truffaut went back to his father-in-law to finance his next film, a bit reluctantly to be sure, since the older man was the producer of such super-productions as Henri Verneuil's *La Vâche et le prisonnier* (*The Cow and I*, 1959), starring Fernandel—exactly the kind of film most reviled by the *Cahiers* critics. The first step in the making of *Les Quatre cents coups* (*The 400 Blows*, 1959) was to audition for a young actor to play the lead role. When Truffaut saw Jean-Pierre Léaud, he was astonished by the instinctive tension projected by this street urchin, and the collaboration that was to last until Truffaut's death in 1984 was launched. Léaud was perfect for the semi-autobiographical,

↑ *Les Quatre cents Coups*

low-budget project since he came from socially disadvantaged conditions similar to those Truffaut had known as a child, and was obviously untrained in the 'art' of acting.

Shooting began in November 1958 in a little sixth-floor apartment in the rue Marcadet in Paris, and from there spilled out into the place Clichy, where Truffaut had spent his own youth. Much of the dialogue of the film was unrehearsed; indeed, Truffaut shot the scene in the correctional facility where Antoine is interviewed at length by a 'spychologist' with no prepared text at all. No counter-shots of the psychologist were included in the original take, and the result was so stunning that Truffaut decided to include it in the film without any cuts or traditional counter-shots. For the end of the film, Truffaut followed Léaud out onto a beach in a makeshift truck cut down for the purpose, Henri Decae perched precariously on the hood with his Cameflex barely secured. After years of a steady diet of artificial and academic studio productions, the French New Wave shot as if with a 'candid' camera. Real apartments and the city of Paris provided the sets, and the only actors in the film turned out to be cameo walk-ons by Jean-Claude Brialy and Jeanne Moreau, who happened to be in the neighborhood. Almost in spite of themselves, the critics found

Les Quatre cents coups to be every bit as 'true' as Truffaut had angrily promised only a year previously. The film's selection as the French representative to the Cannes festival was sweet revenge indeed—Truffaut had gone from pariah to prince faster than a frog in a fairy tale. His victory was to be compromised however, by the death of his adoptive father, André Bazin, who succumbed to leukemia only one week after shooting had begun. In gratitude, Truffaut dedicated his film to the founder and intellectual leader of *Les Cahiers du cinéma*, and *auteur*, in the deepest sense, of the *nouvelle vague*.

The New Wave is christened

By the opening of the Cannes Festival in 1959, the inchoate movement that was surely not yet a movement had been officially baptized 'La nouvelle vague' by Pierre Billard in Cinema58. Billard was reacting in part to the numbers of directors making their first films. Measured purely in numbers of new directors, the industry peaked in 1958. Whereas the number of films made by new directors had averaged sixteen between 1950 and 1958, that average more than doubled (to thirty-three) over the following four years. Indeed, the press had long been busy preparing the way. In October 1957, Françoise Giroud launched a series of articles in *L'Express* entitled 'La nouvelle vague', in which she examined the sociology of youth culture in France—this well before anyone thought to apply the phrase to the emergent cinema. As if to bear witness to the reality of the term, Marcel Camus's *Orfeu Negro* (*Black Orpheus*, 1959) carried off the golden palms at the festival; Alain Resnais's *Hiroshima mon amour* (1959) was to have represented France, but was pulled at the last minute for political reasons. Indeed, Resnais's 'Left Bank school', which included Chris Marker and Agnès Varda, had, unlike the *Cahiers* group, taken a much more politically engaged stance towards new filmmaking. Despite its withdrawal, Resnais's *Hiroshima mon amour* created an explosion of its own for its remarkable experiments with film time and memory, and its radical questioning of all recognizable cinematic discourses and continuity. Resnais spoke of creating a new form of reading, offering the spectator as much freedom of imagination as the reader of a novel. Godard promptly proclaimed *Hiroshima* 'the end of a certain kind of cinema', a gesture that helped generate the belief that something radically new had happened.

Adding to this myth of the New Wave, seventeen promising new directors organized a colloquium at La Napoule in Cannes to affirm their opposition to the industry's status quo, while *Arts* dedicated its entire fall issue to this 'event'. The participants, captured in a publicity photo, included Truffaut, Roger Vadim, Claude Chabrol, Jacques Doniol-Valcroze, Jacques Rozier, and, hidden as always behind his dark glasses, the young Jean-Luc Godard. But if they obligingly produced a joint statement for the eager press, they could agree only on vague general principles: they encountered 'un désaccord total sur le détail' (complete disagreement on the details) (*Arts*, June 1959).

Indeed, when *Le Monde* published a survey in August of 1959, asking 'Does the New Wave exist?', Claude Chabrol, Georges Franju, Louis Malle, Roger Vadim, and several others bluntly answered: no. For his part, Chabrol suspected that the New Wave label was merely a Gaullist publicity stunt equating de Gaulle with renewal, and shamelessly marketing the young directors like a brand of soap. On the other hand, Edgar Morin's survey of the 'New Wave' (*Communication*, June 1961) concluded not only that the New Wave films were responsible for attacking the sclerotic, crisis-riddled French film industry, but that they also shared common tendencies, such as unaltruistic heroes, and themes, such as the perils of love. Morin's approach to 'understanding' this 'wave' is extremely telling, for his very question about themes and heroes tells us that French film criticism was still, in the main, mired in literary models, unable to appreciate film as film, unable to address the real changes that were taking place. André Bazin's question 'What is cinema?' and his insistence on analysis of *mise en scène* and the specific language of film remained well outside the ken of most film critics. In general, criticism had not caught up with cinematic practice. This might well explain why, when queried about a 'New Wave', and ill-equipped to evaluate it in purely cinematic terms, many critics and filmmakers of the time failed to see anything novel. And yet, from our present perspective, if there is anything other than statistics that defines the 'New Wave', it is the revolution in film practice that would eventually cause a concomitant sea change in writing about film that would, in turn, allow us to appreciate what was new in the 'New Wave'. The other explanation for the general confusion about the label is that the film which, more than any other, exemplifies the New Wave had yet to be made.

Godard joins the fray

If Jean-Luc Godard appeared in the photo at La Napoule, it was because his low-budget short subject *Tous les garçons s'appellent Patrick* had included a homage to Truffaut's vitriolic attack on the French film industry in *Arts*. Godard's major contribution to the 'Wave' began only after the dust of Cannes 1959 had settled; yet it is safe to say that no other single film exemplifies what is new in the New Wave as completely as *A bout de souffle* (*Breathless*, 1959).

Godard had grown up in a well-to-do French family (a fact that always surprises one since he generally looks, as Françoise Giroud said, as if he'd just stepped off an overnight train trip spent in a third-class compartment). A candidate for a graduate degree in literature at the University of Grenoble, he grew restless with traditional education and left Grenoble (as well, he claims, as walking out of the entrance exam to IDHEC, though in fact the school rejected him). Rejected also by his grandfather after raiding the family safe, Godard discovered an adoptive uncle in Henri Langlois at the Paris Cinémathèque, and both a new home at *Cahiers* and a new social circle, who gathered at the journal's headquarters every night after the cinemas emptied. An avid fan of American films, Godard saved enough money to finance his first short, *Opération Béton* (*Operation Concrete*, 1954), a documentary about the construction of a dam which the construction company ended up purchasing. The decisive moment in Godard's film career came when the director Marc Allégret introduced him to Pierre Braunberger, a young producer who was eager to assume the risks of financing interesting low-budget films. Braunberger agreed to finance *Tous les garcons s'appellent Parick*, and Godard's career was launched. Indeed, because of the proven success of *Le Beau Serge*, *Les Cousins* and *Les Quatre cents coups*, producers suddenly saw small, low-budget films as having significant enough economic potential to gamble on other new directors. In addition to Braunberger, Georges Beauregard had become a friend of the *Cahiers* group because of his early support of Jean Renoir, and Anatole Daumann (who was to produce most of Resnais's early successes) made the significant financial contributions necessary to launch several other new directors.

Godard met Beauregard while working as a press agent at Fox, and immediately got the producer's attention by castigating the film Beauregard had just produced. Beauregard's reaction was to ask Godard to write a screenplay of *Han d'Islande*, but Godard, unable to complete the assigment, asked Truffaut for his screenplay, *A bout de souffle*. Truffaut had written this story as a sequel to the life of Antoine Doinelle of *Les Quatre cents coups*, but later abandoned the project. When Godard approached Jean-Paul Belmondo in a café near St Germain des Prés about a role in his film, Belmondo was so confused by Godard's demeanor that he initially thought he was being approached for other reasons.

When shooting began, Godard would write the day's *découpage* or shooting script while at breakfast, and, arriving at the set, pull a few greasy pages out of his pockets and distribute them to the cast. The two concerns that had most preoccupied Godard as a film critic—the documentary aspect of filming and the invention of a pure cinema—quickly came to the fore in this project. As Godard would say, he wanted to film life—to discover life in film, and discover film in life—so that cinematic images would function as lingering traces of life. His approach to filming *A bout de souffle* was that of a man discovering an art form as if for the first time. It was no coincidence that, when Godard later spoke in praise of Henri Langlois at the Cinémathèque, he began by an eloquent homage to the Lumière brothers' first documentary films of Paris.

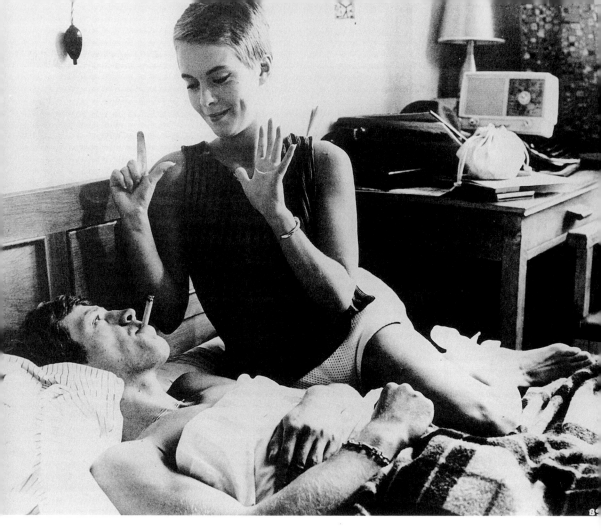

↑ *A bout de souffle*

Certainly everyone around him had the uneasy impression that Godard was making it up as he went, and as he himself wrote to Pierre Braunberger:

We are really shooting on a day-to-day basis. I write the scenes while breakfasting at Dupont Montparnasse. When we view the rushes, the entire team, including the cameraman, find the photography awful [literally, *dégueulasse*, the word Jean Seberg addresses to the dying Michel Poiccard at the conclusion of the film]. But I like it. The important thing is not that things are filmed in such and such a way, but simply that they get filmed, and that they're not out of focus. My biggest job is to keep the technical crew as far as possible from the place we're shooting (Douin 1989: 19–20).

For a month, Godard pushed Raoul Coutard around Paris in a cart, as the latter, using a hand-held camera, captured Belmondo and Seberg on film especially designed for this outdoor project. And for every car that Belmondo steals in Godard's film, Godard himself breaks a fundamental rule of cinema 'grammar'. In the first five-minute segment of the film, Godard will break the 180-degree sight-line rule and will make jump-cuts within a scene. Shifting back and forth between the back and passenger seats of the car, Coutard's nervous, subjective manipulation of the camera makes us acutely conscious of his presence there; indeed, a second camera shot of the passing car reveals him 'hiding' in the back seat. Just as Michel Poiccard, Belmondo's character, improvises his every next infraction of the law, Godard improvises an aesthetic rebellion along with him. But both director and actor make their allegiance to Hollywood (and not the French film industry) a point of honor: Belmondo poses beside movie publicity shots of Humphrey Bogart and imitates his mannerisms, while Godard makes a Hitchcock-like cameo appearance to finger his gangster to the cops and hasten the genre-dictated death of his hero. Both allusions are followed by iris fade-outs to 'signal' their homage to film history.

As if in anticipation of the wholly discontinuous approach to editing he would adopt beginning with *Pierrot le fou* (1965), Godard edited his film without the usual academic concerns for story continuity. Thus, the gendarme is seen already crumpling to the ground before we hear the shot that kills him. Dialogues are cut without regard to rules of shot countershot grammar, and scenes are pasted together without the usual narrative justification. As Godard tells it, because he committed the error every first-time director makes of creating a film 100 per cent too long, he had to cut 'indiscriminately' to get the film reduced to an acceptable length.

The question that arises repeatedly for the viewer of this film is not, 'What will happen?'—for, as Godard himself explained, the rules of the genre dictated that the hero must die. Rather, the question that returns insistently to our consciousness is Bazin's: 'What is cinema?' It is not so much the story (conventional enough by Hollywood standards), nor the characters (for all their existential aimlessness), but precisely the *mise-en-scène* and montage of this work that positions the film as a paragon of New Wave cinema. (For proof of this one has only to compare *A bout de souffle* with Jim McBride's remake, *Breathless* [1982], to appreciate how entirely Hollywood the story and characterizations are when returned to conventional film grammar and editing. McBride so successfully flattens out all of Godard's revolutionary cinematic gestures that the film becomes nothing more than an empty copy of what was already an imitative gesture—albeit a rebellious one.) It is not empty posturing, then, for Godard to claim in 1962: 'As a critic, I already considered myself a cinéaste. Today I still consider myself a critic, and, in this sense, I'm even more of a critic than before. Instead of writing film criticism, I make a film into which I introduce a critical dimension.' It is Godard's proto-Brechtian cinematography as much as any other factor that enables us today to understand just how revolutionary *A bout de souffle* was by highlighting the metacinematic aspect of his

■ The Paradox of New Wave Sound

One of the ironies of the New Wave revolution in technology was that, by adopting hand-held Cameflex cameras to maximize the reality of the street, the young directors deprived themselves of the sounds of the street. Since the hand-held camera's noisy motor made live synchronized recording virtually impossible, Godard would frequently shout his instructions to his actors in the middle of shooting dialogue. In the first five minutes of *A Bout de souffle*, Godard so confuses diegetic and extradiegetic sounds that the spectator can no longer tell the 'real' from the 'imaginary'. At one point, Belmondo fires the gun he has found in the stolen car's glove compartment out the car window, but the 'authentic sound' of gunfire does not match the playful image. In the same sequence, Belmondo will turn and tell the film's audience, 'Allez vous faire foutre!' (Up yours!) in flagrant disregard of the rule that forbids actors from looking (much less speaking) directly at/to the camera.

Most directors opted to re-record sound on-site without the camera motor running, or relied on an on-site tape recorder or note taker. In two cases at least, this search for realism led to bizarre solutions. When Jacques Rozier filmed *Adieu Philippine* (1963), the tape recorder used on the set turned out to be defective and Rozier had to spend five months attempting to lip-read from the film's images what the largely improvised dialogue must have been. Certainly the general tendency of post-sync sound was at odds with the image of the New Wave. But Godard, faced with sound sync limitations, turned the situation to his advantage. While making his short subject *Charlotte et son Jules* (1960), Godard had planned to have Belmondo do the post-sync dialogue but could not afford to pay his actor for the extra work, and so used his own voice instead. As usual, Godard turned carbon into gold: Luc Moullet argues that because of Godard's slightly out-of-sync recording, the whole film takes on a marvelous fantastic quality. Moullet termed this experiment 'a revolutionary approach to cinematic dialogue which renewed the art of filmmaking' (*Cahiers* 106, April 1960). Thereafter, however, Godard tended to film his dialogues with his characters turned away from the camera as much as possible.

film. *A bout de souffle*, significantly enough, would win the Berlin Festival's prize for *mise-en-scène* in 1960. Jean Pierre Melville was to say, 'No New Wave style existed. If it were to exist it would be purely and simply the style of Godard.' It was François Truffaut, however, who paid Godard his highest compliment: 'Godard pulverized the system and, like Picasso, made everything possible' (Frodon 1995: 52). This from a man who also said, 'The New Wave was neither a movement nor a school, nor a group: it was a quantity, a collective name invented by the press to group fifty or so new names who burst forth in a two-year period in a profession that had scarcely accepted more than three or four new names a year' (*France Observateur*, October 1961).

The wave crests and recedes

Despite Truffaut's skepticism, three years after his initial success at Cannes, *Les Cahiers du cinéma* devoted its December 1962 issue to 'La Nouvelle Vague', and in the following year, film critic Raymond Durgnat was cataloguing *The First Decade of the New Wave*, despite his uncertainly as to whether to call it a 'school' or a 'movement', so diverse were its tendencies. In 1962, then, *Cahiers* was officially proclaiming as New Wave directors: Eric Rohmer, Jacques Rivette, whose *Paris nous appartient* (*Paris Belongs to Us*, 1958–60) stitched together a 'labyrinth of scenes appearing to obey some internal but inexplicable law'; Jacques Doniol-Valcroze, co-founder of *Cahiers* and director of the sensual and amusing *L'Eau à la bouche* (1959); Jacques Demy, whose *Lola* (1961) captured the aimlessness and magical spirit often ascribed to New Wave films in general; and Jacques Rozier, whose *Adieu Philippine* (1960–62) was hailed as the 'paragon' of the New Wave by the *Cahiers* editors who declared: 'after this film all the others ring false.' In all, *Cahiers* listed 162 new directors of feature films. Although they claimed to have counted only those directors who had made their first feature film after 1959, they added numerous 'precursors': Alexandre Astruc, Jean-Pierre Melville, Agnès Varda, and Robert Bresson—the latter, well before any of the New Wave directors arrived, had been experimenting with cinematic language in a series of rigorously anti-theatrical films, culminating in his 1959 masterpiece, *Pickpocket*. This extensive list of precursors implicitly compromised the New Wave's claim to novelty, especially since so much of what was advanced looked like a revisitation of the avant-garde spirit of L'Herbier, Clair, and Delluc back in the 1920s.

Moreover, novelty for novelty's sake quickly came under fire. Truffaut's *Tirez sur le pianiste* (*Shoot the Piano Player*, 1960), Godard's *Les Carabiniers* (*The Riflemen*, 1963), and Chabrol's *Les Bonnes Femmes* (*The Good Time Girls*, 1960) were all failures at the box office, and Truffaut would not see another commercial success until *Jules et Jim* in 1962. So numerous were the first-timers, and so inexperienced were the vast majority, that Truffaut was moved to object that the New Wave was merely a quantity of unknowns who had 'rushed' the industry through the opening he and the *Cahiers* group had created. The sworn enemy of the 'tradition of quality' chose a celebratory issue of *Cahiers* to complain that the emphasis on newness had gone to people's heads, and that films should not try to be new in every aspect but should be anchored to the traditional cinema. Indeed, by 1963, with the exceptions of Godard and Resnais, every other New Wave director had either moved on to less experimental commercial films or disappeared from view. In any case, Truffaut claims, by 1962 critics had become 'even more hostile than the film industry to difficult films' (*Cahiers* 138, December 1962). But, Truffaut crowed, there is still something to be proud of: 'By comparison with American directors, we're all intellectuals, so we can take a different tack: the discipline we follow in our work makes our films more complete and complex [than their American cousins].' To be sure, there were a few attempts at reviving the New Wave label by co-authorship: a documentary entitled *La Nouvelle Vague par elle-même* (*The New Wave in its Own Words*, 1964) included interviews with New Wavers Godard, Rivette, Rozier, Demy, and Chabrol; and Barbet Schroeder's *Paris vu par . . .* (*Paris as seen by . . .* , 1965) included shorts by Jean-Daniel Pollet, Jean Rouch, Jean Douchet, Rohmer, Godard, and Chabrol. But Truffaut's absence from the latter film is symptomatic, and rather than serving as a manifesto, the film served more as the last testament of whatever movement there had been. Indeed, the very notion of an independent low-budget cinematic practice had all but disappeared from view. By 1968, 90 per cent of box-office takings in French cinemas was shared among eleven major French distributors and seven American ones. In other words, independent films were reduced to a mere 10 per cent of the market.

Legacies of the New Wave

From our present perspective, then, the New Wave appears riddled with paradoxes: a 'group' that was not one; an insistence on the new despite an acknowledged debt both to classic Hollywood directors and to French filmmakers of the 1930s and 1940s; an endorsement of auteurism by many directors who didn't write their own screenplays; an anti-industry movement that could not have succeeded without significant governmental support; a 'revolution' without any discernible political doctrine; and a disdain for quality by young directors, most of whom rushed to create commercially successful films and thereby hastened a return to the industry's status quo. Nor can the New Wave be said to have reformed mainstream French cinematic practice. Hollywood spectacles and traditional French comedies continued to dominate the French box office from 1958 to 1968.

Surely the most significant legacy of the New Wave derives from Godard's and Resnais's radical breaks with the dominant cinema's illusion of narrative seamlessness and visual continuity. They did not so much invent a practice as articulate, and thereby expose, cinematic *découpage* (cutting and rearrangement of shots) as an ontologically fragmented, discontinuous discourse. Godard's jump cuts, self-conscious actors, playful sound track, and idiosyncratic use of film grammar, and Resnais's experiments with narrative discourse foreground a meta-cinematic practice. As the *Cahiers* critics themselves put it in an interview with Eric Rohmer in 1965:

Today the cinema is an art which looks at itself, turns in on itself. The first object of the cinéaste is to ask the question: what is cinema, what has it been up til now, what can it become? . . . Is it even possible to continue to make films today without beginning by asking this question? (*Cahiers* 172, November 1965).

This new self-consciousness of cinematic language and cinematic ontology not surprisingly coincided with the emergence of structuralism, semiology, and Lacanian psychoanalysis in France, together creating an aperture in critical thinking that has had a lasting and profound effect on our understanding of the medium itself.

Further reading

Andrew, Dudley, *André Bazin* (Oxford: Oxford University Press, 1978). Translation by Serge Grünberg (Paris: *Cahiers du cinéma*/Editions de l'étoile, 1983). The definitive biography and interpretation of the work of one of the most influential voices of the New Wave.

De Baecque, Antoine, *La Nouvelle Vague* (Paris: Flammarion, 1998). An invaluable collection of *Cahiers* interviews with the major New Wave directors, Rivette, Chabrol, Truffaut, Resnais, Godard, Demy, and Rohmer.

—— and Charles Tesson (eds.), *La Nouvelle Vague: une légende en question* (Paris: *Cahiers du cinéma*, 1998). An entire special issue of *Cahiers* devoted to a re-evaluation by members of the original group as well as younger critics. Excellent essays on new technologies of the New Wave and on the importance of the studios in French postwar production.

Douchet, Jean, *La Nouvelle Vague* (Paris: Hazan/Cinémathèque Française, 1998). Trans. Robert Bonanno, *The New Wave* (New York: DAP, 1999). A kind of scrap-book of the New Wave generously endowed with excellent photographs of all aspects of the movement. Includes sections on precursors, the film industry, the studio, technical advances, and a biographical dictionary of members of the movement.

Douin, Jean-Luc, *La Nouvelle Vague 25 ans après* (Paris: Cerf, 1983). Douin has assembled a number of provocative evaluations of the movement, but the real value of this book is the collection of short interviews with New Wave participants including the composer Georges Delerue and cameramen Nestor Almendros and Raoul Coutard, plus producers, screenwriters, and directors.

Durgnat, Raymond, *Nouvelle Vague: The First Decade* (Loughton, Essex: Motion Publications, 1963). Important primarily because of its early publication and the inclusion of filmographies of thirty-five New Wave directors from Jean-Gabril Albicocco to Henri Zaphiratos.

Frodon, Jean-Michel, *Histoire du cinéma français, 1: L'Age moderne du cinema français: De la nouvelle vague à nos jours* (Paris: Flammarion, 1995). A solid history of the movement, with evaluations of the contributions of the major New Wave directors.

Hillier, Jim (ed.), *Cahiers du cinéma: The 1950's: Neo-Realism, Hollywood, The New Wave* (Cambridge, Mass.: Harvard University Press, 1985). An excellent selection of articles by and interviews with New Wave directors and critics.

Labarthe, André S., *Essai sur le jeune cinéma* (Paris: Le Terrain Vague, 1960). Written before Godard had released *A Bout de souffle*, this essay is remarkable for the sense of what is really important in the New Wave and what will last.

Siclier, Jacques, *Le Cinéma français, 1: De 'La Bataille du rail' à 'La Chinoise', 1945–1968* (Paris: Ramsay/Cinéma, 1990). An invaluable guide to the history of the New Wave, with pertinent and perceptive treatments of many of the films of the period.

9

FROM EALING COMEDY TO THE BRITISH NEW WAVE

Sarah Street

The years 1945–60 were of crucial importance for British cinema, in terms of its experience as an industry and for developments in aesthetic trends. The period as a whole saw immense changes in the context of cinema-going, witnessing the peak year of 1,635 million cinema admissions in 1946, followed by a steady decline to 1,182 million in 1955 and then to 501 million by 1960 (Eves 1977: 41). The decline was caused by a combination of factors including competition from television, the rise of consumer culture, the stagnation of inner cities, and the ascendancy of the nuclear family (Docherty *et al.* 1987: 25). There were also changes in the composition of the audience, which became younger (aged 16–24), shifted from being predominantly working-class to lower-middle-class, and saw an increase in male attendance which equalized the domination by female patrons which had held sway from at least the late 1920s (Harper and Porter 1999: 67; Hiley 1999: 47). Despite this background of fluctuating economic and social conditions, the British film industry produced some of its finest films, notable stars, and distinguished genres. The following survey will detail the major characteristics of the film industry; the impact of changes in society; British films at the box office; dominant aesthetic trends; and the advent of the 'New Wave' at the end of the 1950s.

The film industry and social change

Of key importance in assessing British cinema during this period is the character of the film industry, its constraints and opportunities. The status of the film industry was immeasurably enhanced after World War II, when for many critics the British cinema 'came of age'. The maturation of the industry was expressed by its formation into vertically integrated companies, whose ownership of cinema chains provided a degree of protection against fluctuations in the market which in the past had made it extremely difficult for British films to counter American competition. Because during and after World War I the British film industry faced a constant battle to access screentime, most films shown in British cinemas were made in Hollywood. By the late 1940s two companies, a 'duopoly' dominated the scene: the Rank Organization and the Associated British Picture Corporation (ABPC). As early as 1944, between them these companies owned a quarter of all cinemas and a third of cinema seats. Their domination of the market increased thereafter, to such an extent that they were in danger of constituting monopolistic combines (Street 1997: 12–14). The benefits provided by a somewhat protected market had therefore to be offset against the danger of concentration of power in a few hands.

A major development was the ascendancy of the power of distributors such as Rank and ABPC, since distribution was the crux of the financial sponsorship of film production. One consequence was the existence of producers, such as 'the Archers' (Michael Powell and Emeric Pressburger), and Ealing (Michael Balcon), who while not directly connected with these major companies made use of their financial and distribution networks. The only company to rival the duopoly during this period was British Lion, acquired by Alexander Korda in 1946, but this company was weakened by its lack of exhibition interests and unstable financial fortunes throughout the 1950s. This industrial organization produced a relatively stable number of films throughout the late 1940s and 1950s. Thirty-nine feature films were produced in 1945, a figure that rose to 125 in 1950. For the next two years there was a temporary decline in annual production, but in 1953 the figure had risen to 138, increasing to 150 in 1954. For the remainder of the 1950s annual production fluctuated, but even in 1960 a total of 122 films were produced (British Film Institute 1998: 28).

A belief in the film industry's strategic importance 'in the national interest' ensured that the government continued to be involved in its affairs. Since 1927 the state had imposed a regulatory mechanism popularly known as 'the quota' to ensure that a proportion of screentime was available for British films. This statutory provision for renters and exhibitors to acquire and show an annual percentage of British films was extended in 1938, and again in 1948 and 1960 (Dickinson and Street 1985). The Cinematograph

Films Act 1948 was significant in the ascendancy of distributors, since it abolished their statutory quota. No longer obligated to handle British films, distributors made fewer financial commitments to British film producers, leaving the production industry unstable and even more vulnerable to American competition than in previous years.

The most significant element of state support during this period, however, was the establishment of the National Film Finance Corporation (NFFC) in 1949. It represented a fundamental shift in state support from adjusting the market to providing financial assistance for producers. A fund was created that gave money to distributors, in the first instance British Lion, who then allocated funds to producers. In this way many significant British films were financed, including *The Third Man* (Carol Reed, 1949), *The Small Black Room* (Michael Powell and Emeric Pressburger, 1949), *The Wooden Horse* (Jack Lee, 1950), and *The Happiest Days of Your Life* (Frank Launder, 1950). While the funds were never large, the NFFC nevertheless assisted over 750 British films by the time it was wound up in 1985 (Street 1997: 16). A second, if ultimately less helpful, instance of state intervention in the affairs of the film industry was the Eady Levy, instituted in 1950 and abolished in 1985. The Levy created a production fund from a tax on cinema admissions, the proceeds of which were distributed to producers on the basis of box office success. The problem with this type of assistance was that it only benefited the most popular films, and since several American companies produced films in the UK that were registered as British, a good deal of the money went to non-British producers. While success was rewarded, the Levy did little to assist filmmakers who were interested in experimental work, or who did not have access to the large cinema chains.

As well as these prevailing economic conditions, British cinema was influenced by wider societal trends. The postwar period was characterized by an increase in state intervention in the economy and 'modernizing' trends such as a greater number of married women in the workforce which placed traditional institutions like the family under strain and scrutiny (Geraghty 2000: 21–37). It was also a period of increased consumer expenditure. To a greater or lesser extent, many British films engage with these issues, and as Geraghty (2000) has shown, many produced in the 1950s responded to the pressures of modernity in a conservative manner. Indeed, producers' ideologies were often reflected in their films, producing a varied array of perspectives on issues that were pertinent to the period, including gender relations, the role of the state, youth problems, and class. As will be evident in the following survey of popular genres and aesthetic developments, the films were also influenced by their generic heritage, many of them belonging to a trajectory of generic history that pre-dates World War II. A gradual awareness of the changing composition of the audience also had an impact on film content, as producers aimed to reach their increasingly youthful clientele toward the end of the 1950s.

Gainsborough Studios

While American films continued to dominate British screens after World War II, British films were nevertheless popular. During and immediately after the war, costume melodramas produced by Gainsborough Studios did particularly well at the box office, while in the 1950s British comedies and war films provided serious competition for Hollywood's films. Gainsborough's *The Wicked Lady* (Leslie Arliss, 1945) is probably the most celebrated film of the historical/costume genre, outstripping *Brief Encounter* (1945) at the British box office as the war ended. Although it was a melodramatic 'bodice-ripper' set in the seventeenth century, it nevertheless tapped into the wartime mood with its tale of female transgression. Margaret Lockwood, one of the most popular British stars in the immediate postwar years, played Barbara Skelton, a 'wicked' adulteress who masquerades as a highwayman when her privileged lifestyle fails to provide her with the excitement and adventure she craves. On the road, she encounters highwayman Jerry Jackson (James Mason), with whom she has a passionate affair, and is set on a course of theft and murder. Although Barbara dies at the end of the film, and would appear to have been duly punished for her misdemeanours, she is by far the most compelling character in the film. Harper (1994) and Cook (1996) have convincingly argued that, in spite of the film's historical setting, contemporary women related to the dilemmas Barbara faced. With increased female employment and a far more transient and mobile population, World War II presented people with choices they would never have had the opportunity to exercise in peacetime. In particular, marriages were tested by long separations and extramarital romances. These experiences, temptations, and volatile feelings were not dissimilar to Barbara's desire to break free from a life of tedium and duty, her guise as a highwayman providing her with adventure, romance, and danger. In this way films such as *The Wicked Lady* (1945) (and *Brief Encounter* [David Lean, 1946], though from a more guilt-ridden perspective) engaged with wartime sensibilities, presenting strong female characters in a manner that was rare in subsequent years. Like their heroines, British costume melodramas were less prevalent in the 1950s, when comedies and war films became ascendant.

Comedy: from Ealing to *Carry On*

Since the 1930s, British comedies had regularly provided domestic audiences with characters and themes that related to regional identities and an indigenous sense of humor. In subsequent years British comedy was a popular, resilient, and varied genre, producing characters derived from music hall/variety traditions, such as Norman Wisdom's 'the

■ Alec Guinness (1914–2000)

Sir Alec Guinness was a popular actor whose career in British films was most active in the postwar years and the 1950s. Guinness was born in London in 1914, left school aged 17, and was employed by an advertising agency. He enrolled on an acting course and later studied at the Fay Compton School of Dramatic Art, after which he worked as a professional actor. After making his first uncredited film appearance as an extra in *Evensong* (1934), Guinness was later cast by David Lean in two roles that were to establish his screen career, as Herbert Pocket in *Great Expectations* (1946) and as Fagin in *Oliver Twist* (1948).

Some of his most distinctive work was for Ealing Studios, 1949–57, in a variety of roles in comedy films: *Kind Hearts and Coronets* (1949), *The Man in the White Suit* (1951), *The Lavender Hill Mob* (1951), *The Ladykillers* (1955), and *Barnacle Bill* (1957). His acting versatility was demonstrated particularly well in *Kind Hearts and Coronets*, a black comedy in which he played eight characters, all members of the doomed d'Ascoyne family of aristocrats, who are one by one murdered by their penniless relative Louis Mazzini (Dennis Price) so that he can inherit the dukedom. The aristocrats played by Guinness included an eager young photographer, a parson, an admiral, and Lady Agatha D'Ascoyne, whose balloon is shot down by Louis as she distributes suffragette leaflets over London ('I shot an arrow in the

⊕ *The Man in the White Suit*

air; she fell to earth in Berkeley Square'). In Alexander Mackendrick's *The Man in the White Suit* Guinness plays a scientist frustrated with the commercial interests who wish to halt the development of his invention of an indestructible fabric. This film was notable for its combination of comedy with insight into prevailing debates about industrial relations and economic competition. Guinness's style of comedy was understated, intelligent, and laconic.

After the international box-office success of *The Lavender Hill Mob,* films starring Guinness were particularly well received in the USA, where he became a well-known star and was hailed as Britain's most lucrative export. His distinctive voice was also an integral aspect of his appeal; soft, but authoritative. All his understated performances demonstrated his ability to capture extremely well-observed nuances and the minutiae of human behaviour. *The Last Holiday* (1950) was well reviewed by American critic Bosley Crowther, who described Guinness's ability to suggest 'intense emotional moods through his perfect command of stoicism' (*New York Times*, 14 November 1951, p. 39). He plays a mild-mannered, hard-working man who is told he has only a month to live. He spends his savings on a holiday in a fashionable seaside hotel and becomes involved in the lives of the other guests. He assists them when they are in trouble and we conclude that his 'last' holiday has been a valuable experience in gaining friendship and respect. When he discovers that the original diagnosis was incorrect, it is ironic and tragic that he is killed in a road accident. The role demonstrated his ability to convey pathos through playing characters who while not distinctive are in some ways compelling.

Another film to do well in the USA was *The Ladykillers*, which utilized Guinness's talents at disguising his appearance. He demonstrated his versatility once again by playing 'the Professor', a comical but sinister character in a black comedy about a criminal gang who hide out in an old lady's house while masquerading as a 'chamber ensemble'. (In his role as the Professor, Guinness is often mistaken for British actor Alistair Sim, who had appeared in British comedies including the *St Trinians'* films. Sim was also known for being able to disguise his appearance and for appearing in drag, as Guinness had done in *Kind Hearts and Coronets*.)

Guinness appeared in films produced by other independent production companies, including *The Captain's Paradise* (1953), in which he plays a married sea captain who is a bigamist, and *The Card* (1951), an adaptation of Arnold Bennett's novel about a washerwoman's son in the late Victorian period who succeeds in life initially by deception and then by relying on his bravado and wit. He also appeared in an adaptation of Graham Greene's novel *Our Man in Havana* (1959), which co-starred Noël Coward, who described Guinness's performance as 'faultless but dull'. Guinness made several films in Hollywood and was awarded an Academy Award for Best Actor and the New York critics' Golden Globe award for his performance as Colonel Nicholson in the UK–US production, *The Bridge on the River Kwai* (1957). He collaborated on the screenplay of *The Horse's Mouth* (1958), an offbeat black comedy film directed by Ronald Neame and based on a novel by Joyce Cary. He formed a production company with writer Daphne du Maurier to produce *The Scapegoat* (1958), a film based on her novel which starred Guinness as an Englishman on holiday in France who is tricked by his double, an aristocrat, into assuming his identity. Michael Balcon was also involved in the production, which co-starred Bette Davis. Throughout this time Guinness continued to pursue a stage career, working with Tyrone Guthrie, John Gielgud, George Devine, and Peter Brook.

In his later career Guinness worked in television, most notably as George Smiley in the 1980s series based on John Le Carré's novels *Tinker, Tailor, Soldier, Spy* and *Smiley's People*. In Hollywood his most memorable role was as Obi-Wan Kenobi in *Star Wars* (1977), *The Empire Strikes Back* (1980), and *Return of the Jedi* (1983). While Guinness did not enjoy playing these roles, they undoubtedly introduced him to a younger audience to whom his past career in British comedies of the 1950s was virtually unknown.

Gump', who through slapstick comedy lurches from disaster to disaster in films such as *Trouble In Store* (John Paddy Carstairs, 1953). Ealing Studios was responsible for producing many of the most highly regarded comedies that were box-office successes in Britain and overseas. Ealing's main box-office successes were in the late 1940s and early 1950s. Films such as *Hue and Cry* (Charles Crichton, 1947), *Passport to Pimlico* (Henry Cornelius, 1949), *Whisky Galore!* (Alexander Mackendrick, 1949), *Kind Hearts and Coronets* (Robert Hamer, 1949), *The Lavender Hill Mob* (Charles Crichton, 1951), *The Man in the White Suit* (Alexander Mackendrick, 1951), *The Titfield Thunderbolt* (Charles Crichton, 1953), and *The Ladykillers* (Alexander Mackendrick, 1955) represent the most celebrated of Ealing's comic output. At Ealing, Michael Balcon's stable of directors and actors was fairly constant. The studio maintained a degree of continuity of personnel that was rare, including directors such as Alexander Mackendrick, Charles Crichton, Basil Dearden, and Charles Frend, as well as Balcon's use of Alec Guinness, an actor who was particularly popular in the USA. In their different ways, several of Ealing's comedies engaged with British ambivalence about the continuation in peacetime of wartime restrictions such as rationing. In their nostalgic elevation of British communities and their values, which are pitted against trends of bureaucratization and the ascendancy of the market economy, key Ealing films such as *Passport to Pimlico* indeed represent, as Barr (1977) has argued, conservatism and a general refusal to engage with the challenges posed by postwar society. On the other hand, several Ealing comedies are more subversive in their engagement with themes such as black comedy and sexual repression, particularly in *Kind Hearts and Coronets*, and the assertive and resourceful side of community action in *Whisky Galore!*

As a studio, in the 1950s Ealing became increasingly subject to financial stringencies exerted on the company by the Rank Organization. A 1947 agreement between the two companies entitled John Davis, Rank's managing director, to exert pressure on Michael Balcon to scale down many productions, a move which in retrospect can be seen as contributing to the studio's decline. On the whole, however, Ealing's comedies represent an important and respected trend in British production, and many of the most successful comedies of the 1950s were similarly preoccupied with responding to postwar conditions, in particular to the transformation of key institutions which for many represented an aspect of modernity that was to be feared.

The perspective from which many films of the 1950s examined British society was with reference to its institutions: the National Health Service, the army, the education system, the legal profession, and industrial relations. One of the most popular series was the *Doctor* films (*Doctor in the House*, 1954, *Doctor at Sea*, 1955, and *Doctor at Large*, 1957), featuring Dirk Bogarde, Britain's most popular star of the 1950s. Produced by Betty Box, the only major woman feature film producer in the 1950s, and directed by Ralph Thomas, these films represent the dilemmas of a young doctor trying to make a name for himself in a profession dominated by increasingly residual but nevertheless tenacious traditions. The *Doctor* films engage with the medical profession during a period of transition, when the regulations of the National Health Service were being integrated into a reluctant profession. While the comedies certainly contained elements of critique, they were perhaps limited by generic constraints, which meant that satire was gentle rather than biting: traditional structures were the subject of mild rather than penetrating ridicule. Geraghty (2000: 69) has argued that in this way the comedies combine a 'curious mix of rebellion and stultifying conformity', referring to their ambivalence about modernity. Yet, as Porter (2001: 91) has argued, as the decade progressed, British comedies focusing on institutions also point to a critique of archaic management practices, resulting in an erosion of wartime values amidst calls for greater efficiency and flexibility. The popular *Carry On* series, which dominated British comedy from the mid-1950s, similarly critiqued a range of British institutions including the medical profession in *Carry On Nurse* (1959). In general, *Carry On* represents a maturing criticism of institutions which was extended to cover education and the army in *Carry On Teacher* (1959) and *Carry On Sergeant* (1958). In this way British comedies of the postwar period are a key register of social attitudes and responses to the pressures of modernity.

Other institutions were featured in comedies of the period, particularly education. Probably the most anarchic films, which celebrated and even promoted progressive attitudes toward gender and sex, were *The Happiest Days of Your Life* (1950) and the *St Trinian's* series that it spawned. These films satirized British public schools and, particularly in the case of *The Happiest Days of Your Life*, the encroachment by the state's bureaucratic structures on the autonomy of traditional institutions. The films can be termed anarchic in the sense that they present female sexuality as explosive and dangerous, unlike the majority of British films in the 1950s, which sought to contain women's desires in a more conservative manner. The schoolgirls are unruly young women, exploiting the school system which restricts their desires while at the same time, in its own disorganized state, unwittingly promotes the very disobediences on which they thrive. *The Happiest Days of Your Life* was written, directed, and produced by Frank Launder and Sidney Gilliat, whose collaboration extended to the *St Trinian's* films and produced many distinctive British films in the 1940s and 1950s. Another important British team to focus on British institutions was John and Roy Boulting. *Private's Progress* (1956) satirized army life, while *Brothers in Law* (1957) took on the legal profession. *I'm All Right Jack* (1959) expresses ambivalence about trade unionism and community action, demonstrating the extent to which Ealing's nostalgic vision of the values of the wartime community had been eroded.

War films

War films were also extremely popular up until the mid-1950s, almost exclusively with male audiences. These were enhanced by a plethora of popular British stars including Jack Hawkins, Kenneth More, Dirk Bogarde, and John Mills. While female stars had predominated in British films during the 1940s, the following decade was characterized by a preponderance of male stars. Many of the films centered on narratives about male identity and notions of heroism that relate to uncertainties about gender roles in the 1950s. Women were marginalized in films that centered on all-male environments, including ships, planes, and prisoner-of-war camps. Key examples of the genre are *The Cruel Sea* (1953), *The Colditz Story* (1954), and *The Dam Busters* (1955); films which examined heroism, the complex relationships within the male group, and the emotional tension of wartime. While these films hardly celebrated war, they nevertheless looked backwards to a decade when, despite the upheavals of war, being British depended on certain notions of class, hierarchy, and codes of male heroism. Geraghty (2000: 195) has usefully compared war films of the 1950s to the simultaneously popular comedies, remarking that 'they both provide a space in which the demands of modern citizenship can be resiliently shrugged off, an opportunity for relaxation in the old-fashioned spaces of the cinema'. So while many films engaged with social pressures resulting from such trends as the increase of women in the workforce, the expansion of consumerism, and the advance of state intervention in the economy and in areas of social life, they often did so through a skeptical lens.

British stars and stardom

British film stars, as noted above, were an integral aspect of the rising popularity of the two key genres of comedy and war films. Whereas in the 1940s female stars such as Margaret Lockwood and Anna Neagle dominated the polls, in the 1950s Dirk Bogarde, Jack Hawkins, and Kenneth More eclipsed other British stars and even some of Hollywood's. Dirk Bogarde was one of the most popular British film stars of the 1950s. He was the mainstay of the Rank Organization's 'Charm School' promotion of British actors and actresses. Of Dutch extraction, Bogarde (his full name was Derek Van Den Bogaerde) was born in London in 1921 and appeared in amateur dramatics before experiencing success on the London stage in the immediate postwar years. His first break into films came when producer Ian Dalrymple of Wessex Films, an independent company that released films through the Rank Organization, hired him for *Esther Waters* (1948), a period film in which he plays a young groom. One of his most significant early roles was as a troubled youth in *The Blue Lamp* (1949), a typical role for Bogarde. He tended to be offered parts as volatile, enigmatic characters who struggle with life. Bogarde's major box-office success occurred, however, when he played Dr Simon Sparrow in *Doctor in the House*—the first of the *Doctor* films, in which he appeared until 1963.

In their study of cinema audience tastes in the 1950s Harper and Porter (1999) note a key change in the mid-1950s, when teenagers replaced housewives as regular cinemagoers. Bogarde was popular with this younger audience, as well as Hollywood's stars. The rest of the audience consisted of occasional cinemagoers who tended to prefer British stars such as those noted above. As in the 1940s, British stars were subject to scrutiny by fan magazines such as *Picturegoer* and were often compared to Hollywood's stars, though using slightly different criteria. In general the concept of stardom as applicable to British actors depended on notions of 'Britishness', which involved displaying an essence of decorum. In the case of female stars this also involved being perceived to be 'ladylike', while for male stars a chivalric demeanor was desired. The reputations of most British stars were enhanced by advertisement of their experience of stage acting, the assumption being that they had learned a craft and maintained high professional standards. British stars were praised for not seeking glamour for its own sake and for displaying a sense of patriotic duty to the nation and to the profession. In its reportage of the private and public lives of many British stars, *Picturegoer* conformed to this differentiated image.

Occasionally stars who deviated from the norm presented the magazine with problems. Diana Dors was a popular star working for the Rank Organization. With her platinum blonde hair and sexually charged pout, she was groomed as a British version of Marilyn

Monroe. Both she and Dirk Bogarde were presented by what became popularly known as the 'Rank Charm School', which involved a huge publicity campaign to glamorize British stars. It was hoped they would be brought closer to Hollywood's notions of stardom, which depended on glamour, mystery, intense adulation, occasional gossip, and scandal. Most stars feared being pigeonholed into a particular role. This was the case both with Margaret Lockwood in the 1940s, who resented being forever identified in the public imagination as 'the wicked lady', and with Diana Dors, who fought to leave her image as a 'bad girl' behind in pursuit of more challenging roles (Street 1997: 134–5; 2000: 79–107).

Some British stars gained a following in the USA, although this was never extensive. Alec Guinness has already been noted, but other British stars who also made an impression included in the late 1940s Stewart Grainger and James Mason, who both moved to Hollywood. Deborah Kerr was another British star who was noticed in British films and subsequently offered roles in Hollywood. After appearing in *I See a Dark Stranger* (1946) and *Black Narcissus* (1947), she attracted offers from Hollywood studios, including Paramount and MGM. A seven-year contract with MGM facilitated her move to Hollywood where she was groomed as a major star. Particularly after World War II it was hoped that British actors would pursue parallel careers in both Britain and Hollywood, but it was more often the case that, once they had made the move, British stars stayed in California.

British films were popular with metropolitan audiences in the USA. They were usually screened in art cinemas, which increased in number during the 1950s. The most popular films and genres were Shakespearean adaptations, particularly *Hamlet* (1948); Ealing comedies; Powell and Pressburger's *The Red Shoes* (1948); and Hammer horror films, which were marketed with care for American consumption. British films had always found it difficult to obtain screenings in the USA, but during the 1940s and 1950s the Rank Organization made considerable efforts to find distribution outlets through the major Hollywood studios. This strategy was in part successful, and British films were also able to participate in the expansion of the art market during the period, often appearing to be more attractive to American exhibitors as imports than foreign-language films. As a percentage of foreign films imported into the USA during the 1950s, British films regularly represented at least 20–30 per cent of the total, reaching a peak in 1954, when they occupied 34 per cent of the import market (Street 2002: 223). Anglophile critics such as Bosley Crowther, writing in the *New York Times*, assisted the favorable reception of many British films overseas.

Aesthetic trends in British cinema

Throughout the period covered by this chapter, British cinema adopted many guises and was subject to several stylistic influences. The style most commonly identified with British cinema (and praised by critics) was realism, and indeed, many films, particularly in the 1950s, were dominated by the attributes of realism. These consisted of stylistic restraint; characters and situations that were 'believable', often equating with perceived notions of social reality; black and white cinematography; acting styles that privileged emotional restraint; and a general fidelity to the documentary tradition established in the 1920s and 1930s and identified with John Grierson. A key genre demonstrating fidelity to realism was the 'social problem' genre, which later proved to be a key influence on the New Wave. Many other films clearly belong to this tradition, for example, *The Dam Busters*, *The Cruel Sea*, and *A Night to Remember* (1958), the film adaptation of Walter Lord's account of the Titanic disaster, which claimed to be the most realistic film account of the event. Persuading audiences that this was the case was a common trait in realist cinema: rolling credits at the start of the film showed that specialist advisers had been used to develop the script; the film's marketing emphasized the trouble taken to build a scale model of the ship, and the narrative closely followed the events of Lord's meticulously researched book.

Despite the ascendancy of realism, however, it was seldom the case that realism was a style unmediated by other traditions (Geraghty 2000: 79). Similarly, while *Brief Encounter* has commonly been associated with realism, as Dyer (1993) has shown, an acting style that conveys emotional restraint need not necessarily be devoid of deep emotional reson-ance more commonly associated with melodrama. *Odd Man Out* (1947), again a film usually linked with realist aspirations, in places utilizes a camera style associated with both Impressionism and Expressionism. Care must therefore be taken in applying these terms to British films, since there were many coexistent trends that account for their variety and eclecticism.

Critical re-evaluation of the so-called 'lost continent' of British cinema, namely the non-realist traditions of Powell and Pressburger, Gainsborough melodrama, and Hammer horror, which were not always given the critical approbation they deserved at the time of release, has led to a reassessment of the character of British cinema. This period is crucial in that it displays evidence of experimentation in aesthetic form, most notably in the work of Michael Powell and Emeric Pressburger. Their films were notable for their use of color, experimentation with studio techniques, and the idea of the 'composed film'.

Another genre associated with bold use of color and stylistic experimentation is Hammer horror. Gaining popularity from the mid-1950s, Hammer's films were perfectly suited to appeal to the increasingly younger audience. The classic phase of films directed by Terence Fisher included *The Curse of Frankenstein* (1956), *Dracula* (1958), *The Hound of the Baskervilles* (1959), and *The Mummy* (1959). As Hutchings (1993: 60–66) has shown, these films relate to British society in intriguing ways, particularly in their placement of characters who represent 'the professional' who must restore order to the chaos that has

■ Powell and Pressburger

The films of Michael Powell and Emeric Pressburger constitute a distinctive corpus in the history of British cinema. Their partnership began in 1939, when both were working for Alexander Korda at Denham studios on *The Spy in Black*, an espionage thriller. Powell had already gained experience directing films for Gaumont-British, while Pressburger, a Hungarian émigré who had come to Britain in 1933, had written screenplays in France and Germany. They went on to collaborate for eighteen years, forming the 'Archers' company in 1943, for whom they made their most celebrated films.

The films of Powell and Pressburger acquired a reputation for being experimental during World War II, when they combined propaganda with spectacle. *The Lion Has Wings* (1939) and *One of Our Aircraft is Missing* (1941) in particular were admired for their contribution to the war effort. *The Life and Death of Colonel Blimp* (1943), a film that drew on the buffoonish cartoon character created by Sidney Low, was, however, controversial for its satirical portrayal of the military, and was criticized by both Winston Churchill and the Ministry of Information. While several critics admired their films, they were on the whole regarded as being at odds with the prevailing style of British cinema, which was more wedded to the codes of realism. Although it is important not to exaggerate the extent to

⊕ *A Matter of Life and Death*

which they eschewed realism, they were drawn to subject matter that involved fantasy and illusion. This was demonstrated particularly in their spectacular experiment with time and color in *A Matter of Life and Death* (1946), a film in which David Niven stars as a pilot on the verge of death. In collaboration with set designer Alfred Junge, Powell and Pressburger created an imaginative and innovative representation of heaven (in black and white; color for earth) for scenes in which the pilot has to present a case to remain on earth to marry an American woman with whom he has just fallen in love. They also worked extremely well with cinematographer Jack Cardiff on this film, consolidating his experiments with Technicolor, which featured in many subsequent collaborations.

As well as experimenting in the studio, Powell and Pressburger utilized location shooting whenever possible. Powell was particularly keen to research suitable natural settings for their films, most notably in *I Know Where I'm Going!* (1945), a film that employed location shooting on the Western Isles of Scotland. But Powell was not always able to travel to authentic locations, and in their adaptation of the novel by Rumer Godden, *Black Narcissus* (1947), the Himalayas were recreated in a Pinewood studio. The use of color was extremely significant in this and other films, particularly *The Red Shoes*, which was a huge success in the USA. Set in the tempestuous world of ballet, it was able to take advantage of a 'ballet craze' that was especially prevalent in New York and other major cities, and was listed for many years in *Variety* as a rare top box-office draw from Britain. With *The Red Shoes,* Powell and Pressburger created the film after the musical score had been devised—thus creating an example of 'the composed film', with which they experimented further in subsequent films including *The Tales of Hoffmann* (1951). Another new technique they utilized was the 'independent frame', a method of creating effects in a studio in an economical manner.

Linked to a melodramatic tradition, their films dealt with situations of extreme emotional resonance, demonstrated by the depiction of sexual longings within a community of nuns in *Black Narcissus*. This film was considered to be unsuitable for exhibition in the USA, where the Catholic Legion of Decency pronounced it 'condemned' until Powell and Pressburger agreed to cuts for its American release. Despite this focus on female characters, in keeping with many other British films of the period, their films often marginalized women and seemed to be more preoccupied with male activities and dilemmas, such as the clash of egos between composer Julian (Marius Goring) and Lermontov (Anton Walbrook), leader of the ballet company in *The Red Shoes*.

In the 1950s Powell and Pressburger produced several films, but these were less successful. Their last collaboration was a wartime drama, *Ill Met by Moonlight* (1956). Powell continued to work as a director, his most controversial post-Pressburger film being *Peeping Tom* (1959), which many contemporary critics found abhorrent for its portrayal of a serial killer. The film was later heralded as a key film in the evolution of the horror genre. Pressburger continued to write screenplays and novels, but undoubtedly his best work was with Powell. Both reinforced each other's strengths and, despite disagreements, readily acknowledged their mutual interdependence.

In the USA the films of Powell and Pressburger were championed by art film enthusiasts and subsequently by Martin Scorsese and Francis Ford Coppola, directors who declared them as decisive influences on their own work. In recognition of this, Powell was invited to Hollywood in 1981 as director in residence in Coppola's Zeotrope studio. Powell died in 1990 and Pressburger in 1998. The full appreciation of their reputation as innovative film-makers has accumulated over the years. Indeed, in a critics' poll of top ten films conducted by *Sight and Sound* in 2002, very few British films featured with the exception of those produced by Powell and Pressburger, who must now be regarded as Britain's most significant writer–director partnership.

resulted from a breakdown in patriarchal authority (for example Peter Cushing, as Dr Van Hesling, pitted against Christopher Lee, as Count Dracula, who has awakened erotic longings in his female victims). In this sense these films can be related to the wider trend noted earlier of films concerned with masculine angst. As far as their aesthetic style is concerned, it is important to recognize that Hammer's films combined restrained camera and conventional editing style with luxuriant sets and color. In their desire to draw on, but break free from, the classic traditions of horror established by Universal Studios in the 1930s, Hammer's films represented a distinctive contribution to the evolution of the horror genre.

The origins of the New Wave

In some respects the New Wave of feature films produced between 1959 and 1964, which dealt with 'social problem' issues, marked a major turning point in the history of British cinema. It popularized films with working-class subject matter, and associated British cinema with critically applauded films made in the rest of Europe (the French *nouvelle vague* and Italian Neorealism) by directors who saw themselves as contributing to a social and aesthetic experiment. Yet it is important to recognize that the New Wave had distinct origins in previous British films that explored social issues, such as *It Always Rains on Sunday* (Robert Hamer, 1947), *The Blue Lamp* (Basil Dearden, 1950), and *Yield to the Night* (J. Lee Thompson, 1956). Their immediate roots lay in the 'Free Cinema' documentaries screened at the National Film Theatre, London, 1956–9, and produced by Lindsay Anderson, Karel Reisz, Tony Richardson, and others. These practitioners were concerned to produce films that celebrated 'the poetry of the everyday', unrestrained by the pressures of commercialism and big-studio production. Realism was the order of the day, with black-and-white cinematography, location shooting, and unknown actors. Filmmakers drew on the lyrical documentary tradition represented by the wartime work of Humphrey Jennings. Several documentaries were made, including Lindsay Anderson's *O Dreamland* (1953), about a Margate amusement arcade, and *Every Day Except Christmas* (1957), about the people who worked in Covent Garden market. Karel Reisz, who went on to direct *Saturday Night and Sunday Morning* (1960), made *We Are the Lambeth Boys* (1959), a film about a London youth club. This phase allowed the directors to experiment with the documentary form, which proved to be a good basis from which to develop ideas for feature films.

The shift into feature film production was facilitated by the publication of a key group of novels by relatively unknown working-class writers including John Braine, Alan Sillitoe, and David Storey, as well as new playwrights including Shelagh Delaney and John Osborne. The feature films that resulted concentrated on class structures as their major concern, especially the frustrations of young people who wanted to break free from the physical and emotional restrictions of social class. The phenomenon of the 'angry young man' was epitomized by Jimmy Porter (Richard Burton) in *Look Back in Anger* (1959), Joe Lampton (Laurence Harvey) in *Room at the Top* (1959), and Arthur Seaton (Albert Finney) in *Saturday Night and Sunday Morning*. Their anger was directed against a social system that made it difficult for them to be upwardly mobile, or to move away from their home town where they were pressured to marry a local girl and follow their parents' lifestyle. Unfortunately, in many of the films this problem becomes fixated on the female characters, who are depicted as clinging creatures who wish to hold back their angry young men, trapping them into a lifetime of hard, repetitive, low-paid work to pay for consumer durables and to bring up a family. The only film to depict this scenario from a female perspective is *A Taste of Honey* (1961), adapted by Shelagh Delaney from her first play.

During the following decade, British cinema entered a distinctive phase when many significant films and bold aesthetic styles were deployed. Arguably this development would not have been possible without the groundwork laid in the late 1940s and 1950s. Not only did the New Wave have its roots in the 'social problem' film of the 1950s, but subsequent examples of aesthetic experiment can be related to the films of Powell and Pressburger and to Hammer horror. The theme of social institutions continued to fascinate directors, most notably Lindsay Anderson, whose film *If . . .* (1968), set in a public school, is regarded as a key example of British cinema's engagement with the traditions of art cinema. Writing in *Sight and Sound* in 1960 (vol. 29, no. 1: 7), critic Penelope Houston commented: '1959 has been a year of intense vitality, an amazingly confident contrast to the uneasy fifties.' In the excitement of witnessing the ascendancy of the New Wave it was tempting to dismiss the films of the previous decade as anachronistic. Yet trends clearly do not emerge out of nowhere, and it is crucial to interpret the 1960s as part of a continuum inextricably linked to British cinema's previous engagement with distinctive themes and styles. Despite the changing composition of cinema audiences, for many fans during the postwar years, British cinema was undoubtedly a popular cinema, with key stars and genres.

Further reading

Barr, Charles, *Ealing Studios* (London/Newton Abbot: Cameron & Tayleur/David & Charles, 1977). This book provides an excellent overview of the history, aesthetics, and ideological preoccupations of Ealing Studios.

Cook, Pam, *Fashioning the Nation: Costume and Identity in British Cinema* (London: British Film Institute, 1996). Useful for analyzing the 'look' of British films, in particular melodramas of the 1940s.

Dickinson, Margaret, and Sarah Street, *Cinema and State: The Film Industry and the British Government, 1927–84* (London: British Film Institute, 1985). The first study of the relationship between the film industry and the government; policy decision-making and the economics of the British film industry.

Docherty, David, David Morrison, and Michael Tracey, *The Last Picture Show? Britain's changing film audiences* (London: British Film Institute, 1987). A useful survey of the changing nature of film audiences; provides useful statistical information.

Dyer, Richard, *Brief Encounter* (London: British Film Institute, 1993). Analysis of this classic British film in relation to performance styles and to debates about realism.

Eves, Vicki, 'The Structure of the British Film Industry', *Screen* 2 (1) (Jan./Feb. 1997: 41–54). Analysis of the major structural underpinnings of the British film industry; useful text in relation to other economic analyses.

Geraghty, Christine, *British Cinema in the Fifties: Gender, Genre and the 'New Look'* (London: Routledge, 2000). The first major book to concentrate on the 1950s; contains many film analyses in relation to contemporary discourses about modernity.

Guinness, Alec, *Blessings in Disguise* (London: Hamish Hamilton, 1985). A useful, if idiosyncratic, autobiography that demonstrates Guinness's divergent attitude toward his stage and screen performances.

Harper, Sue, and Vincent Porter, 'Cinema audience tastes in 1950s Britain', *Journal of Popular British Cinema* 2 (1999): 66–82. Interesting analysis of fracturing audience compositions and their various film preferences.

Hutchings, Peter, *Hammer and Beyond: the British Horror Film* (Manchester: Manchester University Press, 1993). Classic study of the horror genre in relation to its history, aesthetics, and ideological preoccupations.

Porter, Vincent, 'The Hegemonic Turn: Film Comedies in 1950s Britain', *Journal of Popular British Cinema* 4 (2001): 81–94. Useful genre study of comedy as it related to changing ideological imperatives in the 1950s.

Street, Sarah, *British National Cinema* (London: Routledge, 1997). Overview of British cinema throughout the century, its economic history, dominant generic modes, and non-mainstream cinema.

—— *British Cinema in Documents* (London: Routledge, 2000). Case studies illustrating methodological issues relating to British cinema's relations with the government; censorship; fans and fan culture; and the cinema audience.

—— *Transatlantic Crossings: British Feature Films in the USA* (New York: Continuum, 2002). The first major study of the distribution and reception of British films in the United States.

10

THE NEW GERMAN CINEMA

Thomas Elsaesser

The newness of the 'new'

The New German Cinema: was it more than a passing fad, the convenient label for films from West Germany between roughly 1965 and 1983? Were the audiences who in the 1970s flocked to see the latest film by Rainer Werner Fassbinder, Wim Wenders, Werner Herzog, or Hans Jürgen Syberberg intrigued by the strange talents of a new generation of European *auteurs*, or did the fact that these directors all came from Germany register as the key feature (Gilliat 1977)?

In the United States, critics soon spotted a trend. 'The Germans are coming,' warned Andrew Sarris, and *Time* magazine opined that 'the German Cinema is the liveliest in Europe' (Sarris 1975; Canby 1977; Clarke 1978). Invented by journalists, aided and abetted by Anglo-American film scholars, the label stayed, and has come to connote more than the sum of its parts: New German Cinema now stands for a country, a decade, a generation, even a mood of melancholy self-reflection mostly among males. But it was also a movement of anti-establishment protest, where women, gays, and other disadvantaged or diasporic minorities found an authentic voice.

In Germany itself, the resurgence of filmmaking that began in the mid-1960s was initially known as 'Young German Film', and only with the international acclaim that came in the 1970s did 'New' replace 'Young' in West Germany. But the perception that the New German Cinema was a distinctly 'national' cinema and a break in the country's film history was not just due to foreign critics or film scholars. Several filmmakers picked up on 'German' and highlighted it in their often rather self-consciously chosen titles: such as *Deutschland bleiche Mutter* (*Germany Pale Mother*, 1980), *Die bleierne Zeit* (*The German Sisters*, 1981), *Deutschland im Herbst* (*Germany in Autumn*, 1978), *Hitler—ein Film aus Deutschland* (*Hilter—A Film from Germany*, 1977), or *Heimat: eine Chronik in elf Teilen* (*Heimat*, 1984). These served as a reminder of just how acute and unresolved the question of Germany's (post-WWII) national identity still was in the 1970s. At the time, Germany was divided into two sovereign states, the Cold War extract allegiance from both East and West Germany to their respective superpowers, the Soviet Union and the United States, and the Nazi past still loomed over West German society precisely because it was so rarely discussed in the open. International interest in the New German Cinema might well have been less keen had it not been for a series of extraordinary political events shaking West Germany during the mid-1970s, of which the notorious exploits of the Baader–Meinhof group (the RAF) were only the most startling. Many cities—Berlin, Hamburg, Frankfurt—had known student unrest since the mid-1960s, and the Vietnam War, May 1968, and the stationing of NATO nuclear missiles on West European soil provoked often violent protest and led to widespread anti-American sentiment. The spotlight on a convulsed West German body politic gave a focus to very diverse films, and a sense of unity of purpose to those who had written and directed them.

In the eyes of the outside world, the filmmakers became unofficial ambassadors, and their task was to reassure the world that German youth had not entirely taken leave of their senses. 'We are legitimate German culture,' Werner Herzog was fond of proclaiming. But the common denominator 'Germany' has nevertheless to be set against the fact that, in retrospect, the majority of films remembered as 'New German Cinema'—*Der Händler der vier Jahreszeiten* (*The Merchant of Four Seasons*), *Angst essen Seele auf* (*Fear Eats the Soul*), *Die Ehe der Maria Braun* (*The Marriage of Maria Braun*), *Aguirre der Zorn Gottes* (*Aguirre Wrath of God*), *Kaspar Hauser*, *Stroszek*, *Fitzcarraldo*, *Alice in den Städten* (*Alice in the Cities*), *Im Lauf der Zeit* (*Kings of the Road*), *Der amerikanische Freund* (*The American Friend*), *Ludwig Requiem für einen jungfräulichen König* (*Ludwig Requiem for a Virgin King*), *Unser Hitler* (*Hitler—A Film from Germany*), *Die verlorene Ehe der Katharina Blum* (*The Lost Honor of Katharina Blum*), *Die Blechtrommel* (*The Tin Drum*), *Abschied von Gestern* (*Yesterday Girl*), and *Die Patriotin* (*The Patriot*)—were the work of a mere handful of directors (Fassbinder, Herzog, Wenders, Syberberg, Kluge, Schlöndorff) and thus also typical of European *auteur* cinema. Yet while these films (including the collectively produced *Germany in Autumn*) were highly personal works, their cumulative effect was to transform the image not only of German cinema in the context of European art cinema but of West Germany itself, as a country which, though prosperous, indus-trious, and at peace with its neighbors, was nonetheless deeply troubled, even self-tormented, leaving 'no room for laughter'. Part of the ambivalence—the possibly excessive praise abroad and the certainly excessive hostility at home—toward the New German Cinema during and since its miracle decade of the 1970s may have come from doubts—not least by Germans themselves—as to how to interpret this 'new' Germany, manifested in its cinema.

From the perspective of European cinema, what was so new about the New German Cinema? Any one of three different factors: a new model of production (based on the so-called *Filmförderungsystem*), a new function for authorship (the so-called *Autorenfilm*), new patterns of exhibition (the role of television, the *kommunale Kino* initiative). To this must be added the public and critical response to the New German Cinema abroad after 1974, fed by two complementary interests: the curiosity about the violent and bloody post-1968 social upheavals just mentioned, and a growing fascination with Germany's Fascist past that these events once more thrust into the limelight. Such intrigued but also vigilant and suspicious eyes as came to scrutinize the films, notably in France, Britain, and the United States, did much to define what the New German Cinema was about also for its own makers. Choosing their topics more and more with an international—art house and festival circuit—audience in mind, they reinforced the label German, but now refracted in the mirror held up to West Germany in the eyes of others (geographical neighbors, allies, former enemies) (Elsaesser 1986: 535–49).

Manifestos and self-definitions: from Oberhausen to Hamburg and back

Within Germany, several landmarks lined this history and divided it into the Young and the New German Cinema: the Oberhausen Manifesto of 1962; the first government-sponsored film subsidy law (*Filmförderungsgesetz*) of 1967; the co-production agreement with television in 1974; the discussions in 1978 around *Germany in Autumn* and the television screening of the American series *Holocaust*, followed by an intense, media-led soul-searching about ordinary Germans' role in the persecution of German Jews; the 'Hamburg Declaration' of 1979; the award of the first Oscar for a German film, *The Tin Drum*, in 1980; and R. W. Fassbinder's death in 1982. These dates, debates, and turning points are typical of the inextricable tangle between politics and film politics, the past of the nation catching up with the present of its filmmakers. The dates suggest a steady curve of rise, climax, and decline, peaking in 1977. But from another point of view they trace a cyclical pattern or a pendulum swing. The 1962 Oberhausen Manifesto (the occasion—a film festival—was by general consent the birth date of the Young

German Cinema) called for a 'new [kind of] feature film'[1] and a director's cinema, while in the 1979 Hamburg Declaration filmmakers proclaimed a cinema at the service of the spectator, with a new commitment to documenting 'reality'. Also in the late 1970s, critics spoke out against what they saw as the tyranny of television, which had been greeted a few years earlier as the cinema's white knight riding to the rescue (Blumenberg 1997a; 1997b). In 1982 the 'author's film'—the aesthetic, film-political, and economic cornerstone of the New German Cinema—was accused of ruining the German cinema's chances with a public, an argument the old guard and industry lobby had been tirelessly repeating in the trade journals for the previous twenty years (Rohrbach 1983: 318–26). Some insiders saw more power to the producer as the only viable future strategy, while a new generation of filmmakers at the fringe began demanding another Oberhausen, to depose the reigning dynasty of star directors (von Praunheim 1977).

The Young German cinema

Calling the Oberhausen rebels 'Young German Cinema' had made it seem like a confrontation between generations. 'Papas Kino ist tot,' ('Dad's cinema is dead') declared a sticker handed out at the festival in 1962. But, as Edgar Reitz admitted in an interview with Jan Dawson, this was simply a translation of the slogan that had made the French *nouvelle vague* notorious three years earlier (Dawson 1980/81: 14–20). In France, the revival of more personal filmmaking was preceded by a renewal of film culture, prompted by a reassessment of the work of Hollywood directors: what came to be known as the 'politique des auteurs' (Hillier 1985). In West Germany, the theoretical as well as the cinephile dimension was less apparent, the activists being united more by outright opposition than by a re-evaluation of their cinematic patrimony. In fact, the signatories of the manifesto were an ad hoc group, comprising mostly Munich directors of sponsored documentaries and experimental films who had gathered in Oberhausen for the annual festival of non-fiction shorts. Among this group there were people 'who had never made a film of their own and had no intention of making one—one was a composer, two were cameramen, there was also an actor' (Dawson 1980/81: 14–20). The Manifesto ostensibly targeted the German commercial film industry, seen as an old boy network of the formerly Nazi film industry closing ranks. But both the idea of independence and the underlying aesthetics were ambiguous. Addressing themselves to ministry officials rather than to audiences, the Oberhausen group chose a documentary festival to call for the 'new feature film'! Their main impact would be as a pressure group, lobbying parliament and the regional state governments for more money and new funding structures to sponsor feature films the way official bodies had hitherto supported shorts and documentaries.

Radical aesthetic and formal innovations were left to a more categorical avant-garde (represented by Jean-Marie Straub, Vlado Kristl, Hellmuth Costard, and Harun Farocki), who were also implacably hostile to the film industry, but no less opposed to the spirit of Oberhausen, just as they would dismiss the New German Cinema that followed.

That the fronts were never as clear as the manifestos suggested becomes obvious when one looks at the economic infrastructure of the German film industry as a whole. Unable, during the 1950s, to generate enough capital to compete with Hollywood, the German film industry had to be propped up by a whole series of government measures.[2] The West German commercial cinema, no different from that of other European countries, experienced during the 1960s a seemingly irreversible decline. Some of the causes were economic, some aesthetic (as its opponents claimed), but most of them sociological and demographic, culminating in the erosion of the traditional family audience with the advent of television as the dominant entertainment medium. The challenge was to make films differently, for younger audiences, with smaller teams, portable equipment, out in the streets, rather than in the studio with constructed sets and contractual labor. Just as had happened in France a few years earlier, the call was taken up by a new generation of directors, with varying degrees of success.

It was Alexander Kluge who emerged as the figurehead of the Young German Cinema, especially after *Abschied von Gestern* (*Yesterday Girl*, 1966) was awarded the Silver Lion at the Venice Film Festival. Two years later he won the Golden Lion for *Artisten in der Zirkuskuppel: Ratlos* (*Artists at the Top of the Big Top*, 1968), suggesting that the Young German Cinema had found its style: part ciné-vérité, part philosophical parable, with a didactic, Brechtian tone, but more cryptic and whimsical, preferring loose episodes and montage sequences to scripted stories with psychologically motivated characters. But Kluge the filmmaker proved less influential than Kluge the film-politician, for it was due to his professional expertise as lawyer and lobbyist that the German cinema developed a unique system of financing and subsidy. As a movement, Oberhausen disintegrated almost as soon as the ink had dried on the pamphlets, but as the starting signal for this quite different campaign to reform the relations between the cinema and the state, Oberhausen was to have momentous consequences.

The uncertain beginnings and eventual dissipation of the Young German Cinema suggest that if one sticks to the founding myth of Oberhausen, then neither the model of the European *auteur* cinema nor the *nouvelle vague*'s love and appreciation of Hollywood quite applies to the first German New Wave. In fact, one would have to argue that the films made between 1965 and 1968 had to be rewritten, almost written off as a false start, in order to get from the Young to the New German Cinema. In terms of style, outlook, even themes and politics, the New German Cinema of the 1970s had little in common with the Young German Cinema, except perhaps that the outstanding figures of the New German Cinema—the second generation, so to speak: Fassbinder, Herzog, Wenders—still had strong Munich connections, as opposed to coming from Berlin or Hamburg, the two other filmmaking centres. However, if in retrospect one can now discern a clear difference in tone, style, and subject matter between Young and New German Cinema, this was not so at the time. For instance, while the term 'young' emphasized generational conflict (the 'old' being the directors who started in the 1930s and 1940s and were thus tainted by their careers during the Nazi period), there was no similarly obvious way of distinguishing membership of the New from the Young. Successive phases of both the Young and the New German Cinema contributed to an almost imperceptible shift in attitude towards a common cinematic heritage, transforming hostile rejection into either camp celebration or cautious reappraisal of that legacy, gradually blurring the edges of the dichotomies that seemed so fundamental in the early 1960s.

Commerce, culture, and the *Autorenfilm*

The economic basis for the phenomenon of the New German Cinema must be sought in the Young German Cinema's political attempts to gain subsidies for film production via the national and regional funding structures, which evolved during the 1960s and 1970s. It is even possible to write a history of the films themselves, their subject matter and styles, according to the type of subsidy and the policies of the funding bodies. The trend toward filmed literature, for instance, in the mid-1970s (with Kleist, Büchner, and Fontane the clear favorites) was dubbed the rise of the *Gremienfilm*, a reference to the selection committees that decided on subsidy, whose members, reputedly, could only be impressed by a script bearing a prestigious (literary) name. Likewise, the 'women's film' of the early 1980s or filmed biographies can be related to different conjunctures in the overall media politics, in this case, of public service television which, in the name of balance, want to reach special interest groups.

But West Germany's film policy developed gradually and almost continuously from the late 1940s onwards. What changed in the 1960s was the opening up of new funding channels (the *Kuratorium Junger Deutscher Film*, the Federal Ministry of the Interior's film prizes, the *Filmförderungsanstalt*, the Berlin *Förderung*) and new legislation that brought the diverse bodies and their piecemeal measures into a common framework. Yet this legislation needed several amendments before the film subsidy system could be said to work as an effective production stimulus for small-scale *and* large-scale productions; for independent author-producers *and* more experimental filmmaking; for commercially oriented producers as well as for first-time projects from previously non-represented groups such as women filmmakers. This central feature of the West German situation—that politics and critical prestige took precedence over popularity and box office—could be described as the victory of culture over commerce.[3]

What was remarkable about the German experiment was that the money necessary for making films no longer relied on the capitalist system, purportedly regulating itself through market forces. It had shifted, within less than fifteen years, to one operating largely outside these conditions. This not only left traces on the films themselves, it also changed the function of the cinema within the culture at large. In the new situation, the films had a semi-official status, and the filmmakers occupied the roles of representatives. Whether they liked it or not, their 'first audience' were the committees, and thus the state as guardian of the arts and national culture, to which was added public service television as the guardian of cultural diversity and political consensus.

Discourses of social legitimacy and authorial justification were a prominent feature of the new cinema, involving it in politics even more than in aesthetic debates. The cinema became part of the so-called extra-parliamentary opposition (APO) of radicalized students and other protest groups, who felt themselves disenfranchized or unrepresented and who demanded radical social change. Compared to other European New Waves, it was striking how many militant platforms but also how many committees the directors felt obliged to sit on, and how few admitted to a simple passion for cinema. The intense media debates and the discussions filmmakers sought with their audiences were indicative of the directors' changed status.[4] They had to be spokespersons on social issues, since the new cinema rarely filled the cinemas; but it found compensation by occupying a public sphere, where it stood for solidarity, the class struggle, and sexual emancipation, rather than for *mise-en-scène*, deep focus, the long take, or montage, as did French auteurism.

Nonetheless, Germany, too, needed the art cinema category of the *auteur*, but with a notably different definition. Authorship became an evident focus for both production and reception, now inflected by the role of public figure and spokesperson, as well as the author's function within the funding system as a legal entity and contractual partner. Although the notion of authorship in European art cinema in the 1960s often had progressive connotations, the fact that many of the films produced under state sponsorship failed to reach the cinemas either in Germany or abroad indicated that the *Autorenfilm* could also be seen as retrograde, establishing a filmmaking ghetto whose radical politics or critical agenda that the state had successfully neutralized and rendered ineffectual by making this cinema part of official culture. But the need to attain credibility with a national audience, both for the sake of their professional self-image and in order to counter the accusations of nepotism on the committees, made some directors rethink their strategy in the late 1970s. This was the purpose of the Hamburg Declaration, where directors sought more active ways of responding to what they perceived to be particular audience expectations, such as social relevance and intervention in local problems by documenting communities in distress or regions in decline and by taking up ecological issues or the plight of disadvantaged groups and ethnic minorities. Thus, parallel to the *Autorenfilm* and what it implied in terms of a personality cult, there was a search for an audience at home. This less-often-discussed motivation determined the subject matter of much of New German Cinema during the 1970s, with several hybrid genres of fiction film, essay film, and documentary feature emerging.

Television and the 'audience-film'

Despite its hybrid forms, however, the New German Cinema was primarily a narrative cinema. Directors whose films were based on strategies of continuity other than narrative ones, such as Harun Farocki with his essay films, or who, like Werner Schröter, used forms of narrative derived from music and opera, had a much more difficult time with subsidy commissions and funding authorities (see Fassbinder 1984: 78). By contrast, the most easily subsidized genre were adaptations of literary works, either classics or contemporary authors, indicating that this state-sponsored, official cinema was too timid when picking original subjects or tackling live political issues, one of the main complaints also of the Hamburg Declaration (see Kluge 1977; Lenssen 1983; Zwerenz in Pflaum 1978: 22–5).

The emphasis on filmed literature may also have been an unintended consequence of the second revision of the Film Subsidy Law, which introduced various 'quality' thresholds in order to exclude blatantly commercial or exploitative productions from automatic subsidy. But the most momentous change of this 1974 revision was to bring in television as a co-producer on a structural, legally binding basis. The Television Framework Agreement between the television networks and the Film Subsidy Board specified the amount each of the two national and the many regional channels were to allocate to feature film productions, which would receive regular cinema distribution before being aired on television. The framework agreement also provided development funds and screenwriting subsidies.

With television entering the subsidy system as the filmmakers' major partner around 1974, this search for new audiences was both accentuated and modified. For television broadcasters—in the days of the public service remit, the scarcity of channels and the absence of the remote control—the audience was, in one sense, already constituted: it was the family audience that had abandoned the cinemas. But this was not the audience the New German Cinema author was likely to reach. The challenge was to reach audiences who had never been cinema-goers; the danger was to be at the mercy of programming schedules and end up in late-night or otherwise unpopular time slots. Nonetheless, the directors benefited from the principle of *Öffentlichkeit* (public accountability) as defined in the statutes of German broadcasting, which guaranteed the right of minorities or special pressure groups to be represented on television. This gave rise to an enormous demand for films on a variety of social issues, which, thanks to the *Autorenfilm*, officially belonged to the New German Cinema. A niche opened up between current affairs television and experimental filmmaking. It gave, for instance, many women filmmakers their first opportunity, making the German cinema of the 1970s and 1980s a center of the European women's film.

On the one hand, the policy changes that brought the national television networks into the film-funding system as co-producers, commissioning editors, and exhibitors of the finished product helped ease the severely congested distribution situation for first-time filmmakers and women directors. On the other hand, from the mid-1970s, domestic audiences began to return to the specialized art cinemas, many of which had in the meantime changed hands. The postwar film-club movement had not been able to sustain itself after the decline of Neorealism and the fading presence of the grand European *auteurs* such as Fellini, Visconti, Rossellini, Bresson, and Bergman. Many of its so-called *Gilde-Kinos* (the equivalent of the French *cinéma d'art et essai*, which showed non-commercial films) had to close, or became small houses showing first runs of recent releases. In cities such as Frankfurt (Kommunales Kino), Hamburg (Abaton), Berlin (Arsenal), municipally funded cinematheques arose in their stead. These drew a younger audience for program that—depending on the personality of the programmers and their local knowledge—gave priority to social themes, to international productions, cinephile fare, avant-garde experiment, or auteurist retrospectives. Called 'program cinemas' (*Programmkinos*), they found an ally in late-night television, which serviced a newly awakened film culture, showing award-winning films from the world's festivals, as well as commissioning work by German and international directors, such as those featured in the celebrated *Kleine Fernsehspiel* (Little Television Play) of ZDF (Second German Television) under the direction of Eckart Stein.

Without television as its partner, the New German Cinema would certainly not have 'happened' on the scale that it did. Yet as Kluge, acknowledged architect of West German film policy and critic of each successive government measure (which always seemed to fall short of his own, bolder and more radical proposals) never tired of pointing out, the German Cinema of the 1970s attained even its international reputation not *because of* the West German funding system and television, but *in spite of* them (Kluge 1979). This may have been a polemical exaggeration, but it points to the fact that the benefits of the subsidy system were by no means unanimously recognized. While for many outside observers the most noteworthy aspect of the New German Cinema was the fact that a cultural 'ecology' was flourishing inside a capitalist economy, the view from the inside looked different—witness the Hamburg Declaration, which can now be understood as the culmination of this audience-oriented counter-current to the author-oriented subsidy system:

the strength of German cinema lies in its diversity . . . the funding system has become a maze of bureaucratic controls . . . the imagination must not be administered. . . . The German cinema of the 1980s can no longer be remote-controlled by television broadcasters, committees and special interest groups as it has been up to now. . . . We have proven our professionalism, we are no longer merely a guild. Our only allies are the spectators (*Hamburger Erklärung* 1979: 27 (my translation)).

At first glance this was a 180-degree turnaround from the Oberhausen Manifesto, which had explicitly appealed to a guild mentality of craftsmen and artists. Fifteen years later, filmmakers once more seemed to demand the freedom of the marketplace. Rejecting the very concept of state funding for the cinema, and not just its abuses, they appeared to be arguing against the *Autorenfilm*, as well as against the major positions that had fostered both the Young and the New German Cinema. But the declaration could also be read as a revolt by the home base, irritated by the increasing and exclusive attention paid to the star directors Fassbinder, Herzog, Wenders, Schlöndorff, Syberberg, and a few others. The Hamburg Declaration spelled the end of a development, but not so much that of state funding for the cinema, or the involvement of television. Rather, it marked the point where the New German Cinema began to experience the consequences of its own growth and the end of solidarity, both politically and film-politically. After Hamburg, filmmaking in Germany began losing its specifically 'national' or official character, to become for the most part one element in the highly diffuse, diversified, and fragmented sector of the television industry. One can even conclude that the surge in filmmaking in West Germany between the late 1960s and early 1980s followed the transformations of the international media and entertainment industry, which (with the growth of commercial channels and the opening up of subsidiary outlets, such as video) was able to draw on and absorb a number of as yet unaffiliated, non-unionized directors, cameramen, and other related personnel, on a freelance basis. It could exploit them by giving them for a time the illusion of being independent film artists. With the stabilization of this labor market in the early 1980s, the 'wave' that was the New German Cinema ebbed away, leaving—apart from a vast number of individual films rarely shown in cinemas either at home or abroad—the few internationally known *auteurs*, most of whom might arguably have made a career for themselves even without the film-funding system or elaborate, government-sponsored promotion campaigns.

Wenders, Herzog, Fassbinder, and the pure cinema film

Foremost among these international *auteurs* were Wim Wenders, Werner Herzog, and Rainer Werner Fassbinder. While Fassbinder was turned down by the Berlin Film Academy, Wenders is one of the very few directors of his generation to graduate from a film school (in Munich), where he made his first full-length feature film, *Summer in the Cities* (original title) in 1970. Also active as a writer and critic, he became a co-founder of the Filmverlag der Autoren, an important distribution initiative started by directors (note that both 'Verlag' and 'Autor' refer to the literary publishing business). Given his extensive film culture—he spent a year in Paris—Wenders was the most cinephilic defender of 'pure cinema' and auteurism, especially conscious of the Hollywood legacy, but also anxious to take his place within German film history: the grandson, as it were, of the legendary figures of 1920s and the Paris-Hollywood émigré directors of the 1930s.

Falsche Bewegung (*False Movement*, 1975) and *Im Lauf der Zeit* (*Kings of the Road*, 1975) brought Wenders critical, commercial, and popular success, and with it, bigger budgets: *Der Amerikanische Freund* (*The American Friend*, 1977) led to a US contract with Francis Ford Coppola, to direct *Hammett* (1982). A sobering experience, it was reflected in a number of the director's subsequent films: *Nick's Movie*, on and with his director friend Nicholas Ray; *The State of Things*, a 'film-within-a-film' feature about a disastrous European-American co-production starring Sam Fuller and Roger Corman; and *Paris Texas* (1984), shot in the US, but a Franco-German production, which became a cult film, not least because of Ry Cooder's score, Sam Shepard's script, and riveting performances by Harry Dean Stanton and Nastassja Kinski. Refocused on Germany since his *Der Himmel über Berlin* (*Wings of Desire*, 1987), a meditation on the impossibility of a 'return' and a poetic homage to Berlin, Wenders has made the condition of exile, of being 'on the road', and the difficulty of coming home (*Alice in the Cities*, 1974) his continuing preoccupation in both *Bis ans Ende der Welt* (*Until the End of the World*, 1991) and *In weiter Ferne, so nah* (*Far Away, So Close*, 1993), the latter looking at a post-unification Berlin, caught between a still murky past and ever more nomadic urban existences. Perhaps too readily seen as the European reinventor of the American road movie, Wenders shares his detached observational stance covering deep narcissistic wounds with the Austrian writer Peter Handke, who has written three scripts for Wenders. A director with an unmistakable visual style and rhythm, he often works with the same team, including cameraman Robby Müller, editor Peter Przygodda, and the actors Rüdiger Vogler, Bruno Ganz, and Hans Zischler. Since the phenomenal success of *Buena Vista Social Club* (1999), a stylish and evocative documentary about Ry Cooder's 'rediscovery' of a group of senior-citizen

Cuban musicians, Wenders has found it more difficult to win audiences for his more sombre reflections on millennial anxieties in *The Million Dollar Hotel* (2000).

For a while, Werner Herzog overshadowed even Wenders as the figurehead of the New German Cinema abroad. A self-taught, self-confessed visionary Romantic, Herzog made shorts and documentaries (*Herakles*, 1962; *Spiel im Sand*, 1964) before directing his award-winning script *Lebenszeichen* in 1967. Another *auteur* with a strong personal signature, even when doing remakes of such classics as F. W. Murnau's *Nosferatu* (1978) or literary adaptation of a work by Georg Büchner (*Woyzeck*, 1979), Herzog has a single subject which he varies, depending on the central character's self-image as overreacher and prophet, or as underachiever and holy fool. This impossible blend of humility and hubris in the human animal is best embodied by the actor Klaus Kinski (with whom Herzog made five films) and the non-professional Bruno S. (*Kaspar Hauser*, 1974; *Stroszek*, 1977). Herzog's trademark is the search for extreme locations (in South America, Australia, North and Central Africa), outlandish situations (such as pulling a riverboat across the Andean mountains), and larger-than-life characters (self-doubting explorers, opera-loving rubber barons, slave traders, and conquistadors), whose exploits nevertheless let a strange and touching humanity emerge from impossible odds. His best-known films are the megalomaniacal quests of *Aguirre* (1972), *Fitzcarraldo* (1982), and *Cobra Verde* (1987), all starring Kinski, about whom he also made a posthumous portrait documentary, *Mein liebster Feind* (*My Best Fiend*, 1999), a title that perfectly sums up Herzog's ironic imagination, always inspired by intimate contradiction.

'I am my own best enemy' might have been Rainer Werner Fassbinder's motto, whose turbulent life, sado-masochistic relationships with his collaborators, and frequent public scandals ensured that he became a living myth, with the reputation of a monster. His brief, intense, and immensely productive career was cut short in 1982, when he died of a drug overdose, having made more than forty films in less than fifteen years. Now considered the most important filmmaker of postwar Germany, Fassbinder claimed that from a very early age onward, 'the cinema was the family life I never had at home'. This passion for the cinema—classical Hollywood, commercial German cinema, American avant-garde, and cheaply made porn films—can be seen especially in his early films. They emerged in parallel with directing-scripting-acting efforts on stage, with the Munich Action Theater. There, he worked with Peer Raben and Kurt Raab, Hanna Schygulla and Irm Hermann, who subsequently became the most important members of his film factory company.

His major successes began with *Fear Eats the Soul* (1972), *The Merchant of Four Seasons* (1974), *Fox and his Friends* (1975), and *Despair* (1978). By 1976 Fassbinder had become an international star, yet his work continued to receive mixed notices from national critics, many of whom only began to take him seriously after the foreign press

■ Rainer Werner Fassbinder (1945–1982)

Fassbinder was not only a German director. A unique filmmaker by any standards, he is comparable, on a European scale, only to Jean-Luc Godard, whom at first he much admired. If the 1960s were the decade of Godard, with each film of his eagerly awaited and a source of endless discussions, the 1970s in Europe were Fassbinder's decade, in the way that, in the United States, the decade belonged to Martin Scorsese and Francis Ford Coppola.

Fassbinder died in 1982, at the age of 37 (he was born barely a month after the end of World War II in May 1945). His parents were bourgeois intellectuals from a prosperous town in Bavaria. After not finishing school and generally drifting until he was 20, his productivity was astonishing: more than forty films between 1967 and 1982, during barely fifteen years.

The secret of so many films in such a short space of time was an Andy Warhol-like female-star-and-mini-studio-system, where the same core group of actors, editors, and technicians worked under a charismatic-demonic director on one project after another. For the impossible feat also relied on a manic, possibly drug-induced creativity, in which life and work, work and life constantly mingled and interfered. Fassbinder himself promoted the romantic myth of a brief, violent life, typical of the doomed artist who burns the candle

⬇ *Die Ehe der Maria Braun*

at both ends. He led a nomadic existence, between airplane trips and car rides (where he usually conducted love affairs or business deals, or wrote film scenarios or plays). But beneath the stereotypes of the fast-living artist-*auteur*, Fassbinder was also a calculating artistic production machine, with a finger in all kinds of cultural pies: apart from writing, directing, and producing films, he was artistic director of at least three theaters (in Munich, Bremen, and Frankfurt); he made television drama series and a TV variety show; he wrote plays for the theater (his collected plays make up three volumes), and he even wrote radio plays; he acted in other people's films (by Volker Schloendorff and Wolf Gremm), and contributed critical essays (on Douglas Sirk, Michael Curtiz, and Claude Chabrol); he wrote or signed manifestos, protest notes, and open letters; and he gave dozens of (extremely astute) interviews. His work intersects with—in fact, slices violently into—the softest tissue of German culture since 1945: the homelessness of postwar Germany in its own national history, a feature of West Germany more sorely felt than even the nation's territorial and ideological division. 'No place to hide nor to abide' might have been the motto of this whole generation, born at the end of, or just after, the war. Unlike some of his filmmaking contemporaries (Herzog, Wenders, and, later, Wolfgang Petersen), his chosen self-exile was not to go abroad, but to move to the margins: being openly gay at a time of legal discrimination and public harassment of homosexuals, he instinctively sought the company of social marginals, whether because of their sexuality, their economically precarious existence, their ethnic provenance, or their emotional vulnerability, much like the outsiders, underdogs, petty criminals, prostitutes, has-beens, and no-hopers who people his films.

In 1971 Fassbinder adopted as his mentor Douglas Sirk (Detlef Sierk), who was then living in retirement in Switzerland. What Fassbinder reputedly owes to Sirk is the discovery of melodrama as a viable European, art-cinema genre for social critique. But Fassbinder also saluted in Sirk the man who, before making his Technicolor weepies at Universal Studios, had been one of the German film company Ufa's most successful directors of domestic German women's films in the 1930s. Like Sirk, Fassbinder saw himself as fighting social oppression 'from within'. He knew that the Ufa entertainment films, especially the comedies, musical revues, and women's films from the late 1930s to the mid-1940s, were just about the only emotional 'home' that Germans still inhabited after the catastrophe of Fascism.

Fassbinder died too early to have imagined the fall of the Wall and a post-unification Germany, but his work gives a vivid picture of how the cinema can shape the image of a nation in the eyes of others, across the depiction of how its people deal (or don't) with otherness. If in the house called Europe, Germany is now accepted as the chief resident, and thinks of itself as its most responsible tenant, Fassbinder's protagonists and their often desperate stories are a reminder of how precarious this lease once was. It makes this most untypical of German directors finally one his country's most exemplary, because uniquely 'credible', representatives.

had hailed him as a genius. At once fiercely independent and opportunistic, Fassbinder used state subsidy, worked with commercial producers, and set up international co-production deals in order to finance his films (and personal lifestyle). Some of his most ambitious projects were co-funded by television, where, thanks to the producer Peter Märtesheimer at the prestigious WDR, Fassbinder in the late 1970s turned to recognizably German subjects. Together with Märtesheimer, he made *The Marriage of Maria Braun* (1979), his commercially most successful film and the first in his 'postwar German trilogy' (followed by *Lola*, 1981, and *Veronika Voss*, 1982). His testament film was the con-troversial fourteen-part television adaptation *Berlin Alexanderplatz* (1980), which is one of the underrated masterpieces of world cinema. In the event, it was Fassbinder who proved not only the most prolific but also the most charismatic director of the New German Cinema. Strategically adapting Hollywood and German genre formulas (in *Liebe ist kälter als der Tod* (*Love is Colder than Death*, 1969) and *Angst essen Seele auf* (*Fear Eats the Soul*, 1972), as well as making films on contemporary subjects (*Mutter Küsters Fahrt zum Himmel* (*Mother Kuster's Trip to Heaven*, 1974) and *Die Dritte Generation* (*The Third Generation*, 1979), his output is an exact barometer of the New German Cinema's attempt at finding a balance between addressing domestic spectators and international art house audiences. Ironically, it was precisely this combination of formula cinema and contemporary subjects that secured Fassbinder a place as an art-cinema *auteur*, as well as pointing the way to the subsequent generation of 'postmodern' directors, who no longer recognized a division between film 'art' and popular movies.

Mastering the past (*Vergangenheitsbewältigung*)

In the New German Cinema, the national past was depicted not only across a fractured and broken relationship to authority, and paternal authority in particular. Many films confronted, often in an allegorical manner, the historical conditions under which West Germany came into being: out of the collapse of a dictatorial regime and utter destruc-tion of a country, a people was rescued from itself and gradually rehabilitated thanks to hard work and US aid. Without simplifying too much, one can say that successful films of the New German Cinema could only have one of two subjects: German history this cen-tury and the German family within this history. Straub's *Nicht versöhnt* (*Not Reconciled*, 1964) and Kluge's *Abschied von Gestern* (*Yesterday Girl*, 1965) were at once prescient and premature in this respect. Kluge explained his title (literally 'goodbye to yesterday') with a reference to Germany's past: 'It is meant to provoke a contradiction, because you never can say goodbye to yesterday. If you try to, you get as far as tomorrow, only to discover yesterday all over again.' The contradiction turned out to be permanent, for

West German filmmakers became obsessed with loss: personal memories and child-hood experiences had to be relinquished, tainted as they were by an ideology that had managed, in Kluge's words, to 'maintain the German family idyll right next to the concentration camp'. At first, there was little sign that German audiences were ready to reflect on any of these issues. But such was the force of 'the return of the repressed' or the power of 'the gaze of the other' that history reimposed itself with a vengeance in the following decade. The possible afterlife of Nazism and Germany's 'inability to mourn' either for itself or for the victims of the Holocaust became *the* topic of the 1980s, with *Our Hitler* (1977), *Germany in Autumn* (1978), *The Tin Drum* (1979), *The Marriage of Maria Braun* (1979), *The Patriot* (1979), and *Germany Pale Mother* (1980).

The approach was invariably oblique and indirect: In *Hitler—A Film from Germany*, for instance, Syberberg chose to focus more on Hitler's valet and the neurotic anxieties of Heinrich Himmler than on the dictator himself, who appears as a mere puppet and mouthpiece of the Germans' collective anxieties, fantasies, and premonitions. It was a risky strategy, and while some (notably Susan Sontag) hailed the film as the first cinematic masterpiece to come out of West Germany, because it laid bare the emotional roots and seductive power of this monstrous figure for 'ordinary' Germans, others (notably Saul Friedlander) thought the director had succumbed to the fascination still emanating from the Nazi cult of 'kitsch and death'. In contrast to Syberberg, Kluge used documentary and newsreel footage, family snapshots and fictional scenes in *The Patriot* for a cut-up representation of the many layers that made up a sense of living in a present shot through with an unassimilated and barely understood history.

In another reckoning with German history, Fassbinder decided to tell typical movie stories, using classical realism, heightened by melodramatic stylization and artifice, but above all, to let the viewer know how much our version of history is already permeated by its representation through the cinema itself. What Fassbinder had learned from the American cinema, he skillfully extended to the German cinema of the 1940s, 1950s, and 1960s, producing a sense of disturbing familiarity. This, too, was a controversial move: for Fassbinder, a return to history meant establishing above all a continuity within the official doctrine of the clean break, and thus an acknowledgement of collusion of the present with the past on the basis not so much of an ideological sympathy but of a surfeit of images about Nazism, so that in the stories he told, the repressed of German history did seem to return: the *unheimlich* (uncanny) did become *heimlich* (all too familiar).

The most 'documentary' approach was that of Edgar Reitz's fifteen-and-a-half-hour *Heimat*, the history of a family caught up in German history, from 1900 to the 1970s. Despite worldwide success, *Heimat* was accused of offering a revisionist history, in which roots and the rural community were so central that neither the persecution and murder of the Jews nor the suffering of the civilian population during the bombing raids on the cities during World War II seemed to have a place.

New German Cinema: the last of the national cinemas?

Nothing, in a sense, unites the films made in Germany in the 1970s and early 1980s as much as *how* films were made in Germany. Typical are not the national character, but the cultural mode of production; not the antagonism with Hollywood or the Romantic legacy of high art, but the Film Funding System and the Television Framework Agreement. However, an analysis of the dominant narratives points to certain elements of a national mythology valid for the New German Cinema as a whole. These turn upon a number of key notions, such as the family and paternity, *Heimat* and exile, the wild child and the return of the prodigal son. Especially in the films mentioned at the beginning as having attracted an international public, certain thematic and stylistic constellations repeat themselves. They make the preoccupation with (male) identity and the (female) nation—in their emotional, gendered, and familial repercussions—into a sort of super-genre, that of 'mastering the past' (*Vergangenheitsbewältigung*), which in turn provided a repertoire of motifs for very different directors. Their work resulted in quite distinct—and eventually clichéd—interpretations of German history, notably of the Nazi period and its immediate postwar history. Certainly, the years from 1974 to 1984 were the German cinema's most reflective, introspective, nostalgic, but also self-critical and cinematically vital decade for half a century. It was, ultimately, the filmmakers devoted to 'mastering the past' (Fassbinder, Syberberg, von Trotta, Schlöndorff, Sanders-Brahms) and to the 'pure cinema film' (Wenders, Herzog, Fassbinder, Schröter) who sustained the international reputation of the New German Cinema and supplied the political arguments at home which allowed the subsidy system to survive.

With the critical successes of these *auteurs*, the New German Cinema entered film history. The scholarly reception in turn helped to rewrite German film historiography of the previous decades, reviving interest in and suggesting links with the first German art cinema and the avant-garde during the 1920s. Inviting many parallels with so-called 'Expressionism', the question arose whether the New German Cinema was the manifestation of a profound as social and spiritual protest as Weimar cinema had been. Or was it perhaps a counter-revolution, with the 'pure cinema' author's film representing a new (German) irrationalism, the vanguard of a wave of depoliticization, defeatism, and disenchantment? Paradoxically, it was with films expressing the post-1968 mood of disillusionment and melancholy self-reflexivity that the German cinema gained not only new spectators in Germany itself but an international audience, and with it a world reputation.

⬆ *Der Himmer über Berlin*

Given its radical origins, the New German Cinema clearly belonged to the anti-authoritarian emancipation impulse of the 1960s and the new social movements around gender, class and ethnicity of the 1970s in the rest of Europe, as well as the United States. But the militant spirit of the directors seemed in stark contrast to the somber mood of the films, as if—in the words of Lotte Eisner, commenting on the collectively produced *Germany in Autumn* (1978)—German filmmakers needed a good portion of despair, confusion, and sorrow in order to find their true creative stride.

When Hollywood returned to Europe in the 1980s with its blockbusters, to become once more the benchmark for big screen entertainment, it seemed that the different 'national' movements had only existed in order to fill a gap, flourishing for a decade or two, while the larger shifts in the technological and economic environment of the mass media were taking place, as national film industries 'lost out' to Hollywood, and much of art cinema 'lost out' to television. At the peak of their success, many German *auteurs*, who had outgrown the subsidy system and become involved in international deals and co-production contracts, also tried their luck in the United States. Neither Wenders nor Herzog, neither Schlöndorff nor Percy Adlon can be said to have accomplished this transition—they all returned to Germany. Yet two directors of about the same generation,

Wolfgang Petersen and Roland Emmerich, along with Michael Ballhaus, the cameraman who had worked for years with Fassbinder, did manage to 'succeed', but on Hollywood's terms: they became Europeans making films in Hollywood for a global audience. This, perhaps more than the Hamburg Declaration, more than the end of the social-liberal coalition government of Willy Brandt and Helmut Schmidt, or the death of Fassbinder, rang the changes on the New German Cinema in the early 1980s. Tom Tykwer, Germany's oustanding director of the post-unification 1990s, can be compared with Lars von Trier and Jean-Pierre Jeunet, but he is also closer to Wong Kar Wai than, for instance, to his fellow German director Detlev Buck. In order to survive, national cinemas have tried to become global by learning to be local, as the European cinema is once more redefining its place within world cinema, while its *auteurs* are still expected to represent the nation at film festivals and in university film courses. The New German Cinema instantiated the template for these developments, but—as the last of the European national cinemas—it proved to be no exception to the rule.

Further reading

Bergfelder, Tim, Erica Carter, and Deniz Göktürk (eds.), *The German Cinema Book* (London: British Film Institute, 2002). A representative collection of essays, arranged by topics (popular cinema, stars, institutions, cultural politics, transnational connections) covering the whole history of German cinema, but particularly strong on the post-WWII period up to the present.

Collins, Richard, and Vincent Porter, *WDR and the Arbeiterfilm: Fassbinder, Ziewer and others* (Television Monograph 12: London: British Film Institute, 1981). Highly illuminating case study of a politically controversial genre and a politically controversial broadcaster trying to bridge the gap between television and the cinema and creating a new forum for social debate through popular forms of entertainment.

Corrigan, Timothy, *New German Cinema: The Displaced Image*, 2nd edn. (Austin: University of Texas Press, 1994). A series of very perceptive essays on the major directorial figures, giving sympathetic accounts and in-depth readings of their thematic and formal preoccupations.

Elsaesser, Thomas, *New German Cinema: A History* (London/New Brunswick, NJ: Macmillan/Rutgers University Press, 1989). Analytical study of the 'New German cinema', situating it in institutional contexts and outlining both the economic and artistic determinants. The chief argument is that, divided between films intended for a domestic audience and an international public, this 'new wave' became significant, partly because of the turbulent politics in Germany during the 1970s, and partly thanks to productive misunderstandings between the filmmakers and their critics/admirers.

—— *Fassbinder's Germany: History Identity Subject* (Amsterdam: Amsterdam University Press, 1996). Besides an overview in the form of an extensively commented filmography and a series of detailed readings of key films from both textual and contextual perspectives, this study stresses the import-ance of Germany, its film history, and the representation of its recent history in the director's work.

Haake, Sabine, *German National Cinema* (London: Routledge, 2002). Attempting a coherent account of all periods of German cinema, this study stresses the continuities across the historical breaks and thus contextualizes the New German Cinema more broadly also within developments in East German cinema during the 1960s and 1970s, as well as taking the narrative into the 1990s.

Kaes, Anton, *From Hitler to Heimat: The Return of History as Film* (Cambridge, Mass.: Harvard University Press, 1989). Widely used collection of essays on the relationship between history, representation, and cinema, focusing on a number of key films by key filmmakers from the 1970s and 1980s, such as Syberberg, Fassbinder, Kluge, and Reitz.

Knight, Julia, *Women and the New German Cinema* (London: Verso, 1992). Sympathetic study of German women filmmakers and the strategies they pursued for gaining access to the state-funded television and filmmaking institutions.

Pflaum, Hans Günther, and Hans Helmut Prinzler, *Film in the Federal Republic of Germany* (Bonn: Inter Nationes, 1992). Biographical-filmographical dictionary of 'new' German filmmakers, sandwiched between a critical overview-essay and useful information about film culture and film institutions in Federal (united) Germany.

Reimer, Robert C., and Carol J. Reimer, *The Nazi-Retro Film: How German Narrative Cinema Remembers its Past* (New York: Twayne/Toronto: Maxwell Macmillan, 1992). Very useful annotated checklist of films dealing with aspects of Germany's Nazi past, both fictional and documentary. Trenchant without being partisan in its judgements.

Rentschler, Eric (ed.), *West German Filmmakers on Film: Visions and Voices* (New York: Holmes & Meier, 1988). Extremely valuable collection of statements, manifestos, and short essays by German directors about film aesthetics, film policy, and cultural self-definition.

Notes

1. For the full text of the Oberhausen Manifesto, see Pflaum and Prinzler (1983: 5).
2. The paradox was that the Old German Cinema had never been truly commercial and the New German Cinema never truly independent. See Joe Hembus, 'Bonner Film-AG', in Hembus (1981: 202).
3. For a comparative perspective, see Vincent Porter, 'Television and Film Production in Europe', *Sight and Sound* (autumn 1977), and his 'British Film Culture and the European Economic Community', *Sight and Sound* (summer 1978).
4. The Frankfurt *Römerberggespräche* of 1977, devoted to the future of the German cinema, were held under the programmatic title: 'Sie schlagen uns das Kino tot' (They are murdering our cinema).

NEW CURRENTS

Europe at the end of the twentieth century was marked by a tension between two opposing movements: unification and fragmentation. The creation of the European Union in 1992 was accompanied by the 'Balkanization' of East-Central Europe, which resulted from the collapse of the Soviet Union and the resurgence of old national and ethnic antagonisms that had been suppressed during the Cold War. At the same time, national boundaries were also being redrawn (or ignored) by market capitalism, which forged an increasingly complex network of global connections in finance, trade, manufacturing, transport, and communications, and which, aided by the spread of the Internet, imposed English as the *lingua franca* of the international marketplace.

Cinema has been at once a means of disseminating this global culture and a product of it. Films help publicize cultural values, fashion, music, and stars to a world audience. They are also subject to the dictates of increasing uniformity brought by globalization, witnessed in the rise of the multiplex cinema in the 1980s across Europe, which encouraged the exhibition of fewer films on more screens. This decline in diversity is also apparent in the growing number of English-language films being made in Europe, in co-productions that are sometimes derided as incoherent 'Europuddings' because they are trying to be all things to all people, while failing in fact to be anything to anyone.

On the other hand, many intra-European collaborations have been quite successful, both critically and commercially. For example, Krzysztof Kieślowski, often considered the most quintessentially 'European' of late twentieth-century directors, gained financial backing and utilized actors and technical personnel from Poland, France, and Switzerland to produce his landmark *Trois couleurs* trilogy. The Bosnian director Emir Kusterica filmed *Il était une fois un pays* (*Underground*, 1994) in Prague with German and French funding. At the same time, big-budget collaborations between, in particular, Great Britain and the United States produced such well-regarded and commercially successful films such as *The Full Monty* (Peter Cattaneo, 1997), *Shakespeare in Love* (John Madden, 1998), and *The English Patient* (Anthony Minghella, 1996).

Yet there are still distinctive voices in European cinema that manage to produce films with artistic and commercial appeal without relying on Hollywood. In the last two decades of the twentieth century, European films by directors Pedro Almodóvar, Giuseppe Tornatore, and Jean-Pierre Jeunet (to name just a few) made a perceptible impact in the world market, renewing the vitality of the 'arthouse' circuit. At the same time, younger talents such as Cédric Klapisch, Lynne Ramsey, and Lukas Moodysson have emerged, who are introducing new generations of filmgoers to the pleasures and challenges of European cinema.

Though many of the films and movements examined in this section are no longer 'new' (or 'current', for that matter), they all in some way mark a break with the postwar period, reflecting the stylistic influence of music videos and television advertising, and of new technologies such as digitization (which, like television before it, has not brought about the death of cinema but has worked in conjunction with it). For all their newness, however, these movements also pick up on earlier traditions. The 1980s witnessed the return of the big-budget spectacle and the lavishly produced historical epic, last prominent in the 1950s. Then, the move away from politics in the 1980s (the *cinéma du look*, the heritage film) was followed in the 1990s by a renewed interest in the margins of society and in exposing the excesses of consumer culture, evidenced in a return to realism that displays a sense of urgency not seen since the 1940s.

European cinema may, thus, be branching out in new directions, but it still owes much to its roots. Despite the major changes redefining the role and even the composition of Europe in the twenty-first century, cinema remains a significant force in the construction and expression of cultural identity. The threat of homogenization wrought by unification has not prevented distinctive voices from emerging; nor has the pain of fragmentation and the reassertion of national and ethnic identities quelled collective creations, many of which indeed manage to be much more than the sum of their parts.

THE *CINÉMA DU LOOK*

Sue Harris

French cinema in the early 1980s witnessed a definitive challenge to the author-ity of the generation of directors, actors, and technicians schooled in the intel-lectual and naturalistic modes of *nouvelle vague* (New Wave) filmmaking. Once proud and innovative critics of the *cinéma de papa* ('old cinema'), the practitioners of the 1960s and 1970s increasingly found themselves out of favor with audiences, whose numbers fell dramatically over a twenty-year period. As the 1980s began, so new aesthetic modes with new narrative priorities made a tentative appearance on French screens; and as the 1980s advanced, the work of new filmmakers with a taste for extravagant spectacle progressively eclipsed the 1970s vogue for historico-politico-realist filmmaking. As the *cinéma du look*, a celebration of the visual and sensory elements of the filmic text, became established as a contemporary norm in France, critics and journalists sought to find an appropriate label for this latest cohort of young Turks. Variously termed 'post-modern', *les néo-baroques* (new baroque), or the filmmakers of the *Forum des Halles* (after the 1980s designer-chic Parisian shopping center), it is somewhat ironic that the generic label that attached itself most forcefully was that of the 'new' New Wave.

The filmmakers of this new New Wave were in fact far less a school of filmmaking, with its implied shared ambitions and ideologies, than their 1960s predecessors. The first to emerge as a new force in French filmmaking was Jean-Jacques Beineix, the elder statesman of the movement with credentials in TV advertising and pop videos rather than

⬆ *Diva*

in big-budget filmmaking. His film *Diva* (1981), now a benchmark film in the *cinéma du look* corpus, was produced with a budget of only 7 million francs, and was initially only a very minor hit in Parisian cinemas. It was not until almost a year after its release, with a clutch of nominations for the *Césars* (the French version of the Academy Awards), that the film began to find success with a wider audience. Beineix's arrival on French screens was swiftly followed in 1982 by that of the much younger Luc Besson, a high-school drop-out with a penchant for the fantastic. His début film, *Le Dernier Combat* (*The Final Combat*, 1983), produced with a budget of only 3.5 million francs, was also the recipient of two major awards, this time at the 1983 Avoriaz Science Fiction and Fantasy Festival. Finally, in 1984, Léos Carax directed *Boy Meets Girl* (original title), and was embraced by critics as the third newcomer in what was to become an influential trio of directors active in this new aesthetic mode.

Although not a school in the generally understood sense of the term, Beineix, Besson, and Carax launched their careers in close enough proximity to be considered a phenomenon. And again, although each director's work is distinctive, they share enough common ground to be considered as an identifiable movement in modern French filmmaking. The directors share a number of priorities in their filmmaking, and these are most evident in their innovative approaches to questions of genre, characterization, narrative form, and aesthetics. As a body of work, the films exert what Fredric Jameson has identified as a 'visual spell: an enthrallment to the image in its present of time' (Jameson 1990: 130). These films share a distinctly oneiric quality, in which the world and the inhabitants of the diegesis are recognizable but 'uncanny', and in which narrative events are framed less by processes of continuity, logic, and cause and effect than by the random, the accidental, and the arbitrary. If a single defining framework prevails in the *cinéma du look*, it is that of the image, the spectacle that stands apart from the narrative dynamic, and offers discrete moments of heightened sensory pleasure to the viewer.

Genre

Cinéma du look films are generically influenced by expressly popular genres previously explored in both literature and filmmaking. The crime thriller is a recurrent reference in the work of all three directors, forming the core narrative thread of *Diva*, *La Lune dans le caniveau* (*The Moon in the Gutter*; Beineix, 1983) *Subway* (Besson, 1985), *Mauvais Sang* (*Bad Blood*; Carax, 1986), *Nikita* (Besson, 1990), *Léon* (Besson, 1994) and *The Fifth Element* (Besson, 1997). Science fiction features heavily as a generic reference in Besson's *Le Dernier Combat* and *The Fifth Element*, while the feel of grainy television documentary is captured in films such as *Boy Meets Girl* and *Les Amants du Pont-neuf* (*The Lovers on the Bridge*; Carax, 1991). Indeed, much of *Le Grand Bleu* (*The Big Blue*; Besson, 1988) with its langorous shots of the ocean and marine life, resembles a televised natural history program (indeed, Besson went on to make a documentary about sea life, *Atlantis*, in 1991). Romance is another staple element of *cinéma du look* films, with the 'boy meets girl' storyline underlying almost every film in the corpus, and even giving a title to one of the form's earliest examples. Beineix's *37,2 le matin* (*Betty Blue*, 1986) is the film that distills this particular narrative to its purest form, conveying a preoccupation with madness and sexual obsession via the photographic compositions common to postmodern television and cinema advertising. Underlying these generic forms are a series of other popular influences: comedy permeates the dialogue, gestures, and appearance of many characters in the films, and action often respects the broad lines of cartoon strip narrative with its excessively slick, choreographed gestures. Characters such as Fred (Christophe Lambert) in *Subway*, or Nikita do not ask to be read at the level of psychological realism, but rather as types within a given narrative form, whose composition is the logical extension of the wider generic conventions at play.

Narrative events in the more deliberately fantastic films of the *cinéma du look* (those closest to science fiction or the thriller genre) are frequently a pretext for elaborate visual compostion, the trigger that will lead to a major set-piece spectacle that may be violent, musical, or simply highly theatrical. The events leading to the formation of the rock band in *Subway*, for example, are little more than a prelude to its sole, energetic performance in the final sequence of the film. At all other levels, the events that precede this sequence are inconsequential, and are therefore not subject to the same laws of logic and continuity as the genres that are referenced. Thus the elaborate car chase that opens the film exists primarily as a cinematic quotation, a playful wink to the viewer. Its primary narrative purpose is to establish, via a vertiginous descent into the labyrinthine tunnels of the subway, the spatial topography of the subsequent performance space.

Characterization

In terms of content, the work of all three directors focuses on marginality as an expression of national, class, and generational identity. The characters in their films are a curious mixture of the chic and the down-at-heel, the attractive and the grotesque, the intellectual and the brutish. Throughout the corpus we witness the actions of marginal or marginalized characters, people who live on the edges of society (*Diva*, *Le Dernier Combat*, *Nikita*, *Le Grand Bleu*, *Léon*, *Les Amants du Pont-neuf*), if not actually far below it (*Subway*), in a literally simmering and potentially explosive underworld. There is frequently a sense that the world of the *cinéma du look* constitutes a freak show, in which hastily drawn caricatures—the macho police officer, the exotic singer, the passionate lover, the cold-blooded killer—have come to life. Indeed, character construction is inherently simplistic, closer to that of cartoons and fairy tales than to that of modern cinematic representation. This is especially the case at the level of secondary, transient characters, such as *le gros Bill* ('Big Bill') in *Subway*, a fairground strongman whose actions are simply an extension of his function as a type. He, like the broad canvas of characters in the films, is but a single element in a self-contained world that is characterized both by simplicity (*le gros Bill* is the sum of his visible parts) and ambiguity (the narrative continually suggests that he might represent more than this). The leading protagonists generally fall into the category of young hedonistic misfits, at ease with a consumerist ethos and skilled in the generic mores of popular culture. In some critical circles, they were read as expressive of what became know as *le style Forum des Halles*, a fashion of the early 1980s for designer brands in clothes and accessories. The recently built modernist underground shopping mall, the Forum des Halles in Paris, was in its day the emblem of contemporary metropolitan fashion, and these characters were among the most accessible mediatized embodiments of this aspirational material culture.

Indeed, what we have in *cinéma du look* films is the representation of a culture of individuals that sets store by objects and brands: recording equipment and music, watches and jewelry, classic vehicles and state-of-the-art weapons; a shallow, superficial society concerned with how it looks more than who it is. The image is itself a source of mutual recognition and identity for *look* protagonists that extends beyond the screen and into the audience, and which is referenced again and again in the actions, lifestyles, and vocabulary of its key players. Furthermore, a mastery of both urban space and sophisticated technological equipment is key to the lifestyles, indeed the survival, of the majority of the protagonists in the films (see the examples of Jules [*Diva*], Fred [*Subway*], Nikita [*Nikita*], Léon [*Léon*], and Leeloo [*The Fifth Element*]), and art itself is represented in the worlds of the films as something inextricably bound to capitalist modes of production and consumption. The desire to own the Diva's voice, like the desire to own Leeloo's ancient stones, sets in motion a series of events in which material possession is determined by the successful negotiation of space and technology.

This rigorous focus on the surface qualities of characterization represents, to some extent, the disintegration of the unified subject of earlier cinematic traditions. Thus, exterior characterization is a major contributing factor in creating the 'surface sheen' effect (Jameson 1990: 130) so characteristic of *cinéma du look* films. As superficial visual icons, rather than psychologically drawn individuals, the characters stand in stark contrast to the intellectual formation, or broad comic stance, of many post-1968 film protagonists. Instead of using political discourse or satire, their provocation is inherently performative: their carefully cultivated designer look, whether upmarket like that of Helena in *Subway* or down-at-heel like that of Alex in *Les Amants du Pont-neuf*, is what confers an identity upon them, uniting them as a peer group, while setting them apart from the ordinary. While they may be disenfranchised by dint of being young and poor at this period in France's history (their material acquistions often bear little relation to actual economic security), they are victims of the fallout of previous political positions, rather than activists who seek to circumvent the reality of their circumstances. Thus the *cinéma du look* introduced a new type of character into French cinema, one whose primary function is to 'be' rather than to 'do'; one we look at and appraise visually, rather than engage with emotionally; one we understand as a performative essence rather than a psychological construct.

Narrative form

The intensely theatrical pause that is deliberately spectacular either in terms of action or composition is a narrative staple of the *cinéma du look* style. Many of the films of the *cinéma du look* feature performative set-pieces that are embedded in the narrative. Cynthia Hawkins's recital (*Diva*), Alex's fire-eating (*Les Amants du Pont-neuf*), and Diva

Plavalaguna's concert (*The Fifth Element*) are sustained moments of narrative intensity that exert a visual and auditory compulsion over the viewer. Likewise, the Roller's acrobatic skating (*Subway*), Nikita's punk ballet (*Nikita*), and and Alex and Michèle's drunken straddling of the Henri IV statue on the Pont-neuf bridge (*Les Amants du Pont-neuf*) are all inadvertent performances that distract the viewer from the otherwise linear narrative evolution. Similarly, high-intensity violent action frequently has the quality of a choreographed performance: the pursuit of Jules on a motorscooter through the subway (*Diva*), the assassination in the Train Bleu restaurant (*Nikita*), and Leeloo's defeat of the warrior aliens (*The Fifth Element*) are examples of moments in which the visual entertainment value of the action is extended well beyond its function as narrative motor. Elsewhere, surprising collisions of style and tone impose a break in the narrative flow. Often, it is just as we are in danger of losing ourselves in the complexities of plot and character that a visual rupture occurs, forcing spectators to review and rethink the image before us. In *The Fifth Element* for example, the sci-fi coherence of the flight to Flauston Paradise is abruptly sacrificed at the sight of the sumptuous baroque decor and costumes of the ornate Italianate theatre in which Diva Plavalaguna performs. Similarly, in *Les Amants du Pont-neuf*, verisimilitude is abandoned in a momentary visual lapse which sees Alex and Michèle become drunken cartoon figures in a giant world of empty wine bottles and cigarette boxes. Less comically perhaps, the endlessly repeated photographs of Michèle that adorn the subway walls dazzle and repel in equal measure, with the recognizable object, in its excess, becoming a grotesque and bewildering spectacle of confusion and fear.

These broadly defined moments of performance generally have a free-standing quality in the *cinéma du look*, overshadowing the minute details of plot constuction and compelling us to prioritize sensual visual interludes over action-driven narrative events. This remains consistent even at the level of the static image: the films are replete with almost photographic stills that stand outside the action as moments of pure visual pleasure. In *Diva* there are numerous shots of a rectangular water feature in Gorodish's appartment, and the photographs of Alba, or the views of the lighthouse in which the protagonists seek sanctuary, exist primarily as serene and glossy images to be savored by the viewer. From shots of dolphins breaking the sea surface (*Le Grand Bleu*) to the explosions of the bicentennial fireworks (*Les Amants du Pont-neuf*), the *cinéma du look* delights in capturing beautiful images, and in thereby creating 'a present of uncodified intensities' (Jameson 1990: 149) which overwhelms as much as it diverts. As the examples here have shown, playful visual distortions, discontinuities, and digressions underpin the project of the *cinéma du look*, which relishes the possibilities of visual over discursive narrative, the visual consumption of the surface over empathetic emotional engagement.

Style

In aesthetic terms, the films of the *cinéma du look* corpus explore color, light, sound, and space in such a way as to foreground elements that tend to be hidden in conventional filmmaking. This implies a close relationship between the artistic expression and the technological apparatus that enables its production, a relationship that is at the heart of postmodernist theories of cultural production such as those advanced by Jameson. The films of the *cinéma du look* make extensive use of filters to create a palette of primary colors in which reds, blues, and yellows become the dominant elements of *mise-en-scène* and composition. In some cases, color is used as a supplementary element of narration, as for example when a bloodied Jules, pursued by Saporta's thugs, decends into the red-hued hell of the arcade (*Diva*). Elsewhere, the use is more globally conceptual: the interrogation of national identity that Carax mounts in *Les Amants du Pont-neuf*, where the reality of exclusion in modern France is juxtaposed with a celebration of 200 years of liberal republicanism, is underpinned by a Godardian distillation of the dominant colors to red, white, and blue, the tricolor colors of the French flag. The visual gratification of color in postmodern films has been noted by Jameson, who views it as 'a source of particular pleasure (or fascination or *jouissance*)' and even as 'a libidinial apparatus' (Jameson 1990: 130, 142).

Lighting in the *cinéma du look* is frequently used to clear stylistic effect. Many of the films favor interior locales, thus relying on a combination of stark artifical lighting and dark unlit corners. *Subway* takes place almost entirely underground, as does much of *Nikita*; many scenes in *Le Grand Bleu* take place in the darkness of ocean water, while *The Fifth Element* favors sterile, neon-lit white interiors. In the pitch blackness of a subway corridor, Fred (*Subway*) picks up a neon tube to guide his path, and with that simple gesture is transformed into an iconic figure—a Luke Skywalker of the Paris métro. When Nikita does finally escape the dark labyrinthine 'Center' for the first time (*Nikita*), she finds herself in a nocturnal urban street, an environment which then gives way to an oppressively baroque enclosed restaurant from which there is almost literally no escape. Much of the subsequent action of the film takes place at night or within artificially lit confined spaces, and even when a natural outdoor environment beckons (as in the Venice episode), Nikita's opportunity to penetrate it is cruelly limited. More frequently, those films that explore the outdoors use lighting in creative ways, using the ocean itself as a filter in *Le Grand Bleu*, or saturating the screen with high-intensity sunlight in *37,2 le matin*. Beineix's *Roselyne et les lions* (1989) is unusual in that much of the film has a naturalistic feel to it, with natural lighting dominating in the *mise-en-scène*. As we approach the climax of the film, however, light is used to intensify the elements of performance that are so crucial to the narrative; strategic theatrical lighting is deployed to reveal Roselyne as a privileged performer, set apart from the kind of prosaic naturalism that previously surrounded her, and from the limited performance space of the circus ring. Light permits her to transcend her construction as the apprentice lion-tamer of the narrative, and become a cinematic image, separate in time and space from all other elements of the film.

The *cinéma du look* has a distinctive sound that combines music, percussive rhythms, and the amplification of ambient sound. The hybrid soundtrack of *Diva*, which in 1982 received Césars for both sound and music, established an auditory model that we might consider as typical of the form: from the opening bars of *Diva*, we listen as much as we look, to an audacious soundtrack that combines high opera (Wagner and Catalani) with percussive rock, classical interludes with rhythmic synthesizers. The opening moments of Besson's films in particular are as audibly determined as they are visually. *Subway* sees Fred, resplendent in a tuxedo and punk hair, fumbling with his car's cassette player: thus the diegetic music on the casette becomes the pulsing soundtrack against which the action unfolds, and is brought to a logical end only by the crashing of the car and thus the destruction of the diegetic musical apparatus. *Le Grand Bleu*, *Nikita*, *Léon*, and *The Fifth Element* are all characterized by a scrolling or travelling movement on a ground surface, in each case set against an intense rhythmic beat that picks up gradually as the opening action unfolds. *Les Amants du Pont-neuf* is distinguished more by musical interludes than by an ever-present Besson-like soundtrack (for example, the two-hour-long *Fifth Element* boasts a musical content of around one hundred minutes), but music is nevertheless used in ways that echo Beineix's hybridity: as the protagonists dance on the bridge under a sky full of fireworks at the climax of the bicentennial celebration, so the traditional music of the Parisian *bal populaire* (the working-class ball) cedes to African beats, before culminating in the *cinema du look*'s signature heavy rock beat. All the while, the ambient noise is exaggerated on the screen: the sound of the fireworks and later of the swishing waterskis are amplified, with the unfamiliar, distorted sound compelling the viewer's ear as much as the eye. Carax overlays the action with a medley of ethnic and generational sounds that, in their fusion, constitute a backdrop to modern French life, as well as a pseudo-diegetic soundtrack to the visible dance action of the protagonists.

In terms of awards and soundtrack sales, the *cinéma du look* has been hugely successful. In 1982, *Diva* was awarded four Césars, including those for sound and music. The music for all Besson's films has been composed by Eric Serra, a self-taught guitarist whose filmic career was launched with Besson's *Le Dernier Combat*. He went on to win Césars for the score of *Subway*, and later *Le Grand Bleu*, of which over three million copies of the soundtrack were sold in France. He has also been the recipient of other French industry prizes such as the *Victoire de la meilleure musique du film* (best musical soundtrack award) for *Subway*, *Le Grand Bleu*, and *Léon*. Technical expertise in the domain of sound is a trademark of the *cinéma du look*, with many of the films in the corpus being nominated for international awards in sound and music over the years. Besson's English-language film *Messenger: The Story of Joan of Arc* (1999) is the most recent work from this group of directors to receive a Best Sound César.

Finally, the *cinéma du look* style is recognized by its frequent reliance on a compositional framework that respects clear geometric principles. Interior spaces are often expressly modernist, with clear-cut lines that exaggerate their horizontal and vertical axes: Gorodish's apartment in *Diva* is an extensive, virtually empty space, whose compositional lines are broken up with elaborate antique objects (the free-standing iron bath) and with repeated circular movements (Alba's roller skating). The action spaces of the final segment of the film are an immense derelict warehouse and a phallic lighthouse, both vertiginous constructions that dwarf the human elements within the frame. The horizontal trajectory of the underground network is emphasized in the labyrinthine topos of the metro in *Diva* and *Subway*, and a sense of anonymity and human vulnerability is poignantly communicated by the endless linear corridors and automated doors of the government 'Center' in *Nikita*. Baroque elements like the circular staircase leading to Amande's dressing room (*Nikita*) are all the more intrusive, and therefore visually compelling, in such an otherwise stark environment. The possibilities of geometric composition are taken to an extreme in *The Fifth Element*, where the minimalist lines of ancient Egypt give way to an extravagantly futuristic New York, in which the Manhattan grid system is applied vertically as well as horizontally, and movement takes place at high speeds in all possible directions.

Even when the spaces used are less aggressively geometrical, the clarity of the line is still obvious: starkness and sterility are conveyed by the overwhelming whiteness of the gently curving metro corridors of *Les Amants du Pont-neuf*, and the painted beach huts of *37,2 le matin* take on the aspect of coherent blocks of color indicatative of a high degree of attention to composition. The importance of line is further explored in the trademark cross-cutting of many of Besson's films in particular: composition within space is here exaggerated by a technique of comparison such as the scene of the Diva Plavalaguna's concert/Leeloo's battle with the aliens (*The Fifth Element*): both figures are centred in the frame, their actions are choreographed with fluidity and coherence, their relation to their space is seen in each case as continuous, and both use their space as a stage on which to perform.

This prioritizing of aesthetic elements constitutes to a large extent a rejection of the post-New Wave practices of location and improvised shooting, and a return to the production priorities and methodologies of the classic studio system. That the set of *Subway* should have been designed by no less a figure than the celebrated 1930s designer Alexandre Trauner gives some idea of the store that a director like Besson sets by careful control of the cinematic environment. Likewise, many of the scenes in *Les Amants du Pont-neuf* take place not on the actual bridge itself, but on an exact replica that was constructed at huge expense in the South of France after Carax ran over schedule in his filming. Studio filming, with its possibilities for precise control of variable elements such as color, light, sound, and space, lies behind much of the visual extravagance of the *cinéma du look*. The imaginative, often absurd stylization of an environment is intrinsic to the form; however arbitrary individual elements might appear within a given narrative, they are the result of a highly professional, highly skilled attention to the very smallest details of cinematic composition.

Conclusion

From the vantage point of the twenty-first century, the *cinéma du look* is a historically contained, late twentieth-century phenomenon. Initially derided for its flashiness and criticized by august bodies such as the journal *Les Cahiers du cinéma* as being 'all style and no substance', the *cinéma du look* developed a cult following in France and on the international art-house circuit, and by the early 1990s *Diva* had been critically hailed by Fredric Jameson as 'the first French postmodernist film' (Jameson 1990: 55). It is now considered a landmark film in modern French production, a benchmark for modern filmic experimentation.

In terms of the span of the movement, its era can be limited to 1980–1994 (*Diva* t o *Léon*), a period that coincides almost too neatly with the first socialist presidency in France for over forty-five years. Indeed, Jameson's essay 'Diva and French Socialism' (1982) situates Diva in terms of this very precise historical context, arguing that May 10, 1981, the date of Mitterrand's election, 'draws a line beneath the disappointing neo-romantic and post-Godard French production of the 1970s, and allow [*sic*] *Diva* (1981) . . . to emerge (rightly or wrongly) with all the prestige of a new thing, a break, a turn' (Jameson 1990: 55). Given that the *cinéma du look* emerged in the early 1980s against the backdrop of an intensely optimistic political climate, a generous reading might account for the form's absence of politics as symptomatic of a new kind of youth cinema, a cinema that has had its traditional oppositional voice stilled by the concrete reality of elected liberal politics. The *cinéma du look*, it could be argued, was untouched by politics, because the desires of 1968 had been realized with the election of Mitterrand, General de Gaulle's former adversary. And with the need for a political voice removed, the voice of fun, experiment, and visual pleasure could once again assert itself in the cultural apparatus of the nation.

Such a reading would lend itself to the inevitable conclusion that the demise of the *look* form should be understood in terms of the climate of generalized political disaffection that marked the end of socialist power and the return of the right in France under Jacques Chirac in 1995. Having witnessed first-hand the failure of the socialist dream, it could be argued that the mature *cinéma du look* is compelled to address the issues of which it is a product, and thereby loses itself in a sociopolitical commentary to which it is ill-suited. *Les Amants du Pont-neuf* is one of the most politically challenging films of its era, yet the message about exclusion, the assertion that there is something rotten at the very heart of modern French life, was overwhelmed and ultimately lost in the furore that surrounded the budget and production history of the film, as well as the spectacular romantic fantasy of the aesthetically, more than psychologically, damaged protagonists.

The *look* as visual style continues to be expressed in the work of Luc Besson, but *Léon* in 1994 marks the beginning of a new tendency that positions the *cinéma du look* as international blockbuster rather than as experimental French form. *Léon*, *The Fifth Element*, and *Messenger: The Story of Joan of Arc* all boast elements of the *look* style developed in France over a fourteen-year period, but the transition to English language, Hollywood stars, and US production modes is so significant a departure as to enable one to categorize these films as a series in themselves, distant cousins rather than devoted siblings to the French corpus. And yet, if this discussion has found its examples again and again in Besson's *The Fifth Element*, it is because this film, more than any other, actively celebrates the *cinéma du look*, and its almost childlike delight in pastiche and inter-textuality; *The Fifth Element* is a film that recognizes its parentage, and pays adoring homage to it.

The visual ambition of the *look* aesthetic has nevertheless found a continued expression in France, and this is most compelling in overtly political youth-targeted films such as *La Haine* (*Hate*; Kassovitz, 1995). While rooted very securely in psycho-socio-realism, *La Haine* uses a visual code that is very close to the *look* aesthetic: a limited palette of contrasting colors (black and white as opposed to primary colors); a frantic pace in which narrative is conveyed by ellipsis rather than causal logic; a cinephilic delight in quotation (one thinks of the Scorsese and Spike Lee references that permeate the film); an appeal to the auditory as well as visual senses (the ticking countdown, the hip-hop music, the excessively rich urban slang spoken by the protagonists). Nevertheless, the dominant impulse toward spectacle that we find in the *cinéma du look* has, in *La Haine*, been relocated as only one element among many at the service of a sociopolitical message, rather than as the driving force of film form in and of itself.

While Besson's career continues apace, it is perhaps the case that the purest expression of the look may well be those films such as *Le Pacte des loups (The Brotherhood of the*

■ Luc Besson (1959–)

Luc Besson has been the most commercially successful and internationally visible of the directors of the *cinéma du look*. From an inauspicious debut as a young, self-taught, independent filmmaker (his first production company, Les Films du Loup, produced *Le Dernier Combat* in 1983), he has become one of the most influential figures in the French industry, directing, writing, and producing major features in both European and US cinema. While he is credited as director on only nine films to date, his presence as a creative force in international filmmaking extends far beyond this modest portfolio. With two further production companies to his name (Les Films du Dauphin and Leeloo Productions), as well as alliances with major international companies such as Gaumont, Warner, and Fox, Besson has been the artistic and financial force behind many recent box-office hits, including the *Taxi* series (Pirès, 1998; Krawczyk, 2000 and 2003), *The Kiss of the Dragon* (Nahon, 2001), and *Les Rivières pourpres 2* (Dahan, 2003). The esteem with which he is regarded by his peers is also impressive: from uncredited adviser to camera operator on *Astérix et Obélix: Mission Cléopâtre* (Chabat, 2002), his unseen contribution to French practices has been extensive.

Two principles appear to underlie Besson's practices: the first is his preference for working almost artisanally with a core technical and artistic crew in ways reminiscent of the collectivist practices of directors such as Renoir and Carné in 1930s France. Thus, actors like Jean Reno, Milla Jovovich, and Gary Oldman appear in a number of his films, while the composer Eric Serra has scored the music for every Besson film to date. Thierry Arbogast has

⬇ *The Fifth Element*

worked as Besson's cinematographer on all films since *Nikita*, while Dan Weil, who has also worked with Beineix, was the production designer for *Nikita*, *Léon*, and *The Fifth Element*. Even in personal terms, Besson has tended to stay close to his circle of intimates, having very public relationships with two of his leading ladies: he has a daughter with Anne Parillaud (Nikita) and was married to Milla Jovovich (Leeloo). The second principle that has remained constant in Besson's work is his true affection for his fan-base: he prefers, for example, to release his films not, as is conventional in the industry, in an *avant-première* destined for press and critics, but rather directly into general release, thereby achieving what he sees as a dialogue with those whose reactions matter most to him.

Wolf; Gans, 2001) and *Le Petit Poucet* (*Tom Thumb*; Dahan, 2002) that are entirely the product of digital technology (computer graphic imaging (CGI)). At the time of writing, the French remain ahead of other European industries in developing a credible corpus of CGI films. Perhaps this continuing engagement with, and innovation of, the apparatus of aesthetic expression will prove to be the abiding legacy of the *cinéma du look*.

Further reading

Austin, Guy, *Contemporary French Cinema: An Introduction* (Manchester: Manchester University Press, 1996). An accessible account of recent trends in contemporary French cinema. See particularly ch. 6, 'The *cinéma du look* and fantasy film' (pp. 119–41), in which Austin talks about the careers of Beineix, Besson, and Carax.

Ezra, Elizabeth, 'The Latest Attraction: Léos Carax and the French Cinematic *Patrimoine*', *French Cultural Studies* 13 (2) (2002: 225–33). A close reading of *Les Amants du Pont-neuf* as a modern example of the 'cinema of attractions'.

Forbes, Jill, *The Cinema in France after the New Wave* (London: Macmillan 1992). Discusses *Diva* as an example of a postmodern thriller in a chapter entitled 'Hollywood-France: America as Influence and Intertext' (pp. 47–75).

Hayward, Susan, *Luc Besson* (Manchester: Manchester University Press, 1998). An overview of the directorial work of Besson up to *The Fifth Element*.

Izod, John, 'Beineix's *Diva* and the French Cultural Unconscious', in Elizabeth Ezra and Sue Harris (eds.), *France in Focus* (Oxford: Berg, 2000), pp. 181–93. A Jungian psychoanalytical reading of *Diva*.

Jameson, Fredric, *Signatures of the Visible* (London: Routledge, 1990). Includes the seminal essay '*Diva* and French Socialism' (pp. 55–62), in which Jameson posits *Diva* as the 'first postmodernist French film'.

Powrie, Phil, *French Cinema in the 1980s* (Oxford: Oxford University Press, 1997). Provides a comprehensive account of the period in which the *cinéma du look* emerged. See particularly ch. 10, 'Diva's Deluxe Disasters' (pp. 109–20) and ch. 11, 'Subway: Identity and Inarticulacy' (pp. 121–9).

—— (ed.), French Cinema in the 1990s (Oxford: Oxford University Press, 1999). See particularly Graeme Hayes, 'Representation, Masculinity, Nation: The Crises of Les Amants du Pont-Neuf, (pp. 199–210), and Susan Hayward, 'Besson's "Mission Elastoplast": Le Cinquième Élément (1997)' (pp. 246–57).

—— Jean-Jacques Beineix (Manchester: Manchester University Press, 2002). An overview of his work.

Reader, Keith, 'Cinematic Representations of Paris: Vigo/Truffaut/Carax', in Modern and Contemporary France 4 (1993): 409–15. A discussion of how the spaces of Paris, including the Métro, have been represented in the work of three French filmmakers from different periods.

12

THE NEW ITALIAN CINEMA

Gaetana Marrone

The slow but constant rise of what has come to be known as the New Italian Cinema from provincial obscurity to international recognition is often described as a story beginning ambiguously in the mid-1970s, coming of age boldly with the filmmakers who emerged during the 1980s (Tornatore, Amelio, Archibugi, Avati, Luchetti, Mazzacurati, Vanzina, Salvatores), and reaching a climax with Roberto Benigni's top-grossing film *La vita è bella* (*Life is Beautiful*, 1998). Almost fifteen years have elapsed since a young and relatively unknown Giuseppe Tornatore was awarded the Grand Jury Prize at Cannes, the Felix (the European Oscar), the Golden Globe, and the Academy Award for his *Nuovo Cinema Paradiso* (*Cinema Paradiso*, 1988), an exploit that had eluded *auteurs* such as Federico Fellini. The story of what Vito Zagarrio (1998: 11) has called 'The Next Generation' finds in Tornatore not only the personal creativity that appeared at one time to be suppressed in the period following the many great artists of postwar Italian cinema, but also the embodiment of a type of cinema engaged in coming to terms with the unstable and tarnished identity of the nation it represents. The television age, with deregulation and the digital camera, proved to be an era of transformation. It engendered a popular culture largely molded on American programming and electronic technology. The Neorealist masters and the ideological *auteurs* of the 1960s have been ousted by a group of independent filmmakers who embrace a more flexible means of production in order to adapt to the necessities of a new era. They have brought critics to

■ Giuseppe Tornatore (1956–)

Best known outside Italy as the director of *Nuovo Cinema Paradiso* (*Cinema Paradiso*, 1988), Giuseppe Tornatore has had a fast-rising career. The son of a Sicilian labor leader, he was born and raised in Bagheria, near Palermo, and was drawn early on to Left-wing politics. He started out as a photographer, capturing the emotional character of the people around him. In 1981, as a documentary filmmaker, he began a close collaboration with Raitre, the cultural channel of Italian television. In 1982, he won his first award for best documentary with *Le minoranze etniche in Sicilia* (*Sicilian Ethnic Minorities*) at the Salerno Film Festival. After a short while he made a compelling first feature film, *Il camorrista* (1986), starring Ben Gazzara in the role of a charismatic Camorra boss, inspired by Raffaele Cutolo, one of the most sinister criminals of recent times. Tornatore's next film, *Nuovo Cinema Paradiso*, a nostalgic testament dedicated to the vanishing cinematic culture, gained him international prominence. It is a flashback to the postwar era, set in a small Sicilian town, where personal and cinematic realities are closely intertwined. Tornatore sets up a dream world and reproduces for his audience a childlike wonder at the emotional power of cinema. This theme continues with *L'uomo delle stelle* (*The Star Maker*, 1995), featuring a con artist who poses as a talent scout from Rome, traveling through several Sicilian villages during the 1950s. Equipped with a professional-looking movie camera, lighting, and colored backdrops, he promises the fame of the silver screen to whomever nurtures the dream of escaping a reality of misery and violence.

⬇ *Nuovo Cinema Paradiso*

The sociohistorical process recounted in these films is one of passive accommodations and compromise. After *Nuovo Cinema Paradiso*, Tornatore's preoccupations shifted notably toward class conflict, family, and loneliness. In *Stanno tutti bene* (*Everybody's Fine*, 1990), an aging Sicilian widower, played by Marcello Mastroianni in a memorable performance, travels around the country paying surprise visits to his five grown-up children, only to discover that they lead disappointed lives in an impersonal and overcrowded Italy. *Una pura formalità* (*A Simple Formality*, 1994) focuses on one man's painful soul-searching, which leads him to commit suicide. It stars Gérard Depardieu as a famous novelist suffering from writer's block and Roman Polanski as a devilish inspector. In *La leggenda del pianista sull'oceano* (*The Legend of 1900*, 1999), the story of a boy born on a transatlantic steamer who never steps off the ship and over the years becomes a virtuoso pianist, and in *Malèna* (2001), the protagonists are painfully aware of a time lost. With these two films, the director offers an original account of one character's drama and his unique way of coping with the world.

Deeply immersed in all aspects of cinematic culture, Tornatore pays special attention to his actors and has been consistent in his technical approach as well as his use of extraordinary set designs and cinematography. Film critic Tullio Kezich has compared his *Legend of 1900* to Chaplin's *The Immigrant* (1917) and *America America* (1963) by Elia Kazan. Tornatore's cinema is a tribute to the art of filmmaking as collective memory, constantly evolving and open to poetic solutions and inventions.

rethink questions of aesthetics and authorship: how were these filmmakers to find stories and create images that break away from those of the privileged past?

Since the mid-1970s Italian cinema has experienced a more intense critical transformation than that of any other European country. Tangible factors included the dismantling of the centralized studio system of Cinecittà, the economic restructuring of film production radically constricted by Articolo 28 (Clause 28 of Act 1213 regulating the cinema), the withdrawal of American finance, and the participation of collaborators with little or no training in the craft. The reorganization of distribution also led to a sharp fall in ticket sales for domestic films, which plummeted in the 1980s, and many of the films subsidized under Clause 28 (originally designed to assist first-time directors in making their films outside commercial channels) were shelved and never released. Moreover, television replaced routine cinema going. While the battered Italian cinema industry survived with its genres as best it could, the 'new' filmmakers grew up in a disorganized way, their landscape geographically and culturally fragmented. Their films explored diverse identities to include the family, the South, political corruption, linguistic pluralism, ethnic minorities, and mass culture. They are small-scale productions, thus attracting a limited audience. Gian Piero Brunetta has defined these filmmakers as *sperduti nel buio* (lost in darkness), borrowing the title from Nino Martoglio's film made in Naples in 1914 (1993: 518). It took nearly two decades for Italy to recapture the prestige it had once enjoyed as a producer of a dramatically invigorating cinema.

Critical Directions

Born under the constellation of a crisis, the most serious and dramatic in the history of our film industry, the New Italian Cinema was forced to move and develop in a state of complete precariousness. In other words, it is a cinema born under uncertainty because it was abandoned and ignored. Abandoned because, in order to realize their films, the new *auteurs* were constrained to become their own producers . . . and ignored because, once their films were completed, they were confronted with absolute indifference, not only by the market, but also by the people in the film industry (producers, distributors, critics)*.

This introductory statement by Franco Montini (1988: 7) to his *Una generazione in cinema* poignantly describes the actual conditions under which first-time directors ventured to work in the film industry. Most of their films were not even shown. The title of Felice Farina's debut film, *Sembra morto . . . ma è solo svenuto* (*He Looks Dead . . . but he has only Fainted*, 1986), is often cited as a motto for their productions, particularly in the 1980s. Farina's dark comedy about a brother and sister's mishaps in Rome is a portrayal of detached realism, projecting a disorientation unknown to previous filmmakers. Until this point, most film historians had been mourning the death of Italian cinema. The long-lasting crisis of the 1970s appeared to have left nothing but an irreplaceable void. Some compared the New Italian Cinema to 'an iceberg', with only a fragmented part floating to the surface (Morandini 1989); others evoked 'opaque images' (Miccichè 1998) and 'landscapes of catastrophe' (Brunetta 1993). During a 1998 retrospective of Italian cinema in Pesaro, Lino Miccichè spoke emphatically of a *cinecidio*, or cine-killing. In an article published in *La repubblica* on 3 August 1997, Montini himself questioned whether contemporary films showed an exceptional power and originality that could rescue them from a gradual loss of vigor. He polemically entitled his article: 'Cinema italiano: Chi l'ha visto?' (Italian Cinema: Who's Ever Seen It?). The New Italian Cinema is difficult to analyze not only because these filmmakers belong to a diverse background but also because they are often blamed for lacking ethical and aesthetic strengths. With a huge number of first-time directors (more than 300 between 1975 and 1989), the New Italian Cinema has yet to be recognized as a school or a movement. In order to fully understand the work of this disparate group of directors, it is necessary to address their films as a reflection of Italian national life during a period of vital self-definition.

* All translations of works in Italian quoted here are mine.—GM

Film subsidy, television, and art cinema

In Italy, the process that led to a radical transformation in the film industry began in 1968, when rapidly changing political conditions and a deterioration of social institutions contributed to a general sense of malaise. By the mid-1970s the country experienced inflation, terrorism, drugs, organized crime, and the struggle between political factions generated a climate of profound uncertainty, in which young filmmakers adopted contrasting positions on the nature of national identity. Moreover, these positions reflected a shift from established production structures. Whereas in the past the major directors never worked in isolation and always relied on the collaboration of highly professional circles, there is no such interrelationship among the new filmmakers nor indeed among actors, cinematographers, editors, or screenwriters. For instance, the film editor Simona Paggi (Academy Award nominee for *La vita è bella*) began experimenting with the computer Avid technology because traditional editors such as Gabriella Cristiani refused to work with electronic media. As a result, an irregular group of new editors emerged. Cecilia Zanuso and Marco Spolentini adapted their television and commercial experience to feature film. These days, due to budget restraints, several screenwriters also direct their own scripts, such as Amelio, Luchetti, Calopresti, and Pieraccioni. Directors of photography and actors, too, have moved through different camps. Established Italian film stars have been replaced by TV personalities and new faces. Michele Placido had the lead in the popular television mini-series *La piovra* (*The Octopus*, 1984) and later directed *Pummarò* (1990); Enrico Lo Verso's everyday face closely identifies with the roles he has played for Gianni Amelio. As for the cinematographers, many started with directors who were financed by Clause 28, because the older generation of Rome-based cinematographers (Rotunno, Tovoli, etc.) were reluctant to work with substantial production cuts. In the 1970s, the average shooting schedule had dropped from eight or nine to six or seven weeks, and to four or five weeks in the 1980s. Many renowned professionals such as Luca Bigazzi, Dante Spinotti, and Renato Tafuri built their reputation photographing early films for Silvio Soldini, Giacomo Battiato, Gabriele Salvatores, and Giuseppe Bertolucci. This generation was forced to experiment in order to reinterpret the present and look to the future. For those who moved into the 1980s and 1990s, finding their own voice meant that the present would be occupied by terrorism, urban social disintegration, and a market ruled by Hollywood products.

In 1979, the Italian film industry recorded a general and growing decline in attendance. Ticket sales had dropped by nearly half, and the situation worsened during the 1980s. By the early 1990s only 90 million tickets were sold, a collapse from 514 million in

1976. Furthermore, from an annual release of up to 300 films at the end of the 1960s, with more than half being Italian productions, the annual output decreased to about 90 films, with 75 per cent of box office sales going to American films. The failure of the Italian market was due to particular national conditions. The support of the film industry by parliamentary legislation relied on Clause 28, ratified on November 4, 1965. Subsidies, some as high as to $400,000, were allocated to Nanni Moretti (*Ecce Bombo*, 1978), Francesca Archibugi (*Mignon è partita*, 1988), Gabriele Salvatores (*Marrakech Express*, 1989; *Turnè*, 1990), Fiorella Infascelli (*La maschera* [*The Mask*], 1988), and more recently to Sergio Rubini (*La stazione* [*The Station*], 1990), and Mario Martone (*Morte di un matematico napoletano* [*The Death of a Neapolitan Mathematician*], 1992). In the long run, Clause 28 promoted a cinema characterized by critics as 'minimalist'. Moreover, many of the films subsidized were never completed, and no one claimed a profit. In March 1994, Clause 28 was amended to sponsor only fifteen or twenty films a year.

An important role has been played by the law reforming the RAI (Italian National Television), which shifted control from government to a regulatory parliamentary commission, and by the proliferation of private television stations after July 1976, whose programming was organized around the broadcasting of films, mostly American imports. Ironically, the pressure to import was enforced by the crisis of the film industry and by the shutdown of half of the cinemas between 1978 and 1982. During the 1980s, certain corporate giants emerged to fill the gap created by deregulation. The market was dominated by Silvio Berlusconi's Fininvest (today's Mediaset), which owned the three major private networks (Canale 5, Telequattro, Italia 1), and by the Cecchi Gori Group. Together they created Penta Film (1989–94), thus controlling 25 per cent of film production and distribution in Italy. Berlusconi had built his reputation out of popular TV programming and advertising sales. His strategy was to carefully select imported international shows (films, soap operas, cartoons) and to deliver a massive viewing audience that attracted advertisers, thus providing a range of entertainment never experienced before on the RAI's national channels. Mario and Vittorio Cecchi Gori were the undisputed patrons of low-budget box office hits. Their formula was to pre-sell films around the world. They owned television stations (Telemontecarlo, Canale 10, Videomusic), home video, and more than thirty cinemas. From 1988 they also operated out of Los Angeles. Penta Film offered well-packaged products for a middle-ground audience that was steadily deserting the movie theaters. It released traditional comedies directed by Paolo Villaggio, Roberto Benigni, Francesco Nuti, and Massimo Troisi. It also financed *auteurs* such Francesco Rosi, and a newcomer, Gabriele Salvatores (*Mediterraneo*, 1991).

In 1990 the Broadcasting Act (Legge Mammi) ratified this mixed system of public and private networks, with some mild anti-monopoly restrictions. Since 1988, 80 per cent of all Italian films have been produced by one or the other of these groups. The industry's configuration blocked the release of independent art-house films: Italy had increasingly succumbed to blockbuster mentality. Nanni Moretti's seven-minute documentary *Il giorno della prima di Close-Up* (*The Day of the Premiere of Close-Up*, 1997) criticizes these conditions of corporate maneuvering, and expresses Moretti's anxious search for a film by Abbas Kiarostami being shown at his own theater in Rome, the Nuovo Sacher.

Nanni Moretti

The most successful filmmaker of the last two decades, in terms of consistency, quality, and intelligent business practice, Nanni Moretti is considered by many to be the forerunner and mentor of the New Italian Cinema. Always independent in his way of thinking and production approach, he has come to represent 'our critical conscience' (Zagarrio 1998). He places himself in the lead role, as a character who embodies the neurosis of urban life, constantly searching for new values against a paradoxical present. Moretti started his career with a Super-8 cult film (blown up to 16mm), *Io sono un autarchico* (*I Am an Autarchist*, 1976). He achieved his first nationwide success with *Ecce Bombo* (1978), where he dares to cast a jaundiced eye on the literal and cultural body of the post-1968 generation, making fun of the tradition of the Italian comedy (Bondanella 2002). The following films, *Sogni d'oro* (*Golden Dreams*, 1981), *Bianca* (1984), *La messa è finita* (*The Mass Has Ended*, 1985), and *Palombella rossa* (*The Red Dove*, 1989), are political and cultural manifestos of the decade. In 1989, in recognition of his long quest for an authentic cinema, the prestigious French journal *Cahiers du cinéma* gave him front-page coverage.

However, it was not until *Caro diario* (*Dear Diary*, 1993) that Moretti gained international acclaim, particularly in the US. *Caro diario*, which won the Best Director award at Cannes, is divided into three episodes that make up a visual cinematic journal: 'In vespa' (On My Vespa); 'Isole' (Islands); and 'Medici' (Doctors). Using voice-over, Moretti comments on television and mass media overshadowing the art of cinema, the speed of contemporary life and the youth-centered middle-class culture while continuing to address ideological concerns. He achieves results that are as powerful as those of the Neorealist practices of gazing upon everyday life. For example, Sicily is no longer the sacred island of Ulysses; it has been transformed to fit into the Italian identity of the early 1990s, designed to reinforce commercialized media images. Out of the smoking crater comes a postmodern prophecy in the guise of American tourists: a glimpse of future plot development of the popular soap opera *The Bold and the Beautiful* (Marcus 2002). TV has replaced fables and legends. The most compelling scene in the film occurs while riding on his Vespa in a deserted Rome, when Moretti heads toward the abandoned site where Pier Paolo Pasolini was murdered in November 1975. A poet and novelist, Pasolini had turned to filmmaking as an alternative mode for expressing his ideas on contemporary culture and politics. The last part of *Caro diario* shows Moretti's personal struggle with cancer as prominent doctors fail to recognize his symptoms. A more recent film, *La stanza del figlio* (*The Son's Room*, 2001), is about the pain of loss and mourning that not many other filmmakers have touched upon. Nanni Moretti continues to probe the ways in which a filmmaker can forge a different type of cinema, abandoning past formulas and conventions (Landy 2000). In the confusing political climate of these days, he has launched a protest against the conduct of mainstream parties and has formed a movement called I Girotondi (Dance in a ring), which tries to find alternative forms in which to express political ideas.

The 1980s: new industrial structures

By the 1980s, two of Italy's legendary producers, Carlo Ponti and Dino De Laurentiis, had moved to the US. Since the 1960s, Ponti had made a series of international co-productions with MGM, hiring directors such as Michelangelo Antonioni for *Blow-up* (1966), *Zabriskie Point* (1969), *and The Passenger* (1975). De Laurentiis, after the collapse of his ambitious Dinocittà (1964–72), had moved his family business to New York and later to Beverly Hills. In an interview for *Variety* on 14 November 1973, he declared that it was no longer possible to make internationally viable films in Italy. The key to achieving a larger market was seen to lie in the involvement of major American distributors, who could also provide better promotion in Europe itself. The idea was also to make films primarily for American audiences. De Laurentiis embarked on a series of colossal productions, which included *King Kong* (1976), *Dune* (1984), and *Hannibal* (2001). On Oscar night 2001, his enduring commitment to the world of entertainment was recognized with the Irving G. Thalberg Memorial Award, awarded for the first time to an Italian.

The departure of Ponti and De Laurentiis left the Italian film industry in a precarious state. The death of Franco Cristaldi in 1992 made the situation even worse. A highly cultured and scrupulous producer, Cristaldi had worked with Fellini, Rosi, Visconti, Pontecorvo, and Germi. His last discovery would be Giuseppe Tornatore, who creatively reshaped *Nuovo Cinema Paradiso* before the film went on to win at Cannes and at the Academy Awards. Much of the strength of postwar Italian cinema relied on the entrepreneurial vitality of its producers. Endowed with strength of character, courage, and intuition, they all invested in established directors as well as searching out new talent. In 1988, Berlusconi's Reteitalia (Fininvest's movie production branch) began financing *auteur* cinema, enlisting among others Peter Del Monte, Gianfranco Mingozzi, Giuseppe Bertolucci, and Andrea De Carlo, but the results were generally bland. An alternative production strategy proved to be successful with a new generation of actor-directors, many of whom wrote and produced their own films. The general idea was to occupy a different cultural and economic space from commercial productions. In 1984 Pupi and Antonio Avati formed Duea Film. Its singularity rested with the Avatis' conceptualization of its purpose: a factory consisting of freelance craftsmen (musicians, cinematographers, set designers, editors, actors), assigning an annual budget for independent films, with all profits to be reinvested in future productions. The first of these was *Noi tre* (*We Three*, 1984), and films released yearly included box-office hits such as *Regalo di Natale* (*Christmas Present*, 1986), a surreal tale of a strange card game on Christmas Eve; *Storia di ragazzi e di ragazze* (*Story of Boys and Girls*, 1989), in which a young groom and his beautiful country bride join their families to share love, dreams, and friendship during a twenty-course feast for thirty relatives; and *Il testimone dello sposo* (*The Best Man*, 1997), a study of late nineteenth-century middle-class society, and its elaborate matrimonial rituals and strictures on women.

In 1987, in association with Angelo Barbagallo, Nanni Moretti established Sacher Film. He not only produced but sometimes acted in many of the films, including Carlo Mazzacurati's *Notte italiana* (*Italian Night*, 1987), Daniele Luchetti's *Domani accadrà* (*Tomorrow Will Come*, 1988) and *Il portaborse* (*The Messenger*, 1991), and Mimmo Calopresti's *La seconda volta* (*The Second Time*, 1995). Alongside Avati and Moretti, a handful of other companies were committed to an innovative idea of filmmaking. They include Silvio Soldini's Monogatari, founded in 1988 in Milan, and Daniele Segre's I Cammelli, established in 1981 in Turin. Soldini began his career with a one-hour film, *Giulia in ottobre* (*Julia in October*, 1985), the story of a woman's daily routine, which was shot on a shoestring budget ($19,000). From his first feature-length film, *L'aria serena dell'ovest* (*The Serene Breeze from the West*, 1990) to *L'anima divisa in due* (*A Soul Divided in Two*, 1992) and *Le acrobate* (*The Acrobats*, 1997), he portrays his own city of Milan as a cold, claustrophobic metropolis, an incubator for political turmoil and corruption. A set photographer by profession, Daniele Segre is interested in social inquiries focussing upon the marginalization of individuals due to working conditions, drug addiction, and sexual difference. *Manila Paloma Blanca* (1993) is the biography of an unstable actor, Carlo Colnaghi, as he struggles with reality. Segre's work includes many award-winning documentaries shot on video, such as *Ritratto di un piccolo spacciatore* (*Portrait of a Drug Dealer*, 1982), *Vite da ballatoio* (*Ordinary Lives*, 1984), chronicling a ghetto of transsexual immigrants in Turin, and *Dinamite* (*Dynamite*, 1994), on a mining community's efforts to fight pit closures.

The new comedians

In the late 1980s, two of the most popular comics of the period also formed production companies in order to exercise greater artistic control of their work: Massimo Troisi's Esterno Mediterraneo Film (1987) and Maurizio Nichetti's Bambù Cinema & TV (1987). A young Neapolitan actor, Troisi made his directorial debut with *Ricomincio da tre* (*I'm Starting from Three*, 1981). Investing less that $400,000, he went on to break box-office records. The same enthusiastic reception was given to films like *Le vie del signore sono finite* (*The Ways of the Lords are Limited*, 1987) and *Pensavo fosse amore e invece era un calesse* (*I thought it would be Love and Instead it was a Cabriolet*, 1991). Troisi also co-directed, with Roberto Benigni, *Non ci resta che piangere* (*Nothing Left to Do but Cry*, 1984). The popular appeal of Massimo Troisi relied on the Pulcinella stock character and a variety of improvisational routines that reflected the social experiences of young Southerners. The turning point in his career came in 1994 with *Il postino* (*The Postman*), based upon a Chilean novel by Antonio Skármeta and adapted by British director Michael Radford. *Il postino* describes the friendship between the Marxist poet Pablo Neruda and Mario, a young postman who delivers his mail. Through Neruda, Mario becomes a poet himself and uses poetry to win the love of Beatrice. He also becomes a Communist, and at a rally of workers in Naples, he is killed, unable to recite his last poem, 'A Song for Pablo Neruda'. The original story was set in Salvador Allende's Chile during the 1960s. Radford places his version in Italy during the early 1950s, a time of conservative political monopoly (in reality, Neruda had moved to Italy in exile). Troisi died of heart failure soon after filming ended in June 1994. His moving performance enjoyed international critical attention. The main road to success was via the United States, where he became a favorite for Best Actor at the Oscar ceremony.

Troisi learned acting from stage improvisations on the Neapolitan stage, and worked with the essential gestures and mimicry of the traditional *istrioni* (mimes). By relying on what the *commedia* actors used to call the old skills of 'playing the mask', he could be a mime, a lover, a singer, or a comic actor. The beauty of his work lay in the most subtle details: in the gradation of his expressions, in the sound of his words, in the humanity of the events as they unfolded. Troisi could play directly to his audience whether he performed in a social comedy or a commercial film. He had the ability to evoke tears as well as laughter, especially in the acting roles for Ettore Scola's *Splendor* (1988), *Il viaggio di Capitan Fracassa* (*The Journey of Capitan Fracassa*, 1989), and *Che ora è?* (*What Time Is It?*, 1989). In the tradition of Eduardo De Filippo, he could mix dialect with high language, while retaining native sounds and accents. He was an archetypal figure, unquestionably the most creative comic performer of the 1980s.

Maurizio Nichetti's cinema is interesting for its technological experimentations and animation. His first film, *Ratataplan* (1979), mostly in pantomime, became a surprise success at the 1979 Venice Film Festival. In *Volere volare* (*To Wish to Fly*, 1991), the main character is transformed into a cartoon figure who interacts with real actors. In 1989 he continued with a comic reinterpretation of De Sica's *Ladri di biciclette* (*The Bicycle Thief*, 1948), entitled *Ladri di saponette* (*The Icicle Thief*), where he analyzes the impact of television on contemporary society and cinema. He stars as a director being interviewed by a pompous film critic in a TV studio that is about to air his film. The audience is made up of an average middle-class family. Nichetti feels compelled to 'enter' into the TV screen to fix the damage done by commercial interruptions and channel surfers. *Ladri di saponette* does not show any actual footage from De Sica, but Nichetti plays the part of the bicycle thief in a black and white film-within-the film.

During the 1980s, the new Italian comedy flourished, attesting to the endurance of a genre that since the 1960s had sustained the national film industry. At the same time the attacks on television, as a determining factor in the decline of Italian cinema, became a recurring theme in many comedies. Television had altered entertainment for the Italians. By the late 1980s the new comics had entered a critical dialogue, with the traditional values represented by the dominant personalities of the *commedia all'italiana* (Sordi, Tognazzi, Gassman, Germi, Monicelli, Scola), questioning their fixed schemata and rules. The genre underwent a substantial transformation with actor-directors such as Moretti and Nichetti. Between 1981 and 1987 box office hits were entirely dominated by Carlo Verdone, Renato Pozzetto, Enrico Montesano, Francesco Nuti, Benigni, and Troisi. The all-time record for profits (more than $30 million) was held by Roberto Benigni's *Johnny Stecchino* (1991), a farce about a mobster's uncanny impersonator, outdoing *Robin Hood* and *Terminator II* at the box office. In 1994 *Il mostro* (*The Monster*) outdrew *The Lion King* and *Forrest Gump*. Due to the success of the genre, 44 per cent of the films produced in that period were comedies.

Filmmaking at the margins

The 1980s saw the emergence of a new phenomenon: films mainly produced on the margins of the industry. If the *auteurs* of postwar Italy searched for a unified national identity, those of the 1980s and 1990s focussed on the dissolution of boundaries (sexual, generational, and national). Gabriele Salvatores, a Neapolitan director working in Milan, has had a great influence, due to his success in capturing a new section of Italian society on film. From his debut with *Kamikazen, ultima notte a Milano* (*Kamikazen, Last Night in Milan*, 1987), a film about cabaret performers, up to *Marrakech Express* (1989), *Turnè* (1990), *Mediterraneo* (1991), *Puerto Escondido* (1992), and more recently *Amnèsia*

(2001), he bases his plots on the theme of the journey. Salvatores attended the Accademia d'Arte Drammatica at the Piccolo Teatro in Milan and founded the Teatro dell'Elfo in 1972. His background in experimental theater helps him create a refreshing approach to the image. This is evident in his Academy Award-winning film *Mediterraneo*, the story of a group of misfit Italian soldiers slowly undergoing a change of identity after they invade a remote enemy Greek island during World War II. The island represents the inviting and hospitable social space that determines a series of encounters through which there emerges a critique of contemporary Italy. He dedicates his film to 'those who are about to escape', thus making a new beginning possible. From his point of view, utopian hopes help us to stay alive and to continue dreaming. He uses existing light and sets, placing his characters in bright sunlight. Salvatores is able to work flexibly with actors, using low-budget techniques, and continues an ongoing dialogue with youth culture. Ultimately his films begin with reality that evolves into a dream world. 'My introduction to cinema has the hue of desire', he has said in an interview with Mario Sesti:

just like when you hear a story about a faraway journey that makes you want to go and visit . . . I believe that cinema must inspire desires and put dreams in motion . . . However, we are learning film by film, doing a job that no one has taught us. The generation that preceded us has left no children. (Sesti 1994: 92, 94).

The new filmmakers are unified by a spirit of independence. They confront the unprecedented complications of multiculturalism that are affecting the country on a large scale, fracturing the traditional patterns of Italian social history. For example, Aurelio Grimaldi's *Le buttane* (*Prostitutes*, 1994) is a bold exploration of sexual politics; Marco Risi's *Mery per sempre* (*Forever Mery*, 1989) and *Ragazzi fuori* (*Outsiders*, 1990) denounce the underground world of Palermo (prostitution, drug trafficking) by exposing young men forced to live in the streets; and Roberta Torre's *Tano da morire* (*To Die for Tano*, 1997) is the first musical on the Mafia, inspired by the real-life story of slain boss Gaetano Guarrasi, which mixes various media styles combining puppet shows with rock music. These films deal with the unfulfilled desires of individuals, the exploitability of their emotions, and the disillusionment they bring upon themselves. A number of other directors—notably Francesca Archibugi, Ricky Tognazzi, and Sergio Rubini—situate their plots in domestic interiors, in which the tension is built up over a period of time and is divided into cuts or camera movements into close-up. They show how the aspirations and frustrations of everyday people interrelate with socio-historical situations. Particularly, the films of Francesca Archibugi, beginning with *Mignon è partita* (*Mignon has Left*, 1988), the story of a teenage boy falling in love for the first time, to *Il grande cocomero* (*The Big Watermelon*, 1993), *Con gli occhi chiusi* (*With Closed Eyes*, 1995), and *L'albero delle pere* (*The Pear Tree*, 1998), explore the shortcomings of adults as seen through the eyes of their children. Archibugi has acknowledged her Leftist political agenda. Her world is autobiographical, portrayed in a 1960s-style reaction to social convention. Over the past decade, at the level of production, advances have been made by women filmmakers, whose small but growing number included Anna Brasi, Cristina Comencini, Giovanna Gagliardo, Fiorella Infascelli, and Wilma Labate. Archibugi and Torre are still the only ones with international recognition.

The dominant culture's anxieties about the politics of identity are also visible in Gianni Amelio's successful films. Amelio began his career working for RAI television in the 1970s. After a long apprenticeship as an assistant director, he came to public attention with *Colpire al cuore* (*To Strike at the Heart*, 1982), which is considered, together with Mimmo Calopresti's *La seconda volta* (*The Second Time*, 1995), one of the best Italian films on terrorism. With *Porte aperte* (*Open Doors*, 1990), a gripping thriller featuring Gian Maria Volontè as a jurist on a murder trial in Fascist Italy, he received his first Oscar nomination for Best Foreign Language Film. *Ladro di bambini* (*Stolen Children*, 1991) established Amelio as a filmmaker whose extraordinary talent is working with children, in the tradition of De Sica's *Ladri di biciclette*. The film centers on an 11-year-old girl and her 9-year-old brother who are escorted by a young *carabiniere* (military policeman) from Milan to Sicily in search of a permanent foster home. During the journey of several days, a bond grows between the taciturn boy and the policeman, played by Enrico Lo Verso. From time to time, the girl, who was once forced into prostitution by her impoverished mother, also lowers her defenses. The children sadly become aware that their new friendship with the *carabiniere* is bound to end. Amelio's penchant for social criticism resurfaces in *Lamerica* (1994) and *Cosi ridevano* (*The Way We Laughed*, 1998). The first follows the plight of the Albanians as a counterpart to the migration of Italians to the United States; the second portrays two brothers, a workman and a student, who go to Turin in search of a better life and instead are faced with corruption and betrayal. *Cosi ridevano*, winner of the Golden Lion at the Venice Film Festival, evokes a vanished world, a time of opportunity, idealism, and political turmoil. Amelio embodies the last reflection of realist iconography, sensitive to the interaction of character and environment, of society and physiognomy. He undertakes a journey into the sources of Italy's national culture, with a tragic sense of forceful class exploitation.

Roberto Benigni

In 1998 the triumph of Roberto Benigni's *La vita è bella* prefigured the commercial revival of Italian cinema. Benigni's comic persona is closer to Fellini's carnivalesque types than to Zavattini's populist characters. He once worked and trained with both of these masters.

Upon the release of *La vita è bella*—which won three Oscars in 1999, including Best Foreign Film and Best Actor—its director was described in the *New York Times* (October 11, 1998) as Italy's Robin Williams: 'The Funniest Italian You've Probably Never Heard of'. Benigni became successful in a country, the United States, that only very few European actors have been able to conquer. Happily married to Nicoletta Braschi, who acts in all of his films, he is a comedian who is in control of his craft. His white clown persona always rebels against the intellectual establishment. He plays the slightly bewildered Chaplinesque character caught up in forces beyond his understanding, who eventually succeeds by using his wits and a touch of luck. On Oscar night, he joked that he was grateful to his parents for giving him the greatest gift of all: poverty. Benigni's humor is rooted in his upbringing in the communal Tuscan peasantry. He is like an itinerant *jongleur*, whose monologues express the spontaneity of popular culture. He practiced his art through improvised performances in town squares and at political rallies. He also worked in a circus and in avant-garde theaters, where he learned pantomime and acrobatics. During the 1970s he moved to Rome, and eventually accepted a year-long apprenticeship with Cesare Zavattini, whose fabulist approach influenced his first commercial release, *Il piccolo diavolo* (*Little Devil*, 1988), a slapstick farce confected around Benigni's naïve, hapless screen persona. He also appeared in Jim Jarmusch's cult movies *Down by Law* (1986) and *Night on Earth* (1992), and Fellini's *La voce della luna* (*The Voice of the Moon*, 1990).

Benigni began working on *La vita è bella* in 1995 with his scriptwriter, Vincenzo Cerami. During the 1990s, the Jewish experience had become a prominent topic in Italy. Benigni, who happens not to be Jewish, immersed himself in the works of Primo Levi, whose novel *La tregua* (*The Truce*) was made into a film by Francesco Rosi in 1996. The idea grew out of a personal experience: Benigni's father was sent to a German labor camp in 1943, where he nearly starved to death. What shaped the film was the way his father recounted his experience, with a mixture of chilling and whimsical details. Despite controversial critical reviews, *La vita è bella* became an instant success in Italy. It was sent to Cannes at the last moment, and surprised everyone by winning the Jury Prize. In Israel it was so acclaimed that the Mayor of Jerusalem awarded the director a medal of recognition equivalent to the keys of the city. In the film, Benigni plays Guido, a bookseller and free spirit who lives in the Tuscan town of Arezzo in 1939. He pursues a pretty schoolteacher, Dora, whom he eventually marries. Halfway through the movie, Guido is deported with Dora and his 5-year-old son Giosuè to a German concentration camp. In order to keep the boy from the realities of the horror, he concocts an elaborate game of deception, in which he tells Giosuè that if he abides by the rules he will win a big prize.

⬆ *La vita è bella*

Some Italian critics, such as Goffredo Fofi and Giuliano Ferrara, the editor of the Roman newspaper *Il foglio*, led a relentless campaign against Benigni, accusing him of making the Holocaust banal with sentimentality and narcissism. In the United States, the film became the most profitable foreign-language film ever shown. However, detractors insisted on the lack of intellectual rigor and historical accuracy in the representation of the Shoah. In *The New Yorker* of November 16, 1998, David Denby dismissed the film as 'nothing but a mistake', questioning whether comedy can redeem the worst horrors of the century. Stanley Kaufmann (*The New Republic*), Richard Schickel (*Time*), Justin Cartwright (*The Guardian*), Linda Holt (*Times Literary Supplement*), and T. Stubbs (*Sight and Sound*), among others, also argued that the film trivializes the Holocaust. Yet others see profound irony in Giosuè's final words to his mother—*abbiamo vinto* (we won)—as he is triumphantly carried off on an American army tank (Marcus 2002). Benigni's most recent film, *Pinocchio* (2002), which was initially scheduled to be made by Federico Fellini, combines cultural sophistication with mainstream appeal.

At the end of 1992, under the auspices of the Turin Youth Festival of Cinema, film critics and scholars were asked to identify five young directors for the year 2000. They were Bruno Bigoni and Silvio Soldini in Milan, Daniele Segre in Turin, Mario Martone in Naples, and Carlo Mazzacurati, a Venetian based in Rome. Thus, the rebirth of the Italian cinema is perceived as moving towards regional cultural fragmentation, breaking away from Rome, the center of the movie industry. However, a number of films released at the turn of the millennium are continuing to be made in Rome, mainly co-productions with other European countries. They include: Ferzan Ozpetek's *Le fate ignoranti (The Ignorant Fairies*, 2001), a striking apologia on transsexual preferences; Marco Tullio Giordana's *I cento passi (The Hundred Steps*, 2000), a film of civic courage and political indictment reflecting the complex relationship between a young man, his father, and the Mafia; Gabriele Muccino's *L'ultimo bacio (The Last Kiss*, 2001), a telling look at the romantic entanglements of a group of young friends; and Roberto Andò's *Il manoscritto del principe (The Manuscript of the Prince*, 2001), the story of two young men's lives affected by the gigantic personality of Prince Giuseppe Tomasi di Lampedusa, as he writes his novel *Il gattopardo (The Leopard*). In a highly stylized film, Andò addresses the issue of art and culture in their relationship to reality and history.

Today's filmmakers display an astounding range of political agendas, styles, and artistic sensibilities. They have produced a body of work that discloses a new beginning for Italian cinema. This is a cinema constantly redefining itself, while exposing the dynamics of unsettling social and cultural boundaries.

Further reading

Gieri, Emanuela, *Contemporary Italian Filmmaking: Strategies of Subversion* (Toronto: Toronto University Press, 1995). A critique of Italian filmmaking as it moves beyond traditional categories of genre film and authorial cinema.

Marcus, Millicent, *After Fellini: National Cinema in the Postmodern Age* (Baltimore: Johns Hopkins University Press, 2002). A highly original contribution to the study of Italian cinema. This book offers new conclusions about continuities and changes in the mapping of the New Italian cinema.

Marrone, Gaetana (ed.), *New Landscapes in Contemporary Italian Cinema* (*Annali d'Italianistica* 17, 1999). The first comprehensive book on the subject in English. It focuses on *auteurs*, crafts, television, and marketing.

Martini, Giulio, and Guglielmina Morelli (eds.), *Patchwork Due: geografia del nuovo cinema italiano* (Milan: Il Castoro, 1997). Film production is examined in Italy during the 1980s, with emphasis on the geographical dislocation and regional circles of the new directors.

Miccichè, Lino (ed.), *Schermi opachi: il cinema italiano degli anni '80* (Venice: Marsilio, 1998). A critical reading of major directors and films of the 1980s.

Montini, Franco (ed.), *Una generazione in cinema: esordi ed esordienti italiani 1975–1988* (Venice: Marsilio, 1988). An early critical study of the New Italian Cinema.

—— (ed.), *I nuovissimi: gli esordienti nel cinema italiano degli anni '80* (Venice: Marsilio, 1988). A study of film production during the 1980s.

Sesti, Mario, *Nuovo cinema italiano: gli autori, i film, le idee* (Rome: Theoria, 1994). A pioneering book on the new cinema.

—— (ed.), *La 'scuola' italiana: storia, strutture e immaginario di un altro cinema (1988–1996)* (Venice: Marsilio, 1996). Sesti expands his study on film production to the 1990s.

Zagarrio, Vito, *Cinema italiano anni novanta* (Venice: Marsilio, 1998). A comprehensive study of Italian cinema during the last decade of the century.

13

CONTEMPORARY SPANISH CINEMA

Peter William Evans

Spanish cinema has become fashionable. Some of its major directors and stars are in demand and fêted both inside and outside Spain. *Belle Epoque* (Fernando Trueba, 1992) and Pedro Almodóvar's *Todo sobre mi madre* (*All About My Mother*, 1999) won Oscars for best foreign-language film; Penélope Cruz and Antonio Banderas have made more than a dozen films between them in Hollywood; Victoria Abril has worked in France; the films of Medem—e.g., *Lucía y el sexo* (*Sex and Lucia*, 2001)— and Amenábar (*Tesis* (*Thesis*), 1996); *Abre los ojos* (*Open Your Eyes*), 1997)), are exhibited widely, and in the case of the latter this has led to work with international stars like Nicole Kidman in *Los otros* (*The Others*, 2001); and co-productions with Latin America are on the increase. For all that, the great bulk of Spanish films remains held back from wider distribution through the hegemony of Hollywood and the struggle to find exhibition space in cinemas both inside and outside Spain. As a result, an extraordinary film like José Luis Borau's *Leo* (2000) has yet to find a distributor in the UK. Even in Spain, filmmakers struggle to find audiences more acclimatized to Hollywood. Nevertheless, while distribution remains a problem, conditions have never been more favorable since the end of the Republic (1939) for the free expression of ideas in the cinema.

The end of the Franco regime (1939–1975), the abolition of censorship, the victories of the Socialist party (PSOE) under Felipe González (1982–96), entry into the European Economic Community (EEC) in 1986, and subsequently the defeat of the PSOE by the conservative Partido Popular (PP) have all contributed to the roller-coaster changes in direction of the Spanish cinema since 1975. But perhaps the key reforms of the more recent past concern the conditions of production and exhibition. Most recently, since the victory of the PP in 1996 a policy of deregulation has meant that the industry has been left largely to fend for itself. Under the PSOE, Pilar Miró, one of the Spanish cinema's most significant women directors, as Directora General de Cinematografía (1983–5) developed a policy of advanced credit whereby 50 per cent of a film's production costs could be covered before the film's completion. The problem with this system was that the films selected for special treatment were inevitably those that conformed to the tastes and prejudices of the subsidies panel-lists, whose decisions sometimes led to the favorable treatment of often worthy but dull projects that fared poorly at the box office. With the increasing conservatism of the PSOE the Miró Levy gave way to subsidies based on box office earnings. The victory of the PP at the polls led to greater erosion of subsidies as well as (crucially) to changes in screen quotas, authorizing the exhibition of three (as opposed to the PSOE's previous limit of two) Holly-wood films for every Spanish or European film (Jordan and Morgan-Tamosunas 1998: 4).

Despite these setbacks, the 1990s also saw, more promisingly—as the industry became increasingly commercialized—the rise of Spanish production and distribution companies (large concerns like Sogepaq, the distributor, and Sogetel, the production company, as well as a proliferation of smaller ones, like Almodóvar's El Deseo), and collaboration between companies and film distributors and exhibitors, as well as the resurrection of the National Film School under F. Méndez Leite in 1995, all of which has allowed the Spanish cinema to make its mark. Even so, the grip of the multinationals ensures that box-office statistics remain heavily biased in favor of Hollywood. The September 2002 figures, for instance, show that the top-grossing Spanish films were Campanella's *El hijo de la novia* (*Son of the Bride*, 2001), with £6,960,926, and Almodóvar's *Hable con ella* (*Talk to Her*, 2002), with £5,035,855, compared with the top three Hollywood films, all of which have earned over £16,000,000 in the same period (*The Lord of the Rings*, taking in £32,200,490 since December 2001) (*Academia* 82: 9). Hollywood, as ever, continues to reign supreme.

Past historic

In purely filmic terms there has been no radical break with the past, since over the last twenty-five years or so many of the key figures who worked during the Franco period survived the transition to democracy and continue even now to make significant films.

Buñuel, perhaps the single most important Spanish filmmaker, effectively stopped making films in Spain at the outbreak of the Civil War. For all their reliance on Spanish creative personnel, *Viridiana* (1961), *Tristana* (1970), and *Cet obscur objet du désir* (*That Obscure Object of Desire*, 1977)—the first two wholly, and the third only partly, set in Spain—are really the work of an exile whose obsessions and interests can hardly be said to reflect the concerns of his ex-fellow-countrymen and women (he had taken Mexican nationality by then). Buñuel's status as an exile made him in some ways, as far as direct links with Spain are concerned, a filmmaker out of time, someone more locked into the issues of pre-dictatorship Spain. *Viridiana*, for instance, is still rightly regarded as one of the masterpieces of the Spanish cinema, but that may be a judgement inspired more by Buñuel's great eminence in world cinema than by its perceived fidelity in recording the lived realities of 1960s Spaniards. *Le Charme discret de la bourgeoisie* (*The Discreet Charm of the Bourgeoisie*, 1972), *Le Fantôme de la liberté* (*The Phantom of Liberty*, 1974), and *Cet obscur objet du désir* are largely French productions—produced and scripted by Frenchmen, Serge Silberman and Jean-Claude Carrière respectively. Their dependence on Spanish stars Fernando Rey and Angela Molina, the Spanish motifs (the flamenco dancer and singer in *Le Fantôme*) or settings (Seville in *Cet obscur objet*), are perhaps best read as revisited memories from exile, brilliantly forming part of Buñuel's known obsessions rather than addressing directly the new agenda of Spain in democracy. Of the other major directors from Spain's pre-democratic past, Saura, Erice, Borau, Gutierrez Aragón, García Berlanga, and Bardem, for instance, all went on making major films. Among the actors and actresses, Concha Velasco, José Luis López Vázquez, Andrés Pajares, and a host of others whose work crossed the boundaries between irredeemably commercial films and what might loosely be called art films, have continued to make films up to the present day. In the case of the directors and scriptwriters, living as they have done—unlike Buñuel—in Spain, forced to work under the constraints of state censorship, their films have been, so to speak, close to the ground, in direct contact with the upheavals, vicissitudes, and redefinitions of Spanish society.

In some cases the new freedoms led to welcome plain speaking and artistic licence impossible under Franco. In other cases these liberties triggered self-indulgence rather than greater subtlety or coherence. An example of the former includes the work of José Luis Borau, already prepared to take risks in the pre-democratic years, with hard-hitting films like *Furtivos* (*Poachers*, 1975), but whose post-dictatorship work, above all in films like *Río abajo* (*On the Line*, 1984), and most recently *Leo*, address issues related to sexuality even more uncompromisingly. *Leo* raises difficult questions about the darker side of sex, dwelling not only on the perennial contents and discontents of human relationships but also on the recognizable realities of modern-day Spain. Buñuel's *Obscur objet*, like

Leo, is partly about older man–younger woman relations, but whereas the former dislocates the issues from the specificity of late 1970s Spanish society, the latter, on the contrary, grounds them firmly in the context of urgent contemporary problems facing Spain (and most other Western European countries) concerning the exploitation of illegal immigrants. This film is in line with much of Borau's post-Franco work, such as *Camada negra* (*Black Brood*, 1977), scripted by him but directed by Gutiérrez Aragón, and *Tata mía* (*Nanny*, 1984). Both take advantage of the new political atmosphere to interrogate the past. *Camada negra* is an uncompromising exposé of Fascism, focusing, like many films of the immediate post-dictatorship years, on Fascism in the family (e.g., Erice's *El espíritu de la colmena* (*The Spirit of the Beehive*, 1973) or Camino's *Las largas vacaciones del 36* (*The Long Holidays of 1936*, 1976). *Tata mía* has the look of a modern Screwball comedy, in which the sexually repressed daughter of a Franco-sympathizing general leaves her convent on learning of the latter's death. Returning to the family home, the daughter comes across the father's memoirs and various secrets. Like Saura's *Cría cuervos* (*Raise Ravens*, 1975), these films unearth the roots of Spain's recent past. Where *Tata mía* and *Camada negra* concentrate on the darker side, *Cría cuervos*, equally focussed on the lives of individuals living under a repressive order, allows space for the recovery of earlier cultural memories. Geraldine Chaplin as María, the Fascist general's wife, reminisces about her pre-marital hopes of becoming a concert pianist, and her mother, paralyzed and mute—metaphorically silenced by the regime?—spends her days looking at photos from pre-dictatorship days, and listens to a song, 'Mari Luz' (famously sung by Imperio Argentina), that recalls the happiness of pre-Civil-War Spain.

The Civil War, its origins and its consequences, remained a topic of interest for other directors and screenplay writers who straddled the pre- and post-Franco years. The films that deal most effectively with the topic include Saura's *¡Ay Carmela!* (1990), García Berlanga's *La vaquilla* (*The Heifer*, 1985), and Aranda's *Libertarias* (*Libertarians*, 1996). In a film that derives much of its force from the more Goyaesque consequences of war, especially in a late scene that focuses somewhat controversially on the barbaric behavior of Franco's 'Guardia Mora' North African troops, *Libertarias* highlights the contribution of women patriots to the Republican cause. *La vaquilla* and *¡Ay Carmela!*, on the other hand, to a large extent find opportunities for redeeming through comedy the absurdities of war. The latter mocks the prissiness and effeminacy of Italian Fascism in a narrative that concentrates on the politicization of a trio of entertainers who move, with tragic consequences, from indifference to commitment as they stumble into enemy territory. The former, falling perhaps a little short of the brilliance of García Berlanga's pre-democratic films such as *Bienvenido Mr Marshall* (*Welcome, Mr Marshall*, 1952), *Los Jueves milagro* (*Miracles on Thursdays*, 1957), *Plácido* (1961), and *El verdugo* (*The Executioner*, 1963), is nevertheless characterized by the instinct of their director and screenplay writer (Rafael Azcona) for satirical comedy.

The collaboration between Berlanga and Azcona produced some of the landmark films of the pre-democratic period. In their partnership they demystified social and moral crusades, the fantasies of the power-fixated and self-seeking. Their films recall the more world-weary, cynical genius of Hollywood directors Preston Sturges and Billy Wilder and, in Spain itself, the picaresque tradition of Quevedo and Cervantes. Already developing his own jaundiced brand of comedy before *Plácido*, Berlanga found in Azcona a natural partner, whose characteristically black humor had been honed on the satirical review *La Codorniz*. Working again with Azcona on *La vaquilla*, the story of comic rivalry between two platoons of Republicans and Nationalists, Berlanga offers a lighthearted survey of the shared instincts and cultural heritage of individuals divided by ideology. The cast includes Alfredo Landa—already famous for lending his name to a special brand of 1960s/1970s comedy known as 'Landismo'—and another leading actor of the day, José Sacristán. It was made on a budget of 250 million pesetas—the most expensive film in Spanish cinema history up to that point—and is Berlanga's most commercially successful work. The idea and original screenplay date from the 1950s, though neither had found favor with the authorities of the day, including Franco himself, who is supposed to have commented: 'todavía es muy pronto para hacer una película así' (It's too soon for a film of this sort). *La vaquilla* displays many aspects of Berlanga's characteristic humor, in some ways exemplifying Freud's definition of humor as something that 'produces pleasure in spite of the distressing affects that interfere with it; . . . the pleasure of humor . . . comes about . . . at the cost of a release of affect that does not occur; it arises from an economy in the expenditure of affect' (1983: 293). Humor born of distress (e.g., war in *La vaquilla*, poverty in *Plácido*, or capital punishment in *El verdugo*) is Berlanga's stock-in-trade. And even if in a film like *La vaquilla* his comic genius had not deserted him, the demise of the censors failed in other respects to benefit films like *Todos a la cárcel* (1993) or *París Tombuctú* (1999), where the somewhat gratuitous vulgarity of certain scenes makes one wonder whether in this case, as the saying goes, 'contra Franco vivíamos mejor' (Life was better in opposition to Franco).

Pedro Almodóvar

This phrase, however, cannot in any sense be applied to the most commercially successful director in the history of the Spanish cinema, the filmmaking dictatorship Spain was in a sense destined ultimately to produce: Pedro Almodóvar. Most of his films set new records for box-office takings in Spain, and he is perhaps the one filmmaker whose films are certain to get worldwide distribution. Although he had already taken his first steps in filmmaking with some shorts on 8mm from the mid-1970s, the Almodóvar phenomenon began properly in 1980 with the punkish comedy *Pepi, Luci, Bom y otras chicas del montón* (*Pepi, Luci, Bom and Other Girls on the Heap*). His earliest feature film introduces audiences to a characteristic blend of high and low art, *boleros* and classical music, Hollywood and European art cinema, all served up in narratives that explore the complexities of human relationships and all the variants of sexuality, while destabilizing fixed categories of gender. Almodóvar's films are characterized by what, in their allusion to other art forms and film genres (both popular and art-house), Bakhtin might have termed their 'dialogic' structure. If the Franquist cinema—not as represented by the dissident voices of the regime—meant one-dimensionality, post-Franquism allows for the possibility of polyphony and heteroglossia, where the 'otherness' of popular culture or high art is no longer considered an intrusion but a welcome mechanism of dialogue and perspectivism.

In its awareness of the shifting ground of masculinity and femininity *Pepi, Luci, Bom* —often referred to as a *movida* film (representing the Madrilenian youth society of the early 1980s)—ranges over heterosexuality, lesbianism, and male homosexuality, and also offers an affectionate satire of indigenous middlebrow music in the form of the *zarzuela* (Spanish operetta); an homage to comic-book aesthetics; and the rise of Madrid as the capital of the new radically chic Spain, increasingly indifferent to the strictures of the Church and other institutional authorities. *Pepi, Luci, Bom* has the rough aesthetic look of a newcomer to the medium. Although its shock tactics (such as the scenes of the golden shower released by one woman over another, or the *erecciones generales* parody of Spanish politics) continue to inspire Almodóvar even in his most recent film, *Hable con ella* (*Talk to Her*, 2001)—notably in the scene of the outsize vagina's penetration by the shrinking man—his style began to evolve toward a slicker, more voluptuous texture from *Matador* (1985) onwards. The glossy color, loving close-ups, and sensuous camera movements in films like *Matador, Mujeres al borde de un ataque de nervios* (*Women on the Verge of a Nervous Breakdown*, 1988), or *Carne trémula* (*Live Flesh*, 1997) convey alongside the quirky, art-movie characteristics the velvety touch of a Sirk or a Hitchcock. In *Matador* the farcical moments Almodóvar finds so irresistible—such as the Bibí Andersen fortune-telling scene —fail to disrupt the flow of the melodrama and the sensuous aesthetics that rely on Bernard Bonezzi's music, the plangent lyrics of 'Espérame en el cielo corazón', the primary colors of the costumes of its stars, Asumpta Serna, Antonio Banderas, Nacho Martínez, Eva Cobos, and Carmen Maura, and the buzz of modernity associated with the capital city.

Mujeres al borde, reversing the generic pattern of *Matador*, is a comedy bordering on melodrama. It too depends on farce, drawing to some extent on the Spanish cinema's own popular traditions, the inane but highly colorful 1960s and 1970s comedies,

⬆ *Mujeres al borde de un ataque de nervios*

usually directed by Pedro Lazaga or Mariano Ozores. The mambo taxi driver (Guillermo Montesinos), always opportunely available to drive Pepa (Carmen Maura) to various destinations, or the stuttering son (Antonio Banderas) of Pepa's lover (Fernando Guilén), recall the flawed comic heroes of the Lazaga/Ozores films.

Almodóvar's films survey the changing constructions of Spanish masculinity, and seemingly take as their cue the remark made by Pepa (Carmen Maura) in *Mujeres al borde de un ataque de nervios* that learning mechanics is easier than working out the psychology of the male: 'Es mucho más fácil aprender mecánica que psicología masculina. A una moto puedes llegar a conocerla a fondo, a un hombre jamás' (It's easier to take up mechanics than to comprehend male psychology. You can really get to know a motorbike, but never a man). Antonio Banderas, Eusebio Poncela, Liberto Rabal, and many others partly owe their rise to stardom to Almodóvar, having all played their part on screen in the Spanish cinema's deconstruction and redefinitions of Spanish masculinity.

In *Carne trémula*, one of Almodóvar's most elegant films, the underlying structures of old and new forms of Spanish masculinity are explored through the double focus on one man's struggle with the past (David, played by Javier Bardem), and another's (Víctor, played by Liberto Rabal) appeal to the future. The narrative turns on the pursuit of David's wife, Elena (Francesca Neri), by Víctor, who is accused of shooting and paralyzing David.

To some extent, Víctor is motivated by feelings of revenge against David, the cripple whose injuries have led to years of imprisonment. His additional interest in Clara (Angela Molina), the wife of the policeman (Pepe Sancho) who was really responsible for David's injury, represents the displaced desire for his dead mother (Penélope Cruz). In this respect the film recalls Melanie Klein's remarks in *Love, Guilt and Reparation* where, prefacing comments on the interaction between love and hate, she argues that 'the feelings of a man towards a woman are always influenced by his early attachment to his mother' (1964: 87). The baby's first love object—his mother—is both desired and hated, aggressiveness towards the mother arising 'when his desires are not gratified' (1964: 58). Love and hate therefore struggle for dominance in the baby's mind, a struggle that persists throughout life and, as Klein argues, 'is liable to become a source of danger in human relationships' (1964: 60). Destructive urges towards the mother, moreover, lead to guilt (Klein 1964: 62–3). In *Carne trémula*, the inexperienced Víctor, often referred to as a child, is sexually inept. A mother-fixated son whose grief at the loss of his mother seems genuine enough, he displaces feelings toward his mother onto the women with whom he comes into contact, at times playing the good child and at other times releasing in fantasy frustrations and anger from the past, driven by urges for reparation and aggression.

The sensitive handling of human relationships becomes ever surer with each successive film. Almodóvar's brilliance has even led one critic to claim that his most recent film, *Hable con ella*, is 'one of the first great pictures of this century' (French 2002: 1). The focus in *Hable con ella*, as well as in *Carne trémula*, is on the complexities of masculinity. In Almodóvar's somewhat confessional earlier film, *Todo sobre mi madre* (*All About My Mother*, 1999)—he often uses his own mother, Francisca Caballero, in cameo roles—the focus is on the mother's feelings for the son and, in other films, on mother-daughter relationships, concerns that have led to their director's recognition as, among other things, the Spanish cinema's foremost analyst of female psychology. His films are a barometer of the times, measuring changing attitudes to sexuality, relations between the sexes, identity, and above all feminine psychology and the situation of Spanish women in democracy.

With some exceptions—especially *Átame* (*Tie Me Up, Tie Me Down*, 1990) and *Kika* (1993), denounced in some feminist quarters for the impression they give of the Victoria Abril and Veronica Forqué characters' masochistic pleasure in submissiveness to their abusers (Antonio Banderas and Santiago Lajusticia, respectively)—his films have struck a chord particularly with women. They offer a spectrum of strong female characters: at one end the glamorous 'chicas Almodóvar', Maura, Abril, Cruz; at the other, their older or more maternal equivalents, like the Marisa Paredes, Chus Lampreave, Julieta Serrano characters, through whom are dramatized tensions between drives for self-fulfillment and maternal responsibility. No Spaniard since Lorca has more convincingly represented the authenticity of Spanish women.

Women directors

But in recent Spanish cinema women are not to be found exclusively in front of the camera. Prior to 1975, the history of women filmmakers in Spain is notable perhaps above all for the work of Rosario Pi (1899–1967) and Ana Mariscal (1921–95). In democracy the most significant figure has been Pilar Miró (1940–97), whose contribution goes beyond her subsidy policies, to the fine films she made as a director. Her rise to prominence—an achievement not without its struggles against the media establishment and its traditional prejudices against women—is in line with the advances made by women in general from 1975 onwards, developments that, as Anny Brooksbank-Jones notes, had begun well before the advent of democracy (1997). In politics, for instance, Carmen Alborch and Rosa Conde; in feminist initiatives, Lidia Falcón; or in business, the Koplowitz sisters are, like Pilar Miró, the beneficiaries of social change (García de León, 1994). Pilar Miró was also a director (eventually becoming Director-General of RTVE, 1985–8, resigning her post after accusations of inappropriate expenditure of public funds). Her outstanding work in the cinema includes *El crimen de Cuenca* (*The Crime at Cuenca*, 1979), *Gary Cooper que estás en los cielos* (*Gary Cooper Who Art in Heaven*, 1980), *Beltenebros* (1991), *El perro del hortelano* (*The Dog in the Manger*, 1995) and *Tu nombre envenena mis sueños* (*Your Name Poisons My Dreams*, 1996), the last two films reserving key roles for two of the rising stars of the Spanish cinema at that time, Emma Suárez and Carmelo Gómez. In all these films Pilar Miró ensured that the experience of women is given full expression: *El crimen de Cuenca* does this to some extent indirectly by concentrating on fascist brutality, while *Gary Cooper* . . . directly addresses, in a faintly autobiographical way (drawing on her experiences as a producer, though not yet as Director-General), the career and personal problems faced by a woman whose private and professional life are under threat. Even *El perro del hortelano*, an adaptation of a play by Lope de Vega— earning her seven Goyas, the Spanish Oscars—manages to adapt the concerns of another age to the issues of contemporary Spain. Perhaps to some extent inspired by the success of Shakespearean adaptations around that time—e.g., *Henry V* (Kenneth Branagh, 1989) and *Much Ado About Nothing* (Kenneth Branagh, 1993)—Pilar Miró mined the equally rich source of golden-age Spanish drama. Through the ready-made contexts of Baroque society's highly codified and imprisoning social mechanisms, she produced a film that, despite its ancient stage origins, rivals any Nora Ephron romantic comedy in its survey of human relations and desire. The wavering appeal for a high-born lady of a man of lowly origins allows reflection on the complications of love as well as on the wilder forms of desire.

Pilar Miró was the leading lady of women directors, but the stage has become gradually invaded by younger filmmakers, whose work has produced some of the most exciting and innovative Spanish films of recent years. Gracia Querejeta, Marta Balletbó-Coll, Rosa Vergés, Chus Gutiérrez, and Azucena Rodríguez are only a few of the many women directors making their mark. Of these, perhaps the most interesting is Icíar Bollaín. Starting out as an actress in Erice's *El sur* (*The South*, 1983), and continuing to work as such (e.g., *Leo*), she has directed two remarkable films, *Hola ¿estás sola?* (*Hi, Are You Alone?*, 1995) and *Flores de otro mundo* (*Flowers from Another World*, 1999). The former is a kind of women's road movie, Spain's answer to *Thelma and Louise* (Ridley Scott, 1991). The young women friends privilege solidarity and friendship over materialism and self-centeredness in their journey south from Valladolid (*facha*dolid—or *Fascist*-olid—as it has been mischievously christened) to Andalusia. They move from order—in the case of La Niña, the social order imposed by her father, whose aspirations for her go no further than employment in his shop—to disorder and the unforeseen. Significantly, like Marilyn Monroe's Girl with No Name in *The Seven Year Itch* (Wilder, 1955), La Niña is a child yet to discover an identity beyond the constraints of a patriarchal order from which her mother has already fled. Icíar Bollaín's second film, *Flores de otro mundo*, touches on a theme of growing interest, the representation of ethnic and racial difference, something that reflects not only Spain's traditional links with the indigenous races of Latin America but also the recent sharper focus on its own gypsy community and the rising tide of immigration from Africa and elsewhere.

Sameness and otherness

The Spanish cinema has often drawn on the country's historic links with gypsy, Islamic, and Jewish cultures. But with the greater awareness and promotion of regional nationalities, and the creation of autonomous parliaments in 1978 after the advent of democracy, films about race, ethnicity, and immigration clearly parallel changing social, demographic, and political identities.

On the one hand, regionally funded films explore the resurgence of nationalistic feeling in the 'nacionalidades históricas' (Hooper 1995: 44) of what, prior to 1978, had simply been regarded as regional entities (Galicia, Aragon, Catalonia, the Basque country, etc.); on the other hand, mainstream films dramatize the intrusions into Spanish life from the outside—in films like *Flores de otro mundo, Cosas que dejé en La Habana* (*Things I Left in Havana*, Gutiérrez Aragón, 1998), *Bwana* (Uribe, 1996), and *Susanna* (Chavarrías, 1996).

In line with a general trend in the Spanish cinema toward narratives with contemporary settings (Heredero 2002: 58), these films comment on the lived realities of modern Spain. In the latter category—those dealing with immigrant communities—films like *Susanna* have begun to explore in more than rudimentary ways the points of comparison and difference between rival but related cultures. In this film, the *noir*-ish narrative of a loser tormented by the conflicting demands of domestic respectability with a demure wife and the thrilling romance with a young woman from 'Generation X' moves between Spanish and Moorish worlds, the latter now not simply represented one-dimensionally and negatively. Although reflecting the North African immigrant community's position in Spain as the least welcome of all, the Moors are nevertheless treated with some objectivity, especially in scenes where the dialogue is given, with subtitles, in Arabic.

The matter is complicated. While not exactly seen as an object of dread or anxiety—as when in *Bwana* (Uribe, 1996) the Andrés Pajares character and family express shock and horror after coming across the Sub-Saharan African on the beach—the North African community here is still identified with the underworld. Nevertheless, though the family and the wider North African milieu are often characterized by gangsterism, uncouth behavior, and violence, there are redeeming features: the mainly respectful portrayals of the women, and the nobler instincts of Saïd (Saïd Amel), who hopes to escape from the constraints of the more inhibiting elements of his culture, to some extent soften racially coded violent instincts toward the young Spanish prostitute who has betrayed him.

Made in Catalan by a Catalan director, *Susanna* is an example of the rise of regional cinema, often boosted by subsidies from the regional parliaments, the significance of which has tended to mirror the fluctuating affirmation of regional identity by the filmmakers themselves. Basque cinema, too, has also benefited from regional funding, although, as I. Santaolalla has argued, the generation of 'Basque' directors making films in the 1980s—Alfonso Ungría on *Akelarre* (*Witches' Sabbath*, 1983), Pedro Sota on *Viento de cólera* (*Winds of Rage*, 1988), or Jose Maria Tuduri, on *Crónica de la guerra carlista* (*Chronicle of the Carlist War*, 1988)—seemed keener to affirm their Basqueness than more recently, say, Juanma Bajo Ulloa (*Alas de mariposa* [*Wings of a Butterfly*], 1992), Julio Medem (*Vacas* [*Cows*], 1992), or Daniel Calparsoro (*Salto al vacío* [*Leap into the Void*], 1995), all of whom adopt a more detached attitude towards their region of origin (Santaolalla 1998: 331–7). Uribe, for instance, makes no reference to his region of origin in *Bwana*, where the central characters—apart from the North African—hail from Madrid.

And yet, regional nationalism clearly remains an issue, often addressed directly through a focus on cultural traditions. Among the directors who have worked most prominently in this area is Bigas Luna. His 'Iberian trilogy'—*Jamón jamón* (*A Tale of Ham and Passion*, 1992), *Huevos de oro* (*Golden Balls*, 1993), and *La teta y la luna* (*The Tit and the Moon*,

1994)—concentrate on national traditions and cultural idiosyncrasies, above all in Catalonia (and Aragon). *Jamón jamón* was an enormous commercial success, launching the career of Penélope Cruz. Her popularity in Spain parallels the rise of a batch of young Spanish stars such as Emma Suárez, Silke, Maribel Verdú, Aitana Sánchez-Gijón, Ariadna Gil, Jorge Sanz (who started out as a child star), Carmelo Gómez, Eduardo Noriega, and, more recently, Tristán Ulloa and Carla Pérez, who have become, in the light of more ambiguous ideals of femininity and masculinity, the mirrors and wish-fulfillment fantasies of Spanish audiences in the last decades of the century. If Almodóvar's films led the way in challenging the taboos of the past, these stars have enabled Spanish audiences to identify themselves with their attractiveness, youth, confidence, and difference. The new models are a far cry both from the way many mainstream stars (e.g., Fernando Fernán Gómez and Alberto Closas) portrayed the anti-Franco troubled protagonists of the dissident cinema and from the comic half-wits of some of the sillier regime-approved genre films (Esteso, Pajares etc.). In the post-Franco crucible of sex and gender, male stars became feminized (e.g., Jorge Sanz), played homosexuals (e.g., Banderas, Poncela), or took on political roles (e.g., Imanol Arias, Carmelo Gómez), while female stars played assertive professionals (e.g., Carmen Maura, Victoria Abril), in a general trend toward greater self-awareness, prompted by drives for introspection and self-knowledge.

By and large the films in which these stars appear belong to recognized genres: melodramas, comedies, thrillers. But in Spain generic boundaries have never been rigid. Nevertheless, in recent years there has been, as Carlos F. Heredero argues, an even more noticeable mixture of native cultural and formal traditions and Hollywood formulas for thrillers, romantic comedies, science fiction, and fantasy. Moreover, comedies and thrillers are the genres on which Spanish filmmakers continue most often to rely. The fluidity of each of these genres makes for complex definition: so, for instance, while Aranda's *Amantes* (*Lovers*, 1991) and Uribe's *Días contados* (*Numbered Days*, 1994) could both be considered thrillers, the former borders on melodrama through preoccupation with family and love entanglements, while the latter largely avoids the psychological complexities of the thriller through concern with terrorism sponsored by the ETA (the Basque separatist group).

Comedy, too, is characterized by a multitude of variants. Once again, the genre in Spain allows for formal cross-fertilization: Alex de la Iglesia's *Acción mutante* (*Mutant Action*, 1992) and *El día de la bestia* (*Day of the Beast*, 1995) draw respectively on fantasy and religion for comic effect; *Airbag* (Bajo Ulloa, 1997), Santiago Segura's *Torrente: el brazo tonto de la ley* (*Torrente: The Idiot Arm of the Law*, 1997), and *Torrente 2: misión en Marbella* (*Torrente: Mission Marbella*, 2001) on adolescent humor; Miguel Abaladejo's *Manolito gafotas* (*Manolito Four-Eyes*, 2000) on even more juvenile humor; and Gómez

■ Julio Medem (1958–)

Julio Medem is one of the most important emerging directors in the Spanish cinema of the last decade or so. He began by making experimental 8mm, and subsequently 35mm, shorts, before directing a medium-length film, *Martín* (1988), produced by one of the leading figures of the Spanish cinema, Elías Querejeta. This was part of a series commissioned to promote the work of young filmmakers in Spain. Medem's first full-length feature was *Vacas* (*Cows*, 1992), which won the Goya for best newcomer director in 1993. Although the narrative and themes are firmly grounded in his native region, Medem was soon keen to distance himself from overemphasizing identification with exclusively Basque issues. He routinely organizes his films around journey motifs (Santaolalla 1998: 332), as if detaching himself from as well as confirming his cultural heritage. Ever since *Vacas* he has been careful to ensure his films have wider, more universal significance. So, for instance, his next film, *La ardilla roja* (*The Red Squirrel*, 1993), poses questions of individual as well as of regional or national identity.

Terrain, so pivotal to Basque mythology, provides the spatial context for analysis of psychology as well as of cultural identity. The main female character (Emma Suárez) uses her apparent loss of memory resulting from a road accident as an excuse both for reconstructing her own identity and for allowing it to be refashioned by the person responsible for the accident. Clearly in evidence again in *La ardilla roja* is Medem's more poetic, symbolic, formally inventive style. The telluric cow and circle symbolism of *Vacas*, allowing psychological and even metaphysical as well as sociohistorical readings of the film, finds its equivalent here, among other things, in squirrel imagery, a mechanism that guides the viewer toward awareness of parallel real and imagined worlds, between which the main characters seem endlessly to travel. Inspired again by Basque myth, but characteristically keeping a certain distance from it, *Tierra* (1995) maintains Medem's passion for exploring multiple levels of

⊕ *Lucía y el sexo*

reality. In *Los amantes del círculo polar* (*Lovers of the Arctic Circle*, 1998), the circle symbolism of the earlier films resurfaces in a narrative about two individuals whose love for each other is as eternal and uninterrupted, whatever the circumstances of their separation, as the unbroken line of a circle. The film is marked, as ever, by formal experiment, each lover narrating the story of their love. Love is at the heart of Medem's most recent film to date, and *Lucía y el sexo* (1998) (*Sex and Lucia*, 1998), is a more upbeat follow-up to *Los amantes*. A self-conscious meditation on desire (Stone 2002: 158–82) and artistic creativity, *Lucía y el sexo* traces the boundaries between love and sex, confirming Medem, from the point of view of both form and content, as one of the major directors of recent Spanish cinema.

Pereira's *Todos los hombres sois iguales* (*You Men are All Alike*, 1994) on the more traditional conventions of romantic comedy, a subgenre in which Fernando Colomo (e.g., *Alegre ma non troppo*, 1994) and Fernando Trueba (e.g., *Sé infiel y no mires con quién* [*Be Unfaithful with Anyone You Like*, 1985]) have shown themselves to be particularly adept. Black humor persists in the late work of García Berlanga (*Todos a la cárcel* [*Everyone to Prison*],1993; *París-Tombuctú*), and in La Cuadrilla's *Justino, un asesino de la tercera edad* (*Justino, a Senior Citizen Murderer*, 1994). While these are the two most common genres, the Spanish cinema of recent years has made space for much else besides: musicals (e.g., Chávarri's *Las cosas del querer* [*The Things of Love*, 1989]), science fiction films (e.g., Colomo's *El caballero del dragón* [*The Dragon Knight*, 1985]), historical films (e.g., Saura's *Goya en Burdeos* [*Goya in Bordeaux*, 1999], or Aranda's *Juana la loca* [*Juana the Mad*, 2001]), and youth-centered films (e.g., Armendáriz, *Historias del Kronen* [*Stories of the Kronen*, 1994] and León de Aranoa's *Barrio* [*Neighbourhood*, 1998]).

A significant development in recent years has also been increasing co-productions with Hispanic America (e.g., Guillermo del Toro's *El espinazo del diablo* (*The Devil's Spine*, 2001)), Hollywood (e.g., *Los otros*), and the rest of Europe (e.g., *Land and Freedom*, Ken Loach, 1995). The links with Latin America seem especially interesting, given the continent's ties with the mother country. A case in point is *Martin Hache* (1997), directed by Adolfo Aristaráin, starring Federico Luppi, Juan Diego Botto, and Cecilia Roth, all Argentinians—prominent stars now of the Spanish cinema, appearing, for instance, in Agustín Yanes's *Nadie hablará de nosotras cuando hayamos muerto* (*No One Will Talk About Us When We Are Dead*, 1995) (Luppi), and *Todo sobre mi madre* (Roth)—as well as the Spaniard Eusebio Poncela. *Martin* has little of the nervousness surrounding the connections between Spain and Latin America often found in the literary work of, say, Borges and Cortázar. The Luppi character emigrates to and remains in Madrid; his son, played by Juan Diego Botto, travels to Spain, but then returns home to Buenos Aires. To the son, Buenos Aires may be less exciting in some ways than Madrid, but in the wider sense it is home, a place in which 'me siento protegido' ('I feel protected'), a remark that resonates beyond this film to globalized or migratory audiences increasingly disoriented by changing social, economic, or national circumstances.

Co-productions involving, as well as finance, personnel—actors, technicians, directors, producers—are becoming an increasingly familiar, even necessary feature of the Spanish film industry, as it explores all avenues for funding including, crucially, television deals. What may be lost in terms of distinctiveness—to the point where through transnational or global processes the very notion of 'Spanish' cinema begins to disintegrate—is gained through the collaboration of interested parties. As Barry Jordan and Rikki Morgan-Tamosunas argue, 'what is remarkable is the sheer breadth and variety of Spanish film output, which is able to combine successfully the representation of cultural specificities and identities with an attractive appeal to the tastes and concerns of wider, international audiences' (1998: 208).

Carlos Saura remarked some time ago that the Spanish cinema was not just Bardem and Berlanga. Today we could say that however wonderful—like Bardem's and Berlanga's—their films, the Spanish cinema is not just Saura, nor even just Almodóvar.

Further reading

Evans, Peter William (ed.), *Spanish Cinema: The Auteurist Tradition* (Oxford: Oxford University Press, 1999). A collection of essays by Spanish cinema specialists on key films from the 1950s onwards.

Graham, Helen, and Jo Labanyi (eds.), *Spanish Cultural Studies: An Introduction* (Oxford: Oxford University Press, 1995). An extremely useful guide to the cultural contexts in which Spanish films (up to the mid-1990s) were made.

Hopewell, John, *Out of the Past: Spanish Cinema after Franco* (London: British Film Institute, 1986). Still the most comprehensive guide to the history of Spanish cinema since the end of the Franco regime up to 1986.

Kinder, Marsha, *Blood Cinema: The Reconstruction of National Identity in Spain* (Berkeley: University of California Press, 1993). An excellent, provocative analysis of the major trends of the last three decades or so.

Martin-Márquez, Susan, *Feminist Discourse and Spanish Cinema: Sight Unseen* (Oxford: Oxford University Press, 1999). The first sustained analysis of the place of women in Spanish cinema.

Perucha, Julio Pérez (ed.), *Antología crítica del cine español 1906–1995* (Madrid: Cátedra-Filmoteca Española, 1997). Excellent, detailed readings of individual films by different authors.

Smith, Paul Julian, *Desire Unlimited: The Cinema of Pedro Almodóvar* (London: Verso, 2002). Still the best guide to Almodóvar.

Stone, Robert, *Spanish Cinema* (London: Longman, 2002). A clear, stimulating, wide-ranging survey with sharp analyses.

Triana-Toribio, Nuria, *Spanish National Cinema* (London: Routledge, 2003). An excellent study, with a welcome emphasis on popular cinema.

14

EAST-CENTRAL EUROPEAN CINEMA: BEYOND THE IRON CURTAIN

Paul Coates

If the central question of a globalized, multicultural, and postmodern reality is that of the ecology of identity—which identities are sustainable and/or worth sustaining—the events of 1989 posed it with particular intensity to the inhabitants of what was once known as 'the Other Europe', who consider themselves 'Europeans' but who may not necessarily be seen as such by Western neighbors anxious to separate themselves from a perilous 'Wild East' (wherever one thinks it begins) and who define a 'European project' in ways that may yet again exclude more than a few Europeans. The directors featured in this chapter—Krzysztof Kieślowski, Emir Kusturica, and Agnieszka Holland—are ones whose success beyond their countries of origin indicates an ability fruitfully to exploit the co-production imperatives that prevail across a Europe otherwise unable to compete with the massive investment in production that is one of the keys to American global dominance (the other being, of course, a frequent near-monopoly of distribution). This involves a capacity for self-transformation while simultaneously retaining the vital impetus and preoccupations of their earlier, pre-1989 work, and inevitably entails confrontation with the ways in which individual identity interfaces with that of the native cultural sphere.

Meanwhile, any discussion of 'cinema behind the Iron Curtain' once that curtain had rusted away must confront just what habits living behind it had been fostered, and which one these directors would need or want to discard. If it must also interrogate the phrase 'behind the Iron Curtain' itself, however, this is because it may be as misleading as the references to 'East European cinema' that often accompanied it, though less because the particular always eludes and defies generalization than because of the glaring inadequacy of the generalization in question. After all, there were at least two Iron Curtains: the one separating Western from Eastern—or East Central—Europe; the other, separating that area from the Soviet Union. Having exported its ideology and institutional structures into countries that were usually viscerally hostile to them, the Soviet Union had no desire to permit its own citizens' infection by the unpleasantly lively remnants of bourgeois ideology in the Western wing of the socialist fraternity. Moreover, from time to time miniature 'Iron Curtains' would fall between the members of that fraternity themselves, marking different moments in the herculean Soviet effort to turn Eastern Europe into 'Western Asia', as it was satirically described by Nobel prize-winning Soviet poet Joseph Brodsky. Such moments would recall the frantic installation of a screen around a severely endangered patient in the hospital of would-be socialist ideology. To use a different, better-known metaphor: in all cases the attempted integration of these countries resembled the 'saddling of the cow' to which Stalin likened the bringing of Poland—vanquisher of the Red Army in 1920—into the Soviet orbit. Every now and then, 'fraternal aid' led by Big Brother would be needed to quarantine other Warsaw Pact states against possible infection, be it by the Prague Spring of 1968 or the Polish August of 1980.

It is possible to discern a movement in the history of East European cinema from an engagement with politics to complete disengagement from it. That movement may be summarized emblematically—and simplified, of course—through consideration of the two major figures of Polish cinema, as one 'from (Andrzej) Wajda to (Krzysztof) Kieślowski': if one likes, from *Ashes and Diamonds* (1958) to the *Three Colors* trilogy (1993/4). Across the divide between these two notional historical moments, however, the preoccupation with the formulation of an ethics adequate to catastrophe—be it that of war, invasion, or the collapse of elites in a system that had no mechanisms for smooth handovers of power—remains a constant. Also constant is an ethos of (often self-camouflaging) protest. Even apolitical or aestheticizing works could be taken as protests against the pervasive politicization of discourse within the bloc, and so suffer a second-order politicization—though it should be added that aestheticism only represented a sharp cutting edge of protest in the era of Socialist Realism, when the state pilloried it as 'formalism'; the closer the system came to crumbling, the more aestheticism suggested a pusillanimous evasion of the emerging options for more direct protest. The various cinemas of Poland, Hungary, Czechoslovakia, and Yugoslavia, among others, employ different tactics of disruption and opposition, but the aim is always the same: defence of the local and native (often, a *local* 'road to socialism') against a would-be monolithic, alien system. After 1989, those cinemas would then weigh the cost of national habits of staunch defense of such identities: among other things, the habit of persecution of local minorities, such as the Roma, or a prejudicial, sometimes pathological fear of the ghosts of past minorities, particularly of the phantom of 'the Jew'.

From political censorship to economic censorship

At the heart of the system that called itself 'real socialism' lay a series of institutions of political censorship and control. After 1989, however, East European artists awoke to find themselves confronting different forms of filmmaking, and of censorship: the economic imperatives of capitalism displaced the ideological ones decreed by the Politburo. The transition between different forms of filmmaking had been eased, though, by the fact that upon occasions in the late 1980s the economic problems of the Eastern bloc system had generated a move that could be seen as a concession, or an insertion of the thin end of the wedge of subversion (the authorities were content if it simply remained thin): an eventual willingness to contemplate co-productions with Western countries (in addition to the ones with other members of the Warsaw pact that had prevailed earlier). The most daring such works emerged from Hungary and Poland. In this context, Krzysztof Kieślowski's universalization of his work in *The Decalogue* (1988)—which eschews any reference to Polish politics—uses the demands of co-production as a way of traveling into a future Eastern Europe: one lacking the Soviet occupiers, though still struggling to come to terms with their dire legacy.

For Kieślowski, as for other East-Central European directors, co-production with Western countries involved trading a political censorship for an economic one. The compromises required now were different ones. Economic in origin, they were more likely to involve budgets and profit-generating strategies: how to film a sequence most cheaply (a skill already possessed by East Europeans, whose footage had been rationed), who to cast (the European star system as pallid reflection of the solar flares of Planet Hollywood), how to satisfy backers in various countries (usually by international casting, continent-trotting for locations, or the selection of internationally bankable issues, the most obvious being the Holocaust and what Susan Sontag once termed 'fascinating fascism'). Such compromises may be viewed as 'the cost of doing business'. If they do not incur the potential opprobrium of politically motivated compromise, they may still be artistically deleterious, with—for instance—the cocktail that mixed international casting, with use of a majority Western language unknown to many of the cast, often wreaking havoc upon ensemble playing and banishing the drama to unconvincingly abstract never-never-lands. If filmmakers also had to discard habits of smuggling subversion in Trojan Horses of allegory, parable, and allusion, either because the resultant works could become incomprehensible to non-native audiences or because such strategies were no longer necessary, such renunciations could decimate the vocabulary of their filmic languages, or destroy the very things that make a national cinema 'national'. The 1990s development of East-Central European cinema may make one ponder particularly intensely the degree to which national cinemas are diluted and even devastated by fierce globalization and co-production.

Kieślowski: the end of necessity

The work of Kieślowski assumes particular significance in this context. The degree to which it has 'traveled', rendering his last films the best-known 'East-Central European' works of the early 1990s, depends on a talent that includes a knack for avoiding the potentially devastating effects of compromise. This occurs in part because of the close fit between the working conditions that dictated repeated compromise and Kieślowski's worldview—in particular, the preoccupation with alternatives, and alternative worlds, that pervaded his work from top to bottom. It dictated his subject matter (*Blind Chance* gives three possible versions of one life, depending on whether or not its protagonist catches a train), editing practices (generating different versions of 'the same' story, such as *Dekalog 5* and *A Short Film About Killing*), openness to the suggestions of co-workers (the filters for *A Short Film About Killing* being suggested by its cameraman, Slawomir Idziak), and willingness to accommodate producers. Kieślowski may have wanted a poster of Michelle Pfeiffer or Kim Basinger placed alongside Dominique's window in *Three Colors: White*, but he was prepared to accept the cheaper alternative proposed by producer Marin Karmitz, a poster of Godard's *Contempt*, which he had co-produced. Kieślowski would not compromise on essentials, but his definition of 'the non-essential' —both philosophical (linked to his preoccupation with alternative versions of events) and pragmatic—was far broader than that of most directors. His documentarist training had given him an abiding sense of the variability of all footage and an openness to chance that reversed Hitchcockian storyboarding and its attendant sense of predestination. This disposition was tailor-made for production conditions that promoted open, flexible structures.

This flexibility of conception also opens the work to multiple spectatorial approaches: *Three Colors*, for instance, may be viewed as: a painterly essay on the use of color; a philosophical disquisition on liberty, equality, and fraternity; a quasi-documentary inspection of its three lead actresses (and/or love poem to them); a sociopolitical study of the cost and possibility of European integration; a theological probing of chance, probability, and the degrees of divine control; a series of in-jokes and playful auto-allusions (the old people at the bottle bank, the recurrent references to Van den Budenmeyer—the pseudonym of Kieślowski's regular composer, Zbigniew Preisner)—among other things. As the work issues invitations to aesthetes, philosophers, sociologists, connoisseurs of beauty, sociologists, theologians, *et al.*, it also invites every one of us to alternate between these possible identities, to discover new hermeneutic roles for ourselves. It is satisfyingly dense and rich.

If Kieślowski was particularly well placed to exploit the opportunities that arose after 1989, it was because he had long since inhabited a variant of the 'post-political' condition it inaugurated. Just when he entered it is debatable, but it can be seen exemplified in *Blind Chance:* Witek, its protagonist, is a Communist Party member in one variant and a dissident in another, yet remains the same person throughout, played by the same actor, Boguslaw Linda. In the teeth of the Polish propensity to ascribe all virtue to the Romantic, dissident side, political categories self-destruct. As a result, 'the real story'—the version of Witek's biography that frames the work—is the one that renders him banal, apolitical (its brevity and deliberate stylistic triteness may be taken as an index of its perceived banality). It is as if this third Witek has drawn the fullest conclusions from his dying father's anti-injunction: 'You don't have to do anything.' Death dignifies his fate: he alone is 'Everyman', and his protest is the metaphysical one of the screamed 'No' that opens the film.

The later films tease out some of the implications of the implied interconnection of freedom and death, meditating on the degree of continued usefulness of such central elements of the European, Judeo-Christian patrimony as the Ten Commandments or the maxims of the French Revolution. *The Decalogue* employs each one of the Ten Commandments successively as a pretext for a story about characters with little or no regard for them. The relationship between the commandments and the individual, fifty-minute stories is vexed, as each appears to activate—not necessarily 'illustrate'—more than one. It may even be useful to discuss whether or not *all* of them are in play, often in surprising ways, in each story. Véronique Campan (1993: 15–24) discerns an absence of the Second Commandment's prohibition of graven images, which consequently hovers over the entire sequence. Whether or not the Second Commandment really is absent may be disputed, particularly in the light of its incorporation into the First Commandment in the Catholic numbering system Kieślowski utilizes (Coates 1999a: 113 n. 1). Here the most daring conjecture is Slavoj Zizek's thesis that the First Commandment corresponds to

■ *Dekalog* and *The Decalogue*

Kieślowski and his co-scenarist Krzysztof Piesiewicz, of course, did not give the individual sections of *Dekalog* titles aligning them with particular commandments (though some European distributors did). Here, as in *Three Colors*, Kieślowski and Piesiewicz clearly sought a dialogue with spectators about the interrelationships between concrete cases and abstract injunctions. If it is even arguable that all Ten Commandments play through each section, this would echo St James's statement that offences against one point of the Law breach it in its entirety: 'For whoever keeps the whole law and yet stumbles at just one point is guilty of breaking all of it' (James 2: 10, New International Version). (It would be worth considering the implications of this, as James himself does to some extent in the subsequent verse: 'For he who said, "Do not commit adultery," also said "Do not murder."') The best-known enunciation of the commandments is found in Exodus 20: 2–17, where their importance is underscored dramatically by the mystical forty days of Moses's absence from the Israelite camp, his journey to a mountain-top to procure the Commandments, and the thunderstorms surrounding Mt Sinai. Nevertheless, Kieślowski's *Dekalog* owe more to their Deuteronomic reiteration before the Israelites' entry into the Promised Land. This, for instance, orders the bunched final injunctions against covetousness to prioritize the one against adultery, facilitating its isolation as a separate commandment, the ninth. Thus

⬇ *Dekalog 1*

Dekalog 9 would find its starting point in this command, and *Dekalog 10* in the proscription of other forms of covetousness. A slightly edited version of Deuteronomy 5 (NIV) yields the following matches with the sections of Kieślowski's *Dekalog*:

Dekalog 1 (Deut 5: 7) You shall have no other gods before me. (v. 8) You shall not make for yourself an idol in the form of anything in heaven above or on the earth beneath or in the waters below. (v. 9) You shall not bow down to them or worship them . . .

Dekalog 2 (v. 11) You shall not misuse the name of the LORD your God, for the LORD will not hold anyone guiltless who misuses His name.

Dekalog 3 (v. 12) Observe the Sabbath day by keeping it holy, as the Lord your God has commanded you. . . .

Dekalog 4 (v. 16) Honor your father and your mother, as the LORD your God has commanded you, that you may live long and that it may go well with you in the land the LORD your God is giving you.

Dekalog 5 (v. 17) You shall not murder.

Dekalog 6 (v. 18) You shall not commit adultery.

Dekalog 7 (v. 19) You shall not steal.

Dekalog 8 (v. 20) You shall not give false testimony against your neighbor.

Dekalog 9 (v. 21a) You shall not covet your neighbor's wife.

Dekalog 10 (v. 21b) You shall not set your desire on your neighbor's house or land, his manservant or maidservant, his ox or donkey, or anything that belongs to your neighbor.

Dekalog 10, displacing all the others (*Dekalog 1* referring to the Second Commandment, and so on [Zizek 2001: 111–17]). Given the broken relationships in the grim housing block it takes as its setting, the sequence's title suggests its haunting by the issue of whether or not the characters' lives can be aligned with any norms, be they the traditional ones followed by Christians and Jews, some new ones, or simply 'love thy neighbor'. *Dekalog 5* is anomalous both in its style—the green filters that turn Warsaw into the putrid hell of the mind of the future murderer—and in its strong endorsement of a Commandment ('thou shalt not kill'), and so may be called the sequence's 'eccentric center'. For the rest, though, Kieślowski offers a cinema of questions and of the agnostic, open-ended dialogue of which the ethics class of *Dekalog 8*—which discusses the story of *Dekalog 2*—is a model.

The question of the relation with origin and tradition is transposed into a different key in *The Double Life of Véronique*, where it includes Kieślowski's relationship with Poland (and his own work, as it provides a variation on the 'alternative lives' idea of *Blind Chance*), as well as in *Three Colors*, which consider whether or not 'liberty, equality and fraternity' really possess the primacy in human aspiration posited by the French

Revolution. In all cases, one unwritten word would appear to be still more significant: love. Polish Weronika is the other partner in three relationships, none of which is satisfying: with family (she leaves home town and father for Cracow, the home of her aunt); with boyfriend (also left behind, though he follows her—and then, as he rides away, she runs after him); and, unconsciously, with Véronique, whom she sees only once, without being recognized herself. The incompleteness of these relationships may owe something to the absence of the mother (a leitmotif of *Dekalog 1*), particularly given her appearance in the pre-credit sequence, in the two girls' early childhood. One-third of the way through the film, Weronika dies of a heart attack during her concert début. The film's remainder shows her double, Véronique, begin and end a relationship with a man who lures her with posted clues relating to a children's story he has written, arguably manipulating her like one of his puppets. Throughout, she feels herself somehow bereft, as if unconsciously scarred by the death of her soul-sister, which intuitively instructs her in the danger of singing and prompts her to cancel her lessons. If this caution also dictates Véronique's final return to the father, the apparent withdrawal from the world may match and anticipate the renunciation of filmmaking Kieślowski would later announce. Since Weronika and Véronique are doubles (Irène Jacob's widely praised double role), what is the status of their relationship? Does it represent a self-involution resulting from—even causing?— the collapse in the relationships with the surrounding world of each one of them? Or do their different fates reflect two choices confronting a single person (Helman 1999: 128)? What is the effect of Slawomir Idziak's yellow filters? Intriguing, suggestive, but possibly frustrating, does the film comprise a set of unanswerable questions, and if so, does this render it a possibly 'psychotic', finally incomprehensible text (Wilson 2000: 28)?

Three colors: blue, *white*, and *red*

Each section of *Three Colors* successively examines the concepts of the French Revolution in the light of three stories and the three colors of the French flag. Each story concerns love-links broken and possibly mended. Kieślowski himself described the color-concept pairing as a mere pretext for the telling of these stories focussed upon love. It is up to the viewer to decide whether or not this statement is simply the kind of smokescreen to be expected of Kieślowski, a very private person who resolutely refused to say 'which of the characters he stood behind'. One may also wonder whether the colors and concepts really can be peeled away from the stories. After all, both colors and concepts have sufficient openness of meaning to interweave the stories at an unspecifiable multiplicity of points. Each film may well be a set of three things—a concept, a color, and a story—to be connected or disconnected playfully, in a speculative variety of ways, by the spectator.

Consider *Blue*, for instance. In terms of the trilogy's conceptual discourse, it shows Julie 'freed' from composer husband Patrice and daughter Anna by a car crash she alone survives. Seeking to isolate herself subsequently, she is courted by her husband's collaborator, Olivier. Discovery of Patrice's adultery in a sense 'frees' her to complete the score —on which she too may have collaborated—and join Olivier, who truly loves her. Kieślowski asks what liberty is, how much it costs, and whether people really want it. But *Blue* privileges the color blue to an even greater extent, as its title indicates. This inversion of the customary hierarchies that deem abstract notions superior to the concrete, and that link the French Revolution to three *concepts* rather than three colors, suggests either a certain playfulness or a desire for a new revolution, one in our mental habits. How does this color interact with this concept and this story? Interviewed, Kieślowski denied any necessity in the linkage of this concept and this color (Coates 1999b: 170). Spectators themselves have the liberty to agree or disagree, a response that will probably involve defining 'freedom' more broadly than did the French Revolution (blue could be related to the sky and the sublime—for instance—and the *absence* of images of blue sky might reinforce Kieślowski's assertion that his characters do not really desire freedom). How 'freedom' might relate to politics in the sense of the question of the unification of Europe —the intended object of celebration in the Patrice/Julie/Olivier concerto—is also a moot point. If it is doubtful that any necessity links color and concept, how about the linkage of the color and this particular story? Might it function as a musical key? Here one may be tempted to assert a stronger link: 'blueness' may be associated with the minor key in which this story most emphatically unfolds (cf. for instance the 'blue period' of Picasso). The story itself, though, may destabilize any assumed connection between blueness and a minor mood, as it moves from tragic catastrophe and isolation to the exalted solidarity in solitude of the choral finale's review of the characters, possibly tracing a trajectory from one blue to another: from depression's 'minor blue' to 'sublime blue'. That ending, in which the chorus from the concerto accompanies the camera's slide between key characters, may itself dramatize two senses of a hidden (unmentioned) key concept: love. Since the chorus sings the words of 1 Corinthians 13, it may be open to religious appropriation, and the eye viewed in close-up at the end is possibly not just Julie's—to be compared with her eye as seen after the accident—but also the eye raised to a second power, that of the divine owner of the omnipresent gaze, and perhaps also a metaphor for the camera eye. However, Kieślowski stated that he chose this particular New Testament chapter because it eschews use of the word 'God' and speaks only of 'love'. Thus, any transcendence it intimates may not be metaphysical at all. In this context, though, it is worth remembering the enigmas that dot the work, particularly the one involving the provenance of the music, which appears to be strangely ownerless or even pre-existent, much as the truths of mathematics (itself—not coincidentally?—often linked to music) are often said to be. Does it 'belong' to Julie, Patrice, Olivier, or the flautist on the street? The question of its provenance may be read 'realistically', even cynically (Patrice may have stolen it from the disenfranchised flautist (Jankun-Dopartowa 1995: 5)) or 'ethereally', for its drifting status may indicate the existence of a 'collective mind' (or musical *Zeitgeist*?), or its origin in a point Beyond all the characters. Is that minor Beyond in a sense part of a major Beyond (the thin end of its transcendental wedge)? If part of a 'musical *Zeitgeist*', it may in fact be 'nothing special', a status that would corroborate the suspicions of some of its listeners (it is, after all, less memorable than Preisner's score for *The Double Life of Véronique*). If the latter, though, it is clearly a matter of great moment. Should one worry if one cannot really say?

Quite where the Trilogy would go from *Blue*—whose stunning ending may deliberately pre-empt the entire sequence—was an object of some speculation at the time of the films' release. Meanwhile, its comparison with *The Double Life of Véronique*—with which it displays multiple continuities—indicates a greater earthing of the ethereal in the later film. The sequence of *Véronique*, *Blue*, and *White* becomes a movement toward an earth into which it arguably crashes in the last-named film—falls being of the essence of comedy. In terms of the series's rhythm of moods, *White* amplifies the element of jokeyness that remains an undertone in *Blue* (the flautist, the dissonant combination of joke and death in the moment of the car crash). For Kieślowski, the fall to earth is one to Poland and is in part a fall away from Europe—or at least from its everyday comforts. The alternation of the esoteric and the blackly comic shows Kieślowski as no simple mystic or symbolist artist: his willingness to juxtapose strongly contrasting chords indicates a sovereign control that—in the context of this film—may appear mockingly ironic. In terms of the Trilogy's conceptual discourse, *White* examines the desirability of equality by prob-ing its proximity to 'getting even', as the hairdresser Karol Karol (Polish for Charles, as in Charlie Chaplin, Kieślowski remarked) avenges his humiliation in the home country of his beautiful, blonde (that is, super-white) French wife, Dominique. Do his final tears as he stares at her prison window betoken regret at having achieved equality? Indeed, *is* it true equality? He still stands below her window, as he had in Paris at his moment of deepest humiliation, and Kieślowski invites us to compare the two moments and consider the degree of equality between them. Moreover, vendettas always up the ante. If the essence of drama is conflict of high and low resolvable only by the universal death that concludes *tragedy*, the question of the degree of resolution and—conversely—of 'art cinema' open-ness in the ending of this comedy becomes an important issue that involves something more than the work's generic classification. (How truly 'comic'—uncomplicatedly 'funny' —is black comedy? How 'comic' can an affliction like Karol's truly be?) Although the

Orwellian dictum that 'all animals are equal, but some animals are more equal than others' had been of particular interest to denizens of the East European societies whose Soviet prototype had been satirized in *Animal Farm*, Kieślowski applies it to East–West relations post-1989, ironically noting the subcutaneous similarities between an East and a West that think themselves very different. The irony is underlined by the fact that the 'more powerful' Western figure is the traditionally less privileged female, whose name ('Dominique') nevertheless suggests domination, while the male is both Polish (less privileged) and actually impotent. Thus, Kieślowski's discourse on geopolitics also encompasses gender. The color 'white', for its part, might be linked to the utopian nature of equality: never achieved, it is blank, non-existent (utopia as—etymologically—'no-place', which may well be the only place where Karol and Dominique can meet: an internationally homogenized, neutralized place like the Marriott hotel—that enclave of 'the West' in Warsaw—where they make love). Of the three colors at play in the Trilogy, white may be the most conceptual, the most obviously ambivalent, suggesting both weddings and death, and it appears to be used in a more varied fashion than the colors of the other two sections (simply because more widely—and naturally—present in the environment?). Is the resultant relative abstraction that of comedy *per se*, which Henri Bergson famously described as involving a freezing (snow-whiteness?) of emotion? If so, does the work cease to be comic when Karol's tears flow, as tears do at the end of each of the Trilogy's sections?

Like several of Kieślowski's Polish documentaries, *White* investigates mechanisms of control. This thematization of control musically anticipates *Red*, reiterating Kieślowski's insistence on the unity of apparent opposites: the black comedy can be *transposed* into a work that combines a discourse on control with one on fate, reincarnation, and the divine. In *Red*, which is sprinkled with over 400 red objects, a misanthropic judge (Joseph Kern) thaws as he appears to orchestrate a love between a young girl (Valentine) who befriends him and a young man (Auguste) whose experiences precisely replicate elements of his own past. Is Kern God, or just *a* god? If he is just *a* god, is there possibly another deity above him? (Questions raised by *Dekalog 1* recur here, and the two films deserve comparison.) Is he even in a sense Auguste, or even a dream, as Kieślowski himself suggested (Amiel and Ciment 1994: 28)? If brotherhood seems more desirable than either liberty or equality, is it because it is closer to the love hymned in the musical finale of *Blue*? Moving between several European countries, *Three Colors* interrogates the possibility of an integrated, 'European' identity, but its emotional wellspring lies at the point where love and (quasi-) divinity intersect in the question of the nature, possibility, and defensibility of control. Kieślowski described *Red* as cast in the conditional tense (Stok 1993: 218). This being the case, what is the status of the world it depicts? Reality's elements seem subject to slippage, divorce, and remarriage. A foghorn that would appear to belong to the ending (unlikely in a landlocked Switzerland) can accompany Valentine's photo shoot; the key image to emerge from that shoot, meanwhile—that of Valentine looking sorrowful—can be used on a gum poster then reappear as the frame freezes after her rescue from the ferry disaster; and elements of the judge's life can be replayed in that of Auguste. If sounds and images can shift contexts endlessly, does this render them 'depthless' in the manner Fredric Jameson has associated with postmodernism? One may doubt this—and not just because of the vehement disclaimers of postmodernism by Krzysztof Piesiewicz, Kieślowski's cowriter, in interview—the shuffling and reshuffling of material practised by a deity who doubles Kieślowski himself (with his passion for editing), and may either be Judge Joseph Kern or have him as one of his doubles, is not necessarily endless, but rather part of a quest for the right place for it, the home possibly found at the work's end, which brings August and Valentine together in a prospectively happier version of the Judge's life. Nevertheless, Kieślowski holds continually before us the *cost* of such happiness, which is shadowed—perhaps even overshadowed—by appalling waste, be it in the lost lives of the other ferry passengers or the unfulfilled one of the Judge himself. If *Red* is a Last Judgement, how does it relate to the discourse on law of *The Decalogue*? Do Kieślowski's echoes of his own earlier work also generate a sense of homecoming, relocating old themes and motifs in a 'right place' and thereby motivating and justifying his subsequent proclamations of retirement? Are certain works *obviously* 'last works' (*Red* was compared to Shakespeare's *The Tempest*), and, if so, does *Red* fit such a category of evident finality? Appropriately enough for Kieślowski's final contribution to his directorial dialogue with spectators, such questions resist easy answers and may even be finally open.

Kusturica: the mirage of community

The plaudits earned by Emir Kusturica's works may simply reflect an international audience's affection for their sometimes overblown bravura, their Felliniesque, carnivalesque relish of the tang and 'color' of gypsy communities; but their particular ongoing relevance lies in the status of the former Yugoslavia—Kusturica's homeland—as the possible nightmare terminus of Western multiculturalism should it too fail to integrate its ethnic minorities, casting them (out) instead as images of the paranoid Other. The negative Other, of course, has an equally fantastic (because purely positive) counterpart: thus for the Slovene Marxist Slavoj Zizek the central issue is whether or not the films become the locus of 'the reverse racism which celebrates the exotic authenticity of the Balkan Other' (Zizek 2000: 5). But the blood-soaked breakup of the former Yugoslavia clearly helped impress Kusturica's work upon the attention of Westerners. The opening line of *Underground*—his most controversial and best-known work—runs 'Once upon a time there was a country.' It can also be conjugated into 'Once upon a time there was a community': as that opening line suggests, Kusturica's project concerns how a director of the former Yugoslavia is to deal with a splintering of community he experiences both as its evaporation and that of his subject-matter. From what position can filmmaking then continue? Kusturica's solution involves utilizing gypsy communities as images of ones that are bounded, knowable, and non-bellicose (because non-aligned with any state or proto-state structures, bubbling inwardly, rather than straining outwards). While the collapse of such a community is the subject of *Underground*, the possibility of its establishment—or re-establishment—lies at the heart of his films organized around gypsy life, *Time of the Gypsies* and *Black Cat White Cat*.

Underground—recipient of the Palme d'Or at Cannes in 1995—grows increasingly surreal with each of its three sections. If the first presents a grotesque, rambunctious, Fellinian image of the love rivalry between two Serbian wartime resistance fighters—Marko and Blacky—the second offers a pungent, somewhat unfocussed allegory of the mentality of a populace enslaved in darkness by Communism. Where section one was entitled 'War' and section two, 'Cold War', section three is the return of 'War', and sees the semi-coherent allegory of the second section tip over into a savagely surreal depiction of the war in the Balkans in 1992. Blacky, who heads a private army, orders the shooting of the profiteer, only later discovering him to be Marko. A blazing wheelchair containing the dead Marko and his wife, Natalija, careers around an upturned crucifix, accompanied by an apocalyptic choral keening. The film ends in a poetic utopia of cleansing and rebirth, assembling all its characters, both dead and alive, on a spit of land whose ends breaks off and floats away as they party to raucous brass music: brother no longer kills brother.

Of the three sections, the final one may well be the most impressive: a savage, poetic lament for the collapse of brotherhood and country that nevertheless generates a final, utopian counter-image. If the first section had been somewhat complacently rambunctious in its celebration of a life force which may be Balkan, Serbian, or a cartoon version of the energy of the Nietzschean Superman, conversely, the second is not entirely coherent: although the dark cellar allegorizes the Tito regime's keeping of an entire population in the dark, the critique relies upon a Communist-style, class-based analysis of the exploitation of the naively plebeian (Blacky) by such would-be intellectuals as Marko. The viscerally powerful, contrasting images of inferno and utopia in the third section render issues of coherence finally irrelevant.

Upon release, *Underground* encountered violent criticism as alleged Serbian propaganda. Dina Iordanova (2001: 118) finds the case for the prosecution weak, though

⊕ *Underground*

she also likens Kusturica to Leni Riefenstahl. The comparison has some validity: both are inclined to write Nietzschean blank cheques for exceptional individuals who may be taken as stand-ins for the artist, and thus for themselves. There is surely a crucial difference between their visions of community, however. Whereas Riefenstahl saw utopia incarnated already in the Third Reich, Kusturica deems it unattainable under current world orders. This may well render the work of the former ultimately political, and the latter's anti-political. Since both victims and villains are Serbs, the accusation of purveying Serbian propaganda can seem all the weaker, though the reader should consult Iordanova's fine, terse summary of the pros and cons of the case (2001: 115–29). Kusturica's position seems rather to be one of defiant anarchism—even incoherence—that finds its ideal in the Roma, who are extraterritorial to established state structures, and so can survive their collapse. Simultaneously, it undermines both the 'political correctness' of an old 'East European' aesthetic and that of a West currently imposing its norms of economic efficiency across the former Soviet bloc.

Less controversial is the earlier *Time of the Gypsies*, which I consider rather than *Black Cat White Cat* because it seems to me the more complex achievement. Its power stems from being both deeply poetic and grounded in the realia of Roma life (it does not suffer the excessive abstraction from any known reality that burdens the equally poetic *Arizona*

Dream). The central metaphors are ones of communal and individual ecstasy in levitation and flight. For Kusturica here, 'getting a community off the ground' is literally that: a process of putting it in the air, as a mirage. Where the nightmare of life *under* history is being underground, the dream is being in the air, where a free community exists. It does so, however, only in *displaced* form, as utopia, as an uprooted aesthetic construct, like the floating island at the end of *Underground*. Kusturica's awareness that such a community exists only in the air, as pastoral, is reflected in the near-pre-industrial rural setting of *Black Cat White Cat*, which was explicitly fashioned to escape the political crossfire into which he had wandered with *Underground*. But it is expressed more interestingly in *Time of the Gypsies*, where the miraculous status of the various levitations (from forks, houses, and Azra giving birth to athletic males leaping on foreign billboards) encapsulates the difficulty of sustaining the energy and ecstasy that enliven his communities. Those communities exclude the individualist, the rootless artist determined to succeed, embodied in the first-person voice of Perhan, whose own dreams of flight could theoretically as well be accommodated in the Arizona and the Arctic of *Arizona Dream*.

Kusturica's notion of art is, however, entirely and fruitfully contradictory, exalting both the cunning and ruthlessness of the individualist Nietzschean will and the communal art of the gypsy bands whose music pervades his work. Its fruitfulness lies in its attunement to film's paradoxical combination of auteurist individualism and absorption in a group. *Time of the Gypsies* is richer than Kusturica's American film because his surrogate comes and goes between home and a delusive foreign land of plenty. Here his obsession with earth-bound birds becomes polysemous. The geese and the turkeys that haunt Perhan signify the *difficulty* of getting off the ground. But they also belong in and feed a community both literally and metaphorically; they do not fly away. As *birds* they represent the flight they themselves cannot achieve; which may be why flight and levitation are associated with death as well as ecstasy. Thus Azra levitates just before dying, while Perhan is told to 'fly' by the woman who shoots him, then sees a spectral white turkey swoop down toward him as he dies. As figures of mediation, these earth-bound birds are scar-signs of a contradiction within Kusturica's dream, which pursues both flight (up and away) *and* community. That contradiction—a possible subject for structuralist analysis—is resolved in part by the use of levitation: being in the air is not necessarily the preliminary to going anywhere. (In *Arizona Dream*, the plane simply circles the house.) On a larger scale—in the macrocosm that encompasses these microcosmic strategies—the gypsies perform the same function. How can they go anywhere, when 'home' is everywhere and nowhere? Gocic usefully contrasts the comic, 'insider' view of Roma culture presented by Kusturica with the more bleak and critical 'outsider' view of the older Yugoslav director Zvivojin Pavlovic (Gocic 2001: 99–105). The power of *Time of the Gypsies*, however, lies in transcending both this opposition and a simply romanticizing 'projective identification' with the Other: Perhan, the exploited visionary, himself becomes an exploiter, and his hard rejection of his childhood sweetheart Azra, and willingness to sell the baby he thinks is not his, threatens him with the loss of soul his grandmother fears may befall him. The richness and density of such metaphorical complexes may render Kusturica's work more multi-layered than even his most authoritative interpreters have realized.

Holland: fluidities and fixities of identity

Although made at the beginning of the 1990s, Agnieszka Holland's *Europa Europa* (1990) has an enormous continuing resonance almost irrespective of the skill of its execution, as the extraordinary autobiography of Salomon Perel that it dramatizes permits a complex simultaneous examination of 'the hero's cultural, national, religious and even sexual identity' (Jankun-Dopartowa 2000: 216). The outrageous ironies of this story would be deeply questionable were they merely fictional contrivances (Holland deviates from Perel's account at only one or two points). They set in with the deadpan voice-over noting the identity between the birthday of this Jewish man and Adolf Hitler. This breathtaking coincidence drily insinuates a sense of almost infinite, fantastic possibility, and suggests an ironic fulfillment of the rabbi's 'May this child live' as he circumcizes him. The clash and interaction of Salomon's various identities makes Holland's work a key text for discussion of the globalized world's dialectic between postmodern identity play and the rear-guard efforts—of residual selfhoods or cultures—to define and retain a single dominant identity amidst the flux. It is a dialectic with profound relevance both to analysis of the origins of the National Socialism that engulfed Perel's life (largely a reaction to the perceived anarchy of the Weimar republic) and to Perel's eventual location of the bedrock of his identity in the Jewishness inscribed in his body by circumcision.

For much of the film, however, that circumcision seems to be Solly's curse. This ironic male version of the affliction of the lower body women know as 'the curse' (menstruation) renders the work peculiarly appropriate to the work of a female director. (Is it therefore also 'feminist', for all Holland's rejection of that label?) For Jankun-Dopartowa, Holland's works recall those of the Czech novelist Milan Kundera, which she first encountered when studying at the FAMU film school in Prague. Like Kundera, she argues, Holland derives the origins of kitsch from the suppression of awareness of the necessity of defecation (2000: 218; Kundera 1985: 248). Meanwhile, Holland's remark of Perel—that 'his penis saved his soul' (Taubin 1992)—recalls the unwillingness to separate body and soul found both in Kundera and in Judaism. Holland's pervasive sense of the body as ungainly, defective, even imprisoning, is most apparent with regard to lower bodily functions in general (including sexual ones; a possible point of divergence with Kundera, whose Don Juanism sometimes glamorizes sexuality). As filmed by Holland, Solly's sexual attractiveness, the apparent passport to bisexual protection, entails his upper body's issue of a promissory note its lower part cannot honor. This sense of the body in conflict is also central to the adolescence through which Solly is passing. If he can never forget his lower parts, it is because adolescence renders his a body awkwardly in the making. In all cases Solly's identity has to be occulted from his environment, his individual 'I' as thoroughly covered as the private parts in which it is lodged. The confusion of different layers of identity as he makes a Feast of Tabernacles booth with Robert while decrying religion as the opium of the masses makes a mockery of the notion of integrated selfhood. For Holland, however, that failure of selfhood may be less a sign of ludic postmodern freedom than the imprint of historical catastrophe.

In interviews, Holland compared her work to Voltaire's *Candide*: its original title was 'A European Education'. Among other things, her study of identities is one of processes of education and indoctrination. If Perel can be both a Komsomol and a Hitler Youth, does this indicate the instability of his identity or the secret interdependence of these— and perhaps all—opposites, with opposition becoming merely skin-deep and the term 'national socialism' furnishing quite a piquantly accurate x-ray of the essence of Stalinism? Is that why, in Solly's dreams, Stalin waltzes with a Hitler whose hands shield his lower body to hide his Jewishness? If Holland's Solly apparently retains an ethnic sense of identity throughout—tracing a Star of David on a steamed window in the Academy, or imitating the hands on a Jewish gravestone just after his rejection by his German girlfriend, Leni—does this actually make him more of a hero of our own (postmodern?) times than the real Solomon Perel, who self-confessedly absorbed Nazi ideology at a profound level (Perel 1997: 100, 178, 181)? Indeed, as in a fairy tale, Solly's acknowledgements of Jewishness are not punished but rewarded, as only when he breaks down and confesses it does he meet with affection—first from the gay German actor Robert, then from Leni's mother. (The question of Solly's contemporariness, of course, includes that of whether or not historical films are ever anything other than modern ones in disguise.)

Amid the ongoing East-Central European efforts to exorcize a persistent anti-semitism and confront the extent and nature of local complicity in crimes once simply and safely attributed to Nazi or Soviet others, Holland's work has lost none of its original relevance. The degree of its possible adherence to a postmodern notion of infinitely malleable identity is also worth discussing. The written injunction of Solomon's father—'Never forget who you are'—reverberates across Solly's life with a succession of deep, unwitting ironies, and may be compared and contrasted with the father's 'You don't have to do anything' in Kieślowski's *Blind Chance*. The father follows up with the question 'Do you keep the sabbath?' For him at least there is a primary identity and it is religious. If Susan Linville is right to argue that denials of the fluidities of identity dovetail easily with the Fascist construction of selfhood (Linville 1995), does that make any fixed identity potentially fascistic? Or can one identity rein in the potential excesses of other ones, as religious believers would maintain, arguing that the demotion of an overarching imperative to love God and neighbor disastrously and inappropriately promotes a secondary identity (Lewis 1989: 19–24)? It could then be argued that National Socialism and Communism spawned kitsch on such a scale precisely because they infused anti-religion with religious elements, be it from cynicism or schizophrenia, with the question of which of the two prevailed varying from one National Socialist or Stalinist to another. Like all the East-Central European texts considered in this chapter, Holland's displays a timely, healthy suspicion that neither Europe nor any one of its individual inhabitants can rest secure in a sense of just who they are, or who—or what—they may become.

Further Reading

This guide refers only to work in English. Much significant work on Kieślowski is to be found in French (Amiel, Campan), while the best work on Holland is indisputably in Polish (Jankun-Dopartowa).

Coates, Paul (ed.), *Lucid Dreams: The Films of Krzysztof Kieślowski* (Trowbridge: Flicks Books, 1999). The only English-language study to incorporate Polish perspectives on Kieślowski.

Gocic, Goran, *Notes from the Underground: the films of Emir Kusturica* (London: Wallflower, 2001). The first English-language study of Kusturica: a lively and theoretically provocative introduction.

Haraszti, Miklos, *The Velvet Prison* (New York: Noonday Press, 1987). The most eloquent and incisive analysis of the climate created by East-Central Europe's political censorship.

Insdorf, Annette, *Second Chances, Double Lives* (New York: Hyperion, 1999). A sensitive critical reading of Kieślowski's films, which is strongest in the area of the late works.

Iordanova, Dina, *Cinema of Flames: Balkan Film, Culture and the Media* (London: British Film Institute, 2001). An extremely informative and penetrating study of media representations of the breakup of the former Yugoslavia.

Linville, Susan, '*Europa, Europa*: A Test Case for German National Cinema', *Wide Angle* 16(3) (1995): 38–51. A challenging analysis of the ramifications of the issue of identity politics in Holland's film.

Perel, Solomon, *Europa, Europa*, trans. Margot Bettauer Dembo (New York: Wiley, 1997). Offers the opportunity to confront Holland's film with Perel's own more detailed account of this extraordinary period of his life.

Stok, Danusia, *Kieślowski on Kieślowski* (London: Faber & Faber, 1993). The indispensable interview-based account of Kieślowski's life and self-understanding.

Wilson, Emma, *Memory and Survival: The French Cinema of Krzysztof Kieślowski* (Oxford: Legenda, 2000). A very valuable, theoretically sophisticated reading. (French quotations are not translated, however.)

15

FRENCH CINEMA OF THE MARGINS

Martine Beugnet

Introduction

The construction of modern France's national identity has been underpinned by a certain ideal of democracy based on unity and equality. One of the by-products of these progressive principles, however, was a tendency to centralization and homogenization (the denial of difference) (Silverman 1999). Though in the face of contemporary social fragmentation and multiculturalism this tendency is being questioned, much of French identity and culture remains defined by centralist beliefs. Characteristically, a large part of the country's administrative powers, of its political as well as cultural life, and of its national symbolism, is still anchored within its capital city. This is also true of its cinema. Overall, in its economy and in its strategies of representation, the French mainstream sector tends to reproduce this sense of a strong centripetal force at the heart of the country's national definition, and helps shape some of the myths that enrich the sense of collective identity that derives from it (Hayward 1993). Yet French film production was always sufficient in number and variety to allow for the development, alongside 'hegemonic' types of national cinema, of influential counter-trends that not only question but also, through cross-fertilization, help renew mainstream practices of filmmaking. This chapter will focus on recent French cinema (the late 1980s to the present) that falls within the traditional feature-film category, and is distributed through the conventional networks, but nevertheless thematically and formally diverts from the larger, more established, part of film production. (For practical reasons, this brief overview does not include short films and experimental cinema, which would necessitate a study in themselves.)

Diversity of styles and blurring of genre definitions preclude easy categorizations, but there is a point of convergence among a large number of films released outside the dominant commercial trends in that period. They testify to a renewed interest in portraying the marginal and the mechanisms of exclusion in contemporary France. Films 'set within the real, in order to work on the real' (Blüher 2000: 15), they also question the reduction of cinema to mere entertainment or 'pure spectacle' (Beugnet 2000). René Prédal (2002: 125) further differentiates between the cinema of engagés (politically committed) directors such as Bertrand Tavernier, whose films tend to reconstruct reality in order to demonstrate a point, and a batch of new directors who take 'the real' as their point of departure. Yet the principal characteristic of this filmmaking cannot be equated with Bazinian[1] principles of Neorealist transparency: through a diversity of approaches and styles, the cinema of the 1990s takes its raw material from the real but shapes it and re-presents it to form specific visions of a complex, changing reality.

The return of the real?

In the 1980s, even the most established French genres of the comedy and the *polar* (French thriller) appeared to be taken over by the kind of lavish productions that are best exemplified by the films of the *cinéma du look* and of the Heritage cinema styles. A cinema associated with large budgets, famous actors, massive advertisement, and the promise of spectacular visual pleasures became the dominant trend. As a by-product, the tendency to shy away from the ideological and the critical in favor of nostalgia, entertainment, and 'aestheticism' seemed to rule (Austin 1996; Powrie 1999). Yet even beyond the alternative work of a handful of well-known independent directors, the production of the late 1980s already showed signs of a transformation.

While the style characteristic of the vanishing *cinéma du look* was being assimilated by the action thriller genre (the films directed or produced by Luc Besson in particular), and in spite of the Heritage cinema's continued domination, the period between the late 1980s and 2000 is often discussed in terms of a 'return of the real' (Powrie 1999; Tesson 2001). An unprecedented number of unknown or first-time directors established themselves at that point, and started to develop low-budget styles very much in contrast to the dominant trends. In financial terms, the existence of this 'Young French Cinema'[2] depended not only on the development of less onerous methods of filmmaking (the DV camera especially) but also on the continuing role of supporting national bodies such as the Centre National du Cinéma and of the loan system of the *avance sur recettes*. Combined with funding and commissions from television channels and with the aid offered by regional and local bodies, such state policies have, in spite of their obvious deficiencies,[3] greatly contributed to preserving France's lively non-commercial film sector. In the 1990s, they played a determining role in the surge of first feature films that often presented a critical vision of contemporary society. In many cases however, the directors' determination and ingenuity made up for the absence of adequate financial support (one of the most striking examples being that of Jean-François Richet's *État des lieux* [*Inner City*, 1995], produced thanks to the money reaped in casinos where the director and scenarist spent their unemployment benefits).

Part of the Young French Cinema draws on a literary and cinematic *auteur* tradition, and focusses on educated, middle-class milieus,[4] but it has also generated a cinema of the margins, one that portrays darker areas of French society and deals with issues of impoverishment and alienation. This revival of the social and political concerns in French cinema—borne out, for example, by the 1997 *Appel à la désobéissance* ('call for diso-bedience'), a petition written, signed, and publicized by a group of directors as a protest against immigration policies—emerges against a particular historical backdrop: the failure of left-wing politics and the disenchantment created by the widening socioeconomic gap or *fracture sociale*. In particular, the enduring combination of ethnic divide, unemploy-ment, and lack of opportunities in postcolonial France resulted in an explosive situation in some of the *banlieues*, and in a radicalization of some segments of public opinion. While these connected but complex issues are explicitly or implicitly evoked by its films, the French cinema of the margins also draws on a wide array of cinematic traditions: from the films of *nouvelle vague* veteran *auteurs* to African-American cinema and British realism, these various intertextual references all contribute to the diversity of these films.

Agnès Varda and the tradition of the *auteur engagé*

With its emphasis on personal vision and style, *auteur* cinema has always provided alternatives to the mainstream approaches, both in terms of production techniques and subject matter. *Auteur* cinema tends to be low-budget and idiosyncratic, and rejects conventional characters and narratives in favor of anti-heroes, elliptical narration, and streams of consciousness. For these reasons it has often been dismissed as self-centered, the expression of highly individualistic points of view. However, ever since the release of her first film in the 1950s, the work of Agnès Varda has denied the divide between

■ Agnès Varda (1928–)

Varda's first film, named after a fishing village (*La Pointe courte*, 1954), has been described as a forerunner of the *nouvelle vague*. Thirty-two years later, *Sans toit ni loi* heralded the renewal of French production. In between, Varda has produced a diverse and absorbing body of work that includes feature films, shorts, and documentaries that often blur with the fictional (as with *Jane b by Agnès v* [1993] and *Kung Fu Master*, a portrait of Jane Birkin twinned with a fiction scripted by the actress).

Time and mortality are central themes to her work. *Jacquot de Nantes* was shot as an *homage* to her husband, filmmaker Jacques Demy, who was at the time dying of cancer. The narration moves back and forth from the past (Demy's childhood) and the present, linking the sequences with evocative graphic cuts: from a view of an estuary's landscape, with its sinuous, reedy banks, to a much enlarged view of Demy's arm, with its wrinkles and hair, for instance. In such sequences, Varda uses her extreme close-up tracking-shot technique in order to search, lovingly, for signs of aging and of illness on her husband's skin. Similarly, *Les Glaneurs et la glaneuse* could be described as a cinematic 'vanitas' (a still-life painting evoking earthly pleasures that includes a visual reminder of mortality), in which the evocation of aging and human vulnerability operates as a counterpart to the depiction of the materialism and the tyranny of the 'look' that rule today's society.

⊕ *Les Glaneurs et la glaneuse*

Although they may seem very distant in time, style, and subject, these films have in fact much in common with her first box-office and critical success, *Cléo de 5 à 7*, released in 1961. Shot almost in real time, *Cléo de 5 à 7* follows ninety minutes of the life of Cléo, a beautiful popular singer. Not only as a performer but also as a person, Cléo's identity is defined by her appearance, and she exists through the gaze of others. Early on, a celebrated sequence in a shop where a display of mirrors reflects her image perfectly captures the narcissistic nature of the character. But Cléo has been told that she has cancer. At first, she feels doubly betrayed, by the beautiful body that hides a deathly illness and by her entourage, who are unwilling to share in her anguish. In the second part of the film, however, Cléo learns to confront her new self and to cast her gaze outwardly. The camera work, and in particular the long subjective tracking shots, portrays her discovery of herself as an active observer, one who looks, questions, and listens rather than seeks other people's gazes and attention.

Together with her continuing interest in art and in literature, her training as a photographer profoundly shaped Varda's cinematic vision. Intent from the start on exploring cinema's potential both as a specific language and as a subjective mode of expression, she describes her filmmaking as a form of *cinécriture* ('cinewriting'). Varda always claims authorship of her films, not only through the distinctive stylistic features that she has developed, but also at times through a voice-over commentary, or by appearing in person. Her latest releases reaffirm her commitment to the critical observation of her contemporary world and her belief in a cinema where authorship and political engagement are not antithetical. On the contrary, in Varda's films, the marked presence of the director as *auteur* serves as a reminder of the subjectivity of the cinematic vision, and questions its apparent truthfulness.

subjective approach and the exploration of social issues. Indeed, her insistence on developing her own style of filmmaking has combined with a sustained interest in depicting marginal subjects and in portraying disenfranchised areas of French society. In both *Sans toit ni loi* (*Vagabond*, 1986) and *Les Glaneurs et la glaneuse* (*The Gleaners and I*, 2000), the exploration of the margins prompts an existential questioning and an examination of cinematic practices.

Sans toit ni loi, released in 1986, announced many of the issues that became fundamental to the cinema of the margins that emerged in the following years. The unusual subject of the film, and its radical approach to narrative, visual treatment and characterization, have made it one of the most frequently analyzed French films of the 1980s, and a highly influential text for feminist film theory. Drawing on a documentary aesthetic but endowed with the painterly quality typical of Varda's style, *Sans toit ni loi* is presented as an inquiry into the life of a mysterious young woman found dead in a ditch. Starting with the discovery of the body and a voice-over introduction by Varda, the narrative then alternates between interviews of people who met the girl, a vagabond called Mona, and flashbacks depicting her journey and the various encounters that marked her last few weeks. Long traveling shots set to wistful music form a visual motif that gives the film its pace, and depict the central character moving through the inhospitable, dull landscape of a winter-stricken south. Mona's passage resembles a counter-current; she walks from right to left, resists definitions, and declines to engage with the conventional rules of the existing system of social and economic exchange. Mona provokes and fascinates, does not thank, never pleases, and demands the ultimate gift: disinterested generosity. Her presence is potentially no less frustrating for the spectator than for other characters in the diegesis. The young woman's physical presence is powerful: she dominates the space; she is dirty and she smells. But the conventional process of audience identification is in any case precluded by the character's elusiveness (Smith 1998: 125–8; Hayward 2000: 272). She hardly talks and, in the way she enters and leaves the frame, often eludes the penetrating gaze of the camera. As such, the symbolic weight of her presence becomes just as compelling as her movements and narrative functions: through the character of Mona, *Sans toit ni loi* questions not only social perceptions and expectations but also cinematic stereotypes and spectatorial involvement. The film thus creates a potent figure of refusal, one who rejects objectification and categorization and tragically but unashamedly claims her difference (Smith 1998: 118; Hayward 2000: 270).

The rules of consumption and exchange, both material and visual, are investigated again in *Les Glaneurs et la glaneuse*. This time it is the director herself who takes to the road in order to record the activities of the contemporary gleaners—those who collect refuse for their subsistence, for ethical reasons, or for their pleasure. Indebted to Surrealism, *Les Glaneurs* develops along the principles of chance, and the value and significance of found objects and found images. The film itself is a hybrid, a collage of styles that combines images produced with professional equipment with those shot on a mini-DV camera. A complex narrative structure, carried by the voice-over of the director, mingles techniques that are recurrent in Varda's filmmaking: interviews, documentary descriptions, static tableaux, and a personal commentary where the director's own body becomes a field of investigation. *Les Glaneurs* thus appears as a cross between the documentary, the essay, and the self-portrait (Rosello 2001). At the heart of the project is the critical assessment of some of the effects of mass consumption (of food, of objects, of images). Through its investigation of the nature of waste and its implicit critique of the dominant ideals of standardization, youth, and the new, the film leads to a reflection on social exclusion and aging, Varda eventually turning the camera on herself to track the signs of her own mortality. Gleaning thus suggests a modest alternative to the hegemonic consumerist rules and conventions (of the beautiful, the useful, the cinematic . . .). The director casts herself as a gleaner, collecting images that are usually deemed unworthy of the screen, focussing on that part of the real that tends to be cut off or to remain in the margins of the frame. In *Les Glaneurs: deux ans après* (*The Gleaners: Two Years Later*), released in 2003, Varda goes back in search of the gleaners she met, people often living in precarious conditions. While it reaffirms her ethical choices, this second film also further challenges the traditional role of the filmmaker by highlighting the responsibility of the director towards the subjects of his or her films.

From center to periphery

Geographically, the two films that have been discussed are characteristic of the non-mainstream cinema of the late 1980s and 1990s. It is the less known, downtrodden parts of the Paris and the non-picturesque provinces that are shown. However, for practical reasons involving its concentration of production facilities and of funding sources, but also for historical and cultural reasons, Paris is an inescapable feature of French cinema. The history and architectural organization of the 'City of Light' have made it into a particularly seductive urban spectacle that generations of artists, including filmmakers, have transformed into a myth. Paris on screen has been endowed with a symbolic meaning and romantic aura, which have made it a privileged backdrop for fiction films that only depictions of the south of France can occasionally claim to rival. The 'de-centering' (Blüher 2000) that marks the new batch of films is thus a significant move, and accompanies the shift in focus from the singular hero fighting for the good of all to marginalized individuals and small, endangered communities.

Cédric Klapisch's *Chacun cherche son chat* (1996) is emblematic of this transition. Save for a holiday scene that lasts a few seconds, the film is strictly located within the boundaries of one popular district of Paris, and many of its characters are played by non-professional actors recruited locally. Building sites and demolitions punctuate the film like visual and sound motifs: the small *quartier* (neighborhood) that the heroine, the timid Chloë, inhabits, is undergoing a profound upheaval. Concurrent with the disappearance of the old communities is the loneliness experienced by individuals like Chloë, and the film's *mise-en-scène* and disruptive soundtrack constantly underline the urban coexistence of physical closeness with indifference and isolation. Through Chloë's search for her missing cat, however, the spectator is invited to discover a *quartier* and a microcosm where the young woman finds human contact and, perhaps, love. But although the film evokes the existence of the traditional convivial community with obvious nostalgia, it does not necessarily idealize it. Elizabeth Ezra points out that beneath the depiction of the close-knit community centered on its local café lies a wider principle of exclusion. Protected but also humored by the locals, Djamel, a young man of Arabic descent, is part of the community inasmuch as he takes on the function of 'village idiot', the acceptable, unthreatening 'other'. His presence suggests that such comforting coherence as the traditional social grouping can offer may be established through implicit forms of differentiation and segregation (Ezra 1999: 219–22). Hence, the nostalgia expressed in *Chacun* is of an ambiguous quality: the ways of life and the Paris it looks back on seems an attractive alternative to the dehumanizing fragmentation of today's life, but an obsolete one in the face of a contemporary multiethnic society.

Multiethnicity and the cinema of the *banlieue*

Coexistent with the progressive 'cleaning-up' and 'upgrading' of the popular quarters in the center of the main French cities was the appearance of the suburbs or *banlieues*. Begun after World War II, the process was accelerated in the 1960s, after the independence of Algeria and the surge in numbers of North African immigrant workers in particular. This 'cut-price modernist vision' (Reader 1995: 12) resulted in the establishment of quickly deteriorating *cités* (low-income housing complexes) pervaded by unemployment and petty crime. In the late 1980s and early 1990s, the poverty and general feeling of hopelessness spurred a series of riots. In turn, as illustrated by the growing popularity of the extreme Right, the unrest and the exploitation of the 'insecurity' issue as a political weapon contributed to crystallizing the social anxieties of part of the nation around the 'problem' of immigration and of the *banlieues*. Thus, while increasingly large areas of the center were turned into a showcase of urban consumption and tourism, the *périph'* (short for *périphérique*, or ring road) became synonymous with a frontier, the physical and symbolic boundary with what was cast as a surrounding wasteland. From Carax's *Les Amants du Pont-neuf* (*The Lovers on the Bridge*, 1990) to Laurence Ferreira Barbosa's *Les Gens ordinaires n'ont rien d'exceptionnel* (*There's Nothing Special about Normal People*, 1993), to Siegfried's *Louise Take 2* (1999), or to Yolande Zaubermann's *Clubbed to Death* (1999), the *périph'* does not just mark the crossing from center to suburbs: it signals the passage from 'normal' life to social, economic, and mental alienation, from the land of the living to a kind of purgatory.

The significance of the *cinéma de banlieue* was to address these very issues, but from the point of view of the 'other' side, of those who inhabit the *cités*. The location determines some of the central themes of the films: economic and social exclusion, unemployment and drugs, but also multiethnicity and racism. As such, the *cinéma de banlieue* often overlaps with Black cinema and with *beur* cinema (Parisian backslang for *arabe*),

⬆ *La Haine*

that is, the films directed by Black or *beur* directors and/or focusing on Black or *beur* milieux and characters.[5] 1995 was an outstanding year for the *cinéma de banlieue*: 27-year-old Mathieu Kassovitz's *La Haine* (*Hate*) won the prize for Best Director at the Cannes Festival, among heated and highly publicized controversies. The film is shot in black and white, and its opening credits are set on real footage of battles opposing youths from the *cités* to the CRS (the French riot police). The film apparently veered away from established French values not only in its subject matter but also in its very cinematic references. For all the specificity of the film's location, the topic, the characters and fast-paced dialogues, and the style of filmmaking of *La Haine* provoked comparisons with the work of American directors John Cassavetes, Martin Scorsese, and Spike Lee.

The film depicts one day in the life of a *black–blanc–beur* trio of friends: Jewish Vinz, Arabic Saïd, and African-Caribbean Hubert. The dual structure divides the narrative space between sequences spent in the young men's *cité* and scenes shot in the city center. The center of Paris, where the three youths feel acutely out of place, is shot with light equipment, with shallow depth of field and a monophonic sound track. On the contrary, and although the sense of entrapment is evident in the cramped interiors of the housing complex'es apartments, the external space of the *cité* tends to be depicted through airy, ambitious camera movements and stereophonic sound. One of the most remarkable instances of this is a scene of an impromptu concert. The sequence starts with a tracking shot through a courtyard where children and teenagers hang around and play, surrounded by concrete buildings. It then cuts to the inside of an apartment, where a young man is playing music on his mixing table. The music that he blasts out from his high window into the courtyard mingles the sounds of contemporary Paris with that of the Paris of old, fragments of Edith Piaf's *Je ne regrette rien* (*I have no regrets*) overlapping with bursts of 'Fuck the police'. As if carried by the music, the camera then takes off through the open window to a sweeping aerial shot of the housing complex. The sequence could be contrasted with the later scene where the three friends attempt to enter a typical high-class Parisian house. Trapped in the claustrophobic entry hall, unaware of the code that would allow them to enter the building, they crowd the image caught by a surveillance camera that captures their deformed faces through a fish-eye lens effect. Yet the film does not give a rosy picture of life in the housing complex. The narrative alternates between long sequences portraying its idleness and hopeless boredom and the sudden accelerations of scenes where violence threatens to explode. Playing on a feeling of impending catastrophe, the episodic plot builds on an increasing atmosphere of tension and alienation toward an inevitably tragic climax.

Though the critics were more favorable toward Richet's *État des Lieux* and Thomas Gilou's *Raï*, released the same year, *La Haine* aroused the enthusiasm of the public and took its place among the top five films at the French box office. But some of the reasons for the film's appeal also signal the limitations of the vision it presents. Carrie Tarr notes how films like *La Haine* facilitate identification by portraying attractive youths of different ethnic and cultural backgrounds who have 'a universal appeal because they lock into an international, masculine, heterosexual culture of youthful revolt which elides ethnic differences' (1993: 341). Most remarkable is the near-invisibility of women, a feature that *La Haine* shares with many of the early *beur* and *cinéma de banlieue* films. Rachid Bouchareb's *Cheb* (1991) and Malik Chibane's *Hexagone* (1993) and *Douce France* (1995) stood out in that they included fully fledged female characters, and evoked the schizophrenic situation experienced by young women trapped between the social and racial boundaries of the society at large and the close-knit but often oppressive familial rule.

In recent years, more *banlieue* films have been directed by women (Tarr 2000: 153–71), and more films feature female characters in the central roles. Bourlem Guerdjou's *Vivre au Paradis* (1998) and Yamina Benguigui's *Inch'Allah Dimanche* (2001), for instance, depict the situation of the Algerian women who joined their husbands in the early days of North African immigration. Philippe Faucon's *Samia* (2000) focuses on a *beurette* or 'second generation' Arabic girl. *Samia* was praised by the critics as a film that successfully managed to eschew the temptation of didactic exposition to which much of the *banlieue* cinema succumbs. *Samia* does not set out to demonstrate, yet presents a insightful observation of the life of a French teenage girl of Arabic descent. Less inclined to abide by the rules of the schooling system than her elder sisters, Samia nevertheless refuses to see her future limited to domesticity, whether it is of a private (marriage) or a professional kind (a job as a cleaning lady). Rebellious, she is nevertheless bound to her family through ties of love and oppression. Through the camera work and the *mise-en-scène*, the complexities of Samia's daily life emerge without melodramatic effects. Door frames and sections of walls contain the characters filmed in medium close-up and in close-up, within the cramped space of the family apartment. Samia's mother attempts to act as a mediator among a close-knit trio of sisters, a fading father figure, and a tyrannical brother, driven to religious fundamentalism and authoritarianism by the lack of prospects and daily humiliations of life in a Marseilles *cité*. Filled with the young women's liveliness, the film is not pessimistic. Yet its open ending, so characteristic of recent independent cinema, is ambiguous. Samia smiles wistfully as the ferry that takes her and one of her sisters to North Africa pulls away from Marseilles under the watchful gaze of the brother, but is she merely being sent on holiday? Still, as illustrated by the emergence of the road movie element, as in *Bye bye* (Karim Dridi, 1995), *Drôle de Félix* (*The Adventures of Felix*, Olivier Ducastel and Jacques Martineau, 2000), or in *La Repentie* (*The Repentant*, Laetitia Masson, 2002), hope is to be found by fleeing the *cité*, even if the south and the return *au pays* (to the parents' country of origins) prove to be dead ends.

The new realism of the 1990s

Away from Paris and its suburbs, the new realist cinema of the 1990s chose provincial locations often unfamiliar to the cinematic gaze. Popular suburbs of provincial cities, ordinary towns and villages, inhabited by ordinary people, started to appear on the screens with increasing regularity in the 1990s. The fear of unemployment and poverty, the pressures in the working environment combined with family tensions and depicted through elliptical narratives, replaced the tightly suspenseful plots and heroic actions of mainstream cinema. Dominique Cabréra, Bruno Dumont, Robert Guédiguian, Claude Mouriéras, Sandrine Veysset, and Eric Zonca, to name but a few, are part of a large group of directors, at the time still more or less unknown, who chose to focus on the unglamorous and the banal in order to explore often overlooked aspects of contemporary French society. In some ways this cinema evokes the Poetic Realism of the 1930s and the Neorealism of the 1940s. But its main affinities are to be found in the documentary tradition, in the work of distinctive independent French filmmakers (including Robert Bresson, Agnès Varda, Jean-Luc Godard, and Maurice Pialat) and the films of British directors of the realist trend such as Mike Leigh and Ken Loach. The approach generally evokes modernist fiction in its refusal of psychological description and explanations (Blüher 2000); but it is closer to realist traditions in the importance given to the wider context, the particular economic, geographic or social environment which, though it rarely explains it, may determine the characters' behavior. The dialogue respects regional accents and idioms, and the use of the sequence shot, best suited to group compositions (Darke 1998), underpins the importance given to small groups and local communities. The kind of insularity humorously claimed at the beginning of Guédiguian's *Marius et Jeannette* (1999) (Ungar 2000: 40) does not prevent most of the films from endowing characters and stories with a universal dimension often signalled by their titles. At the same time, the new realism eschews any attempt at rigorous genre categorization: elements of the melodrama may be combined with comedy and satire, while a naturalist depiction can be entwined with elements of the fantastic and the lyrical.

All of Robert Guédiguian's feature films were shot in his native Marseilles, with the same pool of actors, seemingly reviving the precedent established by Marcel Pagnol in the 1930s (but in complete contrast with the cinematography of the more recent adaptations of Pagnol's stories, as in Claude Berri's blockbusters *Jean de Florette* and *Manon des sources*, both 1986). Comedy, romance, and melodrama mingle in Guédiguian's didactic tales, and his sympathetic description of small popular neighborhoods earned his cinema the denomination of 'warm realism' (Ungar 2000: 50).

Also situated in the south, Sandrine Veysset's films present a far bleaker vision. *Y'aura-t-il de la neige à Noël?* (*Will it Snow for Christmas?*, 1996), her first feature, is often mentioned as one of the most accomplished examples of the new realist trend. In spite of its small budget and its uncompromising portrayal of rural life, it proved extremely successful among critics and public alike. The film depicts the life of an 'illegitimate' family, a woman and her seven children, who live on a farm owned by the children's father. The south of France as depicted in Veysset's film is the antithesis of the kind of 'visual tourism' proposed in the lush production of the Heritage cinema. In spite of its documentary feel however, *Y'aura-t-il de la neige à Noël?* includes thematic and stylistic elements of the naturalist melodrama and a fairy-tale dimension. Combining actors with non-professionals, the film is set almost solely on a farm and its surrounding fields. The narrative structure follows the rhythm of the seasons and of agricultural activities: work is, as in most of the new realist films, a central feature of the diegetic world. The careful depiction of the social, geographic, and economic environment allows the film to bypass essentialist discourses in its depiction of gender relations (Beugnet 2000). In this,

Y'aura-t'il de la neige à Noël? is typical of the new realist approach at its best, where visual suggestion, resistance to the objectifying gaze, and attention to detail become tactics against stereotyping and reductionism.

Generally shunned by mainstream cinema, the harsh realities of the industrial north have also proved a crucial source of inspiration to Neorealist directors like Xavier Beauvois (*Nord* [*North*], 1992), Edwin Baily (*Faut-il aimer Mathilde?* [*Should Mathilde be loved?*], 1992), Laetitia Masson (*En avoir (ou pas)* [*To Have (or Not)*], 1994), Eric Zonca (*La Vie rêvée des anges* [*The Dream Life of Angels*], 1998), and Thomas Vincent (*Karnaval* (*Carnival*), 1999). Bruno Dumont succeeded in making a mark with *La Vie de Jésus* (*The Life of Jesus*, 1997), and received the coveted Cannes Festival's jury award for *L'Humanité* (1999), amid heated controversy. Through the unrelenting depiction of cruelly mundane settings and ordinary characters, Dumont explores in effect the metaphysical dimensions of human existence. With their focus on destiny and choice, evil, guilt, and redemption, his films have been compared to Robert Bresson's cinema (Prédal 2002: 82). The dialogue is scarce; the close-ups and the length of the shots in static framing are uncomfortable and add to the defamiliarizing effect of the representation. Part of *L'Humanité*'s reflexive quality stems from its reference, diegetic as well as formal, to realist paintings of the late nineteenth century. The film's painterly compositions sometimes reveal the hidden beauty of the land, but more often underline the latent violence and anxiety permeating an environment whose brutal banality and void impregnate the soul. The recurrent violence and crudity of the imagery (the close-up on the mutilated body of a murdered young girl at the beginning of *L'Humanité*, for instance) bring Dumont's cinema close to those more radical trends of contemporary cinema that could be designated as a 'cinema of abjection'.

A cinema of abjection

Part of the cinema of the margins invokes an implicit or avowed tradition of French and American literary counterculture (De Sade, Rimbaud, Bataille, Genet, Artaud, but also Burrows, Bukowski, and the 'punk' and 'trash' tendencies), with cinematic references ranging from German Expressionism, Rainer Werner Fassbinder, Pier Paolo Pasolini, and David Lynch, to porn and gore. Transgression is the main principle, the thematic and aesthetic crossing of the frontier of the acceptable into the sphere of the abject. Some directors concentrate on taboo subjects (violent crimes, rape, incest), and draw on the conventions of genres such as gore and pornography, that have been marginalized by both mainstream and art cinema. Often, the body as flesh is the raw material of the filmmaking; assaulted, mutilated, violated, it becomes a war zone, symbolic of the attack that is supposedly performed by the same token on social, cultural, and cinematic conventions. Abjection, the violent repulsion against and expulsion of bodies felt as alien or threatening, also works as a metaphor for the processes of exclusion through which a social 'body' seeks to 'purify' itself (Beugnet 2001). The cinema of abjection focuses precisely on those 'aberrant' elements: criminals, psychopaths, monstrous beings or those perceived as such, creations of the very system that must eradicate them.

As in Gaspar Noë's controversial works, in Dumont's films the apparent naturalism of the setting and characters is subsumed in a form of enhanced or 'hyper' realism. But although the abject quality of the real is made more visible through the recurrent and sustained extreme close-ups that punctuate *L'Humanité*, these ultimately serve as a reminder of mortality and as an invitation to transcendence. The technique recalls Varda's use of the extreme close-up to describe the human body. In *Les Glaneurs et la glaneuse* in particular, her inquiry into the 'abject' quality of aging is also an invitation to explore and to discover.

On the contrary, in Gaspar Noë's films, the relentless focus on the drab and the abject merely enhances the grotesque and fearsome nature of the reality depicted. Both *Carne* (1992) and *Seul contre tous* (*I Stand Alone*, 1998) center on the life of an unemployed butcher, progressively drawn into an obsessive world of violence, prejudice, and incest. Through various techniques (the voice-over monologue, the intertitles, and the 'gunshot' style of the editing in particular), the film constructs a distorted and seemingly highly subjective vision, but one that ultimately resembles the discourse of the tabloid press. Though the butcher reappears briefly in the prologue, Noë's *Irréversible* (2002), charts, in reverse order, one night in the life of a different set of characters. Like Noë's previous works, *Irréversible* caught media attention, this time for its graphically represented and extended rape scene.

The same recourse to graphic violence is to be found in Kassovitz's *Assassin(s)* (1997), a film designed to de-glamorize the classic character of the professional killer. *Assassin(s)* presents a pessimistic vision of a society dominated by the stupefying effect of television and the corrupting influence of the obsolete father figure.

Both Noë and Kassovitz's films depict masculinity in crisis, but also include reductive, degrading, and occasionally aggressively violent portrayals of women. Yet central female characters have their place in this cinematic trend, though often in the films of female directors. Women feature prominently among the filmmakers who deal with transgression, thus reclaiming certain territories of the cinematic depiction of sex and violence that were traditionally defined as essentially masculine. Virgine Despentes and Caroline Trinh Thi's x-rated *Baise Moi* (*Rape Me*, 2000) is a brutal depiction of two women's revenge though sex and murder that emphasizes precisely those conventionally repressed 'abject' qualities of femininity and the female body. In *Romance X* (1999) and *A ma sœur!* (*To My Sister!*, 2001), Catherine Breillat borrows elements of the pornographic and gore genres respectively to investigate the mechanisms of contemporary gender relations. In these films, the logic of a reality that is steeped in conventions and hypocrisy, in internalized patriarchal values and power games, expresses itself through pornographic practices and sadomasochism, through murder and rape. Systematically unromantic, Breillat's films deconstruct the myths associated with love and sex: emotional, sexual, and physical violence is irremediably confused with love, affection, and desire, and ultimately functions as the norm.

Gore is also a defining feature of Claire Denis's *Trouble Every Day* (2001), a story of sexual cannibalism that includes scenes of murder with graphic visual and sound effects. The haunted characters of *Trouble Every Day* have brought back from Guyana a murderous disease that slowly consumes them and turns them into monsters. As in Claire Devers's *Noir et Blanc* (1986), a *huis clos* that locks a black man and a white man in a sadomasochistic relationship, in Denis's work (*S'en fout la mort* [*No Fear, No Die*], 1990, *J'ai pas sommeil* [*I Can't Sleep*], 1994, *Beau travail* [*Good Work*], 1999), the exploration of transgression is coexistent with an investigation into the lasting effects of colonialism. The unravelling of the contemporary malaise that affects both ex-colonized and ex-colonizers leads to the depiction of perverse, destructive forms of alienation. Usually contained through internalization, and through the repression of memory, their seemingly random, lethal self-expression sets in motion society's own mechanisms of retribution.

Conclusion

France has always boasted a strong counterculture, one that repeatedly challenges a long-standing tradition of centralization and normalization. In fact, the central system tends to nurture and, in turn, seeks to integrate marginal expressions: as one author points out, France provides a rare example of 'state-funded cinema of dissent' (Darke 1999: 26). This constant tension and exchange has so far ensured the renewal and persistence of a diversity rarely equalled in other national cinemas.[6] The developments of the 1990s are also a reminder of the reflexivity that operates between cinema and the wider society, as films simultaneously mirrored and informed the realities that they portrayed, by contributing to the debate on contemporary society, national identities, and representation. The emergence of various trends of cinema of the margins appeared as a salutary disturbance, both to a highly formalist school of French film criticism that had long shunned any debate on ideology and strategies of representation, and to a dominant but devitalized mainstream cinema.

Further Reading

Beugnet, Martine, *Marginalité, sexualité, contrôle dans le cinéma français contemporain* (Paris: l'Harmattan, 2000). Includes a discussion on the representation of marginality in film, and of several of the films mentioned.

Flitterman-Lewis, Sandy, *To Desire Differently: Feminism and the French Cinema* (Urbana: University of Illinois Press, 1990). Together with Smith's book, Flitterman-Lewis's book and articles are indispensable to a study of Varda's films up to the 1990s.

Hayward, Susan, and Ginette Vincendeau (eds.), *French Film: Texts and Contexts* (London: Routledge, 2000). Contains an article on *La Haine* as well as on *Sans toit ni loi*.

Marie, Michel (ed.), *Jeune cinéma français* (Paris: Nathan, 1998). A good introduction to up-and-coming French directors.

Mazdon, Lucy (ed.), *France on Film* (London: Wallflower Press, 2001). Contains useful studies on the films of Klapish and Veysset.

Smith, Alison, *Agnès Varda* (Manchester: Manchester University Press, 1998). An illuminating analysis of Varda's work.

Notes

1. Film Theorist André Bazin famously advocated the primacy of the 'pro-filmic', i.e., of a reality that should not be tampered with—that film should capture rather than reconstruct.
2. The expression chosen by Michel Marie (1998), for his book on new directors, was translated by Chris Darke (1999).
3. Carrie Tarr (1993: 321) remarks that in order to obtain the *avance sur recettes*, 'A proposal must either show evidence of commercial appeal (a sound script, the use of stars, entertainment value) or potential to be a self-expressive *auteur* film.'
4. See, for example, the films of Arnaud Desplechin, Olivier Assayas, Pascal Bonitzer, and Pascale Ferran.
5. The Arabic population, France's largest ethnic minority, is the majority in many of the suburban housing complexes.
6. Though recent reorganizations of the funding system, and the sale of Canal Plus, one of the main commissioning television channels, are likely to deal a blow to the production of non-mainstream films.

NEW DIRECTIONS IN EUROPEAN CINEMA

John Orr

The turn of the century has brought a new reckoning for European film. It is still diverse and inventive but deeply under threat from the external power of Hollywood and the internal power of television. Outside France and the UK, few national cinemas can begin to challenge the dominion of either. Yet within many European countries there are, annually, films in distribution that provoke and stimulate and deserve far wider audiences than they get. Here television is both friend and foe. As medium, it encourages different habits and expectations from cinema. But television channels like the French Canal Plus and British Channel Four have also been vital lifelines, casting a wide net for new talent, co-funding projects in development or from origin, and easing the connections between cinema screen and other media through which films are viewed: TV transmission, VCR, and DVD. Seen as promotion packages, big-budget productions, and star vehicles, most European films cannot hope to compete against the Hollywood studio product. However, as artworks and as forms of entertainment, they can.

Yet Canal Plus and Channel Four also operate in fragile circumstances. At the time of writing Vivendi, the parent company of Canal Plus, is under deep pressure through its expansion into the American market. FilmFour, the pay-TV channel and production/distribution arm of Channel Four set up in 1998, faces crisis because of poor performance. Moreover, the collapse of Kirsch, the German media group, will have a big knock-on effect for European film funding. The problem is one of audiences as well as money and distribution. Transatlantic competition also comes from the pulling power of the American independents. With the emergence of the Sundance Institute in Utah and its annual Festival, there is a forum for autonomous, low-budget films whose audacity has captivated European audiences. Festivals at Cannes, Berlin, Venice, and Edinburgh are a focus of European response, but their influence on the younger generation of filmgoers is limited. In the UK, for example, the last decade has simply not seen the emergence of a new generation of cineastes despite the spread of collateral funding and low-budget technology. Rather, it has seen the consolidation of a previous generation where directors like Ken Loach, Neil Jordan, Terence Davies, Peter Greenaway, Stephen Frears, Mike Figgis, and Mike Leigh have made the most of their opportunities. For young filmmakers the second feature can often be a make-or-break occasion, when talented first features give way to uncertainty the second time around after poor box office or adverse reviews. In the UK, at least, there is a dearth of young talent that, thankfully, has key exceptions: the tenacity of Michael Winterbottom, the boldness of Shane Meadows—yet to make a commercial breakthrough—and the flair of Lynne Ramsay and Christopher Nolan, who both have.

In spite of financial gloom, we can still feel buoyant about the diversity of European film and excited for its future. The range of themes remains wide, approach to form is adventurous, and there is a desire to explore a wider spectrum of social worlds. The challenge for the critic is evident. The creative surge of filmmaking is centrifugal: the critical response must be centripetal. What out of this vast, dispersed creativity can we unify through film aesthetics? The answer is a lot. Structures can be found, categories forged, and continuities asserted. We can start first with the wider context of change. Like North America and East Asia, the European Union and its close neighbors are current beneficiaries of that mixed blessing, the information age where cultural densities of speed, movement, innovation, and contact have multiplied exponentially in the last twenty years. Capital may not quite be global but it is ubiquitous and this is a manifestation of its triumph. The information age is, as Paul Virilio has claimed, a hypermodern age where modernity, in all its forms, has reached unprecedented levels of intensity (Virilio 1996: 23–45). Against the fake rhetorical claims of cool, comfort, know-how, info-superhighway, and multi-cultural bliss that make up the hype of the hypermodern, the new cinema has a more subversive vision, a brittle world of disconnected beings adrift in a sea of transient encounters (Orr 2000: 13–19). The ideology of connection so vital to the new worlds of media is re-formed here as *disconnection*, a human condition that becomes the prime imaginary of hypermodern film. In many of the great European films of the last decade, the *Three Colors Trilogy*, *Naked, Satantango*, *Live Flesh*, *Nil by Mouth*, *Le Vent de la nuit*, and *Code Inconnu*, disconnection becomes the abiding theme.

The innovating features of hypermodern film that revolve around the key motif of human disconnection often take the modernist surge of the 1960s, and especially the French New Wave, as prime inspiration. Yet we can also see a rather different profile. For much of contemporary film the Bazinian legacy of the 1940s has become primary and the modernist idiom secondary. In Western Europe, certainly, the major tendencies of our day are diverse *re-formations* of realism in which different modernist tropes are stylistically integrated. Any European chronology such as Fredric Jameson's, intimating a straight transfer of modernist to postmodern film from the 1970s onward, either through history evoked as nostalgia and pastiche (*The Conformist*) (Jameson 1991: 180–91) or by trans- forming the consumerist spectacle of the image into a postmodern beauty aesthetic (*Diva, Three Colors: Blue*) (Jameson 1997: 93–106), seems hopelessly wide of the mark. For what we have is chronological inversion. Bazin's 1940s aesthetic loops the modernist moment of the 1960s to drive the re-formations of the real: sometimes in ways Bazin would have admired, sometimes in ways he would have thought impossible. This gradual switch from neomodern to hypermodern film is an acceleration of image density matched by a retrojection of form (Orr 2001: 239–48): that is, self-conscious recovery of the social (in the Bazinian sense) as a dominant force field of narrative. Yet this retrojection makes no sense without the intervening tropes of European modernism familiar to us in Bergman, Fellini, Antonioni, and the French New Wave. Bearing this in mind, we can now set out a loose transformational taxonomy for the turn of century, using four basic categories: neo-Bazinian realism; traductive realisms; hyperrealisms; the hypermodern avant-garde. For sure there is overlap, a constant merger and blurring of boundaries. Yet all four forms are vital and equal components of the new direction in European film. Let us take them one by one.

Neo-Bazinian realism

A more awkward term for this tendency might be 'neo-Neorealism', but Italian Neorealism would be too narrow a base for what is happening here. André Bazin's aes- thetics have been stretched wider in the last decade and met in a number of exciting ways (Bazin 1967; 1971; Andrew 1976: 134–79). Bazin had seen cinema as a window opening onto the world, a form of social exploration both in its documentary and fictional forms. It would reveal to us, he had imagined, more of the everyday world in which human beings lived at all levels of society, many of them previously excluded by the commercial dictates of cinema as a culture industry. Many of the practical means he saw as facilitating this new kind of cinema still thrive, more so now than ever. There is still low- to medium-budget cinema, location-based, often using non-professionals, but focusing now on social malaise—exclusion, violence, and poverty—in a more consumerist age, an age of plenty generally displacing an age of want, and where the excluded still miss out. The neo-Bazinian aesthetic usually stresses ensemble acting (with improvisation and comic diversion) and obviates star quality. It forges, by and large, an invisible, not a reflexive or self-conscious, narrative. The major cineastes working in this field tend be veterans rather than newcomers. Among the names that spring immediately to mind are Ken Loach, Mike Leigh, Robert Guédiguian, Bertrand Tavernier, Gianni Amelio, and Gilles McKinnon, while the most powerful of the newcomers are Eric Zonca, Sandrine Veysset, Lynne Ramsay, and Lukas Moodyson. In addition we can mention those popular, self-conscious tributes to Neorealism set nostalgically during its brief reign, *Nuovo Cinema Paradiso* (Giuseppe Tornatore, 1988) and *Il postino* (*The Postman*, Michael Radford, 1994). In narrative, most neo-Bazinians readily mix the comic and the serious, sorrow and laughter, and their social subjects are usually those with few resources, flawed, fragile, often besieged but always defiant. All the best directors have a distinct flair for shooting on location with minimal budgets and for injecting a sense of milieu, above all a tangible sense of place, into their narrative concerns.

We could add to this the 1990s films of veteran Eric Rohmer, for though his subjects are largely bourgeois, Rohmer has pursued his fertile yet subtle aesthetic of the *conte* (tale) as an open fable, prompting the spectator to autonomous judgment. This, it should be noted, is Bazinian and not Brechtian, and has persisted in European film from the late 1950s, when Rohmer was a *Cahiers du cinéma* critic and Bazin his editor, to the start of the twenty-first century—a long pedigree. For Rohmer, to make a social or psychological judgement is also to make a moral one, and one suspects the same is true of the narrative approach of Ken Loach. Where Rohmer's great subtlety, like that of Kieślowski, is to make morality deeply embedded in situation, speech, and gesture, most neo-Bazinians opt to extrapolate it and make it more up-front, more explicit. They opt, that is, to give it a humanist transparency. Here the neo-Bazinian form invites a kind of open ascendancy from one plane to the other, from the ambiguous to the articulated. Over the last ten years Loach has become the maestro of the articulated judgement.

Ken Loach

In Loach's London film *Riff-Raff* (1991), about casual building workers with few rights, the spectator is challenged to make a judgement about Robert Carlyle's repudiation of his Irish lover (Emer McCourt), when he finds her injecting heroin in their makeshift squat.

Should he forgive her even though he has just returned from a funeral in Glasgow, where his brother died from addiction? Are we to assume that his attitude is right? At the end of the film when the building workers, deprived of basic rights and working conditions, decide to burn down the Victorian hospital they have converted into luxury apartments, again we have to ask if their attitude is justified. It can be argued that Loach stacks the cards heavily in favor of the action that takes place, but the onus is still on the spectator and the dramatization of issues central to the plot. In Loach's Manchester film *Raining Stones* (1993), when workless Bruce Jones gets involved in dodgy scams to pay for his daughter's first Communion dress and tries a risky revenge on a loan shark threatening his family, how do we judge his actions? Is he putting himself and his family in unnecessary danger, or is he right?

In part we judge based on our own sense of the authentic, on the exactness of nuance, on the realities of milieu, dialogue, and motivation and this, for Loach, provides an organic connection to judgement. To this end his camera follows actors through well-observed settings, unselfconscious and without indulgence. Loach has spoken of his fondness for the medium-long shot that allows frequent panning, allowing spectators the distance to make critical judgements and actors the space to explore freer expression (Fuller 1998: 40–42). His avoidance of long tracking shots equally minimizes our awareness of the camera. Yet his camera is also there with his subjects, among them, as in his Spanish Civil War feature *Land and Freedom* (1995), where his ensemble of comrade volunteers (Trotskyite *Poumistas*) in action is crucial in setting the tone and style of narrative. Even in this war situation Loach's focus is not so much the dramas of action as their consequence, on the effervescence of their daily life at the moving front, on camaraderie rather than violence. And even on a big foreign shoot like this with European co-funding, his £3 million budget remained modest, a feature he has in common with Rohmer and many other neo-Bazinians. The profitability of their films, ironically, derives from the moral economy of their cinematic attitude, a refusal of excess, and the knack, now quite crucial, of attracting audiences in European countries other than one's own. In Loach's case, indeed, his European audiences have been much larger than his British ones (Christie 2000: 70–72).

Loach's success has sparked a revival in the neo-Bazinian narrative of the British city with Coky Giedroc's dark fable of prostitution in London and Glasgow, *Stella Does Tricks* (1996), Mike Leigh's prize-winning *Secrets and Lies* (1995), and two dark comic parables of industrial redundancy, *Brassed Off* (Mark Herman, 1996) and Peter Cattaneo's box-office hit *The Full Monty* (1997). In a way *Raining Stones* set the scene for all of them, since it is an astute fable about the survival of disaster. Its taut narrative echoes that of De Sica's classic *Bicycle Thieves*, with Bruce Jones's stolen van (that nearly precipitates disaster) working as narrative equivalent of Ricci's stolen bicycle half a century earlier.

The device may be old hat, but here in a more affluent world, as Loach demonstrates, expectation outweighs resource. Yet we are still aware, as cinema evolves, that we are now watching things differently. We are closer on the ground in all these films. There is a nervy and fragmented feel, a plunging into situation that takes its cue, quite probably, from the 1980s work of Alan Clark, who in television films like *The Firm* had minimized obvious storytelling, encouraged ensemble acting in public spaces, and used Steadicam (which Loach seldom does) to generate kinetic energy for a hypermodern age. Clark's Steadicam could be intrusive and pitiless, a sign of his refusal to over-humanize his subjects. Loach's humanism, by contrast, makes him draw back and never lose sight of his Bazinian roots. Here he is prompted into finding a primal goodness beneath the frailties of human nature.

This humanism ironically shows Loach's indifference to nature. In *Land and Freedom*, Catalan landscape is little more than functional backdrop with no visual identity. The comrades at the front may vote on collectivizing land, but Dovchenko this is not. A strong contrast to Loach is found in Gianni Amelio's neglected masterpiece *Lamerica* (1994) where Enrico Lo Verso, a flash entrepreneur in designer clothes, is stranded in the arid countryside of post-Communist Albania when one of his suspect ventures goes wrong. In trying to escape he is then forced to join a long trail of Albanian migrants crossing the Adriatic to Italy. Amelio's ironic contrast of affluent Italian and poor Albanians ending up, quite literally, in the same boat is part of his Neorealist heritage. But his fluent spatial framing of the landscape as hostile and beautiful, but formidably other, shows the modernist legacy of Antonioni at his best. This blending of the mimetic and the neo-modern where nature and culture are equally balanced is vital to the esthetic power of a film that must rank with Guédiguian's Marseilles-based *La Ville est tranquille* (*The Town is Quiet*, 2001) as a landmark Bazinian movie in the new idiom.

Other forms of period fusion are apparent. The 1970s ensemble aesthetic of Robert Altman and Woody Allen, with their fondness for narrative digression, are taken back into the realist esthetics of Loach, Leigh, Winterbottom, and Lukas Moodyson, whose warm retro-tribute to a 1970s Swedish commune, *Together* (2001), is a low-budget gem of ensemble acting. Meanwhile the Scottish memory film has its own modernist predecessors. Set in late 1960s Glasgow, Mackinnon's *Small Faces* (1995) echoes the sensuous and lyrical energy of 1960s cinéastes like Truffaut and Bertolucci while Ramsay's *Ratcatcher* (1999), set in Glasgow of the late 1970s, is indebted to the austere minimalism of 1970s directors Bill Douglas and Terrence Malick, whose disparate influences it blends (Petrie 2000: 191–217). Yet all of these films, we could argue, go back even further, to the Bazinian source of the European collective, Jean Renoir, and Renoir it is whose remarkable vision has given to the re-formation of the realist aesthetic its sure touch and its longevity.

Traductive realisms

This is a new film form where a crucial departure from the aesthetics of Bazin kicks in, though his legacy is never overturned. Bazin's paradigm of representation remains, but the ontology of realism changes dramatically. One of the startling reinventions of realism here has been a double subversion of style and of theme on the plane of the social. Of stylistic changes, there is immediate evidence. Many of the classic forms of Bazinian *mise-en-scène* are set aside: depth of focus, multi-planar composition, the long take, the medium-long shot, and eye-level (or shoulder-height) camera set-up. Others remain crucial—location shooting, the primacy of the social (or the political), the world of the excluded, demotic idiom, tangible sense of place—yet these are treated through a new *unbalancing* of perspective. This mimetic re-forming does not abandon the ontological image, nor is it a follow-up to its radical deconstruction in the earlier modernisms of Buñuel or Resnais. It is, rather, a *deformation* of the ontological image, an anti-style aesthetic that is even further removed from the formalism of the 1960s than it is from the Neorealism of the 1940s. This deformation comes from reworking the role of the camera as a hyperactive presence that may be not reflexive in the Godardian sense but is still disruptive of normal perception. It is a third way, if you like, between Bazinian perspective and self-conscious, avant-garde cinema. Here *mise-en-scène*, not montage, is usually the prime site of deformation. Here traducing means a simultaneous transforming and transgressing. The traductive image is a challenge to the social code at the same time as it is a transgression of classic style.

This emergent form of traducing or *traductive* realism is thus a double violation, a transgressive fusion of style and image. It can be restated as follows. On the one hand a partial break with classic representation that is still socially mimetic; on the other a fuller break from a Bazinian humanism locked into ideals of progress at ground level, and where the humble are exalted by the power of the image. Since 1990 de-formation of the image has often been a *re-formation* predicated on precise excess in the use of the shot: the intense use of close-up, often decentered (Kieślowski, Leigh's *Naked*, Philippe Garrel, Claire Denis, Jacques Audiard, Pawel Pawlikowski); the empowering but disruptive tracking shot (Agnès Varda, Alan Clarke, Jacques Doillon's *Jeune Werther* [*Young Werther*, 1993]); the hyperactive rush of hand-held camera (Kieślowski, the Dardenne brothers in *La Promesse* [1996] and *Rosetta* [1999]); the extreme long take of the static figure (Bruno Dumont's *La vie de Jésus* [1997]) or the use of the sequence shot to mystify, not illuminate (Michael Haneke's *Code inconnu* [*Code Unknown*, 2000]); the telephoto *mise-en-scène* (Gary Oldman's *Nil by Mouth* [1997]) and tight tunnel-vision framing (Audiard's *Sur mes lèvres* [*Read My Lips*, 2001]) or the extreme telephoto shot (the hospital scene at the start of

Kieślowski's *Blue* (1993)). Neo-Bazinian film offers us a balanced look: traductive realism an *unbalanced* look. Seen through the prism of the unbalanced look, deformed narrative then becomes the image-sign of deformed being, the defaming and deforming of fictional character. Here narrative movement may well involve the disruption and lyrical digression that Gilles Deleuze saw as seminal to modern cinema. Yet there is something extra and crucial, a narrative of falling, of ignoble descent. If traducing is a crossing of the moral line as well as a disruption of form, a going across, it is also an implacable going down.

We can evoke this anti-style aesthetic of 'going down' by cueing Julia Kristeva's startling essay of 1980 on the nature of abjection, *Powers of Horror.* Here abjection is an intermediate state between subject and object, the 'in-between, the ambiguous, the composite' (Kristeva 1982: 4). It is not the alienation of self into object but the suspension of identity in a world devoid of meaning where abjection is a safeguard, a choice for the liminal in the instance of the void. It is the choice to be stranded as protection against the void. The downward flight is a conscious exposure by the abject being to the very dangers from which it seeks to protect itself, and ultimately from death. For Kristeva, 'the corpse, seen without God and outside of science' is 'the utmost of abjection' (Kristeva 1982: 4), the true sign of death infecting life. So it is that Agnès Varda's *Sans toit ni loi* (*Vagabond*, 1985), five years on from Kristeva's book, should in its opening sequence zoom in on Sandrine Bonnaire's frozen corpse and usher in the cinema of the abject that is so pivotal to our world of film. Bonnaire's journey as a homeless drifter, which we see in flashback, is a study in abjection, a conscious self-defilement that ends in death but also a risky trajectory that instantiates something against nothing, substance against the void.

In the 1990s many great films—*Blue, Nil by Mouth, Live Flesh, La Naissance de l'amour* (*The Birth of Love*), and *Naked*—take the abject journey out of the open countryside and into the labyrinth of the city. All seem to echo Varda and the earlier work of Maurice Pialat and John Cassavetes by reinstating the body as cinematic presence. Yet beyond the naturalism of Pialat and the jagged psychodrama of Cassavetes lies an anti-determinism in which the resolution to be abject is a perverse but contingent act. This, in effect, is a new form of existential cinema to displace that of the French New Wave: its proximate philosopher no longer Sartre but now Kristeva. At its most powerful in British film, and in clear contrast to Loach, it lies in the abject odyssey of the displaced males in *Naked* (Mike Leigh, 1993) and *Nil by Mouth* (Gary Oldman, 1997) (Orr 2002: 104–14). In Leigh's film, Johnny (David Thewlis) is a fugitive adrift in London, a millennial sociopath prophesying doom and daring his own nemesis. In Oldman's film, his South London family villains (Ray Winstone and Charlie Creed-Miles) are caught despite their bravado in a deep male identity trap, which, aided by a cocktail of drink and drugs, gradually draws them down, on parallel tracks, into the void. Their embrace of the horror of defilement as an imaginary shield to ward off nothingness is a strategy of risk that can go either way, ending in redemption or disaster, but usually in disaster.

A prime exemplar in low-budget film is Carine Adler's debut feature, *Under the Skin* (1997), profiling Iris, a young woman played by Samantha Morton who has much in common with the male desperadoes of *Nil by Mouth* and *Naked*. Traumatized by her mother's death through cancer and wearing her cast-off wig and fur coat as mementos, Morton's journey of flight through city locales and streets, in this case Liverpool, is Adler's spatial rendition of breakdown—or rather break-up, the break-up of body and soul. Brief and brutal encounters, casual sex, and the search for religious epiphany are interwoven patterns of Morton's desperation, shot expressionistically as a subjective world displacing the naturalized world of work and home she has forsaken. Morton's adriftness captured through a following camera reminiscent of Kieślowski's *Blue* has an iconic quality, a mesmerizing star quality that Lynne Ramsey uses to even greater effect in her recent feature film, *Morven Callar* (2002). Here Morton's Morven, a laconic anti-heroine from a Highland fishing port, plots after her boyfriend's suicide an abject, wayward trip (literal and psychedelic) through a disenchanting world. Adriftness and abjectness are the states of being that Ramsay converts through her imaging of Morton into tactile and visual textures of experience that unbalance perspective in order to get beneath the skin of the real.

Another debut film (with no budget, but shot at weekends with a little help from Working Title) charts its own version of the abject journey. Christopher Nolan's *Following* (1999), predecessor to his cult thriller *Memento,* films in black-and-white 16mm the odyssey of a voyeuristic writer (Jeremy Theobald) who stalks faces around London streets only to hit, by chance it seems, on a well-heeled burglar. He then learns the joy of violation that comes with the trade of breaking and entering. Hand-held following shots, source sound, and bleak locations give the film a seedy *cinéma-vérité* feel that matches the writer's willing descent into violation, the buzz of robbing the unknown Other. As in *Memento,* Nolan manipulates time through montage to create surprise and suspense. Yet abject flight is at the centre of noirish flashback and flash-forward. Stark rearrangement of sequence enhances it, firming up the link between abject falling and the American idiom of the *noir* fall-guy: that is, falling as acting out of chance encounters matched against the falling that is falling for a pre-arranged set-up, falling into a trap.

Hyperrealisms

The hyperrealist form that has emerged in recent European film is a creationist impulse that still retains its central contact with a contemporary world. We can refer to its aesthetic as the burning intensity of the copy where an imprint of the real becomes a starting point for its stylization and refinement, at times to the point of nonexistence. The modernist origins of this impulse lie in the work of Fellini and his great composite *œuvre,* from *La dolce vita* onwards, that re-formed the spectacularity of modern life through the film image. Increasingly Fellini would reconstruct Rome in *Roma* or Rimini in *Amarcord* in meticulous detail on the spacious backlots of Cinecittà. The social referent would be reformed, the historical referent re-imagined or, as in the topography of *Rome,* a whole section of the city's ring road, ending in the unlikely cul-de-sac of a cardboard Colosseum, remade on a back lot. Here cinematic world displaces social world yet retains its imprint for expressive ends. Instead of diluting the original, the copy enhances, irradiates, and intensifies. It starts out by absorbing the spectacular into the real and ends by absorbing the real into the spectacular.

A prime exemplar for the 1990s is Léos Carax's *Les Amants du Pont-neuf (The Lovers on the Bridge,* 1991), where a section of the famous Parisian bridge was rebuilt on a studio lot in Montpellier. Yet the hyperreal is gleaned not only from the ultra-stylization of the exterior as look, whether in studio or *in situ,* but also upon the spectacularity of *mise-en-scène.* We can think here of those epiphanic spectacles that define the nature of hyperreal film itself. Here are five that spring immediately to mind: the cascading firework display over the Seine in Carax's film; the chasing of the lost suppository at the start of Danny Boyle's *Trainspotting* (1995); the church roof lifted off by a storm during rites of mourning in Peter Mullan's *Orphans* (1998); Francie's vision of Sinead O'Connor as the blessed Virgin in Neil Jordan's *The Butcher Boy* (1997); the huge boulder that tumbles into Ray Winstone's Spanish swimming pool in Jonathan Glazer's *Sexy Beast* (2000). All are instances of the fantastic at the heart of the natural and all are unexpected, a source of breathless delight. The burden of the banal and expected is lifted by fantasy without transcendence, a style technique we also see in the Spanish films of Julio Medem and Bigas Luna. Sequence can then revert to normality, ever stylized, the natural as breathing space before the next epiphany that repeats the irruption, an eternal return of spectacle at the heart of the mundane.

Here, though, abjection is often transformed into pure style statement: the designer eyepatch that Carax gave Binoche, or the sexy anorexia of Ewan MacGregor as screen icon of heroin chic. The subjection of the abject to the spectacular can be highly suspect. But why is the irruption of the spectacular not, as some critics argue, an instance of the surreal? It is not surreal because the style epiphany is an aesthetic of surface and not of depth. Forget Freud, leave out Lacan: what counts here is the transparency of un-hidden meaning. As pure statement, the un-hidden can be, like much of Carax, portentous. As humor in *Trainspotting, Jamón jamón (A Tale of Ham and Passion), Orphans,* or *Sexy Beast,* it can be darkly funny. And if you cannot read the bisexuality in *Sexy Beast* without having to read Freud on narcissism first, then you cannot read anything. The return of the repressed is ever upfront: at its best, the new European *cinéma du look* is a comic-book glitter-conscious unconscious sending itself up, and never far from the cartoon and the commercial that now drive the visuals of popular culture.

The hyperreal thus throws into relief the wider cultural links of cinema. Here we might contrast *Last Resort* by Pawel Pawlikowski, an Anglo-Polish TV documentary maker, with *Sexy Beast* by Jonathan Glazer, an award-winning director of film commercials. The two best British features of the year 2000, the first concerns a Russian woman and her young son applying for UK asylum and being quarantined in a seedy resort town on the south coast. The second concerns English expatriates on Spain's Costa del Sol, criminals retiring from London to a life in the sun. *Last Resort* is traductive realism, since its shows Pawlikowski's desire to capture the dream-like claustrophobia of the asylum experience. But his alternation of close hand-held shots (with extreme close-up) and wide shots of the desolate town is matched by his documentary sense of time and place (Margate in winter), his integration of chance encounter into semi-scripted filming, and his use of non-professionals in minor parts.

Just as *Last Resort* reveals a documentary sense transformed, *Sexy Beast* reveals an advertising ethos transposed. Pawlikowski traduces the documentary: Glazer stretches the power of the TV ad's thirty-second look into narrative hyperreal. His was a script worked over endlessly to produce the power of the minimal phrase and the absorption of Pinteresque effects. Not only do Glazer's gangsters, Ray Winstone and Ben Kingsley, not act naturalistically: they don't talk naturalistically either, and the Spanish villa in which they meet never seems a 'natural' place. The film pays fantasy homage to the ace bank job that is part of gangster folklore; it pastiches with sly cunning the lifestyle of expatriate villains and hones the idioms of gangster tough talk, which it formalizes to frightening but comic effect. Meanwhile it also undermines the psychopathic tendencies of Ben Kingsley's Don Logan by outing his homophobic angst. And Ray Winstone as 'Gal', a sexually ambivalent shortening of Gary, is anything but the 'sexy beast' of the title. His bloated sun-tanned body floating in his swimming pool is pure travesty, an anti-object of desire. Set in southern Spain as Cockney hyperreal, this is more than apt homage to the world of Buñuel. Yet, in film terms, it has moved on. It creates its own world out of an actual one, and in the end virtual *mise-en-scène* triumphs over actual location. The swimming-pool diamond heist back in London is a set-piece spectacular and the triumph of a virtual world. If it looks like a dystopian movie ad; then, given Glazer's background, this is hardly a surprise. But it works.

The Scottish take on the hyperreal is best known in *Trainspotting* but is at its most visionary in Mullan's *Orphans*, where the parallel worlds of grieving siblings are portrayed

⬆ *Trainspotting*

as intervals of comic nightmare on the night-time streets of hyperreal Glasgow. Here the departure from Loach can be witnessed on the screen itself. In *Riff-Raff* Mullan had acted briefly as Robert Carlyle's brother in the Glasgow funeral scene where cremation turns to farce. The Loach episode, richly comic, remains Bazinian. Eight years on Mullan's film, by contrast, turns Glaswegian rites of mourning into one long night of hyperreal disaster. In its visionary aesthetic it has only been matched in recent years by Jordan's *The Butcher Boy,* which uses digital mattes to manipulate the eruption of fantasy into the daily world of impressionable Francie (Eamonn Owens), the damaged boy complicit in the tragicomic destruction of his childhood. Jordan's small country town in rural Ireland becomes as hyperreal in setting as Mullan's Glasgow streets. This is Francie's world but also an actual world, a given moment (the end of the 1950s) in history. Both are material worlds, location worlds shot where they are meant to be set, and fanciful worlds at the same time: both directors blend seamlessly together the polar opposites of their vision. There is no relationship here between surface and depth but instead the flattening out of all things, the everyday and the oneiric, the natural and the fantastic, onto a single plane. This is the cinematic imprint of the hyperreal for the start of the new century.

The hypermodern avant-garde

In European film, we usually associate avant-gardes with wider artistic tendencies. The early films of Luis Buñuel and Jean Cocteau were closely connected to the rise of Surrealism in Paris, the early films of Fritz Lang and Robert Wiene to the triumph of German Expressionism. In the early 1960s the avant-garde work of Chris Marker, such as his famous formal experiment in *La Jetée* (*The Jetty*, 1962), parallels the modernist revival of the French New Wave and the time experiments of Alain Resnais. In the 1980s the renaissance of UK low-budget filmmaking, with television support from Channel Four and encouragement from the British Film Institute, allowed the experimental work on Super 8 and pre-digital video of the maverick gay director Derek Jarman to flourish. This tradition of experiment has continued in documentary, where recently the great European directors have often worked outside their own countries and indeed their own continents. In 1986 Marker made *Sans soleil* (*Sunless*), his intimate essayistic narrative on the city of Tokyo, and at the turn of century he made his great cine-biography of Russian director Andrei Tarkovsky. Chantal Ackerman's latest and possibly greatest documentary, *From the Other Side* (2002), is set on the Mexican–American border, while Werner Herzog went to Kuwait for his brooding, apocalyptic vision of Gulf War aftermath, *Lessons in Darkness* (1992).

This creates a paradox for us. In twentieth-century European culture avant-gardes have formed themselves around a revolutionary politics with which they have often had an embittered relationship. Yet in a post-Communist Europe this function has practically disappeared. After Marker and Jarman, both radical figures of the Left, something of a hiatus has developed in the last decade, particularly since Jarman's tragic death. So while we have discerned recent *tendencies* in narrative exploration, we have identified few *movements* or *collectives* in filmmaking itself. If we are looking for a tangible movement, then we are, in a way, compelled to speak of Dogme 95.

Dogme 95

With its ten 'rules' of filmmaking, the Danish movement founded in 1995 by Lars von Trier and Thomas Vinterberg—and confirmed by Kristian Sevring and Soren Kragh-Jacobsen to make up Dogme's original Gang of Four—is many things. It is a polemic, a cabal, a manifesto, a tongue-in-cheek form of publicity, a practical guide to filmmaking, and a pastiche of the Ten Commandments (Kelly 2000: 1–16). Dogme is rightly seen as at the cutting edge of innovation, of low-budget technologies, and on-the-hoof filmmaking.

They have consciously set the movement up as a global exemplar, the way forward for low-budget filmmaking throughout the world. As we shall see, Dogme 95 is not a modernist but a hypermodern avant-garde. There are now Dogme films made in the US, Argentina, Belgium, Sweden, Estonia, and South Korea. At the Edinburgh Film Festival in August 2002, the twentieth Dogme picture, *Strass*, shot on location in Brussels, received its UK premiere. In addition, Dogme enthusiasts like Mike Figgis have been inspired to make their own experimental films. Thus *Timecode* (2000) and *The End of Innocence* (1999), while clearly not Dogme films, are unthinkable without it.

Von Trier is the movement's key *auteur*, its latter-day Godard, and comparisons with the French New Wave are inevitable. Yet here Dogme, in order to avoid the accusation of plagiarism, has made a pre-emptive strike. The manifesto's tenth commandment denies a credit to the director, and the manifesto also denounces the Nouvelle Vague's 'bourgeois' cult of auteurism. Yet anyone who knows Dogme can name names. We think of von Trier and Vinterberg as its prime movers, and as the *auteurs* of *The Idiots* (1998) and *Festen* (*The Celebration*, 1998). Leaving names off the credits, in their case at least, has fooled no one. And von Trier has probably made the only Dogme film he is ever likely to make. The eclectic shape of his career, from Middle-European pastiche *Europa* (1991) through surreal hospital soap *The Kingdom* (1994) to the hand-held melodrama of *Breaking the Waves* (1996), the true precursor to Dogme 95, defies any conformity to rules. His musical, *Dancer in the Dark* (2000), a hideous milestone in digital kitsch, further makes the point. If it can't regulate the flamboyance of its inventor, let alone anyone else, Dogme remains perversely paradoxical.

This is the nub of its dilemma. On the one hand, it is a model of inspiration for low-budget filmmaking but little more. On the other, its rules *are* dogmatic. The demand for Academy 35mm seems, for example, a little odd in the age of digital video. Its refusal of violence seems strange in civil societies that have become increasingly violent. And Dogme films themselves break the rules. Both *Festen* and Harmony Korine's (American) *Julien Donkey-Boy* (2000) were shot on digital, while Jacobsen's *Mifune* (1998) was shot on 16mm. Korin violates the anti-violence edict at the very start of his film, when there is a brutal killing. The anti-genre edict is flouted by *Mifune*, a revisionist and very funny romantic comedy, but also by *The King is Alive* (2000), a revisionist and histrionic disaster movie. And so the list goes on. In one self-consciously ironic way, the rules are there to be broken. On the other hand, the seal of approval given by the Gang of Four to 'bona fide' Dogme films is a way of maintaining their hold on filmic innovation and maintaining, in the process, their own profile in the film world.

Paradox proceeds apace. Stylistically, Dogme is a breath of fresh air, but is still one-dimensional in its idea of style. Its irreverence for bourgeois norms is also a breath of fresh air: yet in Danish Dogme most characters are bourgeois in background, even when rebellious in spirit. No city low-life here, for this is a cinema of the new bourgeoisie: play-fully lampooning all the rules that have hamstrung its predecessors, but in a laxer world where they fail to constrain. Its stress on the here-and-now makes it truly contemporary, but also limits its sense of elsewhere and, despite *Festen,* its sense of the past. It is hypermodern because it is hyperactive, its breathless hand-held style of close-in filming, of instant witnessing, a reinvention of *cinéma vérité* for the age of the miniature camera and a ludic culture of play. It replicates the visual and spatial densities of the culture from which it has sprung, subordinates the look and the editing of the film to the feel of that culture's living tissue, and deforms perspective by eliding distance. It is therefore a kind of traducing realism, but one where its *promesse de bonheur* comes through an ideological abolition of form held in place by its own set of rules! Hence its self-conscious and reflexive mission also takes it precariously into the arena of the avant-garde. Dogme characters play at abjection, cushioned by the option of drawing back at the last moment.

At the same time Danish Dogme has a conservative tinge, a fixed set of themes, a base-line of obsession that is firmly Scandinavian. It replicates the *Kammerspiel* (chamber drama) motif in the dramas of Ibsen and Strindberg and in the tightly framed films of Bergman and Carl Theodor Dreyer. The freer lyricism of Bo Widerberg in *The Pram (1966)* might well be an inspiration for its *ad hoc* style, but Dreyer's religiosity is the shadow that haunts its obsessions, and especially von Trier's great sacrificial heroines, Emily Watson and Bodil Jorgenson, who both seem to replicate the face and fate of Falconetti in *The Passion of Joan of Arc.* In his own way, von Trier reproduces Dreyer's sacrificial motifs (Orr 2002b). *Kammerspiel* motifs—fixity of place and fixed interiors, the face-to-face community: often family, often claustrophobic—guide narrative thrust. *Festen, Mifune,* and *The Idiots* all have their variations on the lone country dwelling. *The King is Alive,* with its marooned Shakespearean players, is set in a deserted African village: *Italian for Beginners* (2002) in a hotel-restaurant complex with adjoining chapel and lecture room for its language class. The face-to-face community is either family or surrogate family— ranging from summer communards in *The Idiots,* 'spassing' as disabled, and the mad dysfunctional family in *Julien Donkey-Boy* through to the cosy language class in Lone Sherfig's whimsical comedy.

Through place and 'family', Dogme's aesthetic lies in hyperactive compression of time and space. It reinvents *Kammerspiel* intimacy for the hand-held camera. Often this can be electric in effect, but it sets Dogme up in opposition to key innovation elsewhere in European film—stylistically the revival of the sequence-shot (*plan-séquence*), and thematically the new metaphysic of *parallel worlds* (Zizek 2001: 78–93). Both cue the

■ Excerpts from the Dogme 95 manifesto

In 1960 enough was enough! The movie was dead and called for resurrection. The goal was correct but the means were not! The New Wave proved to be a ripple that washed ashore and turned to muck.

Slogans of individualism and freedom created works for a while, but no changes. . . . The *auteur* concept was bourgeois romanticism from the very start and thereby . . . false!

To Dogme 95 cinema is not individual!

Today a technological storm is raging, the result of which will be the ultimate democratization of the cinema. For the first time, anyone can make movies. But the more accessible the medium becomes, the more important the avant-garde. It is no accident the phrase 'avant-garde' has military connotations. Discipline is the answer . . . we must put our films into uniform, because the individual film will be decadent by definition!

Dogme 95 counters the individual film by the principle of presenting an indisputable set of rules known as THE VOW OF CHASTITY . . . 'I swear to submit to the following set of rules drawn up and confirmed by Dogme 95:

1   Shooting must be done on location. Props and sets must not be brought in (if a particular prop is necessary for the story, a location must be chosen where this prop is to be found).

2   The sound must never be produced apart from the images, or vice versa. (Music must not be used unless it occurs where the scene is being shot.)

⬇ *Festen*

3 The camera must be hand-held. Any movement or immobility attainable in the hand is permitted. (The film must not take place where the camera is standing; shooting must take place where the film takes place.)

4 The film must be in color. Special lighting is not acceptable. (If there is too little light for exposure the scene must be cut, or else the light must be provided by a single lamp attached to the camera.)

5 Optical work and filters are forbidden.

6 The film must not contain superficial action (murder, weapons, etc. must not occur.)

7 Temporal and geographical alienation are forbidden. (That is to say the film takes place here and now.)

8 Genre movies are not acceptable.

9 The film format must be Academy 35mm.

10 The director must not be credited.'

elsewhere (technically off-screen space) of the contemporary world, life as an endless journey of discovery where the film image is necessarily incomplete. The exploration of parallel worlds, especially of the ironies of chance encounter or chance disconnection, is a key metaphysic of immanence in the new cinema. It is a new form of lateral vision that traces the forked and parallel paths of seemingly unconnected figures and can be found too in the recent films of David Lynch, Tsai Ming-Liang, and Wong Kar-Wai. This contemplation of chance is neither mystical nor transcendental, but a metaphysic of the here and now, an alternate metaphysic to von Trier's heavy sacrificial artifice, a filmic reworking of age-old contemplation, the relationship of free will and design in the nature of the human condition.

The great innovators are those who transcend the conflict between style and substance, which is why, perhaps, von Trier has moved into Dogme and out the other side in pursuit of auteurist ambition. Style does not stand still. Nor does technology. Innovation, by definition, cannot. And in the high-risk zone of filmmaking the industry does not stand still either. The use of digital is heralded as a future of film, but film strikes back. Super 8 and Super 16 can still be blown up to 35mm so that digital offers but one set of options, not only in the realm of the image but, more important, in the realms of editing and sound. This provides us with another paradox. Basic digital now seems the low-cost solution to the Dogme-style camera of spontaneous intimacy, that can do anything quickly, immediately, anywhere. On the other hand, digital editing offers unforeseen opportunities for long-term manipulation of the image and experimentation with sound, for spending more and more time in the edit suite. In a way Derek Jarman had already seen this when he mixed Super 8 and pre-digital video in his low-budget films of the late 1980s. Thus we have an interesting formula: simplification of shooting matched by increasing complexity of post-production.

Digital video still works best as an exceptional case, when the project itself is experimental and beyond the reach of film in its singular purpose. It triumphs only if it has a specific rationale. The four-way split screen of *Timecode* (2000) had allowed Mike Figgis to shoot simultaneously four separate but interwoven stories in a single take stretching over 100 minutes one autumn afternoon in Los Angeles. In projecting the film it enabled Figgis, at its Edinburgh Festival premiere, the opportunity of a live sound mix that could fade up and down the four screens at will and produce a different story focus from that of the final cut made for distribution. Digital editing has also allowed new forms of framing and frames-within-frames, recasting the link between moving images and running text, as Peter Greenaway has shown so ingeniously in his baroque, reflexive meditation on Japanese culture, *The Pillow Book* (1995). Yet both these films are by British directors working on different continents. Given the global reach of cinema, neither is strictly European. The Figgis movie is an ironic send-up of Californian and Hollywood culture: Greenaway's film exhibits high, fastidious production values in East Asia. Neither is really an exemplar for low-cost digital, and at that end of things, film is the medium that still prevails. For digital can still be tough. Thus a key low-budget feature of Scottish origin, *One Life Stand* (2000), written and directed by Miles May Thomas and shot in black and white using the tiny Sony digital VX1000E, has won acclaim at film festivals everywhere but to date as found no one willing to transfer it onto film and distribute it in the cinema.

If prospects sound uncertain here for the European avant-garde, there will always be surprises to lift the spirit. Here is the most recent. Aleksandr Sokurov's tour de force, *Russian Ark*, is a history film recorded instantly onto digital disc: made one winter afternoon with a cast of hundreds in St Petersburg's Hermitage museum, and made moreover in ninety minutes as a single Steadicam shot. In the course of the film, the Steadicam of cinematographer Tilman Buttner travels over two kilometres, and many critics have seen it as showing greater hi-tech virtuosity than the latest megabuck *Star Wars* (Macnab 2002). At its 2002 Cannes premiere it was projected both digitally and on 35mm and—in what is often a good sign—won no prizes in a very average festival. This latest advance, this electric marriage of film and digital perfected by Sokurov, promises a way forward for the avant-garde in European film and for more triumphant tales of the unexpected to rival the wealth and power of Hollywood. We can only hope that promise bears fruit.

Further reading

Aitken, Ian, *European Film Theory and Cinema: A Critical Introduction* (Edinburgh: Edinburgh University Press, 2001). Good, up-to-date discussion of the relationship of theory and criticism.

Darke, Chris, *Light Readings: Film Criticism and the Screen Arts* (London: Wallflower Press, 2000). An astute review series of key French and European films in the 1990s.

Deleuze, Gilles, *Cinema 2: The Time-Image* (London: Athlone, 1989).
   The most powerful discourse on modern European film in any language.

Kelly, Richard, *The Name of the Game is Dogme95* (London: Faber & Faber, 2000). An excellent, in-depth account of the growth and aims of the Danish film movement.

Konstantarakos, Myrto (ed.), *Spaces in European Cinema* (Exeter: Intellect Books, 2000). Very stimulating set of essays on space and urban landscapes in European film.

Kristeva, Julia, *Powers of Horror: An Essay on Abjection* (New York: Columbia University Press, 1982). A powerful intellectual source for the new film narratives of the last fifteen years.

Orr, John, *The Art and Politics of Film* (Edinburgh: Edinburgh University Press, 2000). Contains a critical discussion of contemporary developments in European film.

Petley, Julian, and Duncan Petrie (eds.), *New British Cinema: Journal of British Popular Cinema* 5 (Trowbridge: Flicks Books, 2002). A broad set of essays dealing effectively with new British cinema.

Petrie, Duncan, *Screening Scotland* (London: British Film Institute, 2000).
   The definitive book on Scottish cinema in the twentieth century.

Vincendeau, Ginette, *Encyclopaedia of European Cinema* (London: Cassell British Film Institute, 1995). A very useful reference source for films and filmmakers.

GLOSSARY OF FILM TERMS

180-degree rule The convention of placing the camera on the same side of the action, as if behind an imaginary line, from one scene to the next.

actuality Non-fiction film shot in real surroundings without the use of actors, sets, or props.

aerial shot Usually an overhead shot taken from a helicopter or airplane.

analogue (adj. and, by extension, noun) Pertaining to the representation of visual or audio information using continuously varying values (as opposed to digital technology, which breaks up information into discrete units).

arc lamp/light High-intensity lamp that can simulate sunlight.

art films (also 'art cinema') Usually films that are not overtly commercial, and considered challenging and ambiguous.

Articolo 28 (Italian, 'Clause 28') Italian measure providing funds to assist first-time directors in making non-commercial films.

aspect ratio Ratio of width to height of the film image; Academy Ratio, the international standard for shooting and projecting films, is 1.33 : 1.

attractions, cinema of A style generally associated with 'trick' films made c.1895–1905, in which spectacular feats or tricks designed to amaze the audience were privileged over narrative content.

auteur (French, 'author') A director (who is sometimes also the screenwriter) who exercises considerable creative control, and is thought to leave a distinctive mark on his or her films.

Autorenfilm (German, 'authors' film') German style of film that arose around 1913, based on the work of established literary writers, and which drew many of its directors and actors from the theater.

avance sur recettes (French, 'advance on takings') Program of government loans to film projects that are repaid with proceeds from ticket sales; first established in France after World War II.

avant-garde (French, 'vanguard') Artistic movements that experiment with their chosen medium, often using challenging formal strategies.

boom A pole or other extension device used to position microphones, lights, or cameras during shooting.

bridge/bridging shot A device that connects scenes either visually (such as a clock whose hands spin quickly through the hours to signify the passage of time) or through the overlap of sound, such as the use of music or dialogue carried over from one scene to the next.

Brighton School A group of British filmmakers working in southern England around 1900–08, especially James Williamson and G. A. Smith.

British New Wave See **New Wave, British**.

Cahiers du cinéma (French, 'Cinema Notebooks') Influential film journal founded in 1951 for which many of the French New Wave directors wrote before turning to filmmaking.

caméra-stylo (French, 'camera-pen') Term coined by Alexandre Astruc, which implicitly likens film to the literary arts.

cell One of the many individual drawings used in animation.

cinéaste (French, 'filmmaker') Filmmaker.

Cinecittà (Italian, 'film city') A major studio complex in Rome that was Italy's filmmaking center for decades.

ciné-clubs Film societies dedicated to showing and debating art films.

cinéma de papa (French, 'Dad's cinema') Pejorative term used by French New Wave critics to describe big-budget films made in the late 1940s and 1950s.

cinémathèque (French, 'film archive') Film archive.

cinematograph See ***cinématographe***.

cinématographe (French term) Name of the film camera/projector patented by the Lumière brothers, and used more generally to denote any film camera in the first few years of cinema.

cinéma-vérité (French, 'film-truth', after Dziga Vertov's notion of Kino-Pravda) A documentary style in which the filmmaker provokes some of the action (see **Direct Cinema** for comparison and contrast).

close-up Shot in which a face or object fills most of the frame.

continuity editing Editing designed to convey narrative action unambiguously and unobtrusively.

co-production A film that is funded jointly by two or more production companies, usually based in different countries.

crane shot A shot taken from a crane that gives the impression of smooth movement through space.

cross-cutting Alternation of shots from two or more different scenes to give the impression that they are occurring at the same time.

cut A change from one shot to another.

cutaway Shot inserted briefly into a scene to show action at another location.

deep focus Technique in which both the foreground and background are kept in focus at the same time.

diegesis (adj. **diegetic**) The narrative world of a film.

diegetic sound Sound implied to originate in the narrative world of the film, i.e., sound that can be heard by characters in the film (see also **non-diegetic sound**).

digital (adj. or, by extension, noun) Pertaining to the technology that numerically encodes audio or visual data.

digitization The conversion of audio or visual data from analogue to digital format.

Direct Cinema A documentary style, developed in the late 1950s, in which the filmmaker acts as a passive bystander recording the action, rather than provoking it, as distinct from **cinéma-vérité**.

direct sound Sound recorded at the site and moment of filming.

distributor The agency that supplies films to exhibitors.

dolly shot See **tracking shot**.

dissolve (also **lap dissolve**) An editing technique in which one shot fades out and is replaced by another fading in at the same time.

editing The organization of shots into sequence, which can provide a sense of continuity (see **continuity editing**) or a sense of juxtaposition.

ellipsis Any technique that denotes the passage of time, such as a caption, fade, or dissolve.

emulsion The light-sensitive layer affixed to the strip of cellulose acetate (until 1951, cellulose nitrate) on film stock.

establishing shot A shot (generally an extreme long shot) that orients the viewer by showing the general location of the scene to follow.

Europudding A disparaging term for European co-productions that feature international casts and production teams at the expense of artistic coherence.

exhibitor The venue, or owner of the venue, at which a film is screened before an audience.

Expressionism A film style prominent in Germany in the 1920s, which featured theatrical set design, the use of distorted and exaggerated visual motifs, and highly stylized acting techniques.

extreme close-up A shot in which part of a face or small detail of an object takes up most of the frame.

extreme long shot A shot that shows its subject from a distance, encompassing more in the frame than a **long shot** would.

eyeline match When a shot shows what a character in the preceding shot appeared to look at.

fade-in (noun; verb: **fade in**) A punctuating or linking device between scenes in which the image appears gradually from a black (or other solid-colored) screen.

fade-out (noun; verb: **fade out**) A punctuating or linking device between scenes in which the image disappears gradually until the screen becomes black (or another solid color).

feature film Full-length (i.e., generally longer than forty-five minutes), usually fictional film intended to be shown in cinemas.

fill light Lights or softens shadows left by the key light.

Film d'Art (French, 'Art Film') Named after the French film company established in 1908, and referring more generally to films of that era that self-consciously aspired to gain legitimacy by using respected stage actors and by treating literary or theatrical subjects.

film stock Unused film strip, also known as raw film.

fish-eye lens An extreme wide-angle lens that distorts the image, making the center more prominent and rounding the edges.

focus pull When the focus changes (i.e., is 'pulled') within a shot to shift the viewer's attention to another object or activity (see also **rack focus**).

full shot A shot far enough away from its subject to show a human figure from head to toe in the frame.

GATT The General Agreement on Tariffs and Trade.

gauge The width of a strip of film in millimeters.

genre An easily recognizable category of film that adheres to certain stylistic or narrative conventions, such as the Western, science fiction film, or horror film.

German Expressionism See **Expressionism**.

graphic match The linking of two shots by visual similarity (for example, when a shot of a spinning dryer is followed by a close-up of a car wheel in motion).

Heimatfilm (German, 'Homeland film') Genre of German film popular in the 1950s that presented a nostalgic image of traditional, rural life.

heritage film Big-budget costume drama, usually based on a respected literary work, that presents a nostalgic view of the country in which the film is produced.

high-angle shot Shot in which the camera is positioned above the subject.

high-key lighting Bright, flat light with little contrast or shadow, often conveying a cheerful one.

Impressionism In film, French movement of the 1920s including directors Louis Delluc, Germaine Dulac, Abel Gance, and Marcel L'Herbier, who used filmic techniques to convey character subjectivity.

insert Shot inserted into a sequence, often showing a close-up of what a character is looking at.

intertitle Words shown between scenes describing action or conveying dialogue, used most often in the silent era.

iris A round mask that opens up to introduce a shot or closes to end a shot (or to emphasize a detail).

Italian Neorealism See **Neorealism**.

jump cut An abrupt shift from one shot to another within a scene that creates a sense of discontinuity.

Kammerspielfilm (German, 'chamber talk film') German film of the 1920s displaying an intimate, theatrical style.

key light The main source of artificial light in a shot (see **high-key lighting; low-key lighting**).

Kuleshov effect Named for Lev Kuleshov, the Soviet film theorist who demonstrated that a film's interpretation could be greatly influenced by the juxtaposition of shots through editing.

lap dissolve See **dissolve**.

long shot A shot that shows an entire human figure (see **full shot**).

long take A shot that continues uncut for a relatively long time.

low-angle shot Shot in which the camera is positioned below the subject.

low-key lighting Dim main lighting, often contrasted with bright, harshly lit spots.

mask An opaque device placed in the camera or printer that changes the shape of the photographed image.

master shot Shot of all the action in a scene that is intercut with mid-shots and close-ups.

match cut See **graphic match**.

medium shot A shot in which a human figure shown from from the waist up would fill most of the screen (also known as a 'mid-shot', or, if the figure is shown from the knees up, a *plan américain*).

melodrama (1) A genre whose narrative content favors heavily sentimental or emotional drama, usually revolving around romantic or familial tensions. (2) A style of filmmaking marked by excess in its use of color, camera movement, *mise-en-scène*, and/or music.

mid-shot See **medium shot**.

mise-en-scène (French, 'staging') Everything placed in front of the camera during filming, including decor, props, lighting, costumes, makeup, and the positioning and movement of the actors.

montage (French, 'editing') Editing (see also **montage sequence**).

montage sequence A series of shots edited together to suggest the passage of time and/or to provide symbolic or typical images that summarize a topic.

narrative The structure given to events in a story.

Neorealism Style of filmmaking developed in Italy in the mid- to late 1940s, characterized by the use of non-professional actors, location shooting, hand-held camerawork, and working-class characters.

New Wave, British Group of filmmakers who produced films from the late 1950s to the mid-1960s depicting mainly working-class characters, often set in the industrial north of England.

New Wave, French Group of young French filmmakers who all made their first films between 1958 and 1962.

non-diegetic sound Sound, often music or voice-over, extraneous to the fictional world of the film.

nouvelle vague See **New Wave, French**.

overlapping editing Editing that shows the same action repeated from a different camera position.

pan Horizontal, swiveling movement of the camera.

peplum (Latin, 'robe of state') Italian epic film of the late 1950s and early 1960s set in ancient Rome or biblical times (also called a 'toga-and-sandals' epic).

pixillation Form of animation that uses real people or objects, rather than drawings, in stop-action photography.

plan américain (French, 'American shot') Shot in which a human figure is shown from the knees up.

plan-séquence (French, 'sequence-shot') See **sequence shot**.

Poetic Realism Style of film made in France in the 1930s, featuring doomed romantic (usually working-class) heroes in a gloomy, urban setting.

point-of-view shot (POV) See **subjective shot**.

post-synchronization The addition of sound to a scene after it has been shot.

process shot Any shot that combines live action with footage filmed elsewhere (often used in the background).

production values The presentational quality of a film, usually determined by the amount of money and care that have been expended on it.

profilmic (adj.) Describes that which is filmed by the camera (could be used as an adjective for *mise-en-scène*).

pull (focus) See **focus pull**.

rack focus When the focus shifts within a shot to direct the viewer's attention from one object or activity to another.

realism A set of formal conventions that seek to construct the appearance of everyday life through filmic techniques that do not draw attention to themselves.

reverse angle Camera position opposite that of the preceding shot.

scene A series of shots set in a single location that show a single action.

sequence A series of shots edited together to form a unit, usually unfolding continuously in time or within a single space (sometimes used in place of 'scene').

sequence shot A complex shot that depicts more than one action or location, usually in a long take involving camera movement (sometimes the French term, *plan-séquence*, is used in English).

shot A single, uninterrupted segment of film, taken from a single camera, without cuts.

shot/reverse shot Alternating shots of two people, usually in conversation, from complementary angles.

silent era The period from 1895 to 1927 (in the US) and to 1929/30 (in Europe) before the use of synchronous sound was institutionalized.

social realism Genre of film displaying a naturalistic photographic style, emphasizing social issues, and generally featuring working-class or socially disadvantaged characters (not to be confused with **Socialist Realism**).

Socialist Realism Official doctrine in Soviet cinema and other arts between 1934 and 1953, which promoted Communist ideals through fiction.

spaghetti Western Westerns filmed in Italy or Spain, epitomized by those made in the 1960s by Sergio Leone.

static shot Shot in which the camera remains stationary.

subject The person or object being filmed.

subjective shot (also: point-of-view/POV shot) Shot in which the camera appears to adopt the position of a character, apparently showing what he or she sees.

synchronous sound Sound that corresponds temporally to actions on the screen, such as dialogue matched to characters' moving lips.

tracking shot Shot in which the camera is moved (usually on tracks or in a vehicle) backwards, forwards, or from one side to another; also called a dolly shot.

trick films Films made c.1895–1905 that featured magic tricks or special effects without overt narrative content.

Trümmerfilm (German, 'rubble film') Genre of film made in what became East Germany in the years immediately following World War II, which depicted the harsh conditions of daily life in a gritty, realist style.

two-shot Shot showing two people, usually in conversation, in medium shot or close-up.

vertical integration Business practice in which a film production company also controls other sectors of the industry such as distribution and exhibition.

white telephone films Films made in 1930s Italy featuring upper-middle-class domestic settings.

wide-angle lens A lens that increases the illusion of depth or distance from the subject in a shot.

zoom A shot that uses a lens capable of adjusting from wide angle, where the subject appears to be at a distance, to telephoto, where the subject appears close up (zoom in), or vice versa (zoom out).

REFERENCES

Abel, Richard (1984), *French Cinema: The First Wave 1915–29* (Princeton: Princeton University Press).

—— (1988), *French Film Theory and Criticism* (2 vols., 1907–29; 1929–39: Princeton: Princeton University Press).

—— (1998), *The Ciné Goes to Town*, 2nd edn. (Berkeley: University of California Press).

—— (1999), *The Red Rooster Scare: Making Cinema American, 1900–1910* (Berkeley: University of California Press).

Academia (2002), Aug./Sept.

Aitken, Ian (2001), *European Film Theory and Cinema: A Critical Introduction* (Edinburgh: Edinburgh University Press).

Altman, Rick (ed.) (1992), *Sound Theory Sound Practice* (London: Routledge).

Amiel, Vincent, and Michel Ciment (1994), 'Entretien avec Krzysztof Kieślowski: "La fraternité existe dès que l'on est prêt à écouter l'autre"', *Positif* 403 (Sept.): 26–32.

Andrew, Dudley (1976), *The Major Film Theories* (Oxford: Oxford University Press).

—— (1978), *André Bazin* (Oxford: Oxford University Press).

—— (1995), *Mists of Regret: Culture and Sensibility in Classic French Film.* (Princeton: Princeton University Press).

Arendt, Hannah (1994), *Eichmann in Jerusalem: A Report on the Banality of Evil* (New York: Penguin).

Armes, Roy (1971), *Patterns of Realism: A Study of Italian Neo-Realism* (Cranbury, NJ: A. S. Barnes).

Austin, Guy (1996), *Contemporary French Cinema* (Manchester: Manchester University Press).

Bacon, Henry (1998), *Visconti: Explorations of Beauty and Decay* (New York: Cambridge University Press).

de Baecque, Antoine (1998), *La Nouvelle Vague* (Paris: Flammarion).

—— and Charles Tesson (eds.) (1998), *La Nouvelle Vague: une légende en question* (Paris: *Cahiers du cinéma*).

Bakhtin, M. (1981), *The Dialogic Imagination* (Austin: University of Texas Press).

Barr, Charles (1977), *Ealing Studios* (London: Cameron & Tayler).

Barthes, Roland (1984 [1968]), 'L'Effet de réel', in *Le Bruissement de la langue* (Paris: Seuil).

Bathrick, David, *et al.* (eds.) (1987), Special Issue on Weimar Film Theory, *New German Critique* 40 (winter).

Bazin, André (1967), 'The Evolution of a Language of Cinema', in *What is Cinema?* vol. 1, ed. and trans. Hugh Gray (Berkeley: University of California Press).

—— (1971), 'Neorealism: An Aesthetic of Reality', in *What is Cinema?* vol. 2, ed. and trans. Hugh Gray (Berkeley: University of California Press).

Bergfelder, Tim, Erica Carter, and Deniz Göktürk (eds.) (2002), *The German Cinema Book* (London: British Film Institute).

Bergman, Ingmar (1988), *The Magic Lantern* (New York: Viking).

—— (1993 [1973]), *Bergman on Bergman* (New York: DaCapo).

—— (1994), *Images: My Life in Film* (New York: Arcade).

Beugnet, Martine (2000), 'Le Souci de l'autre', *Iris* 29: 53–67.

—— (2001) 'Negotiating Evil', in Ezra and Harris (2001: 195–205).

Blüher, Dominique (2000), 'Histoire de raconter: décentrement, élision et fragmentation', *Iris* 29: 12–25.

Blumenberg, Hans C. (1997a), 'Glanz und Elend des neuen deutschen Films', *Die Zeit* (2 Sept.).

—— (1997b) 'Im Würgegriff des Fernsehen', *Die Zeit* (9 Sept.).

Bondanella, Peter (1992), *The Cinema of Federico Fellini* (Princeton, NJ: Princeton University Press).

—— (1993), *The Films of Roberto Rossellini* (New York: Cambridge University Press).

—— (2001), *Italian Cinema: From Neorealism to the Present*, 3rd. rev. edn. (New York: Continuum).

—— (2002), *The Films of Federico Fellini* (New York: Cambridge University Press).

Borau, José Luis (ed.) (1998), *Diccionario del cine español* (Madrid: Alianza).

Bordwell, David (1981), *The Films of Carl-Theodor Dreyer* (Berkeley: University of California Press).

—— (1993), *The Cinema of Eisenstein* (Cambridge, Mass.: Harvard University Press).

Braun, Marta (1992), *Picturing Time: The Work of Etienne-Jules Marey (1830–1904)* (Chicago: University of Chicago Press).

Breton, André (1969), *Manifestoes of Surrealism*, trans. Richard Seaver and Helen R. Lane (Ann Arbor: University of Michigan Press).

Brewster, Ben, and Lea Jacobs, *Theatre to Cinema* (Oxford: Oxford University Press, 1997).

British Film Institute (1998), *British Film Institute Film and Television Handbook 1999* (London: British Film Institute).

Brooksbank Jones, Anny (1997), *Women in Contemporary Spain* (Manchester: Manchester University Press).

Brunetta, Gian Piero (1993), *Storia del cinema italiano* (4 vols.: Rome: Editori Riuniti).

Brunette, Peter (2000), *The Films of Michelangelo Antonioni* (New York: Cambridge University Press).

Buñuel, Luis (1984), *My Last Sigh* (New York: Random House).

Calhoon, Kenneth S. (ed.) (2001), *Peripheral Visions: The Hidden Stages of Weimar Cinema* (Detroit: Wayne State University Press).

Campan, Véronique (1993), *Dix brèves histoires d'image: le Décalogue de Krzysztof Kieślowski* (Paris: Presses de la Sorbonne Nouvelle).

Canby, Vincent (1977), 'The German Renaissance: No Room for Laughter or Love', *New York Times* (11 Dec.).

Chatman, Seymour (1985), *Antonioni: or, The Surface of the World* (Berkeley: University of California Press).

Christie, Ian (1985), *Arrows of Desire* (London: Waterstone).

—— (2000), 'As Others See Us: British Filmmaking and Europe in the 90s', in Robert Murphy (ed.), *British Cinema of the 1990s* (London: British Film Institute).

—— and John Gillett (eds.) (1987), *Futurism/Formalism/FEKS: 'Eccentrism' and Soviet Cinema, 1918–1936* (London: British Film Institute).

Clarke, Gerald (1978), 'Seeking Planets That Do Not Exist: The German Cinema is the Liveliest in Europe', *Time Magazine* (20 Mar.).

Coates, Paul (1999a) (ed.), *Lucid Dreams: The Films of Krzysztof Kieślowski* (Trowbridge: Flicks Books).

—— (1999b), '"The inner life is the only thing that interests me": a conversation with Krzysztof Kieślowski', in Coates (1999a: 160–74).

Collins, Richard, and Vincent Porter (1981), *WDR and the Arbeiterfilm: Fassbinder, Ziewer and others* (Television Monograph 12: London: British Film Institute).

Cook, Pam, and Mieke Bernink (1996), *Fashioning the Nation: Costume and Identity in British Cinema* (London: British Film Institute).

—— (eds.) (1999), *The Cinema Book*, 2nd edn. (London: British Film Institute).

Corrigan, Timothy (1994), *New German Cinema: The Displaced Image*, 2nd edn. (Austin: University of Texas Press).

Crafton, Donald (1990), *Emile Cohl, Caricature, and Film* (Princeton, NJ: Princeton University Press).

—— (1993 [1982]), *Before Mickey: The Animated Film 1898–1928* (Chicago: University of Chicago Press).

Crisp, Colin (1993), *The Classic French Cinema, 1930–60.* (Bloomington: Indiana University Press).

—— (2002), *Genre, Myth and Convention in the French Cinema 1929–1939* (Bloomington: Indiana University Press).

Curle, Howard, and Stephen Snyder (eds.) (2000), *Vittorio De Sica: Contemporary Perspectives* (Toronto: University of Toronto Press).

Darke, Chris (1999), 'The Group', *Sight and Sound* 12: 24–7.

—— (2000), *Light Readings: Film Criticism and the Screen Arts* (London: Wallflower Press).

Dawson, Jan (1980–81), 'A Labyrinth of Subsidies', *Sight and Sound* (winter): 14–20.

Deleuze, Gilles (1989), *Cinema 2: The Time-Image* (London: Athlone Press).

Deutelbaum, Marshall (1983), 'Structural Patterning in the Lumière Films', in John Fell (ed.), *Film Before Griffith* (Berkeley: University of California Press).

Dickinson, Margaret, and Sarah Street (1985), *Cinema and State: The Film Industry and the British Government, 1927–84* (London: British Film Institute).

Docherty, David, David Morrison, and Michael Tracey (1987), *The Last Picture Show? Britain's Changing Film Audiences* (London: British Film Institute).

Douchet, Jean (1999), *The New Wave*, trans. Robert Bonanno (New York: DAP).

Douin, Jean-Luc (1983), *La Nouvelle Vague 25 ans après* (Paris: Cerf).

Dreyer, Carl (1970), *Four Screenplays* (London: Thames & Hudson).

—— (1973), *Dreyer in Double Reflection* (New York: Dutton).

Drum, Jean, and Dale D. Drum (2000), *My Only Great Passion: The Life and Films of Carl Th. Dreyer* (Lanham, Md.: Scarecrow).

Durgnat, Raymond (1963), *Nouvelle Vague: The First Decade* (Loughton, Essex: Motion Publications).

Durovicová, Natasa (1992), 'Translating America: The Hollywood Multilinguals', in Altman (1992: 138–53).

Dyer, Richard (1993), *Brief Encounter* (London: British Film Institute).

—— and Ginette Vincendeau (eds.) (1992), *Popular European Cinema* (London: Routledge).

Eisenstein, Sergei (1988), *Selected Works*, vol. 1: *Writings, 1922–1934*, ed. and trans. Richard Taylor (London: BFI and Bloomington: Indiana University Press).

—— (1991), *Selected Works*, vol. 2: *Towards a Theory of Montage*, ed. Michael Glenny and Richard Taylor, trans. Michael Glenny (London: BFI).

Eisner, Lotte H. (1969), *The Haunted Screen: Expressionism in the German Cinema and the Influence of Max Reinhardt* (Berkeley: University of California Press).

—— (1977), *Fritz Lang* (New York: Oxford University Press).

—— (1993), *Murnau* (Berkeley: University of California Press).

Elsaesser, Thomas (1986), 'Primary Identification and the Historical Subject: Fassbinder's Germany', in Philip Rosen (ed.), *Narrative, Apparatus, Ideology*. New York: Columbia University Press.

—— (1989), *New German Cinema: A History* (London: Macmillan/Brunswick, NJ: Rutgers University Press).

—— (ed.) (1990), *Early Cinema: Space, Frame, Narrative* (London: British Film Institute).

—— (1996), *Fassbinder's Germany: History, Identity, Subject* (Amsterdam: Amsterdam University Press).

—— (2000), *Weimar Cinema and After: Germany's Historical Imaginary* (London: Routledge).

Evans, Peter William (1995), *The Films of Luis Buñuel: Subjectivity and Desire* (Oxford: Oxford University Press).

—— (ed.) (1999), *Spanish Cinema: The Auteurist Tradition* (Oxford: Oxford University Press).

Everett, Wendy (ed.) (1996), *European Identity in Cinema* (Exeter: Intellect Press).

Eves, Vicki (1977), 'The Structure of the British Film Industry', *Screen* 2(1) (Jan./Feb.): 41–54.

Ezra, Elizabeth (1999), 'Cats in the Hood: The Unspeakable Truth about "Chacun cherche son chat"', in Powrie (1999: 199–211).

—— (2000), *Georges Méliès: The Birth of the Auteur* (Manchester: Manchester University Press).

—— (2002), 'The latest attraction: Léos Carax and the French cinematic *patrimoine*', *French Cultural Studies* 13(2): 225–33.

—— and Sue Harris (eds.) (2001), *France in Focus: Film and National Identity* (Oxford: Berg).

Fanara, Giulia (2000), *Pensare il neorealismo: percorsi attraverso il neorealismo cinematografico italiano* (Rome: Lithos).

Fassbinder, Rainer Werner (1984), 'Klimmzug, Handstand, Salto Mortale—sicher gestanden', in Michael Töteberg (ed.), *Filme befreien den Kopf* (Frankfurt: Fischer Taschenbuch).

Ferlita, Ernest, and John R. May (1977), *The Parables of Lina Wertmüller* (New York: Paulist Press).

Finney, Angus (1996), *The State of European Cinema* (London: Cassell).

Flitterman-Lewis, Sandy (1993), *To Desire Differently: Feminism and the French Cinema* (New York: Columbia University Press).

Forbes, Jill (1992), *The Cinema in France after the New Wave* (London: Macmillan).

—— and Sarah Street (eds.) (2000), *European Cinema: An Introduction* (Basingstoke: Palgrave).

French, Philip (7 Sept. 2002), 'Coma versus coma', http://film.guardian.co.uk/News_Story/Critic_Review/Observer_Film_of_the_week/

Freud, Sigmund (1983 [1905]), *Jokes and their Relation to the Unconscious*, trans. James Strachey, ed. Angela Richards (Harmondsworth: Pelican).

Freyling, Christopher (1981), *Spaghetti Westerns: Cowboys and Europeans from Karl May to Sergio Leone* (London: Routledge & Kegan Paul).

Frodon, Jean-Michel (1995), *Histoire du cinéma français, 1: L'Age moderne du cinéma français: de la nouvelle vague à nos jours* (Paris: Flammarion).

Fuller, Graham (ed.) (1998), *Loach on Loach* (London: Faber & Faber).

Gado, Frank (1986), *The Passion of Ingmar Bergman* (Durham, NC: Duke University Press).

García de León, María Antonia (1994), *Élites discriminadas: sobre el poder de las mujeres* (Barcelona: Anthropos).

Geraghty, Christine (2000), *British Cinema in the Fifties: Gender, Genre and the 'New Look'* (London: Routledge).

Gieri, Emanuela (1995), *Contemporary Italian Filmmaking: Strategies of Subversion* (Toronto: Toronto University Press).

Gilliat, Penelope (1977), 'Gold', *New Yorker* (11 Apr.).

Gocic, Goran (2001), *Notes from the Underground: The Films of Emir Kusturica* (London: Wallflower).

Graffy, Julian (2001), *Bed and Sofa: The Film Companion* (London: Tauris).

Graham, Helen, and Jo Labanyi (eds.) (1995), *Spanish Cultural Studies: An Introduction* (Oxford: Oxford University Press).

Green, Naomi (1990), *Pier Paolo Pasolini: The Cinema of Heresy* (Princeton, NJ: Princeton University Press).

Guinness, Alec (1985), *Blessings in Disguise* (London: Hamish Hamilton).

Gunning, Tom (1990), 'The Cinema of Attractions: Early Film, its Spectators and the Avant-Garde', in Elsaesser (1990: 121–5).

—— (2000), *The Films of Fritz Lang: Allegories of Vision and Modernity* (London: British Film Institute).

Haake, Sabine (2002), *German National Cinema* (London: Routledge).

'Die Hamburger Erklärung' (1979), reprinted in *medium* 27 (Nov.).

Hammond, Paul (1997), *L'Age d'or* (London: British Film Institute).

—— (ed.) (2000), *The Shadow and Its Shadow: Surrealist Writings on Cinema*, 3rd edn. (San Francisco: City Lights).

Haraszti, Miklos (1987), *The Velvet Prison* (New York: Noonday Press).

Harper, Sue (1994), *Picturing the Past: the Rise and Fall of the British Costume Film* (London: British Film Institute).

—— and Vincent Porter (1999), 'Cinema audience tastes in 1950s Britain', *Journal of Popular British Cinema*: 66–82.

Harris, Sue (2001), *Bertrand Blier* (Manchester: Manchester University Press).

Hayward, Susan (1993), *French National Cinema* (London: Routledge).

—— (1998), *Luc Besson* (Manchester: Manchester University Press).

—— (2000), 'Beyond the gaze and into femme-filmécriture: Agnès Varda's *Sans toit ni loi*', in Hayward and Vincendeau (2000).

—— and Ginette Vincendeau (2000) (eds.), *French Film: Texts and Contexts* (London: Routledge).

Helman, Alicja (1999), 'Women in Kieślowski's late films', in Coates (1999a: 116–35).

Hembus, Joe (1981), 'Bonner Film-AG', in *Der Deutsche Film kann garnicht besser sein* (Munich: Roger & Bernhard).

Herbert, Stephen, and Luke McKernan (eds.) (1996), *Who's Who of Victorian Cinema* (London: British Film Institute).

Heredero, Carlos F. and Antonio Santamarina (2002), *Semillas de futuro: cine español 1990–2001* (Madrid: Academia de las Artes y las Ciencias Cinematográficas de España).

Hiley, Nick (1999), '"Let's Go to the Pictures": The British Cinema Audience in the 1920s and 1930s', *Journal of Popular British Cinema* 2: 39–53.

Hillier, Jim (ed.) (1985), *Cahiers du cinéma: The 1950's: Neo-Realism, Hollywood, the New Wave* (Cambridge, Mass.: Harvard University Press).

Holmes, Diana, and Alison Smith (eds.) (2000), *100 Years of European Cinema: Entertainment or Ideology?* (Manchester: Manchester University Press).

Hooper, John (1995 [1986]), *The New Spaniards* (Harmondsworth: Penguin).

Hopewell, John (1986), *Out of the Past: Spanish Cinema after Franco* (London: British Film Institute).

Hutchings, Peter (1993), *Hammer and Beyond: the British Horror Film* (Manchester University Press).

Iordanova, Dina (2001), *Cinema of Flames: Balkan Film, Culture and the Media* (London: British Film Institute).

Izod, John (2000), 'Beineix's *Diva* and the French Cultural Unconscious', in Ezra and Harris (2000: 181–93).

Jameson, Fredric (1990), *Signatures of the Visible* (London: Routledge).

—— (1997), *The Cultural Turn* (London: Verso).

Jankun-Dopartowa, Mariola (1995), 'Trójkolorowy transparent: Vive le chaos!', *Kino* 29(6) (June): 4–7.

—— (2000), *Gorzkie kino Agnieszki Holland* (Gdansk: slowo/obraz terytoria).

Jordan, Barry, and Rikki Morgan-Tamosunas (1998), *Contemporary Spanish Cinema* (Manchester: Manchester University Press).

—— (eds.) (2000), *Contemporary Spanish Cultural Studies* (London: Arnold).

Kaes, Anton (1989), *From Hitler to Heimat: The Return of History as Film* (Cambridge, Mass.: Harvard University Press).

—— (2000), *M* (London: British Film Institute).

—— *Shell Shock: Cinema and Trauma in Weimar Germany* (Princeton, NJ: Princeton University Press, forthcoming).

—— Martin Jay, and Edward Dimendberg (eds.) (1994), *The Weimar Republic Sourcebook* (Berkeley: University of California).

Kelly, Richard (2000), *The Name of the Game is Dogme 95* (London: Faber & Faber).

Kenez, Peter (2001), *Cinema and Soviet Society from the Revolution to the Death of Stalin* (London: Tauris).

Kepley, Vance, Jr. (1986), *In the Service of the State: The Cinema of Alexander Dovzhenko* (Madison: University of Wisconsin Press).

Kinder, Marsha (1993), *Blood Cinema: The Reconstruction of National Identity in Spain* (Berkeley: University of California Press).

—— (ed.) (1997), *Refiguring Spain: Cinema, Media, Representation* (Durham, NC: Duke University Press).

Klein, Melanie, and Joan Riviere (1964), *Love, Hate and Reparation* (New York: Norton).

Kline, T. Jefferson (1987), *Bertolucci's Dream Loom: A Psychoanalytic Study of Cinema* (Amherst: University of Massachusetts Press).

Kluge, Alexander (1977), 'Das Nichtverfilmte kritisiert das Verfilmte', quoted in Karsten Witte, 'Wer schlägt uns das Kino tot?', *Frankfurter Rundschau* 2 (May).

—— (1979), 'Förderung: die modernste Form der Zensur', *Das Parlament* (6 Oct.).

—— (ed.) (1983), *Bestandsaufnahme: Utopie Film* (Frankfurt: Zweitausendundeins Verlag).

Knight, Julia (1992), *Women and the New German Cinema* (London: Verso).

Konstantarakos, Myrto (ed.) (2000), *Spaces in European Cinema* (Exeter: Intellect Books).

Kovács, Steven (1980), *From Enchantment to Rage: The Story of Surrealist Cinema* (Rutherford, NJ: Farleigh Dickinson University Press).

Kracauer, Siegfried (1947), *From Caligari to Hitler: A Psychological History of the German Film* (Princeton, NJ: Princeton University Press).

—— (1995), *The Mass Ornament: Weimar Essays*, ed. and trans. Thomas Y. Levin (Cambridge, Mass.: Harvard University Press).

Kristeva, Julia (1982), *Powers of Horror: An Essay on Abjection* (New York: Columbia University Press).

Kuenzli, Rudolf (ed.) (1996), *Dada and Surrealist Film* (Cambridge, Mass.: MIT Press).

Kuleshov, Lev (1974), *Kuleshov on Film: Writings of Lev Kuleshov*, trans. and ed. Ronald Levaco, (Berkeley: University of California Press).

Kundera, Milan (1985), *The Unbearable Lightness of Being*, trans. Michael Henry Heim (London: Faber & Faber).

Labarthe, André S. (1960), *Essai sur le jeune cinema* (Paris: Le Terrain vague).

Lagny, Michèle, Marie-Claire Ropars, and Pierre Sorlin (1986), *Générique des années trente* (Vincennes: Presses Universitaires de Vincennes).

Landy, Marcia (1986), *Fascism in Film: The Italian Commercial Cinema, 1931–1943* (Princeton: Princeton University Press).

—— (2000), *Italian Film* (Cambridge: Cambridge University Press).

Lenssen, Claudia (1983), 'Filmstoffe, ballenweise', *Frankfurter Rundschau* 30 (Apr.).

Lewis, C. S. (1989), 'First and Second Things', in *First and Second Things* (Glasgow: Collins/Fount), 19–24.

Leyda, Jay (1960), *Kino: A History of Russian and Soviet Film* (London: Allen & Unwin).

Lichtenstein, Manfred (1990), 'The Brothers Skladanowsky', in *Before Caligari: German Cinema, 1895–1920* (Pordenone: Edizioni Biblioteca Dell'Immagine).

Linville, Susan (1995), 'Europa, Europa: A Test Case for German National Cinema', *Wide Angle* 16(3): 38–51.

Macdonald, Kevin (1994), *Emeric Pressburger: The Life and Death of a Screenwriter* (London: Faber & Faber).

McMahan, Alison (2002), *Alice Guy Blaché, Lost Visionary of the Cinema* (New York: Continuum).

Macnab, Geoffrey (2002), 'Palace in Wonderland', *Sight and Sound* (Aug.).

Mannoni, Laurent (2000), *The Great Arts of Light and Shadow: Archeology of the Cinema*, trans. and ed. Richard Crangle, introd. by Tom Gunning, preface by David Robinson (Exeter: University of Exeter Press).

Manvell, Roger (1947) (ed.), *The Penguin Film Review*, 3 (London: Penguin).

Marcus, Millicent (1986), *Italian Film in the Light of Neorealism* (Princeton, NJ: Princeton University Press).

—— (1993), *Filmmaking by the Book: Italian Cinema and Literary Adaptation* (Baltimore, MD: Johns Hopkins University Press).

—— (2002), *After Fellini: National Cinema in the Postmodern Age* (Baltimore, MD: Johns Hopkins University Press).

Marie, Michel (1998) (ed.), *Jeune cinéma français* (Paris: Nathan).

Marrone, Gaetana (ed.) (1999), *New Landscapes in Contemporary Italian Cinema* (*Annali d'Italianistica* 17).

—— (2000), *The Gaze and the Labyrinth: The Cinema of Liliana Cavani* (Princeton, NJ: Princeton University Press).

Martin-Márquez, Susan (1999), *Feminist Discourse and Spanish Cinema: Sight Unseen* (Oxford: Oxford University Press).

Martini, Giulio, and Guglielmina Morelli (eds.) (1997), *Patchwork Due: geografia del nuovo cinema italiano* (Milan: Il Castoro).

Matthews, J. M. (1971), *Surrealism and Film* (Ann Arbor: University of Michigan Press).

Miccichè, Lino (ed.) (1998), *Schermi opachi: il cinema italiano degli anni '80* (Venice: Marsilio).

Michalczky, John (1986), *The Italian Political Filmmakers* (Rutherford, NJ: Fairleigh Dickinson University Press).

Montini, Franco (ed.) (1988), *Una generazione in cinema: esordi ed esordienti italiani 1975–1988* (Venice: Marsilio).

—— (ed.) (1988), *I nuovissimi: gli esordienti nel cinema italiano degli anni '80* (Venice: Marsilio).

Morandini, Morando (1989), 'Il cinema italiano è come un iceberg, è interessante, ma resta in gran parte sottíacqua', *Cineteca* 5/6 (Sept.): 4.

Musser, Charles (1990), *The Emergence of Cinema*, vol. 1: *The American Screen to 1907* (History of the American Cinema series: New York: Scribner's).

Nowell-Smith, Geoffrey (ed.) (1996), *The Oxford History of World Cinema* (Oxford: Oxford University Press).

—— and Steven Ricci (eds.) (1998), *Hollywood and Europe: Economics, Culture, National Identity 1945–95* (London: British Film Institute).

Orr, John (2000), *The Art and Politics of Film* (Edinburgh: Edinburgh University Press).

—— (2001), 'From Neo-modern to Hypermodern Cinema: 1960 to the Present', in Dan Fleming (ed.), *Formations* (Manchester: Manchester University Press).

—— (2002a), 'Traducing Realisms: Naked and Nil by Mouth', *Journal of Popular British Cinema* 5.

—— (2002b), 'Out of Dreyer's Shadow? The Quandary of Dogme 95', *New Cinemas: A Journal of Contemporary Film* 2.

O'Shaugnessy, Martin (2000), *Jean Renoir* (Manchester: Manchester University Press).

Overby, David (ed.) (1978), *Springtime in Italy: A Reader in Neo-Realism* (Hamden, Conn.: Shoe String Press).

Palmerini, Luca, and Gaetano Mistretta (1996), *Spaghetti Nightmares: Italian Fantasy Horrors As Seen through the Eyes of Their Protagonists* (Key West, Fla.: Fantasma).

Perel, Solomon (1997), *Europa, Europa*, trans. Margot Bettauer Dembo (New York: Wiley).

Pérez Turrent, Tomás, and José de la Colina (1992), *Objects of Desire: Conversations with Luis Buñuel* (New York: Marsilio).

Perucha, Julio Pérez (ed.) (1997), *Antología crítica del cine español 1906–1995* (Madrid: Cátedra-Filmoteca Española).

Petley, Julian (1986), 'The Lost Continent', in Charles Barr (ed.), *All Our Yesterdays: 90 Years of British Cinema* (London: British Film Institute).

—— and Duncan Petrie (eds.) (2002), *New British Cinema: Journal of Popular British Cinema* 5 (Trowbridge: Flicks Books).

Petrić, Vlada (1987), *Constructivism in Cinema: The Man with the Movie Camera, a Cinematic Analysis* (Cambridge: Cambridge University Press).

—— (1993), 'A Subtextual Reading of Kuleshov's Satire *The Extraordinary Adventures of Mr. West in the Land of the Bolsheviks* (1924)', in Andrew Horton (ed.), *Inside Soviet Film Satire: Laughter with a Lash* (Cambridge: Cambridge University Press).

Petrie, Duncan (2000), *Screening Scotland* (London: British Film Institute).

Pflaum, Hans Günther (ed.) (1978), *Jahrbuch Film 1977/78* (Munich: Hanser).

—— and Hans Helmut Prinzler (eds.) (1983), *Cinema in the Federal Republic of Germany* (Bonn: Inter Nationes).

—— and Hans Helmut Prinzler (eds.) (1988), *Film in the Federal Republic of Germany* (Bonn: Inter Nationes).

Porter, Vincent (1977), 'Television and Film Production in Europe', *Sight and Sound* (autumn).

—— (1978), 'British Film Culture and the European Economic Community', *Sight and Sound* (summer).

—— (2001), 'The Hegemonic Turn: Film Comedies in 1950s Britain', *Journal of Popular British Cinema* 4: 81–94.

Powell, Michael (1986), *A Life in Movies* (London: Heinnemann).

—— (1992), *Million-Dollar Movie* (London: Heinemann).

Powrie, Phil (1997), *French Cinema in the 1980s* (Oxford: Oxford University Press).

—— (ed.) (1999), *French Cinema in the 1990s* (Oxford: Oxford University Press).

—— (2002), *Jean-Jacques Beineix* (Manchester: Manchester University Press).

von Praunheim, Rosa (1977), 'So schlagen uns die Etablierten tot', *Die Zeit* 13 (May).

Prédal, René (2002), *Le Jeune Cinéma français* (Paris: Nathan).

Pudovkin, Vsevolod (1970), *Film Technique and Film Acting*, trans. and ed. Ivor Montagu (New York: Grove Press).

Reader, Keith (1993), 'Cinematic Representations of Paris: Vigo/Truffaut/Carax', *Modern and Contemporary France* 4: 409–15.

—— (1995), 'La Haine', *Sight and Sound* 11: 11–13.

Reimer, Robert C., and Carol J. Reimer (1992), *The Nazi-Retro Film: How German Narrative Cinema Remembers its Past* (New York: Twayne/Toronto: Maxwell Macmillan).

Rentschler, Eric (ed.) (1988), *West German Filmmakers on Film: Visions and Voices* (New York: Holmes & Meier).

Richter, Hans (1997), *Dada: Art and Anti-Art*, trans. David Britt (London: Thames & Hudson).

Roberts, Graham (1999), *Forward Soviet! History and Non-fiction Film in the USSR* (London: Tauris).

Robinson, David (1991), 'Introduction', in *Masterpieces of Animation 1833–1908*, *Griffithiana* 43 (Dec.).

Rohrbach, Günter (1983), 'Die verhängnisvolle Macht der Regisseure', in Kluge (1983: 318–26).

Rosello, Mireille, (2001), 'Portrait of the Author as an old Woman: Agnès Varda's *Les Glaneurs et la glaneuse*', *Studies in French Cinema* 1(1): 29–36.

Santaolalla, I. (1998), 'Far from Home, Close to Desire: Julio Medem's Landscapes', *Bulletin of Hispanic Studies* 75: 331–7.

Sarris, Andrew (1975), 'The Germans are Coming, the Germans are Coming', *Village Voice* (12 Oct.).

Screen (1998), 39(2) (summer): special issue, *Cinema and Surrealism*.

Sesti, Mario (1994), *Nuovo cinema italiano: gli autori, i film, le idee* (Rome: Theoria).

—— (1996) (ed.), *La 'scuola' italiana: storia, strutture e immaginario di un altro cinema (1988–1996)* (Venice: Marsilio).

Sherzer, Dina (ed.) (1996), *Cinema, Colonialism, Postcolonialism: Perspectives from the French and Francophone World* (Austin: University of Texas Press).

Siclier, Jacques (1990), *Le Cinéma français, 1: De 'La Bataille du rail' à 'La Chinoise' 1945–1968* (Paris: Ramsay/Cinéma).

Silverman, Max (1999), *Facing Postmodernity: Contemporary French Thought on Culture and Society* (London: Routledge).

Slavin, David (2001), *Colonial Cinema and Imperial France, 1919–1939: White Blind Spots, Male Fantasies, Settler Myths* (Baltimore, MD: Johns Hopkins University Press).

Smith, Alison (1998), *Agnès Varda* (Manchester: Manchester University Press).

Smith, Paul Julian (2002), *Desire Unlimited: The Cinema of Pedro Almodóvar* (London: Verso).

Sorlin, Pierre (1991), *European Cinemas, European Societies 1939–1990* (London: Routledge).

—— (1996), *Italian National Cinema* (London: Routledge).

Steene, Birgitta (1987), *Ingmar Bergman: A Guide to References and Resources* (Boston: G. K. Hall).

Stoil, Michael Jon (1982), *Balkan Cinema: Evolution after the Revolution* (Ann Arbor, Mich.: UMI Research Press).

Stok, Danusia (1993), *Kieślowski on Kieślowski* (London: Faber & Faber).

Stone, Robert (2002), *Spanish Cinema* (London: Longman).

Street, Sarah (1997), *British National Cinema* (London: Routledge).

—— (2000), *British Cinema in Documents* (London: Routledge).

—— (2002), *Transatlantic Crossings: British Feature Films in the USA* (New York: Contunuum).

Tarr, Carrie (1993), 'Questions of Identity in Beur Cinema: From *Tea in the Harem* to *Cheb*', *Screen* 34(4) (winter): 321–43.

—— and Freedman, Jane (eds.) (2000), *Women, Immigration and Identities in France* (London: Berg).

Taubin, Amy (1992), 'Woman of Irony' *Village Voice* (2 July).

Taylor, Richard, and Ian Christie (eds.) (1988), *The Film Factory: Russian and Soviet Cinema in Documents, 1896–1939* (Cambridge, Mass.: Harvard University Press).

—— (eds.) (1991), *Inside the Film Factory: New Approaches to Russian and Soviet Cinema* (London: Routledge).

—— Nancy Wood, Julian Graffy, and Dina Iordanova (eds.) (2000), *The BFI Companion to Eastern European and Russian Cinema* (London: British Film Institute).

Tesson, Charles (2001), 'Cinéma français: le vent nécessaire', *Cahiers du Cinéma* 556 (Mar.): 28–34.

Testa, Carlo (2002), *Italian Cinema and Modern European Literatures, 1945–2000* (Westport, Conn.: Praeger).

Thompson, Kristin (1985), *Exporting Entertainment: America in the World Film Market, 1907–1934* (London: British Film Institute).

—— and David Bordwell (1994), *Film History: An Introduction* (New York: McGraw-Hill).

Truffaut, François (1987), *Le Plaisir des yeux* (Paris: Flammarion).

Turk, Edward Baron (1989), *Child of Paradise: Marcel Carné and the Golden Age of French Cinema* (Cambridge, Mass.: Harvard University Press).

Ungar, Steven (2000), 'Marius et Jeannette: A Political Tale', *Iris* 29: 39–53.

Usai, Paolo Cherchi (2000), *Silent Cinema: An Introduction* (London: BFI Publishing).

Vertov, Dziga (1984), *Kino-Eye: The Writings of Dziga Vertov*, ed. Annette Michelson and trans. Kevin O'Brien (Berkeley: University of California Press).

Vincendeau, Ginette (ed.) (1995), *Encyclopaedia of European Cinema* (London: Cassell British Film Institute).

—— (2000), *Stars and Stardom in French Cinema* (London: Continuum).

—— *French Cinema in the 1930s: Social Context of a Popular Entertainment Medium* (Ph.D. Thesis, University of East Anglia, 1985).

—— and Keith Reader (1986) (eds.), *La Vie est à nous: French cinema of the Popular Front 1935–38* (London: British Film Institute).

Virilio, Paul (1996), *Open Sky*, trans. Julia Rose (London: Verso).

Widerberg, Bo (1962), *Visionen I svensk film* (Stockholm: Bonniers).

Williams, Alan (1992), *Republic of Images: A History of French Filmmaking* (Cambridge, Mass.: Harvard University Press).

Williams, Linda (1992), *Figures of Desire: A Theory and Analysis of Surrealist Film* (Berkeley: University of California Press).

Wilson, Emma (2000), *Memory and Survival: The French Cinema of Krzysztof Kieślowski* (Oxford: Legenda).

Wyke, Maria (1997), *Projecting the Past: Ancient Rome, Cinema and History* (New York: Routledge).

Youngblood, Denise J. (1991), *Soviet Cinema in the Silent Era, 1918–1935* (Austin: University of Texas Press).

—— (1992), *Movies for the Masses: Popular Cinema and Soviet Society in the 1920s* (Cambridge: Cambridge University Press).

—— (1999), *The Magic Mirror: Moviemaking in Russia, 1908–1918* (Madison: University of Wisconsin Press).

Zagarrio, Vito (1998), *Cinema italiano anni novanta* (Venice: Marsilio).

Zizek, Slavoj (2000), *The Fragile Absolute, or, Why is the Christian Legacy Worth Fighting for?* (London: Verso).

—— (2001). *The Fright of Real Tears: Krzysztof Kieślowski between Theory and Post-Theory* (London: British Film Institute).

Zwerenz, Gerhard (1978), 'Die falschen Stoffe', in Pflaum (1978: 22–5).

INDEX